Framing Chief Leschi

Framing

NARRATIVES AND THE

Chief Leschi

POLITICS OF HISTORICAL JUSTICE

FIRST PEOPLES
New Directions in Indigenous Studies

Lisa Blee

The University of North Carolina Press
CHAPEL HILL

Publication of this book was made possible, in part, by a grant from the Andrew W. Mellon Foundation and with the assistance of the Thornton H. Brooks Fund of the University of North Carolina Press.

© 2014 The University of North Carolina Press
All rights reserved
Designed by Rebecca Evans
Set in Charis and Calluna types
by Tseng Information Systems, Inc.
Manufactured in the United States of America
The paper in this book meets the guidelines for permanence and durability of the Committee on Production Guidelines for Book Longevity of the Council on Library Resources.

The University of North Carolina Press has been a member of the Green Press Initiative since 2003.

Library of Congress Cataloging-in-Publication Data
Blee, Lisa.
Framing Chief Leschi : narratives and the politics of historical justice / Lisa Blee.
pages cm. — (First peoples. New directions in indigenous studies)
Includes bibliographical references and index.
ISBN 978-1-4696-1284-3 (pbk : alk. paper)
ISBN 978-1-4696-1285-0 (ebook)
1. Leschi, Nisqually chief, –1858. 2. Leschi, Nisqually chief, –1858—Trials, litigation, etc.
3. Nisqually Indians—Kings and rulers—Biography.
4. Nisqually Indians—Wars. 5. Nisqually Indians—Government relations. I. Title.
E99.N74L473 2013
979.7004'979435—dc23

2013036719

18 17 16 15 14 5 4 3 2 1

THIS BOOK WAS DIGITALLY PRINTED

CONTENTS

Preface ix
Acknowledgments xv

Introduction 1

CHAPTER 1 **Colonialism** 23

CHAPTER 2 **Law and War** 50

CHAPTER 3 **Leschi Stories** 80

CHAPTER 4 **The Leschi Message** 103

CHAPTER 5 **Performing Justice** 136

CHAPTER 6 **Haunting** 159

Conclusion 185

Notes 193
Bibliography 255
Index 281

FIGURES & MAP

FIGURES

1 Portrait of Leschi 4
2 Eugene Ham testifying on the stand in the Historical Court 7
3 Nisqually procession ceremony and celebration at the Washington State Capitol Museum 10
4 Detail of Oregon Territory 34
5 Detail of sectional grid overlaying Olympia 35
6 Historians and researchers examine the site of Leschi's execution 68
7 Scene at Leschi Town training facility 76
8 Tribal members and relatives gather for Leschi's reburial ceremony 116
9 Leschi's headstone in the Puyallup Tribal Cemetery 123
10 Front view of memorial stone near the site of Leschi's execution 128
11 Panel of judges listening to testimony in the Historical Court 137
12 Carl Hultman questions expert witness Alexandra Harmon 156
13 Portrait of Quiemuth 160

MAP

South Puget Sound 2

PREFACE

I was a graduate student in Minnesota in 2005 when the story in the *New York Times* caught my eye. A Nisqually Indian leader had been symbolically exonerated of the charge of murder nearly 150 years after his execution. The full name of the event—the Historical Court of Inquiry and Justice—suggested that a group of people sought out the truth and, through this search, enacted justice. I admired the activists, lawyers, and historians who cooperatively took action for a progressive cause. I joined the national press in applauding the exoneration as good news from Indian Country. The small Nisqually Tribe of western Washington insisted that its experiences mattered and succeeded in shaping the public perception of its people and past. It was a story that just made me feel good. But I also wondered: Was justice done? A year later, I made my first research trip to the Pacific Northwest to find out.

Once I began the process of research and writing, however, I quickly came to realize that my original question took a great deal for granted. It did not acknowledge the ambiguities and complexities of historical memory. It was too narrow to accommodate myriad visions of justice and too simple to address the many possible political implications of historical narratives. The Historical Court did not lend itself to a singular interpretation of justice and cannot be wholly celebrated as a success or wholly condemned as a mistake. I came to see that the better questions were those that probed into ambivalence, gray areas, and liminal spaces and did not return with clear answers: How can memories recalibrate power? How does the quest for justice impact historical consciousness? How do we live with the past and use it to define ourselves, our sense of place, and our values? These questions opened doors but also made demands. I approached my research in South Puget Sound free of expectations and let the stories lead the way, but as a result I had to grapple with the unexpected personal and political dynamics of this case.

In order to understand the Historical Court, I needed to know how and why Leschi (pronounced Lesh-eye) matters in western Washington. Within a short time of moving to Seattle, I learned that Leschi has a significant presence in the region's landscape. I sat in Leschi Park in the Leschi neighborhood, drove down streets named after Leschi in three different towns, and visited Leschi's grave and the memorial near his execution site. I found two Leschi elementary schools, viewed the Leschi mural painted on the Nisqually Tribe's community center wall, and walked through a military training facility called Leschi Town.

Leschi holds an equally prominent, if less visible, place in the region's historical consciousness. Everyone I spoke with from the area knew Leschi's name and the outline of his story. Regional libraries and bookstores offer dozens of scholarly and popular accounts of Leschi's story. On and around the Nisqually reservation, tribal elders teach children about Leschi and celebrate his life in an annual commemoration. The tribal historian converted the basement of her home into an archive of documents related to Leschi and penned a book about him, which I picked up at the Red Winds Casino gift shop. I saw Leschi posters, mugs, and commemorative coins. Generations of Washingtonians, Indian and non-Indian alike, have formed their sense of history, identity, and place in a cultural landscape in which Leschi played a prominent role.

Once you start looking, Leschi seems to be everywhere. Of course, what I observed in the region was not the historical figure of Leschi but rather layers of memories about Leschi. Documents in South Puget Sound reveal that people have talked about Leschi for a long time, while the memorials and place-names anchored these stories in the landscape. Significantly, the stories represent Leschi by drawing on a range of ideas from different historical and cultural contexts: a "friendly" Indian, a peacekeeper, a treacherous "savage," the last of the chiefs, an enemy combatant, a hero, a principled leader, a symbol of a legal mistake. Stories about Leschi in the South Puget Sound region run deep, evolve, build on one another, and disagree and have been used for numerous purposes over time. The Historical Court nominally dealt with the figure of Leschi fixed in his 1850s context, but the participants in the court could never step outside of their local cultural context. History and memory cannot be disentangled.

For the same reason, my intention to investigate the Historical Court and the region's historical memory from the perspective of a disinterested outsider proved impossible. My personal interests and politics led me to this study, and I was invested in the ideals of justice expressed through the Historical Court. I would be a participant in storytelling, as both listener and author. The interviewees, including the chief justice of the Washington Supreme Court, the chairwoman of the Nisqually Tribe, and teachers, historians, and lawyers, explained their roles and what they thought was accomplished with the Historical Court. This was not an objective survey: the way my interviewees perceived me affected what they said, and my training and perception of the speaker affected what I heard. Some interviewees recalled that their commitment to Indian treaty rights drew them to participate in the Historical Court—an event they saw as an expression and extension of their politics. Others explained their participation as motivated by professional obligation, curiosity about Leschi place-names, or relationships with Nisqually people. I admired my interviewees and cared about the personal dimensions to their stories. People shared themselves when they talked about Leschi and the Historical Court. Most of the Nisqually narrators led me through their family histories, and I was sympathetic to the emotions these narrators drew from memories of Leschi. My respect for the interviewees, the personal nature of some of the memories, and political considerations made writing *with* and *about* these stories more difficult than I had imagined.

I struggled with how to advance scholarly critiques of these stories of Leschi while acknowledging the personal stakes people hold in them. While I think of Leschi as a historical figure who embodied all the complexities and contradictions of the human condition, some of my interviewees considered him a wise ancestor and heroic icon and would be hurt by negative or critical depictions of him. After all, the Nisqually participants told me that their intention with the Historical Court was to restore Leschi's good name. I also came to see the Historical Court's serious limitations but felt conflicted about how to treat the words of people who generously spoke with me and had dedicated time, energy, and skill to create the event. I therefore sought to honor the *intentions* of each interviewee even as I interpreted their words in ways they may not have planned. My hope is that possible objections to my interpretations may be overshadowed by the fact that I document how a handful of people tried to positively impact their families, communities, and future generations. While I am ambivalent about the Historical Court, my criticisms of the event are not directed at the participants. Stories are personal, but they also reflect larger cultural logics that warrant investigation and reconsideration. My research on the Historical Court has led me to believe, and I think my interviewees would agree, that building the kind of world we want requires acknowledging the limitations of our best intentions.

In addition to my concerns about writing a scholarly study in a way that respects the personal dynamics of stories, I also struggled with the political implications of my work. Certainly, Indians are not unique in terms of historical memory; Indians' and non-Indians' stories about the past both change over time and reflect historical circumstances and political goals. But the stakes are higher for Indians because the United States has asserted power over indigenous nations in myriad ways, from judging Indian identity to determining the parameters of tribal political organization. I recognize that U.S. Indian policies are informed by scholars' representations and truth-claims about Indians. Especially because I am a non-Indian scholar without ties to the Nisqually community, I hold an ethical obligation to consider the impact my work might have on the people and status of the Nisqually Tribe. I came across too many instances in the historical record in which non-Indian scholars promoted social theories, anthropological claims, and legal arguments that brought harm to Nisquallies. I therefore invited review of my work and chose to exclude material that I deemed potentially harmful to the tribe's interests and that did not add substantially to the story I tell.[1] While I do not champion the Nisqually Tribe's specific interests, I am sensitive to the fact that even the best of scholarly intentions can undermine Nisqually self-determination. Even so, in order to avoid romanticizing or exoticizing Native people, I hold Indians' historical narratives to the same analytical standards as those of non-Indians.

Although I delve into political theory and Indian law, I am not a legal advocate or policy maker. I believe the United States must honor its obligations and agreements with tribes and affirm and support tribal self-government, but my goal is to analyze the production of history and uses of the past, not to offer proscriptive conclusions or recommend specific actions. I do not argue that tribes should or should not work within an American system to achieve their goals; the following chapters show that the Historical Court was neither wholly helpful nor wholly damaging to tribal sovereignty. To proclaim winners or losers would take away from the contingencies and possibilities that motivate people to continue their work for change. My hope is that the histories I present in the following pages open discussion and inspire more thoughtful ways to address the consequences of past actions.

The context for this book is the landscape, archives, and stories in South Puget Sound. It is also the position and perspective that I bring to this project—as a non-Indian historian from outside the region and as an American concerned with social justice and indigenous rights. This book presents a set of stories that illustrate the power of memory and the political and cultural uses of the past. Writing a story about stories forced me to analyze a cultural logic of which I am a part and to interrogate my initial impulse to applaud the Historical Court according to what I assumed was a universal principle of justice. This case study speaks to the way we all have historical encounters read through personal and political lenses and makes visible our ongoing attempt to create and re-create the world through stories. At a fundamental level, the Historical Court offers an opportunity for reflection not just when something goes wrong but also when we try to make things right.

ACKNOWLEDGMENTS

My research in South Puget Sound was greatly aided by the generosity of scholars, archivists, tribal members, and others who were inspired by Chief Leschi and loved to talk about his story. At the University of Minnesota, Karissa White shared her research on Leschi when I was in the early stages of conceptualizing this project. Upon my arrival in Washington, Kitten Leschi shared her scrapbooks and enthusiasm, Melissa Parr discussed her experiences with the Historical Court, and Cecelia Svinth Carpenter provided me with a wealth of information from her extensive personal library. This book would not have been possible without Carpenter's years of dedicated research, her numerous books, and her willingness to educate me—a newcomer to both Washington and Nisqually history. I owe Carpenter, who passed away in 2010, a debt of gratitude for her generosity and teaching.

Along the course of my research on Leschi, several people shared their enthusiasm for local history with me. Walter Neary at Historic Fort Steilacoom read a chapter draft, and his comments prompted me to think in new directions. Fort Lewis Cultural Resource Manager Bret Ruby and Range Officer John Weller took me on a jeep tour of Nisqually historical sites and Leschi Town, allowing me to visualize important places central to this book. Alexander Olson and Drew Crooks reviewed early drafts of chapters and shared their own research with me. Joy Werlink at the Washington State Historical Society Research Center went above and beyond to locate obscure references to Leschi in library collections and to provide photographs. I also wish to thank members of the library staff at the University of Washington Special Collections for their patience and assistance in my research. For generously sharing records and advice, I am indebted to Joan Curtis and Janda Volkmer of the Steilacoom Historical Museum Association and Maria Pascualy at the Washington State Historical Society.

I interviewed several lawyers, Nisqually activists and educators, judges, and scholars who participated in the Historical Court of Justice or are otherwise involved in Nisqually history: Gerry Alexander, Robert Anderson, Cecelia Svinth Carpenter, Alexandra Harmon, Thor Hoyte, Carl Hultman, Cynthia Iyall, Joseph Kalama, Tina Kuckkahn, John Ladenburg, Peggy McCloud, Melissa Parr, Bret Ruby, Bill Tobin, and John Weller. I am grateful for their time, insight, and generosity. Their commitment to justice and history was humbling. It was a joy to research and write about histories that matter to so many people today.

A number of colleagues read earlier iterations of this book and offered comments and criticism that have improved its analysis and shifted its trajectory. My thanks to the members of the University of Minnesota's American Indian Studies Workshop who read several pieces of this project and provided helpful feedback at crucial stages. Barbara Welke and the fellows of the 2009 J. Willard Hurst Summer Institute of Legal History at the University of Wisconsin at Madison gave me excellent feedback as I wrestled with the legal aspects of my work. I presented portions of this work at the annual meetings of the American Society for Ethnohistory, the Native American and Indigenous Studies Association, the Organization of American Historians, and the American Historical Association, and I would like to thank the members of these organizations for their feedback and suggestions. My history department colleagues at Wake Forest read a draft of the introduction and offered suggestions and helpful criticism. In addition, several colleagues read portions or entire chapter drafts and improved the book as a result. Theresa Ventura, Nate Plageman, Jake Ruddiman, and Ben Coates patiently read my work, thought through some of the puzzles with me, and lead me to important sources that shaped my writing in the later stages. My good friend Julie Weiskopf dedicated whole days and her sharp editorial eye to searching out errors in an early draft of this book. Polly Myers, my writing partner for the last eight years, devoted many hours to reviewing this manuscript. She read multiple chapter drafts and consistently offered helpful suggestions and questions. Polly's work ethic has kept me motivated, and her good-natured commiseration kept me grounded.

I have benefited from the support and encouragement of brilliant scholarly mentors. At the University of Minnesota, David Chang, Brenda Child, Kevin P. Murphy, Jean O'Brien, Barbara Welke, and David E. Wilkins offered suggestions about law and political culture that pushed me to develop this book in new directions. In particular, Jean O'Brien and Kevin

Murphy deserve the highest praise possible. In my moments of crisis they offered calm reassurances, and in times of doubt they offered encouragement. I am deeply grateful for their concern, unfailing support, and valuable advice. I can only hope to inspire and energize people the way Jeani does; her infectious laughter and spirited insights have made every conversation an uplifting experience. Kevin has been an extraordinary figure in my academic life in Minnesota and beyond. Since I first met him, he has prompted me to think, teach, and write about public history in challenging and important ways. Jeani and Kevin share a collaborative approach to scholarship and foster supportive relationships with younger scholars; they continue to represent in my eyes the very best of academia. I had the good fortune to meet Theresa Earenfight at Seattle University, who offered me encouragement and wholehearted support (in addition to her office) as I transitioned from graduate student to faculty member. At Wake Forest University I have benefited from the guidance and wisdom of numerous senior colleagues, particularly Paul Escott, Michele Gillespie, Monique O'Connell, and Anthony Parent. My mentors and brilliant aunts, Kathleen Blee and Pam Goldman, reviewed fellowship applications, read portions of the manuscript, and offered astute professional advice. I would like to thank an anonymous reader and Alexandra Harmon for reviewing the manuscript. They caught embarrassing errors and posed critical questions that pushed me to deepen my analysis. I am especially grateful to Sasha for offering guidance and advice at a crucial point in my revision process. Mark Simpson-Vos, the editorial director at the University of North Carolina Press, extended his support for this project from an early stage and patiently helped me navigate through the revision and publication process. I am grateful to Mark for seeing the promise in this book so many years ago, for helping me to figure out what it is about, and for advocating for it. The University of North Carolina Press assembled an excellent editorial team for the final stages of revision. I am grateful to Paul Betz and Caitlin Bell-Butterfield of the Press and to freelancer Dorothea Anderson for their fine editing work. I have had the benefit of many valuable interventions, although the errors or missteps that remain are entirely my own.

I was able to complete this book with the assistance of fellowships, travel and publication grants, and crucial institutional support. The Newberry Library granted me a summer research fellowship and access to its fantastic resources. The American Historical Association's Littleton-Griswold Research Grant, the Council on Intercollegiate Cooperation, American Indian Studies Consortium Graduate Student Award, and the

University of Minnesota College of Liberal Arts Research Grant all allowed me to travel to Washington, D.C., and to Washington State archives to conduct necessary research throughout 2007. With the assistance of writing fellowships from the history department and graduate school at the University of Minnesota, I had the opportunity to move to Seattle and immerse myself in research and writing. The College of Liberal Arts at Wake Forest University granted me an Archie Award in 2010, and the history department provided travel funds for research, conferences, and editing. Wake Forest University also awarded me a junior faculty leave, which provided invaluable time away from teaching to focus on book revisions. Finally, the University of North Carolina Press enabled me to complete this project with a publication grant in 2012.

I received a great deal of support from family and friends who contributed in no small way to my well-being and, by extension, the completion of this book. Thanks to Paul Mosher, Kathy Brewer, Julie Weiskopf, Ali Schneider, and Rebecca McCaffery for their loving spirit and sense of humor and for helping me to keep work in perspective. I am grateful to Amanda Tanner, Ben and Vivian Coates, Sean Dunwoody, Monique O'Connell, Nate Plageman, Jake Ruddiman, Theresa Ventura, Emily Wakild, and Heather Welland for exploring North Carolina with me and helping to make Winston-Salem feel like home. Thanks to Ben and Betsy Boyce for generously providing me with a familiar home base and fun outings during my frequent research trips to Seattle. I want to thank Polly and Jason Myers, an extraordinarily generous couple, for opening their home to me and my family and for always offering a bed, salmon, and much more on my periodic visits to Anacortes. Nathan Roberts offered support and intellectual fellowship over the years of this project, patiently reading drafts and giving smart and honest feedback at critical points. Nathan encouraged me through computer crashes, research setbacks, and bouts of self-doubt, all while introducing me to extraordinary places in Washington. Josh and Anna Blee cheered me on with great love, and the boys teach me more about the wonders of Puget Sound every year. Finally, Tim and Virginia Blee taught me to see learning as a lifelong process and always encouraged me to do what makes me happy. I am constantly humbled and inspired by their commitment to educating and healing others. It is to my parents that I dedicate this book.

Introduction

On a gray and rainy Christmas day in 1854, U.S. officials received several Native headmen and hundreds of Indian spectators at the treaty council grounds on the bank of She-Nah-Nam Creek, known to the Americans as Medicine Creek. The council brought together settlers, territorial officials, and Nisqually, Puyallup, Squaxin Island, and other Native peoples to clarify access to the watershed's abundant resources. The Indian headmen, dressed in their finest ceremonial regalia, hoped to establish good partnerships with the Americans and finally receive compensation for the land, materials, and services taken from them. The U.S. treaty party came to the council with a different agenda. Isaac I. Stevens, the newly appointed Washington territorial governor and Indian superintendent, initiated the treaty negotiations in order to extinguish Indian land title and secure homesteaders' claims.

The council at Medicine Creek was to be the first in a lengthy Northwest treaty tour for Stevens. To expedite his mission, Stevens called on local settlers to identify Indian chiefs and sub-chiefs for the purpose of signing his pre-drawn treaty. Quiemuth was recognized as chief of the Nisquallies; his younger brother, Leschi, was recognized as sub-chief. The negotiations at Medicine Creek were frustrating for the headmen. Stevens did not take the time to understand the needs of the Native communities nor to respond to Indians' concerns about his treaty terms. Leschi and others objected to the proposed Nisqually reservation because it was small and the land was poor and rocky. Even worse, the reserve excluded the best pastureland and river fishing sites in the Nisqually watershed. Despite headmen's protests over the reservation, Stevens collected the requisite signatures the next day and sent the document to Congress for approval. The most significant outcomes of the treaty were the immense land transfer and the political relationship established between the United States and numerous Indian nations: Indians in the southern Puget Sound ceded

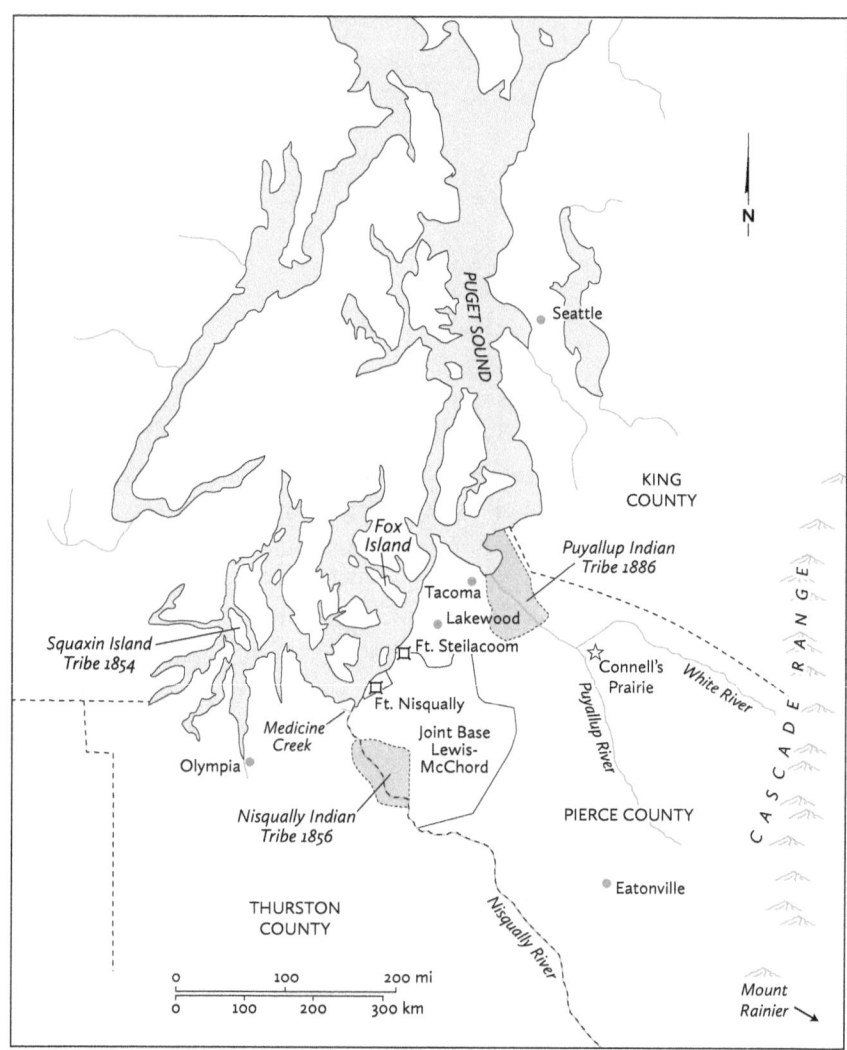

South Puget Sound, Washington

over 2.2 million acres to the United States in exchange for peace, payment, protection, and services.

The territorial newspaper reported that the Indians were satisfied with the treaty, but as Stevens continued on his treaty tour, rumbles of discontent began to grow. In the summer of 1855, war erupted on the eastern side of the Cascade Mountains following Stevens's treaty council with the Yakama Indians. The fighting across the mountains heightened anxieties and suspicions around Puget Sound. The acting governor raised two companies of volunteers from Olympia and sent regular troops toward Yakima at the army's request. The volunteers and regulars rendezvoused at a camp just to the east of the Nisqually watershed. The commander of the joint forces sent an express party from camp with a message for his superior at Fort Steilacoom. The party, including an escort with militiamen Joseph Miles, Antonio Rabbeson, and Abram Benton Moses, traveled through Nisqually country, and on the afternoon of October 31 they encountered a sizable group of Klickitat and Nisqually men and women on a prairie. The Indians dispersed when the express party rode up, but fifteen minutes later the Americans were fired upon from behind. Miles fell from his horse fatally wounded, and Moses succumbed to the bullet wound in his back a few minutes later. Leschi would later be charged with murdering Moses based on Rabbeson's eyewitness testimony.

Nisqually warriors engaged regular and volunteer soldiers in skirmishes throughout the fall of 1855. As the winter rains set in, the heat of war dissipated. By late December, the army commander began to withdraw regular troops from the field. In January 1856, Stevens returned from his treaty tour and directed the volunteers to pursue Indians hiding in the mountains, and he placed neutral Indians into protective custody on island camps. The U.S. Army general for West Coast operations criticized Stevens for prolonging violence with his aggressive policies. In late January, a group of Indians attacked the hamlet of Seattle and killed two settlers. Leschi was assumed to have led the attack, but he denied any involvement. In fact, Leschi attempted to negotiate a peaceful resolution to the conflict during that time. In March 1856 the American forces and allied Native warriors engaged in their final and decisive armed confrontation, and the defeated Indians retreated to the east. A couple of months later, Leschi surrendered to the army near Yakima. Governor Stevens finally disbanded the western Washington volunteers and in August met with the neutral Indians held in custody to discuss the reservation boundaries. The Nisqually people demanded and received an expanded reservation that included prairies, village sites, and a stretch of the Nisqually River.

This was not the end to the matter, however. Governor Stevens insisted that the only way to end the war and stabilize the region was to put Indian war leaders on trial. The U.S. Army reportedly assured Leschi he would not be held liable for the war, but, not honoring this amnesty, territorial officials brought civilian charges against him. Based on Rabbeson's testimony, a grand jury indicted Leschi for the murder of A. B. Moses. Notably, Rabbeson was both the primary eyewitness and the foreman of the grand

FIGURE 1 Portrait of Leschi by an unknown artist, ca. 1895. (Washington State Historical Society)

jury. A mere four days after he was delivered into custody, Leschi stood trial for murder, on November 17, 1856. Despite the hasty organization of Leschi's trial, it followed the letter of the law: Leschi was indicted by a grand jury and was represented by two capable defense lawyers who were given the opportunity to review the evidence against him, a federally appointed judge presided over the speedy and public proceedings, and the jury was composed of local white men. As the primary eyewitness, Rabbeson once again testified that he saw Leschi shoot at the express party. After a day of testimony and a night of deliberations, the jury reported that the members were deadlocked. The judge dismissed the jury and ordered the prisoner to be held for another trial.

In the second trial, on March 9, 1857, Rabbeson once again served as the prosecution's principal witness. Rabbeson's testimony was jumbled and confused. He stated he did not know any of the Indians the party initially encountered on the prairie but later claimed that Leschi had been in the group and must have traveled by separate trail in order to ambush them. Many of the witnesses for the defense contradicted or discounted Rabbeson's testimony. Another express party member testified that the low light conditions on the prairie had made it difficult to identify anyone with certainty. Two witnesses recalled conversations soon after the incident in which Rabbeson told them he could not distinguish the Indians on the prairie or identify them by name. Leschi did not take the stand in his own defense. After a night of deliberation, the jury returned its unanimous guilty verdict. The judge sentenced the prisoner to hang by the neck until dead. Leschi's lawyers appealed to the Territorial Supreme Court, but the justices upheld the ruling. Leschi was hanged in a field near Steilacoom on February 19, 1858, in Washington Territory's first judicial execution.

In South Puget Sound—a region stretching southwest from Seattle to Olympia and west from the Cascade Mountain Range to Puget Sound—the key facts of Leschi's story are relatively well known. And yet Leschi's story is not as simple as it appears. I have chosen certain details and events that reflect how Leschi's story might be told today. But it has not always been told the same way over time. Framings have shifted, plot points have changed, actors have grown significant or faded away, motives and intentions have evolved, and heroes have turned to villains and villains have turned to heroes. There are many different perspectives on those events of the 1850s, and Leschi's story is not always as it seems. This is not just a philosophical point—it is also a political one. The histories we tell do work for us. They create identity, communities, and nations. They make us feel proud, ashamed, or angry. One of the most important uses of the past is to make amends—a social and political act with the potential to maintain *or* change relationships of power in the present and for the future. Leschi's story has done, and continues to do, a great deal of work. Nearly 150 years and a few miles from Leschi's execution, a group of people once again gathered together to negotiate their relationships to one another. Their goal was to discuss the historical record about Leschi in an effort to reconcile differing histories and reckon with the past.

On the overcast Friday afternoon of December 10, 2004, judges, lawyers, historians, activists, and audience members dressed in suits, robes, and ceremonial Coast Salish regalia crowded into a modest auditorium in the Washington State History Museum in Tacoma. The room was filled to capacity, and video cameras recorded the event and aired the proceedings on closed circuit in the museum mezzanine for the overflow crowd and on public access television.[1] The participants convened to review the surviving record of Leschi's trials and decide not only what happened in the 1850s but also what they should do about what happened. Theirs was an ambitious undertaking: changing history. The participants dubbed their novel creation the Washington State Historical Court of Inquiry and Justice.

Chief Justice Gerry Alexander described the endeavor as "uncharted territory." Unlike other trials, there were no living witnesses, the court records were sparse and suspect, and the defendant had been executed nearly 150 years earlier. The judges had never before heard a case that presented quite the temporal, procedural, and political challenges as did the task at hand. "The passage of time makes it extremely difficult to [reconstruct the case]," Alexander told a *New York Times* reporter before the court convened. "But it is like a regular trial, because what you are doing at a trial is searching for the truth. So we're searching for it as best as we humanly can."[2] The best, the *only*, way to bring justice and determine the truth from the foggy past, Alexander maintained, was through a symbolic court.

The Historical Court was the result of a lengthy negotiation that had begun years earlier. In 2001, Sherman Leschi gave Cynthia Iyall the project of "[taking] care of Leschi."[3] Sherman was a direct Leschi descendant, and Iyall, a young Nisqually woman descended from Leschi's sister, took her elder's command seriously. Nisqually family stories maintained Leschi's innocence, but how could these stories stand up against the official ruling of the territorial courts? Iyall turned to the tribal historian, Cecelia Svinth Carpenter, who had worked for years to amass an archive documenting Leschi's life and trials. Carpenter believed the historical record proved that Leschi could not have ambushed Miles and Moses on the prairie and that Rabbeson's testimony should have been dismissed. Carpenter felt confident that these documents could prove Leschi's innocence in court if given the opportunity. Other tribal elders supported Iyall in council meetings when she proposed the idea of a legal exoneration for Leschi.[4]

At about the same time as Iyall was considering how to proceed with a trial, the Washington State Historical Society was developing an exhibit, titled Treaty Trail, set to open in December 2004 to coincide with the sesquicentennial of the Medicine Creek Treaty. Melissa Parr, a member of the curatorial staff, was familiar with Carpenter's historical research and contacted her about the museum's plans. Carpenter recognized that Parr might bring important resources to Iyall's plan, and Parr, as a public historian, believed in the educational importance of telling Leschi's story to a broad public audience.[5] Iyall, Carpenter, and Parr organized as the Committee to Exonerate Chief Leschi and over the following two years made connections with legal professionals, politicians, and academics in pursuit of their goal.[6]

The committee met with Chief Justice Gerry Alexander to establish the structure and agree upon the witnesses for the December 2004 event. Alexander insisted that the court carry only symbolic significance and that the judges' decision would not be guaranteed. The expert witnesses

FIGURE 2 Eugene Ham testifying on the stand in the Historical Court as other witnesses watch from the audience, December 10, 2004. From left to right: Billy Frank Jr., Shanna Stevenson, Dorian Sanchez, Cecelia Svinth Carpenter, Cynthia Iyall, and Connie McCloud. (Hearst Newspapers, LLC/Seattle PI / Karen Ducey)

and lawyers, Alexander maintained, should provide different views on Leschi's case in order to capture the adversarial spirit of a courtroom. In the end, the petitioners offered seven experts for their case: Cecelia Carpenter; Charles Wilkinson, professor of Indian law at the University of Colorado; Shanna Stevenson, historic preservation officer for Thurston County; Captain Eugene Ham, attorney in the office of the judge advocate general at Fort Lewis Army Base;[7] Captain Paul Robson, army lawyer at Fort Lewis; Alexandra Harmon, professor of American Indian Studies at the University of Washington and member of the Washington State Bar; and Kent Richards, professor of history at Central Washington University. Four Native American representatives joined the experts: Cynthia Iyall; Dorian Sanchez, chairman of the Nisqually Indian Tribe; Connie McCloud from the Puyallup tribal council; and Bill Frank Jr., an enrolled member of the Nisqually Tribe and the chairman of the Northwest Indian Fisheries Commission.

The seven judges on the court panel came from the Washington Supreme Court, Division One and Division Two Court of Appeals, Thurston and Pierce County Superior Courts, and Lummi Tribal Court.[8] They volunteered to participate not out of professional obligation but because of curiosity, a sense of community service, or personal interest. Alexander contacted the Pierce County prosecuting attorney, Gerald Horne, to ask if his office would also participate. Horne agreed to do so and appointed prosecutors Mary Robnett and Carl Hultman to represent the respondents. The respondents would argue to confirm Leschi's 1857 conviction, although Hultman admitted to personal sympathy with the petitioners' cause. In fact, Carl and his wife, Sharon, who worked as a designer and writer at the Washington State Historical Society, had reviewed the surviving evidence of the case, actively built support for the Historical Court, and offered legal advice to the Committee to Exonerate Chief Leschi at an early stage in its planning.[9] The petitioners, meanwhile, selected their legal team: Bill Tobin and Thor Hoyte, Nisqually tribal attorneys; Robert Anderson, director of the University of Washington Native American Law Center; John Ladenburg, Pierce County executive; and Tina Kuckkahn from the Longhouse Education and Cultural Center at the Evergreen State College.

The Washington Historical Court of Inquiry and Justice was a singular creation born of grassroots networking, felicitous timing, and patient negotiation. On December 10, the participants established the appearance of a courtroom, with a bailiff, panel of robed justices, petitioner and respondent counsel tables, and witnesses, who were administered an oath en masse. The museum auditorium had all the trappings of a courtroom, but clearly this was a different animal. The time for the court was limited to a mere four hours, the format did not follow appellate procedure, the decision carried no legal weight, and the judges sat on the bench because they were particularly interested in the case rather than disinterested. Indeed, the court event was unique and not easy to define. The *Olympian* newspaper referred to it as a "tribunal," Alexander called it a "symposium" and "historical court," the tribe's legal counsel called it an "educational opportunity," and the Nisqually planners called it simply "the exoneration."[10]

The arguments presented in the Historical Court further illustrate the complexity of an undertaking that blurred the past and present. In their opening statement, the petitioners' counsel laid out a two-pronged argument in favor of Leschi's exoneration. First, they would show that the 1856 murder indictment was premised on insufficient evidence and that the case should not have advanced to a jury. Second, Leschi's 1857 trial was marred by legal error, and if granted a new trial that followed the proper rules of law, Leschi would not have been found guilty beyond a reasonable doubt. The expert witnesses presented a detailed narrative of Leschi's case and built an argument for jurisdictional error: Leschi was an enemy combatant who should not have stood trial in a civilian court for a killing committed during a time of war. The Native representatives, meanwhile, departed from legal arguments and explained how the loss of their leader was a source of ongoing pain and how the possibility of exoneration offered them hope. In the closing statement, the petitioners' legal counsel appealed to the judges to take the opportunity to do the right thing and deliver justice to Leschi and his descendants.

The respondents' counsel—representing the state and defending the territorial court's 1857 conviction—countered with an argument against meddling with history. Robnett opened with the claim that Leschi had received a fair trial by the legal standards of the 1850s and to change a ruling to satisfy political whims would imperil the authority of the rule of law. Hultman reasoned in his closing argument that it was hubris to dismiss legal professionals in the past as biased when only shreds of evidence remain of what they had seen and experienced. If society appreciated the professionalism of judges and lawyers today, it stands to reason that those involved in Leschi's case also deserved the benefit of the doubt. For their part, the expert witnesses presented historical material from the 1850s from various legal and military perspectives. The military lawyers acknowledged that laws had changed over the last 150 years but drew attention to continuities. Richards, the author of a biography of Isaac Stevens, highlighted differences and warned against judging the past by today's standards.

The opposing arguments offered in the Historical Court represented different visions concerning the role of the past in the present and how to address the past's enduring impacts. This was not just a philosophical debate—it was also a political one. More was at stake than determining Leschi's guilt or innocence; the legitimacy of American courts, the character of Indian nationhood, the bounds of cultural and political pluralism, and equality before the law were also at issue in the symbolic court. After three and a half hours of testimony and argument, the panel of judges took a brief recess to consider their decision. The Committee to Exonerate Chief Leschi waited in anxious anticipation. Finally, the judges filed back into the auditorium and Justice Alexander issued the court's decision:

> We have unanimously concluded . . . that on October 31, 1855 . . . a state of war existed between the federal Territory of Washington and several Indian tribes, including the Nisqually Indian tribe. A. B. Moses

FIGURE 3 Nisqually procession ceremony and celebration at the Washington State Capitol Museum following Leschi's exoneration, December 10, 2004. (Washington State Historical Society)

was a combatant in that war as a member of the Territorial Militia, and . . . his death occurred in this war, and therefore Chief Leschi should not, as a matter of law, have been tried for the crime of murder. Therefore, because that is the case, the historical court would exonerate Chief Leschi.

The audience broke into applause. Press coverage from around the country lauded the verdict for clearing Leschi's name and celebrated the quasi-legal structure as an innovative way to confront a long-standing injustice against indigenous people. Leschi's exoneration, they agreed, was generations in the making and long overdue.

But what exactly was attempted and what was achieved that December day? Did the Historical Court intervene in the past and make amends for its effects? What course did it set for the future? This book addresses these deceptively simple questions by delving into the epistemologies of justice, memory, and history at play in the Historical Court. My goal is to deconstruct the Historical Court as an exercise of assimilating different interpretations of the past into a single historical "truth" and definition of justice.

The Historical Court provides insight into the way in which different cultures and political interests construct history, build a relationship between the past, present, and future, and put memories to work. I am not concerned only with what happened—Leschi's trials in 1857 and 2004—but also with the claims people made about what happened, what it means, and how it should shape the future. This book offers a history of Leschi's conviction in 1857 and exoneration in 2004 as events fixed in time as well as symbols that gather significance outside of their time frames and as windows into the political dynamics of historical production and identity formation.[11] By considering the politics of those historical narratives in South Puget Sound, this book will show that the 1850s and 2004 were not the only moments in which Indians and non-Indians negotiated their political relationship. This study is drawn from a specific case, but the issues it presents are not limited to South Puget Sound. Across the country and around the world, people struggle to reckon with the past. This case study shows how and why historical justice is a perpetual but unfulfilled goal.

Historical justice is a paradoxical process in which the past is put to work to make amends for its effects. Instead of ending conflicts about the past, however, this process contains a circular logic that ensures repeated struggles. Historical justice nominally separates history from memory to find the "truth." Supreme Court Justice Alexander insisted that sifting through the facts would lead the judges to determine what really happened so they could then decide what *should have* happened according to so-called rationally applied law and the universal principle of justice. The Historical Court at first glance appears as confirmation of common values and shared politics. Participants in the Historical Court—representing a range of perspectives and drawing various meanings from the past—might find satisfaction in the decision to exonerate Leschi: the judges protected the logic and perception of fairness in the U.S. legal system; public historians provided an educational event; and Nisqually activists cleared Leschi's name. Although the Historical Court offered a mechanism through which these various and competing interests found common ground, the result was not a resolution or a single vision for the future. To deny the entanglements of history and memory ignores how the past continues to haunt the present and obscures ideological and cultural continuities that perpetuate injustice. This haunting, in turn, leads to continuing conflict over the meaning of the past and prompts people to demand a resolution to ongoing grievances. The logic of historical justice leads back to itself; it is at the same time the solution and the problem.

Liberalism helped create the problem of injustice the Historical Court sought to address, but it also provided the theoretical tools to remedy it. Philosophical liberalism emerged in the seventeenth century and has been expressed through numerous and differing formulations over time.[12] The core ideas in the liberal tradition are individualism, equality, and the existence of universal principles applicable to all humans. Based on these basic presuppositions, progress and reform are possible and rational individuals share a common moral standing.[13] Throughout the period covered in this book, 1854 to 2004, liberal discourse and institutions reflected and shaped historical narratives of Leschi. The background, structure, and exchanges within the Historical Court likewise illuminate the dynamic and contradictory nature of the liberal tradition in American society.

Liberalism provides a crucial context for understanding Leschi's conviction and exoneration because this tradition informs both colonialism and indigenous struggles against colonial domination. On the one hand, there has long been a mutually constitutive relationship between liberalism and colonialism.[14] Settler colonialism is more than the event of invasion fixed in time; it is a structure of discourse premised on the usurpation of Native land and the elimination of Native societies.[15] In North America, from the early years of the Virginia colony, English colonial agents used the beginnings of liberal theory to justify settler colonialism and deny the rights of indigenous people to their homelands.[16] By projecting Western culture and land use as universal models drawn from supposedly natural law, colonizers characterized Indians' resistance as irrational and as proof of their inferior civilization. Of course, principles modeled on Western culture and adapted to support the pragmatic goals of one group are neither natural nor universal. This aspect of the liberal tradition functioned from the eighteenth to the twentieth centuries to justify the dispossession of indigenous peoples in settler societies across the globe.[17]

On the other hand, the liberal tradition also generated debates about the justice of colonial endeavors and the inequality it helped produce. Liberal ideals of inalienable rights, equality, and progress could be mobilized in favor of indigenous peoples.[18] In the United States, for example, indigenous nations adopted the liberal discourse of sovereignty to demand rights and recognition in U.S. courts.[19] Many postcolonial critics of liberalism insist that the problem is not with liberal ideals themselves but with the narrow conditions under which universalisms are conceptualized. Moral universalisms like justice do exist, some political theorists maintain, but must be reformulated through inclusive and genuine negotiation with diverse cultures.[20]

Like its embodiment in the Historical Court, the history of the persistent struggle to align liberal ideals with reality embodies the paradox of liberal reform: the solution is the problem and vice versa. Over the last 150 years, human rights advocates, political philosophers, and social reformers have mobilized liberal ideals to critique the policies, relations, and institutions that liberalism helped to create, with mixed results.[21] For example, liberal reformers in the late nineteenth century pushed assimilationist policies targeted at Native people to promote the ideals of individualism and equality of opportunity, but these policies had destructive effects on indigenous cultural sovereignty.[22] Many of the liberal government policies that followed in the twentieth century likewise had the effect of protecting a core Euro-American culture and treating indigenous people as wards rather than partners or constituents.[23] Proponents of multiculturalism, an ideology in operation in the Historical Court, critique assimilation and have sought a pluralistic society in which all members, regardless of cultural, racial, or religious background, can feel valued and free.[24] Multiculturalism ideally opens opportunities for oft-ignored minorities to educate others about their unique histories. However, critics point out that multicultural discourse can gloss over historical disadvantage, reassert the status quo, and ignore continuing acts of discrimination.[25] For American Indians, multiculturalism can remove the political significance of their claims by reducing indigenous peoples to one among many ethnic, cultural, or racial divisions within society.[26] In the context of long efforts to make ideals match reality, this case study demonstrates how liberal thought contains the tools for its own reform but also how liberal traditions define and limit the bounds of change.[27]

Given the historic entanglements of liberalism, colonialism, and reform, the Historical Court represents a complicated solution to historical controversy. By adopting an adversarial court format to determine a single truth and correlating Western legal performance with the principle of justice, the Historical Court mobilized and reinforced the structure of colonialism.[28] But by working outside of the limited confines of official appellate procedure, the symbolic court created a public space for testimony about Nisqually nationhood and Native perspectives on the past. This duality is significant because historical justice for Indian people is complicated by their unique legal status and political concerns. Unlike other minorities,

Native Americans can hold three sets of citizenship rights (federal, state, and tribal) and maintain their political separateness from state institutions that have long attempted to dominate and dismantle their nations.[29] Political theorists pushing for decolonization debate whether indigenous groups should make demands from within or from outside of Western institutions. Some maintain that indigenous groups that agree to negotiate on terms established by a colonial state forfeit their freedoms and right to self-definition. Others argue that liberalism offers the most promising framework for advancing indigenous interests; strategic negotiation within this flexible system holds the potential to create a truly postcolonial democracy.[30] The Historical Court illustrates a deep faith in liberal institutions while also revealing the limits and opportunities such institutions pose for indigenous peoples' political and cultural concerns.

The Historical Court was unique in that it was the first quasi-legal tribunal in the United States to review the government's legal treatment of a Native American leader. But it is also part of a recent global trend toward addressing historic injustices, which some analysts describe as our "age of apology."[31] Since the 1970s, there have been numerous state-sponsored truth and reconciliation commissions in countries emerging from oppressive pasts as a way to distinguish the new regime from the old and to direct victims' urges away from retribution. By 2004, at least twenty official truth and reconciliation commissions had conducted research and issued reports.[32] The United States has ordered investigations and extended apologies and reparations to the survivors of certain state-sponsored, race-based injustices, most notably for Japanese-American internment (1988) and the Tuskegee syphilis study (1997).[33] In situations in which state-sponsored historical justice initiatives are not forthcoming or desired, unofficial historical tribunals have convened to investigate events of racial violence at the local level.[34] The Oklahoma Commission to Study the Tulsa Riots of 1921 (1997–2001), the 1898 Wilmington Race Riot Commission (2000–2006), and the Greensboro Truth and Reconciliation Commission (2004–2006) all featured reports with victim testimony, but their power was limited to issuing recommendations for ways to reconcile the divided communities.[35]

The symbolic gestures in the "age of apology" should not be dismissed as inconsequential. Politically weaker groups sometimes choose to turn to symbolic politics when concrete action is closed to them.[36] Symbolic measures have the potential to set new standards for discussions of rights, empower future activists, and bring historical matters into the light in a way that contributes to greater public acceptance of indigenous claims.[37] In settler colonial states, indigenous nations must rely upon their colonizers to take responsibility for their own conduct. As Hoopa leader Lyle Marshall noted, "Indian survival depends on the American conscience."[38] The Historical Court adopted the truth commission model of opening a public space for "victim" testimony so that suffering could be acknowledged without passing judgment or prescribing sanctions for the perpetrators.[39] Testimony in public hearings is integral to the process of restoring justice. Even if a wrong from the past can no longer be righted, the act of telling one's story can be cathartic to the victim and to society alike.[40] The Nisqually planners and their legal team adopted this element to press the moral imperative for exoneration in the Historical Court. The petitioners made the point that people continue to suffer because of historical injustices and that the current society owes a moral responsibility to acknowledge and address its source.[41] Like many other apologies, truth commissions, and tribunals around the world, the Historical Court allowed aggrieved peoples to be heard, educated the public about events in the shared past, and appealed to a moral definition of justice.

The symbolic court allowed Native representatives to talk about the past, but it also demonstrated how colonial logic continues to determine the rules of engagement on historical grievances. The reality of Native Americans' political weakness can be seen in the omissions in the Historical Court: Nisqually people could testify about the impacts of boarding schools, but monetary reparations were not discussed; tribal leaders talked about Leschi's defense of Nisqually land and resources, yet the return of lands was not on the table; Nisqually activists used the authority of the court structure to find redress, but they did not claim an enduring place for tribal self-government in larger political and legal systems. Critics of truth commissions, tribunals, and apologies argue that without reparations and changes in the political and economic status of indigenous nations, such gestures are hollow because they do not engage with ongoing colonial domination. Without addressing the true source of historical grievances in settler colonial societies and discussing substantive solutions, symbolic justice initiatives actually extend and naturalize state authority over indigenous affairs.[42] As anthropologist Patrick Wolfe explains, the cultural logic of colonialism is both "more diffuse and more resilient" than can be addressed through a single legal decision—or, in this case, a legal correction.[43] To symbolically exonerate Leschi of his 1857 conviction neither shifts power to the Nisqually Tribe nor dismantles the logic that Leschi's conviction expressed and maintained. It is a feature of a liberal democracy to allow certain room for reform but also to protect traditions that have long structured power.

The Historical Court demonstrates the politics of including Indian testimony within a hybrid quasi-legal truth and reconciliation commission. Native representatives in the court offered unmediated stories about Leschi from their own perspectives. In doing so, the representatives made a powerful statement about the validity of Native ways of knowing and redrew the lines around facts, archives, and the meaning of the past. Yet in order to build a convincing case for Leschi's exoneration for the judges, the Nisqually petitioners and their legal team also had to appeal to Western ways of understanding history. Although views are changing, Western historical perspectives continue to gain public authority by claiming to reflect objective inquiry. This assertion of universal rationality powerfully naturalizes modern historical discourse as scientific fact.[44] Orally based historical traditions run counter to disciplinary rules of history, enabling Westerners to dominate indigenous peoples by categorizing them as nonhistorical and biased and their knowledge as "myth."[45] The Historical Court allowed oral tradition but also retained labels for those offering testimony that ranked the expertise of the speaker: the distinction between "expert witnesses" and "Native representatives" reasserts the exclusion of indigenous historical understandings from the realm of legitimate historical practice.

The historical record used in the tribunal demonstrates further the entanglements of liberal thought and institutions, colonialism and decolonization, and history and memory. The Historical Court attempted to assimilate different perspectives on the past in order to offer a swap: the false history for a righted one; a racist past for a postracial present; a "vindication of tribal history over white man's history," as the petitioners' counsel put it.[46] But our relationship with the past is not so simple. Reckoning with the past means not only acknowledging what happened but also delving into the messy and uncomfortable process of historical production.[47] This book traces claims about Leschi and the region's history to reveal the dynamics of historical narrative production in a colonial context. The United States exerted legal and political sovereignty in South Puget Sound starting in the mid-nineteenth century, which empowered Americans over time to define events, collect "legitimate" accounts for posterity, and authorize certain individuals to create interpretations of this record. U.S. settlers had the greatest opportunities to produce and disseminate stories of relations with Indians, and their stories justified U.S. cultural, legal, and political domination. Native people, although largely lacking access to political power during the same time period, nevertheless produced historical narratives that subverted, co-opted, or adapted colonial ideologies and practices in pursuit of individual or collective self-determination. Given these divergent narrative goals, one would expect two diametrically opposed histories.

But each moment of historical production was shaped by negotiation and shifting political and legal circumstances that ultimately blurred or rearranged the lines between Native and non-Indian, colonizer and colonized. Although it is possible to identify different elements and oppositional goals in settler and Nisqually stories, we cannot find two wholly different and oppositional histories. The dynamism of historical production means a single master narrative is elusive, as is a coherent counter narrative. Colonialism causes memory entanglements and narrative collaborations, leading to a historical record with layered contributors and influences. This is not to say that the power to direct historical production was equal, but a closer look at the discrete moments in the process of history-making reveals some give-and-take. We can see the results of this dynamic in the Historical Court: the same representations that established Leschi's guilt in 1857 led to his exoneration in 2004. The same archive that aided in Native dispossession became a source of Nisqually empowerment generations later.

The Historical Court is significant as a rare event that relied upon the documentary record and Indian and non-Indian testimony to navigate through—and sometimes skirt around—colonial ideology and action. The negotiation around Leschi's story uncovers the nation's deep ambivalence toward its settler colonial foundations—a topic often missing from conversations about the nation's past. Most scholarly literature on U.S. historical memory and conflicting narratives has focused on the enduring legacy of slavery and racial segregation. One American scholar of historical grievances argued that the African slave trade "remains the acid test of historical reconciliation. No other aspect of the nation's past has left such a profound imprint on the present."[48] Certainly slavery created a terrible and significant legacy, but American policies and actions designed to dispossess and exterminate Native Americans left deep and profound impacts on land, people, societies, and the national psyche as well. As the story of Leschi's life and death illustrates, the foundations of the present-day South Puget Sound region's demographics and power structure were forged through a history of negotiation, violence, and coercion. Yet westward "expansion" remains a celebratory facet of the nation's historical narrative, which reinforces the assumption that Native people and their land claims succumbed to an irresistible destiny or inevitable natural force. The process of constructing settler sovereignty in peripheral territories of the United States has been largely silenced and compartmentalized, as evidenced by the enduring assumption that these stories constitute a separate Indian history rather than central elements of American history.[49] The history of U.S. colonialism created scars along racial lines but also initiated contests over political rights, responsibility, and sovereignty that remain unresolved. This book pushes the conversation about U.S. historical memory and reconciliation initiatives into a more complicated landscape of indigenous political claims and non-Indians' reticence to acknowledge the ongoing impacts of settler colonialism. Historical justice is not an event in which the meaning of the past permanently shifts, as the participants in the Historical Court may have hoped. Rather, it is bound up in a larger and ongoing process of reflection, renewal, and re-creation in a liberal democratic settler state.

Organization and Methodology

Studies of historical memory necessarily include a range of source material in various forms—from landscapes to reminiscences and literature to activism—in order to consider the contributions of popular and unofficial narratives to historical consciousness.[50] Such breadth can become unwieldy, but memories of Leschi proved to be of manageable size and variety for a discrete case study. In addition to archival sources, I consulted memorials, maps, novels, museum exhibits, textbooks, newspapers, journals, magazines, and photographs. I had informal conversations with public historians, independent scholars, and lay collectors and conducted formal interviews with individuals involved with the Historical Court or professionally concerned with Nisqually history. This study is distinct from most historical memory studies, however, because I use an ethnohistorical approach that combines historical research with anthropological principles.[51] Ethnohistorians hold three related assumptions about indigenous peoples: they have been active historical agents in shaping history; they know their own histories and can speak for themselves; and they act and interpret events within specific cultural frameworks. My research and interpretations flow from these assumptions, and I make a point of including Indian voices from speeches, oral histories, and anthropologists' field notes whenever possible.

Like other historians, I describe what happened and analyze what it means. This task gets a bit trickier when I also describe how people interpreted the past and analyze how they shaped the meanings of events. To properly examine the production of history alongside its unfolding, I critique some assumptions underlying Western historical methods while also employing some of the same approaches. I do not claim to be above the fray, so some discussion of methodology is in order. Notably, I began this book about deconstructing historical narratives with my own narrative of what happened to Leschi in the 1850s. I did so to provide the reader with necessary background on Leschi, his trials, and the region. This introductory information is not intended as *the* authoritative narrative. If anything, it represents merely the least contested assertions of fact. I invite readers to consider my historical account of Leschi as a starting point, rather than as a comparison, for understanding the political goals of other storytellers in the pages to come. In fact, the remainder of the book is organized specifically to draw attention to the dynamic and multivalent process of historical production.

The title of this book, *Framing Chief Leschi*, draws attention to the active and dynamic ways in which Leschi's story can be told. In a legal context, the title suggests that Leschi was accused of a crime he did not commit. But there are other possibilities. The title also refers to the literary device known as "frame narrative," in which a story is told within a story. This book tells a story with and about stories to explore three related elements of historical memory: the figure of Leschi as an actor fixed in time and place; the ways Nisquallies and non-Indians used his memory in political and legal discourse from 1854 to 2004; and the problems of disentangling history, memory, and contemporary motivations in pursuit of historical justice. Each chapter of the book offers a unique framing for the Historical Court based upon the different political projects at play. The goal of this approach is to assert and model how historical justice—just like the history on which it rests—is too complex for labels of success, failure, and progress.

The following six chapters place the Historical Court in different thematic frames rather than following a chronological ordering from the 1850s to 2004. The reason for this structure is threefold. First, the political interests at play in the Historical Court led participants and the audience to frame events of the 1850s in numerous ways. Although some expert witnesses presented material in chronological fashion, the legal argument and questioning pitched back and forth across time to discuss the meaning, causation, and impact of events. In the same way, the thematic chapters in this book illustrate how interpretation and reinterpretation are critical to the construction of historical narratives. To provide a chronological story would obscure the negotiations that led up to and informed the Historical Court. Second, the organization of this book challenges the liberal notion that we inhabit an ever-improving moral age and that the Historical Court symbolizes society's approach to perfection.[52] To begin with Leschi's conviction in 1857 and end with his symbolic exoneration in 2004 suggests such a trajectory. The thematic chapters complicate the notion of progress by illustrating how the Historical Court can be understood within an ongoing liberal tradition that encompasses both colonial domination *and* indigenous protest. The Historical Court has numerous histories, but it is not the conclusion or the apex of them. Third, my intention in collecting archival documents, oral histories, commemorations, and speeches about Leschi is to parse out the layers of historical production, not to graft evidence onto evidence to compile a single narrative of "what really happened." I am interested in the way diverse storytellers have learned and innovated with Leschi's story over time, and a singular account flattens rather than highlights multivocality. History is slippery in that it simultaneously unfolds and accumulates, and this approach offers more richness and complexity than a chronological telling would allow.

The following six chapters move back and forth through time to show that justice has long been a negotiated matter and one that eluded final conclusion on December 10, 2004. Each chapter turns on many of the same events and figures, which underscores the value and necessity of repetition in the storytelling process. Repetition illustrates two points about stories: first, people *remember* through repetition, and second, the same events can be framed from numerous perspectives to achieve different political objectives. This book's structure invites the reader to engage in the storytelling while showing that a story's framing—where it begins and ends, which events are included or forgotten—can define its political work.

Chapter 1 establishes the historical context for American settlement in the southern Puget Sound from the 1840s to about 1900 while illustrating how liberal ideology worked with the American legal system to facilitate settler colonialism. In order to dispossess Indians, settlers used several technologies drawn from nominally universal ways of experiencing and knowing land, including surveys, population figures, place-names, and ethnographic data. Native people accommodated, adapted, and resisted the settlers' efforts to reorder and claim the landscape, and over time they appropriated some liberal traditions to resist the effects of colonialism. The Historical Court must be placed in the material realities of South Puget Sound—the land itself—and understood in the context of this longer history of settler colonialism and liberal discourse.

Chapter 2 focuses on the contested and malleable nature of law in Leschi's 1857 conviction and 2004 exoneration. Territorial settlers and officials in the 1850s seized on the figure of Leschi to work through the proper use of U.S. law in frontier wars of expansion. Leschi was categorized simultaneously as a criminal and as a warrior, reflecting non-Indians' deep-seated impulse to see settlers as both victims and victors and the nation as both pure and powerful. Their inconsistent application of law during war was central to the petitioners' case for Leschi's exoneration in the Historical Court. This argument was well-fashioned for 2004, when the so-called War on Terror prompted similar questions about the rights of combatants. In the 1850s and in 2004, non-Indians used the mythic figure of Leschi to legitimize law and define the nation as consistently law-abiding even in the midst of wartime legal exceptions.

Non-Indians were not the only people to use Leschi's story to pursue political and cultural goals. Chapters 3 and 4 focus on Nisqually efforts to memorialize Leschi as an icon for Nisqually resistance and cultural values. Native representatives who testified in the Historical Court, like their predecessors, walked a fine line between claiming Leschi and sharing him with non-Indians. Nisqually narratives about Leschi have been shaped by generations of engagement with U.S. institutions, policies, and commemorations. Chapter 3 explores the dynamic and cooperative nature of oral traditions by analyzing an account of Leschi's life as told by several Native storytellers over the course of a century. Nisquallies claimed to have maintained a story of Leschi over generations that served as a counter narrative to non-Indians' history while transmitting unique values. From Native perspectives, Leschi's story can impact people and teach them how to fulfill responsibilities to their ancestors and children. The assertion of a counter narrative, despite the significant amount of borrowing and reciprocal influences in histories of Leschi, represents a claim to a separate Nisqually identity. The Historical Court provided a venue in which Native representatives talked about their values, their historicity, and their ancestors. In so doing, they claimed to honor Leschi and the generations of elders who kept his vision of tribal resilience alive. This chapter shows how "history" and "justice" are culturally situated in Native memory traditions and can function as a crucial element in tribal political action.

Chapter 4 focuses on the political and cultural work of narratives from a different angle. This chapter shows how changing Nisqually conceptions of tribal leadership and treaty rights developed in parallel with their commemorations for Leschi. In three periods of political crisis for the tribe, Nisqually leaders invoked Leschi as a symbol for various tribal political strategies, from accommodation to direct defiance of U.S. demands. The Historical Court was another commemorative event for Nisquallies in which the act of testifying about Leschi's leadership was inseparable from their interpretations of tribal self-determination and treaty rights.

The final two chapters assess how the Historical Court's quasi-judicial format opened opportunities for some Indian claims but also closed channels for action. Chapter 5 focuses on the significance of judicial performance in the Historical Court in the context of the unequal political relationship between Indian tribes and Western courts. The petitioners made the notable decision to pursue a judicial route to address a historical grievance because the courtroom setting and format lent authority to the symbolic ruling. However, the legal rules and restrictions that undergird this authority prevented the petitioners from receiving an actual exoneration. The Nisqually petitioners made compromises and benefited in some ways from the flexible format of the symbolic tribunal, but the Washington State Supreme Court ultimately rescued its own reputation by clearing Leschi's name. The judges appeared to enact public justice without actually making the law more inclusive. The creation of the Historical Court as a quasi-legal tribunal resulted from and reproduced the paradoxes of liberalism.

Chapter 6 argues that the colonial archive, which made the Historical Court possible, is also haunted by colonial violence that the court could not address. The legal framing of Leschi's story allowed for a sort of correction for Leschi, but there was no comparable forum to address the extralegal assassination of Leschi's brother Quiemuth. Indeed, the Nisqually petitioners' success in Leschi's case may have simultaneously planted seeds of hope *and* closed off avenues for addressing other kinds of historical injuries. A theme running throughout these chapters is that nominally universal concepts and experiences—justice, memory, law—are contested, culturally and historically situated, and continually reformed. Historical justice is fraught with contradictions and inconsistencies because it is a reflection of the long-contested process of history making (and reckoning) in a liberal democratic settler state.

CHAPTER 1 **Colonialism**

Mary Robnett, a lawyer for the respondents in the Historical Court, began her opening statement by reflecting on the role of law in society: "[The rule of law] is really the core of our democracy, it's the core of our civilization, our self-rule." Although social mores and political imperatives may evolve over time, Robnett argued, "it is part of our free and democratic and very imperfect society that we have to rely on our laws, our application of laws, and the rule of law in order to preserve ourselves." She emphasized the plural possessive—"our"—to appeal to shared American identity. In so doing, she argued that anyone who considered himself or herself a part of "our civilization" had the responsibility to protect the bedrock of the system, despite a history of legal actions that have not always reflected democratic ideals. The respondents' strategy was to present legality as a set of universal standards that created and maintained order in society. The petitioners' indigenous ancestors did not experience the imposed legal order as a set of universal rules. Rather, they witnessed how liberal traditions, the bedrock of American civilization, enabled and justified settler colonialism in the mid-nineteenth century. In South Puget Sound, like other colonial settings in western North America, so-called universal notions were critical to Indian dispossession and American possession of new territory. The Historical Court judges, lawyers, and witnesses, however, did not seek to determine what, exactly, the law helped to preserve, nor the role it played in extending U.S. sovereignty over the region.

At its core, Leschi's case was only one aspect of a multifaceted colonial process of translating ideologies, values, and self-concepts into action "on the ground" in South Puget Sound. In the Age of Discovery, English colonists used common law, from which U.S. law was drawn, to transfer ideas, values, and social relationships from one location to another and effectively overwhelm other ways of being in the world. Similarly, U.S. law created a framework through which American society could be extended to western North American territories and naturalized in the new locales. Law is so closely intertwined with colonial goals and technologies as to be, according to some theorists, "constitutive of colonialism itself."[1] And yet, focusing too narrowly on the legal facts of Leschi's case runs the risk of obscuring this larger picture: Leschi participated in and resisted a settler colonial order premised on taking possession of land and displacing indigenous people. The land itself is critical here. The ground (and water) constituted the level at which indigenous people and newcomers experienced the material realities of colonialism in South Puget Sound.[2]

Although colonial epistemologies contributed to extending U.S. sovereignty over Native people and much of their homelands by the twentieth century, colonialism in South Puget Sound reflected dynamic interactive politics and not just conquest.[3] Native people recognized how U.S. technologies of colonialism, and the Western epistemologies from which they emerged, threatened their world. But, significantly, they also saw how appropriating these technologies could perhaps provide the means for protecting their claims and ensuring survival. The Western legal system in particular provided a framework in which indigenous people denied the legitimacy of colonial domination and defended their claims within it.[4] The Historical Court was an example of this ongoing dynamic: Leschi's descendants seized upon legality and the notion of justice to address their long-standing grievance over Leschi's legal treatment. In so doing, the petitioners revealed the complicated relationship between liberalism and colonialism in a democratic settler state. This chapter explores the inherent tension in liberalism in order to explain how Americans used colonial technologies to justify and promote Indians' disappearance and dispossession, as well as how Indians strategically embraced facets of Western liberalism to resist its effects.[5]

Knowing the Land

When Natives and Europeans/Euro-Americans looked around the southern Puget Sound in the mid-nineteenth century, they each saw their surroundings differently. These varied geographies reflected different cultural values and ideologies, and the fundamental essence of settler colonialism is that one imagined geography contracted while the other expanded.[6] These geographies informed different historical narratives of the southern Puget Sound as well. On the one hand, to indigenous people the region was a sentient landscape that referenced a long and dynamic relationship with humans. On the other hand, to most colonists it was property that contained the potential for future development and material advancement. These different visions led Native peoples and newcomers to divergent senses of belonging on the land.[7]

One of the Native American representatives in the Historical Court, Connie McCloud, argued that even though much of the tribunal focused on Leschi as an individual, Leschi should not be removed from the larger geography he inhabited. In Leschi's time, the adjacent village groups indigenous to the region stretching along Puget Sound from south of present-day Bellingham to Olympia shared certain cultural characteristics and spoke a common language, which anthropologists and other writers variously described as Puget Salish, Coast Salish, or Lushootseed. These groups include Upper Skagit, Duwamish, Nisqually, and Snoqualmie, among dozens of others. Village groups in the southern reaches of the Sound, including Nisqually, Puyallup, and Squaxin, spoke Whulshootseed, a regional dialect version of Lushootseed.[8] All of the Indian representatives who testified in the court re-created a Coast Salish world for the audience to explain why they valued Leschi's name so highly. Their testimony was nominally about Leschi, but it also encapsulated a worldview and sense of being that could easily be missed in the court's focus on legal facts. Southern Coast Salish geographies, just like most non-Indians' geographic understandings, have changed in details but maintained logical consistency over time.

A word of caution is in order, however, before tracing the general outlines of this Southern Coast Salish geography. Native geographic imaginings represent a matrix of sacred, secular, linguistic, and environmental knowledge—some of which has been lost over time or strategically shielded from non-Indians' view. Most scholarly information about Southern Coast Salish geography comes from anthropologists' notes and Native peoples' printed speeches and writings. The geography outlined below represents particular knowledge the speakers or authors considered appropriate for non-Indian audiences (which may leave out sacred dimensions while following some Western conventions). For example, an important source for Nisqually history is the work of the late tribal historian Hope Cecelia Svinth Carpenter. Carpenter was raised off the Nisqually reservation and attended predominantly white, English-speaking schools in South Puget Sound. She earned an advanced degree in education (her master's thesis focused on treaty fishing rights) and taught state history in

Puget Sound junior and senior high schools.[9] Carpenter conducted archival research on Nisqually history and self-published numerous books that integrated written sources and Nisqually elders' stories. Carpenter's status as tribal historian was based primarily on the fact that she followed Western scholarly conventions; in non-Indian eyes, her expertise came from her academic training and intimate knowledge of the documentary record. Even in Carpenter's geography, which was written from an Indian perspective, the content and form reflects the pressures of colonialism and personal choices. What follows is not a singular authoritative Native geography of South Puget Sound but an outline of geographic logic specific to Nisqually and other Coast Salish people.

One Nisqually oral tradition that appears in several published sources explains how physical transformation of the land was the conscious act of a great spirit determined to teach the ancestors how to live. A long time ago—in time immemorial—people became numerous and ate up all the plants, animals, and fish and turned to eating one another. The Changer saw this abomination and brought forth a great flood that drowned everyone except a few who took refuge on the top of Ta-Co-Bet (Mt. Rainier). The survivors' progeny lost the knowledge of hunting, fishing, and making fire. The Changer took pity on them and taught them to walk upright, gave the men and women tools for their survival and comfort, taught them about good and evil spirits, and provided rules for moral behavior.[10] The great flood changed the people and the land and taught them to live harmoniously together, for if relationships among the people, land, animals, and fish are not honored, basic connections between people (whether kinship, trade, or humanity itself) cannot survive.

The origin story encouraged the speaker and listener to imagine the work of the Changer embodied in the landscape. The South Puget Sound was not only a historical text but also an active world, always in flux.[11] Spirits—willful forces of change—could be encountered anywhere and in any form, endowing the physical environment with sentience.[12] Maintaining relationships within this animated world required both skill and a knowledge-set basic to survival. The relationships among the people, the watershed, and salmon are illustrative. The ancestors established permanent villages and fish weirs on the tributaries of the main river because it was on these sites that salmon passed in great numbers.[13] The people depended upon salmon for survival and saw them as both food and putative kin.[14] Billy Frank Jr. explained in the Historical Court: "We're fish people.

We eat salmon. That salmon flows in our blood, as well as all of our animals out there." According to Frank, Nisqually people literally embodied the interconnected state of the world they inhabited.

In addition to an origin myth, Carpenter published a migration legend that reinforced Nisquallies' social connections and appreciation for the region's diverse resources.[15] A very long time ago, Carpenter wrote, the ancestors migrated north from Central America. They settled in the Great Basin for "time unaccountable," until climatic changes prompted them to move further north in search of water, to the Columbia Plateau. One group caught sight of Ta-Co-Bet and broke away from the others to see what lay beyond the high peak. To the west of the mountain range, the group found lush forests and glacial rivers flowing to the sea, called Whulge (Puget Sound). The ancestors followed one of the rivers from the foothills of Ta-Co-Bet to the prairielands below. They called the prairie grass squalli and, over time, came to know the river by the same name. The people, in turn, called themselves Squalli-absch: "The People of the Grass Country, the People of the River." The people's identity was inextricably linked to language and the region's physical geography.[16]

Carpenter's story, which she attributes to tribal sources, establishes a shared group experience of migration that highlights Lushootseed social and trade connections east across the Cascade Mountains and into the heart of the continent.[17] Connie McCloud expounded on these connections in her Historical Court testimony by describing how Native people maintained wide-ranging relationships across the region: "We traveled the Puget Sound, out to the Straits, we traveled up and down the Pacific Coast, into Canada, across the mountains, trading with the people from east of the mountains to the Midwest. Those relationships were important to us." Leschi exemplified these strong regional ties because, as McCloud reminded the audience in her testimony, Leschi traveled east of the mountains to maintain important connections with his mother's Klickitat kin. The origin and migration stories explain how the people became a part of the geography of rivers, prairies, mountains, travel routes, and kinship connections.[18]

Several Nisqually people tell how the ancestors fixed place-names that reflected their views and experiences in the area. Carpenter characterized Nisqually place-names as "encoded with cultural history" because they communicated historical events, commemorated the names of families, and described the locations for important materials across the homeland.[19]

There are few surviving sources on Lushootseed place-names today because, as Chapter 4 explains, government boarding schools nearly eradicated the language. In the early twentieth century, however, geographer T. T. Waterman recorded the names and locations of dozens of Nisqually places in South Puget Sound. Waterman's *Puget Sound Geography* preserved Whulshootseed place-names with their English translations; the place-names referenced the presence of useful resources (a village at the mouth of the river was "place of hay"), the site's physical appearance (the south shore Narrows were "place of swift water"), or the locations of spirit power (the south shore of a smaller tributary was "power of a shaman"). These place-names exhibit an active historical engagement between the land and the people inhabiting it, effectively "anchoring" people to places with language.[20] Nisquallies fixed their social identities and histories in the landscape and maintained relationships with one another and the spirit powers in their midst. These relationships across space, time, and spiritual realms formed the basis of the Southern Coast Salish geography.

The first Europeans to visit the Puget Sound region, by contrast, saw the land as part of an expanding periphery of imperial influence rather than the center of an interconnected social world. In the late eighteenth century, British, Spanish, and Russian seamen skirted the north Pacific coast to investigate the potential for commercial trade with people living in the resource-rich landscape. In 1792, when British captain George Vancouver sailed into the Strait of Juan de Fuca and traveled south into the inland sea, he pointedly named many notable natural features (including "Mt. Rainier" and "Puget Sound") and assessed the potential for trade with Natives.[21] Just like the Spanish Empire before him, the British agent followed the European legal convention of extending a claim to land by right of "discovery." This concept can be traced back to European religious thought, although imperial powers turned to a variety of legal justifications to support their territorial claims in North America. By the eighteenth century, English legal theorists focused on a secularized legal science of a Law of Nations, based on supposedly rational principles of "civilization," which functioned to protect English interests in property while denying Indians' territorial sovereignty.[22] John Locke reasoned that labor (or "improving" land through specific, culturally identifiable actions like cultivating crops) granted land title and envisioned the Americas as a "wild commons" largely untouched by humans. Locke's thinking influenced European and Euro-American ideologies about their right to claim American lands inhabited by indigenous people.[23] Vancouver's renaming and imperial mapping helped to extend the interests of the British Hudson's Bay Company (HBC) into the region and initiated a process of appropriating Native local knowledge in the service of empire.

The HBC primarily used South Puget Sound as a landed commercial center in the regional fur trade. In 1833, the HBC established Fort Nisqually near Squalli-absch villages on the mouth of the river. The employees traded with neighboring and more distant Native groups and soon diversified operations with the creation of the Puget Sound Agricultural Company in 1838. Dr. William Fraser Tolmie, chief trader at Fort Nisqually starting in 1847 (and promoted to chief factor in 1855), managed a staff of British, French, Native, and Hawaiian men employed in the company's buildings, fields, and pasturelands.[24] Unlike the American settler colonialism to follow, the British did not encroach upon Native land use. The dynamics of trade encouraged the creation of a syncretic economic system based on mutual adaptations. British and Nisqually peoples found some common ground in their geographies and adapted new practices and concepts into familiar frameworks. For example, the Southern Coast Salish imposed invisible territorial boundaries on the land, such as hunting grounds or fishing spots that belonged to specific families, which approximated the British concept of private property conveyed in title.[25] Tolmie encouraged his employees to marry indigenous women and maintained social relationships with village headmen to ensure HBC's access to the land and peaceful operations at the fort.[26] Nisqually people readily adapted some British crops and technologies, such as potato cultivation and plows, in order to enhance their food supply.[27] Nisqually headmen and HBC employees borrowed practices from one another, but, significantly, these exchanges did not represent contests over land or threaten Native access to regional resources.

Americans' advances into the region, motivated as they were by acquiring land for permanent settlement, changed this dynamic. Mid-nineteenth-century Americans considered far western territories as a boon to national stability, individual land ownership, and capitalist exploitation. Britain and the United States settled their respective claims in the region with the 1846 Oregon Treaty, which established the border between the two nations along the 49th parallel to the Pacific Ocean. Native people were not consulted or considered a party to the treaty, reflecting the notion that Natives had no standing in international law and colonial powers had the right to appropriate land for "civilized use."[28] To justify a settler colony in indigenous peoples' homeland, Americans invoked Locke's theory that rightful possession of land derived from usage. Furthermore, as legal historian Stuart Banner argues, government land sale practices and court rulings in the early nineteenth century contributed to Americans' legal notion that Indians merely held a right of "occupancy" rather than ownership over their land.[29]

Although Americans had much to learn about the place, when they looked around South Puget Sound they tended to see what they wanted to see and anticipated: unimproved wilderness occupied by ignorant Native people. In order to appropriate land for their exclusive use, U.S. colonial agents converted Indians' local knowledge and histories into a land management scheme based on abstract data and scientific theory. U.S. laws, meanwhile, facilitated Americans' exclusive land-use practices and induced greater immigration to the region. Americans, much like their imperial predecessors, considered land an economic resource that must be named, mapped, and legally defined to be properly exploited.

By the mid-nineteenth century, U.S. settlers and government officials acted in concert to dispossess Indians of lands to which settlers believed they had a legal right.[30] Armed with confidence in white American cultural and racial superiority, settlers and officials (often one and the same) initiated a process of creation and destruction that transformed indigenous territory into settlement lands.[31] As anthropologist Patrick Wolfe argues, settler colonialism is based on a "logic of elimination" that contains positive and negative dimensions: "Negatively, it strives for the dissolution of native societies. Positively, it erects a new colonial society on the expropriated land base."[32] Native space had to be unmade before American legal land claims could be made.[33] This colonial goal was accomplished by dividing the world into discrete categories that could be further defined and studied.[34] American officials and settlers used three key technologies to convert South Puget Sound into American space: mapping and demarcation; compiling and publishing scientific data; and re-narration of Native people and their histories. Although these technologies operated in tandem and shared common motivations, I trace each of these technologies separately as they operated on the ground.[35]

Mapping and Demarcation

Mapping, cartography, and cadastral surveys have held an important place in empire building and modern state formation because these technologies made land known to Western science and therefore manageable and open for exploitation.[36] Cartography was one facet in a larger process of abstracting local indigenous knowledge into American legal categories that justified Indian dispossession. Mapmaking in colonial contexts represents a form of knowledge-power, which, according to philosopher Michel Foucault, gains dominance by "presenting one's own values in the guise of scientific disinterestedness."[37] Mapping and demarcation in the Puget Sound region were critical processes for reimagining the region as a frontier and as legally rationalized space—in other words, as an eventual and inevitable American place.

In 1841, a fleet of warships carrying the United States Exploring Expedition entered the southern reaches of Puget Sound in an effort to strengthen the U.S. claim to the territory. The Wilkes Expedition landed at Fort Nisqually with the express purpose of mapping the region and determining a passable route through the Cascade Mountains to facilitate American overland migration.[38] U.S. Navy lieutenant Charles Wilkes created an exploration plan while at the fort and followed HBC practice by employing Native guides to lead several mapping teams into the territory's interior.[39] In a survey that proved critical for American development in the region, one party under the charge of Robert Johnson mapped out the Naches Pass and became the first American party to cross the Cascade Range.[40]

American settlers later interpreted Native guides' cooperation as evidence that Indians recognized American superiority and would facilitate U.S. settlement in the region. On the contrary, Native mappers and guides knew that foreign explorers depended upon local knowledge and that the guides could exploit these circumstances to their advantage. One Muckleshoot man later recalled how his father, Chief Koquilton, "pictured out the pass and trail across the mountains" and sent family members as guides to lead the exploration team into the interior.[41] Perhaps Koquilton, operating on the assumption that the exploring party was in search of new trade contacts, hoped to lead the group to his relations across the mountains and secure a political alliance with the newcomers. In previous years, the guides had found ways to benefit from British imperial interests. There is no reason to assume that Koquilton and other guides supported Americans' land claim goals just because they played a role in mapping the region's travel routes.

In any case, the Native guides would have scarcely recognized the American explorers' depiction of their familiar landscape. Social relations drove Native mapping and navigation, while American surveyors focused on absolute and uniform schemes of reckoning space.[42] Western mapmakers did not recognize or record the social-spatial context of the Native world they had entered because their goal was to make the land "known" to science and to promote national claims.[43] The Wilkes Expedition not only mapped out the locations of natural features, but also, just as previous imperial powers had done, claimed these features by naming them. Place-naming is the process of attaching meaning to one's surroundings. In a colonial setting, renaming takes on a political dynamic: just as naming is a process of politically (and ideologically) possessing land, renaming is also an act of dispossession.[44] All told, Wilkes and his teams affixed some 261 names to prominent features in the region in the early 1840s.[45] These features already had names, of course. T. T. Waterman recorded 10,000 Native place-names around Puget Sound in the early twentieth century.[46] But American place-names filled blank spaces on U.S. maps, erasing evidence of indigenous political and social geography and denying Natives' historical presence on the land.[47]

Once the early American explorers conveyed local places into Cartesian space, they sent their maps east, where publishing houses incorporated this data into inventories of the national domain. Cartographers in eastern publication houses rendered the landscape into a two-dimensional text full of symbols of visible and invisible landmarks: dotted lines were trails, hash marks were marshland, solid lines were county boundaries. In combining the physical with the political (the visible with the invisible), mapmakers promoted an implicit understanding of the "natural" order of the landscape based in a specific perspective.[48] In practice, the scientific method was not about eliminating subjectivity but rather imposing a common language through which different subjects could convey local conditions across space. In settler colonialism, however, the shared language did not include all perspectives equally.[49] Maps became a way for those versed in particular knowledge regimes to communicate and bolster their authority over new places to the exclusion of other ways of knowing the land.

A closer reading of surviving maps and atlases of the South Puget Sound region illustrates how American officials used Western science to create a legal basis for Indians' dispossession. Morse's *North American Atlas*, published in New York in 1842, depicted the Oregon Territory as largely blank. Only major waterways—the Columbia River and Puget Sound—are clearly labeled and apparent to the viewer in a sea of white space.[50] Blank space on a map, like silences in any text, communicates messages and exerts a social influence. Blank spaces suggested to viewers schooled in an ideology of expansion that the land was open for the taking.[51] Although the early explorers and mapmakers hired Indian guides and asked questions about the land of their Indian hosts, the blank spaces ignored the existence of the region's Native inhabitants. This cartographic representation supported the stadial theory of civilization, in which human societies move from barbarism to civilization chronologically over time and according to geographic location.[52] Those living on "unmapped" places were assumed to be uncivilized and premodern, their omission on the map representing their social status as outsiders to the scientific culture of mapmaking and civilized society more generally.

In Samuel Augustus Mitchell's 1846 map of the western territories of Texas, Oregon, and California, Indian group names are scrawled across wide areas; "Nisqually" alone takes up the entire South Puget Sound region to the exclusion of all others.[53] The prominence of the Nisqually name is due to the fact that the HBC fort, which was located on Nisqually prairieland and hosted American travelers, provided observers the closest and most immediate access to the Nisqually people over other groups. The wide geographic use of the name, which referenced language more than political identity at the time, could also indicate the extent to which Nisqually headmen established and maintained relations with outsiders by trading or serving as guides and translators.[54] Significantly, Nisquallies' existence was noted, but the map was devoid of symbols for villages, paths, pastures, or other uses of the land. This map supported the popular American idea at the time that Indians made no "improvements" that could support their legal claim to land ownership.[55] Furthermore, locating the Native name within the U.S. territorial domain was a necessary device for asserting juridical control over the area and the people alike. The authority of the map was added to the authority of legal documents that claimed American control over Indian land because Indians composed "domestic dependent nations."[56] Isaac Stevens could feel the double encouragement of America's legal and cartographic claims when he went into rushed negotiations with South Puget Sound tribes in 1854 to extinguish their claim to much of the land. Even before Indian title to the land was legally ceded by treaty, maps communicated an inevitability about U.S. national territorial unity that made Indian land ownership irrelevant, at the same time that maps helped to create the conditions for American settlers' claims.

American settlement in the South Puget Sound region increased in the mid-1850s due to a combination of political developments and legal incentives: the 1846 Oregon Treaty, the 1850 Oregon Donation Land Act

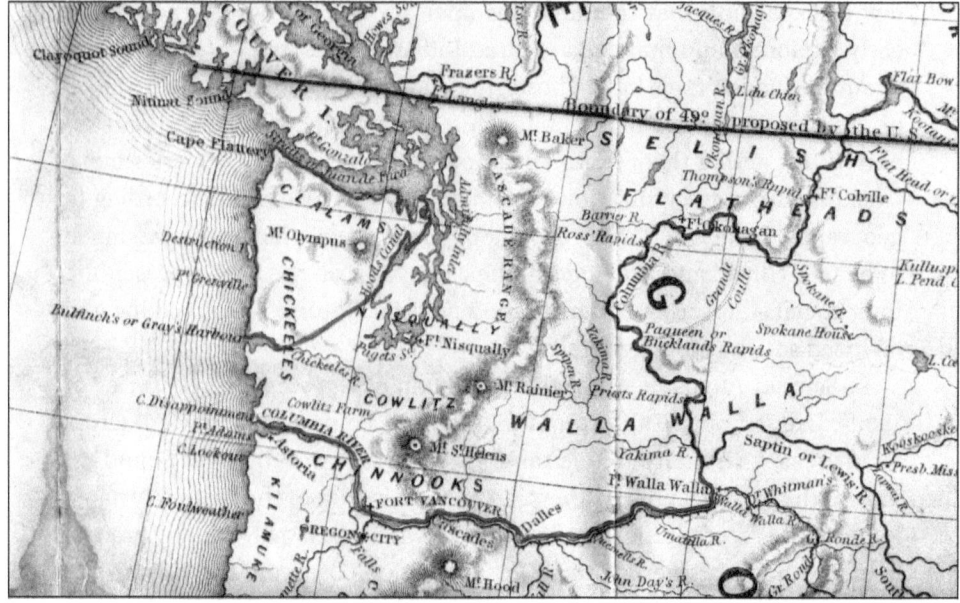

FIGURE 4 Detail of Oregon Territory from S. August Mitchell's 1846 map of Texas, Oregon, and California. (Maps, Coll. No. 1500.026, Department of Special Collections and University Archives, McFarlin Library, University of Tulsa, Tulsa, Oklahoma)

(which was extended to Washington Territory in 1853), the completion of the wagon road across Naches Pass in 1853, and the Medicine Creek Treaty in 1854.[57] Preston's 1856 sectional and county map of Washington offers topographical details of interest to the potential overland immigrant, and several 1857 maps include the names and locations of the passes through the mountains. These maps also include a thick black line tracing the path of a future railroad.[58] Another detailed map of the region indicated where roads, trails, and proposed survey lines were to be located in the following years.[59] For eastern land speculators, these symbols of future development in the region were especially enticing. These roads promised to guide settlers to likely locations for urban growth, and proposed surveys suggested to distant speculators how they might prosper when the values of their strategic landholdings grew with increased settlement.[60] Far removed from the conditions on the ground, these geographic texts helped investors to imagine South Puget Sound as an American frontier awaiting "improvement."[61] These maps educated viewers about how the territory could be politically claimed, economically exploited, and abstractly known.

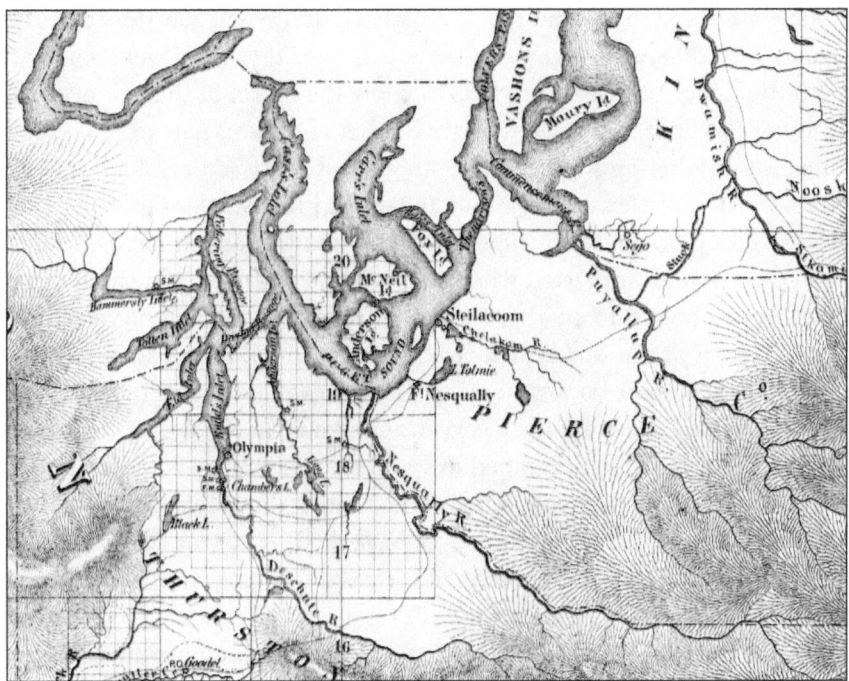

FIGURE 5 Detail of sectional grid overlaying Olympia from Preston's Sectional and County Map of Oregon and Washington, 1856. Note surveyed sections (grid lines), county borders (dotted lines), and proposed railway routes (solid lines). (University of Washington Libraries, Special Collections, UW35583)

On the ground, however, the process of surveying and claiming land was much messier. American settlers followed British understandings that surveying and fencing in land was the process by which the land was claimed and legally rendered as property. American officials used surveys to separate Indian reserved land from land open to American settlement, although questions of land ownership were far from settled. In 1857, a group of armed American settlers confronted British surveyors in a Nisqually Delta land dispute, and, in turn, some Native peoples resisted the work of American surveyors.[62] Native people of South Puget Sound quickly recognized how survey lines threatened their access to land, resources, and social connections across space. Just a few months after the armed settlers threatened the British surveyors, U.S. government surveyors complained to Indian agent Wesley Gosnell that Hohamish Indians (one of the signatory bands of the Medicine Creek Treaty) were removing their surveying stakes from Henderson's Bay, causing the surveyors to have to double-back and repeat their measurement work. When questioned by the agent, the Hohamish men reportedly told him that they were satisfied with the treaty but were "anxious to know the object of the surveyors in running the lines." The agent assumed that the men knew exactly what they were doing and were attempting to prevent settlers from taking claims.[63] One settler recalled that Indians on the Muckleshoot reservation (a group drawn from Upper Puyallup and Duwamish bands in Central Puget Sound) protested when surveyors began to extend subdivision lines from a township nearby. The settler reported: "I could not convince the Indians that the survey meant no harm to them."[64] The settler downplayed the colonial implications of the surveys and failed to grasp the significant consequences for reservation Indians. In the late 1850s, many Muckleshoot Indians succumbed to starvation when they could no longer access clams along the coast. An army captain at the Muckleshoot Agency reported in 1856 that "they should all have died" if not for those who left the reservation to procure salmon at their usual fishing stations.[65] Indians stood to lose access to land where they gathered food and resources not available on the reservation, met friends and family, and maintained connections with places of power. The boundaries between reserved Indian land and nonreserved land on maps became legal realities with material consequences.[66]

Survey lines purported to remake the land into a series of abstract parcels, which, once the measurements had been recorded in territorial records, lent legal weight to settlers' land claims. In recognition of the power of title in this land management scheme, South Puget Sound Indian chiefs in the early 1870s reportedly petitioned for certificates to secure their ownership rights on equal terms with settlers. "They said that they and their people desired to . . . live like white men," one Indian agent reported of the petition, "but that no one knew where his land was, or had a paper showing that he owned any land at all; that neighboring white men frequently told them that the Government would soon take their reservations and sell them." The superintendent of Indian Affairs used the petition to call for surveys of Indian land, but national officials delayed for years the certificates of land ownership the Indian agents had promised to Indian individuals who took surveyed plots.[67] This paternalistic policy reinforced the notion that boundaries, when applied to Indian land, functioned more as a placeholder. Americans expected Indians to disappear (either physically or culturally) and assumed that their reservations could then be systematically recategorized as settlement land. George Wheeler, head of the U.S. Geographic Surveys west of the one-hundredth meridian, expected his surveys on reserved lands to be soon outdated, for "the time is not far distant" when Indians would surrender their lands to "actual settlers . . . on the plea of the greatest good to the greatest number."[68] Some settlers, convinced by land speculators' fantastic predictions for a future metropolis on South Puget Sound, squatted on reserved land and displaced Nisqually families with the expectation that the land would eventually open for sale.[69] Ironically, Wheeler noted with approval that settlers "crowd over the borders of . . . reservations," willfully ignoring the demarcation system that he labored to create and that the settlers held as sacrosanct when applied to their own private property.[70]

The fate of the Nisqually reservation by the end of the nineteenth century seemed to fulfill colonial agents' predictions about the disappearance of Indians and their reserved lands. An official who conducted a reservation survey in 1871 concluded that an earlier survey contained an error that he "corrected" by cutting off a stretch of reservation land that included a tribal cemetery where Leschi lay buried.[71] A few years later, a Northern Pacific Railway survey of the reservation shaved off plots of land belonging to eight Nisqually families. The railroad company then offered to sell their homes back to them at double the price paid for equivalent land in the area.[72] Just as settlers expected and their demarcation system facilitated, reserved Indian land—with its permeable and plastic boundaries—was almost already settlement land.

The technologies of cartography, surveying, and naming would have had little impact beyond the signs and measurements they created if not for the state's power to exert control over the spaces depicted on maps and in cadastral surveys. The second and related way in which colonial agents transformed South Puget Sound into settlement land was through knowledge claims about Indians, which helped to create and justify the legal and administrative system Americans imposed over the region. Colonial agents in South Puget Sound collected particular information about Native people that would both facilitate and rationalize their dispossession. Native people participated in this process to varying degrees and consequently shaped the so-called scientific method and resulting data. Just as guides led newcomers through the landscape, Native informants and ethnographic subjects pursued their own interests while Americans appropriated their place-knowledge to facilitate and justify Indian dispossession.

Americans' knowledge claims about Indian peoples of South Puget

Sound initially worked to ameliorate the legal inconsistencies of settler colonialism of the mid-nineteenth century. In 1850, Congress passed the Oregon Donation Land Act, which provided up to 320 acres to each single male settler in the new territory. Under the act, a few hundred settlers filed claims around Puget Sound and proceeded to fence in fields, build mills along the rivers, and establish farms in the watershed.[73] The act promised settlers land belonging to Indians without first purchasing it from them, which departed from earlier U.S. policy.[74] The 1787 Northwest Ordinance proclaimed that Indian land should never be taken without Indians' consent, and the only ways to exert U.S. sovereignty over new territory was through fair dealings with Indians or in "legal and just war."[75] The federal government did initially purchase Indian lands in the East but came under increasing political pressure to quickly grant western lands to settlers in the mid-nineteenth century, regardless of whether the land had been purchased from Indian owners. The government's practice of granting Indian lands to settlers without even the pretense of "fair dealings" became increasingly common; even lawyers began to think of Indians as merely tenants, rather than owners, of the land.[76] However, the appearance of legal order was important. In an effort to legalize settlers' homesteads, federal officials hastily drafted treaties of land cession to present to Native people. In the early 1850s, officials hoped to acquire land in Washington Territory through legal channels without sparking a costly war.

The first Indian agent for Puget Sound reported in 1852 that he faced difficulties arranging for treaty negotiations because he could not identify Native leaders, did not know how to distinguish the different groups, and poorly understood Indians' resource use.[77] But settlers continued to arrive, and federal officials needed to know much more about Native people in order to draw up acceptable treaties.[78] The officials turned to local "Indian experts"—typically self-taught observers of Indian people and amateur collectors of Indian products and stories. These experts amassed "data" on Native people that federal officials could exploit in order to legally separate Indians from their resources.

The most significant Indian expert in 1850s Washington Territory was George Gibbs, a lawyer from a wealthy Long Island family who had traveled west in 1849 and had filled a number of federal jobs in Oregon and Washington.[79] Gibbs's official duties illustrate the connections between discrete technologies of colonialism: he was a member of the 1853–55 Northwest railroad surveys, secretary of the Washington Treaty Commission, head of the territorial militia, ethnographer, and interpreter for the

American Boundary Commission (in which he translated Indian place-names into English).⁸⁰ In 1854, territorial governor Isaac Stevens hired Gibbs to prepare a report on Puget Sound and join him on his treaty tour across the territory.⁸¹ Gibbs's legal background and his cultivated expertise in territorial management technologies proved crucial for constructing treaties and extending U.S. sovereignty across the Northwest.⁸² Notably, Gibbs was influenced by prevailing mid-nineteenth-century American arguments about efficient land use. U.S. policy makers justified Indian dispossession on the premise that small numbers of Indians "roamed" over great tracts of land, while industrious American settlers wisely settled and cultivated the land in greater concentrations.⁸³ Gibbs mapped this ideology onto the Northwest by drafting the template for the Medicine Creek Treaty, by which Native people of South Puget Sound ceded over 4,000 square miles of land in exchange for three small reservations, annuities, and services.⁸⁴ Gibbs's expertise helped to create both the treaty and a story about the rational and legal foundation of American colonialism.

In anticipation of the treaties, Gibbs provided Stevens with tribal maps, observations on Indian political organization, and recommendations for government management of tribes.⁸⁵ He noted that Coast Salish villagers lacked chiefs and suggested that officials appoint headmen to the positions for the purposes of treaty negotiations and to initiate home rule. Leschi received a piece of paper naming him a "sub-chief" a few months later.⁸⁶ Gibbs observed the importance of fish and clams to Coast Salish diets and reasoned that the Indians needed only small reservations, excluding the fertile plains and bottomlands, so they could continue to feed themselves by fishing and gathering in their usual places without government expense.⁸⁷ But Gibbs's report omitted critical information: upland Nisqually villagers, including Leschi, gathered berries and camas and maintained cultivated fields and horse herds on the region's upland prairies. Gibbs did not offer a government management scheme that took upland Nisquallies' needs into account because this would have compromised the nation's land policy and Americans' stories about their superior land use. Because Americans' legal land claim rested on the Western epistemology equating certain forms of "use" with ownership rights, Gibbs failed to recognize or account for the ways upland Nisqually villagers' land use was similar to Americans'.

In anticipation of treaty negotiations concerning the reservation of Indian land, the U.S. government ordered an updated count of Native people in a treaty area. In 1854, Gibbs conducted an admittedly "hasty voyage through the Sound" to count the members of each Indian band in order to calculate the size of reserved Indian land. To collect his data, Gibbs relied upon settlers' speculations and his own observations because he assumed that Nisqually people had only a vague sense of numbers.[88] In fact, numbers and cadastral surveys enabled an eastern federal bureaucracy to determine land allocation in South Puget Sound based on supposedly scientific rationale while obscuring the cultural assumptions at work.[89]

Gibbs's research method was frustrated by highly mobile Native populations with complicated spatial social connections. Gibbs reported that "their habit of moving about" between locales left him and other settlers with "the impression of great numbers in each," and his best estimate, consequently, was "rather under than over the mark" to compensate.[90] He calculated 184 Nisquallies, a number close to Wilkes's estimate of 200 Nisquallies in 1841. William Tolmie, however, estimated the Nisqually population to be 471 in 1844—double the size of the Americans' 1841 and 1854 calculations. To some extent, Gibbs's and Wilkes's small numbers reveal the devastating impacts of epidemics since the 1780s, but Tolmie's count represents a significant difference from the Americans' numbers that cannot be explained by diseases alone.[91] Without historical perspective on the scale of the demographic upheaval around them, U.S. officials could not contextualize their population figures. Reservation calculations were based on the assumption that Native population numbers were static or declining, and not on the possibility of population rebounds or growth, which would necessitate larger reservations. Wilkes's and Gibbs's low population numbers thus suggest that the officials either lacked familiarity with the region and the nuances of Native identity or expressed wishful thinking. Americans might underestimate the Native population to encourage white settlement, justify smaller reservations, and confirm their own expectations about Indians' inefficient use of the land and imminent disappearance.[92]

Ultimately, the terms of the Medicine Creek Treaty were based on settler Michael Simmons's population estimate of 638 individuals from Puyallup, Nisqually, Squaxin Island, and other autonomous communities in the region. When nearly 700 Native people arrived on the Nisqually Delta for the treaty council on December 24, it became clear that the commission had underestimated the population by at least half. The treaty terms, reservations, and annuities promised in the treaty—all based on miscalculated population statistics, denial of Indian land use and claims, and the expectation that Indians were nearing disappearance—reveal more about the stories Americans told themselves than about the Native people with whom they negotiated.⁹³ Presumed experts on Indians used what their society deemed rational methods—observation and enumeration—to convert popular beliefs and expectations into hard data. These scientific practices and numbers, in turn, provided a "rational" basis for treaties and management schemes while obscuring their origins in colonial ideology.

The third key technology of colonialism was not a state-directed initiative but a collection of activities that more subtly and insidiously used Western science to justify American expansion and to appropriate (and discount) Native knowledge. In the nineteenth century, proto-anthropologists, working independently or in the service of national knowledge, developed theories about the origins of the region's Native peoples that effectively denied Native knowledge and histories. Proto-anthropologists in the nineteenth century were largely motivated by philosophical questions about the origins of modern man and debates over the genesis of the indigenous inhabitants of North America.⁹⁴ Thomas Jefferson believed in the theory of Bering Strait migration and sought proof through study and comparisons of Native American languages, which he hoped would supply final "evidence of their derivation."⁹⁵ Some Native people, from the nineteenth century to the present, dismissed the Bering Strait hypothesis because it invalidated oral traditions of "deep time" events predating the land bridge. The late Lakota writer Vine Deloria Jr. argued that the theory carried "immense political implications" by presenting Indians as immigrants and allowing non-Indians to discount their claims to aboriginal occupancy.⁹⁶

It is not surprising, then, that George Gibbs used and expanded upon Jefferson's vocabulary list to conduct his own ambitious study when he traveled to the Northwest fifty years later.⁹⁷ Gibbs's ultimate goal was to collect all Native languages west of the Rockies to create a comprehensive ethnographic map that would reveal migration routes and, ultimately, the origins of Indians.⁹⁸ In 1854, a few months before the Medicine Creek Treaty council, Gibbs filed a homestead claim near Fort Nisqually and began collecting word lists. As a gentleman farmer, Gibbs hired laborers to tend his crops and home; his Nisqually cook, Jack, was likely the main source for words in Gibbs's "Niskualli Dictionary."⁹⁹ His vocabulary lists eventually contributed to data sets housed in the Bureau of American Ethnology in Washington, D.C. Researchers believed that once Native languages had been collected, classified, and compared, they could rescue Native origins from an unrecorded past.¹⁰⁰ By the end of his years of collecting, Gibbs's vocabulary lists led him to a theory of Coast Salish northwestward migration from the Great Plains. Cecelia Carpenter's published migration legend later corroborated this linguistic data, but Gibbs could not bring himself to publish his findings in his lifetime. No matter what conclusions his ethnographic records and linguistic investigations suggested, he believed firmly in distant Asiatic connections and the Bering Strait migration. He never resolved the issue to his own satisfaction because he refused to acknowledge that Native people not only *have* a history, but they also *know* their history.[101]

Like most nineteenth-century ethnographers, Gibbs believed in a theory of social progress in which societies move "upward" along a spectrum from savagery to civilization.[102] Many ethnographers assumed that precontact Native societies epitomized savagery and were static and unchanged—outside of history—until contact with a "superior" society engendered rapid social "uplift." Early Euro-American proto-anthropologists considered their primary task that of recording or salvaging data on precontact traditions and languages for the use of scholars after Native cultures and people had vanished. Of particular interest to proto-anthropologists were Indian "legends," which served as examples of humankind's primitive stage of social development. In order to obtain the most authentic data possible, North American ethnographers relied on Native informants who claimed to remember the precontact period.[103] Notably, proto-anthropologists "salvaged" Native stories using scientific methods, but these findings were interpreted as examples of timeless cultural products, not reliable scientific data indicative of historical change.

Within this tradition of study and collection, Gibbs interviewed Native informants and exchanged letters with longtime traders familiar with Native customs.[104] One of the most common topics in these letters—with the exception of vocabulary—was the most effective method for extracting "true" information from Native people. According to one American settler, "any legend or interpretation given or related to me I make a note of and after a lapse of time I get the same person to repeat the story and then ask another person if it is correct. And when I find an Indian to tell the same story several times and have it corroborated by others I set it down for fact."[105] This method of cross-checking was (and remains) an important aspect of Western scientific rigor, but it is ineffective when applied to Native stories. Generally, Native societies recognized restrictions on stories and storytelling.[106] Depending on the genre of story, only some Coast Salish individuals with authority could tell (or even knew) certain stories about places and people, and stories themselves had seasons and proper venues in which they could be told.[107] Without taking note of the relations among and between informants, the special authority of each speaker, and the time of year, the proto-anthropologist's method of cross-checking missed stories located in a specific social geography. Although ethnographers claimed that this system allowed them to distinguish truth from fabrication, the approach effectively limited data to only that which fit into Western models of knowledge.

In a similar fashion, Gibbs dismissed oral traditions that challenged the Bible or seemed to resemble Judeo-Christian stories too closely. Just as Gibbs had been especially attentive to differences between Indians' and American settlers' land-use practices, and therefore missed or ignored similarities, he was interested only in stories that met his expectations of Indian difference. After recording numerous Salish versions of the flood epic recounted earlier in this chapter, Gibbs concluded that the stories contain "too much of the flavor of Genesis about them for actual credence." One newspaper editor later used Gibbs's assessment to explain that Native people, like parrots, only repeated what they learned from missionaries—a rhetorical move that reversed the flow of knowledge between Natives and newcomers.[108] The implication was that Native people either recognized the superiority of American culture and replaced their own with it or simply lacked the ability to recount their own histories. Either way, their claim to the land—and the related claims to belonging, autonomy, and cultural preeminence—appeared tenuous and easily severed. In discounting Native knowledge and historicity, proto-anthropologists undercut aboriginal land claims and justified Americans' territorial expansion in the region. Indeed, proto-anthropologists helped settlers to imagine that they had created civilization in a primordial wilderness devoid of rational humans, even as they appropriated Native knowledge about the land to make this claim.

In the early twentieth century, mapping practices, anthropological theories, and Americans' popular expectations about Indians could be combined to instruct the next generation of settlers in the continued appropriation of Native historical presence. In 1906, the first state historian at the University of Washington, Edmond Meany, created a list of 103 "Indian words used as geographic terms," along with instructions for the "correct orthography and pronunciation" for the benefit of the region's schoolchildren. He targeted what he determined to be commonly mispronounced words, including Leschi (which he claimed was pronounced "Leschy" as opposed to the more accurate Whulshootseed approximation of "Lesh-eye"). Meany's notion of correct pronunciation did not include the glottalized ejectives characteristic of Lushootseed phonetics, reasoning that it was unnecessary to teach English speakers to make new sounds to reference local and familiar geography. He insisted that Indian words "are most useful when recast into our own form of speech," since Indian languages faced imminent extinction.[109] In a fashion similar to territorial maps and Robnett's description of law, Meany's pronunciation guide sought to create a standard that included some people and excluded others from a nominally universal experience and perspective.

By anglicizing Lushootseed words, Meany participated in a process of remaking the land in the language and worldview of the colonial power while appropriating and recasting indigenous historical experiences.[110] Translating Lushootseed words into English phonetics meant altering the pronunciation, yet Native place-names gained much of their meaning from their location in language, the structure of which reflects cultural values. This act of phonetic translation emptied the word of its cultural location and separated it from its geographic context in the Nisqually homeland. American students could appropriate Native places by connecting American English language, maps, ethnographic data, and territorial rights.[111] American geographic education reflected liberal and colonial ideologies by negating or erasing different geographic imaginings while purporting to create an orderly system, equally accessible to all.

From the mid-nineteenth century through the first decade of the twentieth century, American explorers renamed the landscape, surveyors divided and categorized the land, experts identified manageable Indian populations, and proto-anthropologists separated Natives from their histories and unmoored their stories from the land. These discrete acts of colonization worked together to make South Puget Sound into American space by unmaking a Native world. Yet this task was never completed, as the survival of Native communities and histories, evident in the Historical Court, can attest. Although the United States came to dominate the indigenous people of the region politically, appropriation was not a one-way street. Long after the fur trade period, the mutual appropriation of knowledge and stories continued to be a feature of the relationship between Indians and non-Indians. This dynamic of exchange and reciprocal influences (albeit in unequal circumstances) highlights the ambiguous role of liberal ideologies and institutions in a democratic settler state. Nominally universal categories, abstract notions, and objective science reflected European and Euro-American epistemology, but these concepts also provided limited pathways for indigenous claims to unique histories, identities, and sovereignties.

Dynamics of Resistance

Native people of the region strategically embraced some American liberal concepts and categories because such a path offered opportunities, even though, paradoxically, such a strategy could work to naturalize settler colonialism and grant legitimacy to a system committed to their dispossession. Nisquallies were not alone in this quandary; groups that sought to undermine colonial law in the nineteenth and twentieth centuries often argued for broadening state jurisdiction in an effort to extend their rights recognized under state authority.[112] While some Puget Salish people resisted the work of surveyors in the mid-nineteenth century, for example, it occurred to others that acknowledging solid political boundaries — recognized on an equal scale with other international borders on maps — might help Indians to safeguard their lands. Conversing with non-Indians about the land in the legal language of property and rights could possibly forestall Indian dispossession while securing better economic opportunities for the tribe.[113] Beginning at the turn of the twentieth century, Native individuals and tribes in South Puget Sound began to sue in U.S. courts to protect their reservation boundaries and allotments, and even to expand reserved lands. These challenges had mixed results, however, because the legal justification for settler colonialism persisted. In one 1916 Supreme Court case, for example, the judges praised the United States for "deal[ing] more liberally with their subject races" than other empires, even though Indians were "generally easy and always tempting to destroy and whom we have so often permitted to squander vast areas of fertile land before our eyes."[114] Yet Native leaders persevered, using the English language forced on them in government boarding schools to write appeals to the U.S. government, Indian agents, and the Bureau of Indian Affairs for relief from suffering caused by land loss.

In the late nineteenth and early twentieth centuries, while the majority of South Puget Sound non-Indian settlers held disparaging and negative views of Indians, a few local non-Indians sought out Native voices and were sympathetic toward them. However, just like the proto-anthropologists who observed and collected data on "authentic" Native cultures, non-Indians were primarily interested in hearing from Indians about precontact times.[115] But as much as "traditional" Indians pleased non-Indian audiences by eliciting a romantic nostalgia for premodern simplicity, the "modern" Indian informants who spoke English and wore suits appealed to Americans' vanity as well.[116] Sympathetic non-Indian audiences saw in boarding school–educated Indians the best of American modernity and the "civilizing mission" reflected back on them. Instead of fomenting resentment or guilt among non-Indian audiences, Native informants and public intellectuals found that their histories built sympathy and goodwill, as long as they strategically embraced Western epistemologies and expectations.

Henry Sicade, a man whose mixed Puyallup-Nisqually ancestry reflects the close ties between the neighboring tribes, provides an important early twentieth-century example of this leadership approach. Born in present-day Lakewood in 1866 and raised on stories and salmon, Sicade attended the Puyallup Indian School through sixth grade in the 1870s and continued his education at the Indian Training School (later Chemawa) and Tualatin Academy in Forest Grove, Oregon.[117] Sicade's experiences in government schools prepared him to communicate with non-Indians on their terms: he knew English, knew the settlers' narratives, and knew their expectations of Indians. Starting in 1917, Sicade served as an informant for ethnographers on South Puget Sound Native history and place-names. T. T. Waterman described him as a man who "more than holds his own . . . in modern commercial life," and a biographer reported in 1936 that Sicade "learned early in life that the best way to get along with the whites was to be one of them, not compete with them."[118] Sicade was among the earliest Native intellectuals to lecture and publish material about Nisqually history for non-Indian audiences.[119] Sicade spoke before scholarly, pioneer, and outdoor recreation organizations and maintained correspondence with local historians. His networking resulted in widespread reprinting of his speeches and letters in newspapers and journals. Using these venues, Sicade sought to show his audience that Indians were rational beings equal to U.S. citizens and, as such, held rights to their land deserving of respect in a liberal democracy.

In his 1917 speech before the Tacoma Academy of Sciences (published twenty-three years later), Sicade provided a history of the region quite different from those available in print at the time.[120] First, he informed his audience that the aboriginal people of the area were properly named Squally, "a name which means, in my mother tongue, the tops and flowers of various roots and herbs," Sicade explained. He reminded his audience that they stood in a place of multiple geographies, still legible in the language and political identity of the Nisqually people.[121] Sicade anchored his ancestors in the land to assert an aboriginal claim to the region that predated U.S. law and geography. Sicade also endeavored to teach his listeners about the oral tradition so that they might recognize the historical content imbedded in stories. Before recounting a story, Sicade explained how he had learned from elders who had themselves been trained to memorize the histories.[122] Sicade's essays and speeches reaffirmed the historical relationships between his people and the land that settlers and officials previously discounted or denied.

Once he established this historic claim, he railed against the injustices of land loss and colonial violence without indicting American presence and laws. In what he described as "sort of a family history," Sicade recounted the Nisqually leaders' anger at the Medicine Creek Treaty terms and the 1856 massacre of Nisqually women and children at the hands of militiamen. He blamed Stevens for perverting the spirit of fair treaty negotiations and criticized the militiamen for failing to exhibit the honorable behavior befitting an American patriot-soldier. Sicade chose to undergo several years of military training at Tualatin Academy, and, as a former cadet, he implied that injustices occurred in the war because a handful of individuals did not live up to otherwise laudable American military principles. Following this mix of indictment and flattery, Sicade made his appeal for his right to land. "There are three thousand Indians now clamoring for land promised them but which they have never received," Sicade said. "I am one of those outcasts; I have never received any of the promised lands and God forbid that I shall ever ask for any."[123] Sicade hoped to prompt his audience to take action to support indigenous land claims, so he adopted a nonconfrontational position that balanced grievances with goodwill.

Sicade explained that Indian land rights were based on U.S. law and aboriginal preemption and, fitting the scientific venue, on the premise of Indians' wise land use. Sicade explained that the Nisqually people expertly used their 3,000-square-mile homeland of sheltered coastline, rivers, islands, grasslands, and foothills by collecting foods "from the salt water, the fresh water, which abounded with fish, and the prairies, which had deer and elk."[124] While settlers' stories claimed that Indians did not make the most efficient use of the land, Sicade reminded his listeners that his people knew the wealth the land was capable of providing. Notably, he did not mention the Nisqually land-use practices and technologies adapted from Europeans, such as pasturing horses, cultivating potatoes, and plowing. While these activities predated the earliest American settlement in the 1840s and would have provided evidence of Nisquallies' industrious land use by Euro-American standards, Sicade emphasized the precontact activities his audience expected. Sicade found some political advantage to acceding to his audience's interests; fishing and hunting in usual and accustomed places across the region were, not coincidentally, the same usufruct rights the Indian signers of the Medicine Creek Treaty reserved for their people.

Sicade did not question the legitimacy of U.S. law. In fact, he found ways to benefit from it. Although the U.S. government denied him an allotment (he was an orphaned minor and attending school when plots were issued), Sicade eventually worked as a surveyor, road construction supervisor, hops farm foreman, and land appraiser in the Puyallup Valley. He acquired land, esteem, and social connections by working within this system, and he served his people by establishing tribal cemeteries, schools, and employment networks during a period of transition and displacement for many Natives around Puget Sound. He knew the value of tribal lands, even as he adapted to a new system of land management that, in some cases, facilitated Indians' dispossession.[125] In his public speeches, Sicade asked for Americans to abide by their own laws and live up to their liberal and democratic ideals. In truly just conditions, Sicade suggested, Indians could benefit individually and prosper as a people in the region—just as their ancestors had done.

Sicade was not the only Native man to turn to the venues and technologies of colonialism to challenge settlers' assumptions. His classmate at the Cushman Indian School, Peter Kalama, the son of a Hawaiian HBC employee and a Nisqually woman, wrote letters of protest to U.S. officials over the loss of reservation lands and offered advice to other tribes in their court cases.[126] And in the mid-twentieth century, tribal leaders used Gibbs's maps in their land claims cases, and, with the establishment of a Native school in the 1970s, teachers began to employ Gibbs's dictionary and legends for language and cultural revitalization purposes.[127] The Nisqually Tribe now incorporates scientific research and salmonid enhancement technologies into its salmon hatcheries management and recovery programs.[128] Nisqually leaders appropriated some of the tools of colonialism and invested in the American liberal project to fight for their land and the power to possess, express, and pass on their stories.

In the 2004 Historical Court, Native representatives embraced a simulacrum of law to challenge a legal injustice—Leschi's 1857 conviction and subsequent execution. Like other leaders before them, the Native representatives hoped to appropriate a Western liberal tradition to challenge its exclusionary and unfair effects. Her voice wavering with emotion, Puyallup representative Connie McCloud testified to generations of assaults on Southern Coast Salish peoples' religion, language, and ways of knowing, which persisted long after Leschi's death. McCloud's testimony affirmed the survival of ancestral knowledge of the land and the relations that held the world together, even though various technologies of colonialism had forcibly transformed the world their ancestors knew. For McCloud, exonerating Leschi would be part of a longer process of reassembling language, land, religion, and ancestors in South Puget Sound.

The historical experiences of settler colonialism in South Puget Sound—for American settlers and Native peoples alike—reveal a great deal of mutual appropriation and reciprocal influence. These interactions do not mean that indigenous people exercised equal power or that Native adaptations signify assimilation. Rather, the entanglements show that non-Indians relied upon and reacted to Native knowledge and activities, and Native people strategically engaged overwhelming colonial power in myriad forms.[129] The material realities of settler colonialism formed the backdrop to these interactions. Leschi's response to the treaty has come to matter a great deal to people in South Puget Sound because it stands in for a larger and longer process of Indian dispossession and settler possession. Leschi's legal fate has continued to be a source of contention because it has the power to reveal, in some ways, the fallibility of a legal system that defines land rights and justifies U.S. sovereignty over South Puget Sound. The Historical Court was about philosophical problems and abstract ideas—truth, justice, history—but it was also grounded in place. As such, it could not escape a fundamental irony: the legal culture the petitioners invoked to exonerate Leschi was part of a tradition used to dispossess their ancestors. "Our free and democratic and very imperfect society," as Mary Robnett put it in her opening statement, was shaped just as much by liberal impulses as by the logic of settler colonialism.

CHAPTER 2 **Law and War**

As the petitioners in the Historical Court of Justice well understood, legality is the basis for legitimacy. The best way to present their case for Leschi's exoneration was not to question the fairness of the legal system that produced Leschi's conviction. Rather, the petitioners' lawyers would need to ground their case in law and highlight the virtuous capabilities of the liberal institution. They would argue for the inherent justice and legitimacy of the law in order to make their argument compelling to the judges. The main issue of debate in the Historical Court was therefore not whether U.S. law should or should not have been applied to Leschi in the 1850s, but rather *how* it should have been applied to him. Both Leschi's 1857 conviction and his 2004 exoneration reinforced the legitimacy of law, even as they revealed law's malleable nature. In this context, did the Historical Court exacerbate the larger problem it was created to address?

In Washington's territorial period, law and courts were put to the task of ordering a settler colonial society in the aftermath of armed Indian resistance. Territorial officials conferred on Leschi an exceptional legal status that made it possible for them to disregard legal restraints on the punishment of former enemies while claiming fidelity to due process.[1] In 1856 and 1857, Leschi stood before territorial courts to answer for the specific crime of murder and the more general accusation of "inciting war." The charges against him hint at the flexible nature of mid-nineteenth-century legality when applied to Indians: Leschi was neither seen as a warrior (for warriors cannot be charged with crimes in civilian courts) nor classified as a citizen (for citizens cannot make treaties or war).[2] Territorial officials and settlers treated Indian warriors as both subject to and outside of U.S. law because the liminal legal category justified and advanced their goals of territorial expansion in the region.

In 2004, the petitioners' legal team in the Historical Court made the problem of legal categories central to their argument for Leschi's exoneration. The petitioners asked the judges to interpret Leschi's alleged actions in the context of *legal* war and consider his status as an enemy combatant.[3] The legal team developed a two-pronged "wartime defense" designed to dismantle the logic of Leschi's exceptional legal status. First, they argued that the judge in Leschi's 1857 trial erred by failing to instruct the jury that a combatant could not be charged with murder for killing an enemy during wartime. Second, they insisted that the territory's civilian courts did not have jurisdiction over an enemy combatant's case, which should have been handled by military commission, if at all.

The issue was not just whether Leschi's trials followed due process, but whether the United States should categorize an Indian warrior as an enemy combatant or a criminal. The petitioners maintained that Leschi should have been treated consistently as an enemy combatant and should have received the legal protections appropriate to that status. The petitioners struck a chord with the judges when they framed Leschi's case in terms of the role and proper application of law in wartime contexts. Questions about how to define war and combatants were just as relevant in 2004, when the United States detained alleged terrorists captured in the so-called War on Terror, as they were in 1855 when American militiamen and soldiers fought Nisquallies in South Puget Sound. Once again, war offered the backdrop for debate over the proper judicial action in Leschi's case.

Warfare is as old as human societies, but the laws of war have a history especially suited for discussion in the Historical Court. Enlightenment military theorists treated warfare as a rational science and, as such, assumed it could be ordered through the rule of law. In the first half of the nineteenth century, the professional officer class in the United States developed principles for this legal code based on eighteenth-century philosophy and the writings of lawyers in maritime prize cases. The organizing principle to this body of law held that soldiers must be distinguished from criminals.[4] This code further developed in the international realm as rules of warfare that hostile "civilized" nations implicitly agree to follow when declaring war. Laws of war were supposedly based on natural order and rationality, which lent these laws the perception of universality and timelessness and its followers the mark of "civilized" peoples. The notions of universalism and continuity invested in the laws of war were especially important to Leschi's case. Although criminal law in Washington Territory was fluid and inconsistently applied, Captain Paul Robson informed the judges that "the United States has always acknowledged [the] doctrine of customary international law as controlling." Robson further explained that the United States recognizes "substantially similar" laws of war, especially concerning prisoner of war protections, to those in operation in the mid-nineteenth century.

Robson oriented the judges, who were all drawn from civilian rather than military courts, to three questions about the laws of war relevant to Leschi's case: When is there a state of war? Who has prisoner of war status? And how should prisoners of war be treated? Robson suggested that these questions had straightforward answers that should form the basis of a consistent body of law and action. If the judges determined that Leschi fit the standard definition for an enemy combatant, they might exonerate Leschi to affirm that consistent standards and definitions form a basis for just action during wartime. Furthermore, if the judges believed Robson's assertion that the United States has "always acknowledged" certain aspects of international law, they would be loath to allow an aberration from legal standards to remain unaddressed.

While the army lawyer presented the case for consistent principles in international legal practice, the petitioners' lawyer, John Ladenburg, argued that the surviving documentary record "is full of examples of the fact that both sides knew that a state of war existed and that Leschi was . . . entitled to protection from state murder charges and state jurisdiction." The facts were not in dispute, Ladenburg insisted. The petitioners' case appealed to a sense of consistency and continuity, presenting the judges with a liberal argument that fairness is defined by the universal application of law, regardless of race, political identity, or the passage of time. In this vein, Ladenburg implored the judges to "correct the historical record" and provide Washingtonians with "the clean vision of history."

But what was the "clean vision of history"? According to the petitioners, the facts were not disputed as much as their interpretation, so a clean vision of history is one in which the interpretation of past events—in this case, war and the application of law surrounding it—aligns with society's values and principles. As the petitioners framed it, the court's decision should represent a new interpretation unsullied by the passions that cloud judgment during wartime, such as fear, hatred, and revenge. The decision could confirm the existence of universal values and laws of war that *should* have won the day in Leschi's time but did not. The petitioners asked the judges in the Historical Court to recognize both continuities and breaks with the past: law and order remained in force in the 1850s just as in 2004, but the society in 2004 could deliberate rationally in a way that biased individuals in Leschi's day could not. In the context of the War on Terror, participants of the Historical Court surely recognized how Leschi's exoneration could make a public pronouncement about America's values and the humane principles embedded in law. The judges' decision could serve the dual and contradictory purposes of redeeming Leschi as a legal enemy and reaffirming the just nature of U.S. ways of war.[5] The symbolic exoneration could signify the victory of ideal liberal principles over the occasional and regrettable perversion of law and breakdown of consistent categories in a wartime context. The petitioners convinced the judges to claim fidelity to static principles of justice in order to change history.

However, the documentary record reaching back to Washington's early territorial period reveals that the definitions of war, enemy combatants, and law have long been contested and variable. Settlers in South Puget Sound wrote about war to defend themselves and degrade their enemy and turned to law to justify their actions or attack their foes.[6] The figure of Leschi was what made these legal and historical gymnastics possible. Leschi, imagined as a murderer or warrior, helped non-Indians define themselves as law-abiding and justified in their actions, even as they selectively enforced or disregarded certain laws in order to punish and/or dispossess Indians. Through their writings, settlers and government officials who benefited from U.S. military and political domination of Indian lands constructed new, cleansed memories of war and settlers' actions.[7] Although Justice Gerry Alexander called the Historical Court "unprecedented," this event was, in some ways, not new. In two wartime contexts in South Puget Sound—the 1850s and 2004—non-Indians defined and redefined the meaning of the Indian enemy combatant in accordance with a range of contemporary goals and concerns. Although separated by nearly 150 years, non-Indians' debates over the merits of Leschi's case similarly worked through the proper place of law to justify or rein in American power in wartime.

The competing impulses to claim and change the past reflect a cultural reluctance to come to terms with an unsettling history, particularly American settlers' and officials' use of flexible definitions of war, enemies, and legal standards to dispossess Indians. As historian John Fabian Witt argues, laws of war embody an internal tension between constraint and vindication, humanitarianism and justice. Throughout American history, laws of war have been used as both a mechanism of restraint and a way to achieve war aims at any cost. In the international realm, Americans have been among the chief creators and conspicuous violators of these rules.[8]

The logic of settler colonialism and ideals of liberal democracy are intertwined, which makes the quest for a "clean vision of history" a complicated act of both erasing and creating continuities with the past, of breaking from and claiming fidelity to just and humane practices.

1850s: War in the Territory

An expanded view of the region's political climate in the 1850s helps to explain how differences of opinion about legal authority in the territory developed into the "Leschi question." In the mid-nineteenth century, increasing sectional divide over the issue of slavery threatened to tear the Union apart, and U.S. claims to western territories only exacerbated the political conflict. In fact, the territorial system of governance was in crisis. According to the Constitution, Congress retained supreme power over federal territories. American territorial residents were treated almost like colonial subjects, with limited power over their governance and representation. The federal government covered most territorial expenses but also appointed the governor and three district judges, who presided over the territory. The potential for tyranny and corruption was significant because the federal officials were largely indifferent to territorial affairs and unconcerned when appointees ignored local concerns.[9] Washington never erupted into the civil wars and armed rebellions that plagued the Kansas, Utah, and New Mexico territories, but it did exhibit all of the symptoms of a dysfunctional colonial holding typical of the period: partisan officials treated federal law and policy as open to their interpretation, settlers defied federal authority yet demanded federal aid, and Americans mistreated peoples whose roots in the region predated U.S. claims.[10] Leschi tangled with people and institutions at the heart of the territory's tensions: he negotiated a treaty with a controversial governor appointed by the president rather than elected by the people; he fought against regular and volunteer troops, the former taking orders from the army and the latter from the governor; and he stood trial in federal district courts with federally appointed judges and locally drawn jurors. It is not surprising that settlers and officials focused on the figure of Leschi to work through questions about the nature of the expanding nation and the limits of popular sovereignty in a federal territory.

Washington became a territory in 1853, and the first governor, Isaac I. Stevens, set up his government in Olympia and built his cabinet with political supporters. The new territorial legislature granted a printing contract to the *Pioneer and Democrat*, which served as the mouthpiece of the government and the Democratic Party. Although the majority of Washington settlers were not ardent Democrats, government contracts helped the *Pioneer and Democrat* to become the most powerful public voice around Puget Sound. Oppositional newspapers struggled to compete without government subsidies and failed to provide alternative perspectives consistently to those advocated by Stevens and the Democrats.[11] In early 1855, George Goudy was elected territorial printer for the *Pioneer and Democrat* and simultaneously served in the territorial militia during the war.[12] These factors would be important to Leschi's case, because the *Pioneer and Democrat* was, in several instances, the sole reporter of crucial information about Leschi and the unrest in the territory.

Divisions among South Puget Sound settlers emerged soon after Stevens's appointment. Settlers around the territorial capital of Olympia, located in Thurston County, generally supported Stevens and shared his suspicions of Indians and resentment of naturalized citizens—those Hudson's Bay Company (HBC) employees who remained in Washington after it became a federal territory and took U.S. citizenship to retain their land holdings. Settlers in Pierce County, just to the northeast of Thurston County, were a more diverse lot, composed of American settlers, British, French, and Scottish employees of the Puget Sound Agricultural Company, and army regulars stationed at Fort Steilacoom. With a longer history of friendly interactions with Native peoples, many Pierce County homesteaders believed that peaceful and mutually beneficial coexistence was possible.[13] The tensions between Thurston County and Pierce County were not determined by political party. Rather, pro-Stevens and anti-Stevens camps pursued different paths to secure U.S. sovereignty over the region. Given this political landscape in a region far from federal concern, the controversy that would envelop Leschi was, as one army officer wrote in his journal, "the wire by which many a machine, social and political, is pulled into action."[14]

The first federal legal "intervention" in South Puget Sound came about in response to a crisis the federal government had created by allowing Americans to take homesteads in the region under the Oregon Donation Land Law Act.[15] American settlers quickly escalated tensions with Indian neighbors around Puget Sound by acting on the assumption that they had a superior claim to land.[16] The territorial legislature's 1854 Civil Practice Act, meanwhile, denied the competency of Indians to testify in civil proceedings in which a white person was a party, which allowed whites to abuse Indians without fear of punishment. Some settlers fenced in Indians' resources and permitted their hogs to run loose over Indians' camas fields and potato patches, and millers and farmers were known to withhold payment to Indian laborers.[17] One of the first directives Stevens received from his superiors in Washington, D.C., was to complete treaties with the region's Native peoples to clarify land title and property rights.[18] The 1854 Medicine Creek Treaty reflected a shift in U.S. Indian policy away from removal and toward reservations, which impacted settlers' ideas about land claims and legal order because Americans formed the minority in the region. The *Pioneer and Democrat* calmed homesteaders' concerns by praising Stevens's efforts to establish political authority over the Native majority. In the December 30, 1854, issue, the newspaper editor claimed that the Medicine Creek Treaty allowed Indians to continue "living in the vicinity of settlements at the sufferance of the whites." The report reassured settlers that the function of treaties was to legally affirm Indian subordination to "whites" without mention of rights Indians retained.[19] Reflecting on the issue fifty years later, the interpreter at the Medicine Creek Treaty dismissed the treaty as nothing more than a courtesy, since "the Indians knew . . . that the Government had possession of the whole country and could do as they pleased with it."[20]

The newspaper's interpretation of the treaty followed national trends in U.S. Indian policy. At the federal level, the Supreme Court wrestled with the nature of Indian sovereignty and the extent to which U.S. laws applied to Indian peoples and lands. As Indian policy shifted from removal to reservation management in western territories in the 1840s, legal decisions trended toward growing plenary power over Indians. Just over two years after the Medicine Creek Treaty, for example, Justice Roger B. Taney argued in *Dred Scott* (1857) that Indians were "in a state of pupilage" and that the United States deemed it necessary to "legislate to a certain extent over them and the territory they occupy."[21] Federal-level decisions dovetailed with the Washington territorial legislature's initiatives to deny Indians legal standing in local proceedings and strip them of legal protections.[22] Indians' ambiguous legal status meant that non-Indian settlers in the territory could choose which laws would or would not apply to Indians. Furthermore, although federal Indian policy imposed few limitations on settlers, many settlers considered Indian resistance as a unique challenge that locals were better equipped to handle than federal law and plenary power. This perception led some settlers in the 1850s to take positions to support the authority of law when it was used to punish Indians for resisting U.S. power but reject it when it did not.[23]

Just because territorial settlers *could* extend legal power over Indians in the region did not mean that they all agreed they *should*. Most HBC employees were sympathetic to Natives' perspectives and saw Stevens's actions as dictatorial. William Tolmie listened to Leschi's complaints about the reservation boundaries after the treaty council and wrote letters attesting to Leschi's frustration with Stevens's unwillingness to compromise.[24] Steilacoom's *Puget Sound Courier,* the short-lived Whig paper published in Pierce County, charged that Stevens was a failed diplomat and that his unjust treaties only succeeded in making Indians angry. The editor of the *Courier* criticized officials for acquiring territory from Indians "without any better title than can be wrested from its proper owners by the display of superior power"; the federal appointees' "impolite and unmanly" course in Washington was no different than that of filibusters who circumvented legitimate political channels in order to personally benefit from the acquisition of foreign territory.[25] One Pierce County settler, Ezra Meeker, later wrote that Indians and settlers built a "community of interest and good feeling," which was ruined when corrupt federal authorities pushed their "fatal policy" of treaty making upon western tribes and settlers.[26] In Meeker's opinion, treaties were based on the legal "fiction" that Indians composed independent nations and were the "rightful owners of the soil." If this were true, Meeker scoffed, "we pioneers were here as interlopers, as marauders assuming ownership without shadow of title." These law-abiding settlers were victimized by a perverse federal law that challenged settlers' stories about themselves and the meaning they gave to homesteading in the West. In Meeker's mind, the federal government's insistence on treaties brought "indescribable calamities . . . upon hapless peoples, both Indians and whites."[27] Tolmie's letters, the report from the opposition paper, and some settlers' anger at federal intervention show how non-Indians' concern about Stevens's governance aligned with Native peoples' complaints about the treaties. Leschi's dissatisfaction about the reservation supported some settlers' critique that Stevens rushed through his duties without adequate knowledge of and careful consideration for local needs and customs.

The events leading up to the Puget Sound Indian War presented similar tensions between federal "outsiders" and territorial settlers. When violence broke out between Indians and the U.S. Army on the east side of the

Cascade Mountains, Acting Governor Charles Mason (who had replaced Stevens during his treaty tour across the territory) raised two companies of volunteers. The regular enlisted men stationed at Fort Steilacoom and the local volunteers from Olympia exhibited markedly different views about the prospect of war with Indians. One army officer noted that the Olympia volunteers left the fort with "the determination of taking the scalp of every red-skin who may be so unfortunate as to fall in their way."[28] The officer's comment suggested that the regular troops were disinterested professionals but that the militiamen delighted in cruelty toward Indians; volunteers seemed excited that the government sanctioned their preferred approach to Indian relations. The officer claimed that the army followed the laws of war, while some volunteers were ready to dispense with discipline and legal restraints to achieve their ultimate goal of exterminating Indians. However, not every settler agreed with that assessment. One Steilacoom resident wrote that the regular soldiers terrorized homesteaders and Indians alike, and in contrast to hardworking locals who invested in the community, low-ranking soldiers squandered their federal pay on alcohol and rabble-rousing. The *Puget Sound Courier* insisted that violence could be avoided outright if federal officials simply remitted to Indians proper and just compensation for their land.[29] It was the irresponsible and illegal actions of outsiders, these settlers maintained, that drove Leschi to fight.

Once the local militiamen were mustered and ready, the tense peace on the west side of the Cascades rapidly eroded. However, the actual start of the war in South Puget Sound is not easy to discern from the surviving records because of varying interpretations of what constitutes an act of war. Western settlers and officials at once feared and expected an Indian "uprising" but did not define an act of war with consistency or agree that Indians had the national character to declare war.[30] Nineteenth-century U.S. military officials classified Indians as criminals for resisting their demands—a position that escalated tensions and made violence more likely.[31] Several settlers and officials in South Puget Sound expected Leschi to plan an attack and were poised to see his actions as resistance to U.S. authority, and thus equivalent to lawbreaking. Tolmie wrote that Leschi sought advice from him after hearing rumors that the Indian agents intended to "incarcerate, and perhaps hang him" for not cooperating with the treaty terms.[32]

The quick succession of events in October 1855 that finally led to open hostilities presents evidence of escalating tensions and distrust but no single definitive start to war. At the beginning of the month, settlers in King County, just to the north of Pierce County, feared that the war between the U.S. Army and Indians on the east side of the Cascades would spread to their area so they began to gather in block houses for mutual protection. Mason responded to the settlers' fears by summoning Leschi and Quiemuth to Olympia on October 22 to secure the leaders' commitment to peace. The brothers promised peace and even acted as interpreters and guides as Mason visited other Native communities in the area.[33] Leschi apparently considered these actions proof of his intentions to cooperate with territorial officials, perhaps even hoping to negotiate better treaty terms by fostering a closer relationship with the acting governor. However, Leschi did not immediately move to Olympia as Mason had requested because he feared it was a trap. After two days of waiting, Mason assumed that Leschi's reticence to move to the capital was evidence of his hostile intent. From Mason's perspective, each day Mason waited was another day for Leschi to recruit warriors and organize an attack. Mason therefore sent a group of forty rangers from Fort Steilacoom to arrest Leschi, interrupt communication between tribes on the east and west sides of the Cascade Range, and break up and disarm any Indian assemblages. Mason considered this a reasonable step to secure the settlers' safety, but it could also be interpreted as an act of war. In that view, Mason initiated a blockade and preemptively ordered the capture and detention of a leader of another nation in order to dictate his political decisions.

When Leschi heard that an armed posse was on the way to capture him, he apparently assumed that the rumors about the government's plan to kill him were true, and he went into hiding with his family. The rangers did not find Leschi but reportedly helped themselves to fifteen of Leschi's horses. On October 27, two rangers and one Indian guide were shot and killed near Connell's Prairie while on a reconnaissance mission. Did the shooters seek to protect Leschi or to retaliate for the property seized by the rangers, or did they aim to send a message to Mason? The records do not reveal whether those who ambushed the reconnaissance party intended to start a war. But within hours, tensions in South Puget Sound broke into open violence. The other rangers heard gunshots in the distance and, acting on the assumption that they would soon fall under siege, fortified a well-stocked Indian longhouse and burned a nearby barn of grain. Late in the afternoon, a large group of Nisqually warriors, perhaps exacting retribution for the destroyed property or in answer to the rangers' mission, attacked the longhouse and engaged the rangers in an all-night gun battle. Early the next morning, an unidentified group of Indians attacked an American settlement fifteen miles to the north, killing eight men, women, and children in what became known as the White River Massacre.[34] The first report of hostile fire on U.S. soldiers and militiamen on the west side of the Cascades—a clear declaration of war from the army's perspective—came three days later, again from Connell's Prairie, on October 31. When soldiers returned to the prairie to retrieve the bodies of the fallen militiamen, they found the remains of the missing rangers as well. October 27, 28, or 31 are the dates most chroniclers mark as the beginning of the Puget Sound Indian War, yet these supposed start dates interpret acts of war from a solely U.S. perspective. Paradoxically, only Indians could start war, and they did so with "criminal" acts.

Once hostilities broke out in South Puget Sound, the territorial newspapers did not hesitate to describe the situation as a war, which implies conflict between nations, although the meaning of an Indian war is particularly fraught. The editors of the opposing newspapers jousted over the terminology to describe the nature of war with Indians. The *Courier* first labeled the hostilities a "civil war," which the *Pioneer and Democrat* emphatically rejected: "Are these heathen miscreants of our nation or kindred? We . . . proclaim boldly we are not of them." The *Courier* countered that if not a civil war, it certainly was not a "foreign war." The Democratic mouthpiece answered that it was simply a war because the governor had recognized it as such, and if Indian tribes' sense of autonomy drove them to fight, the United States would strip them of their national character in order to "conquer a peace."[35] This argument rested on the tortured logic that the United States would need to defeat Indian nations in war in order to disabuse Indians of the notion that they had a legal right to wage war. Settlers and officials knew war when they saw it, but could not bring themselves to see Indian tribes as autonomous nations, even when Indian tribes took actions consistent with those of a sovereign nation.

The *Pioneer and Democrat* in particular focused blame for the war on Leschi. In November 1855, the editor declared: "The Klickatats, Puyallups, and a large portion of the Nisqually Indians have entered into an offensive alliance, to wage war against the whites, under Leschi, a Klickatat."[36] The newspaper pointedly identified Leschi by his mother's kin to support the story that Indians spread the war from the east side of the Cascades to the west out of racial loyalty rather than specific grievances with the Medicine Creek Treaty, which would have made Stevens at least partially culpable.[37] Leschi was specifically named in accounts of violence against settlers because, as Stevens put it in a letter to the superintendent of Indian Affairs, Leschi "was familiarly known to most of our citizens."[38] As the next chapters show in greater detail, Leschi was well known because he cultivated economic and social relationships with many regional settlers and HBC employees. It may have been Leschi's friendly disposition toward settlers before 1855 that sealed his fate as a "known" figure in later reports of violence.[39] On November 16, 1855, the *Pioneer and Democrat* published "a horrid recital of the massacre of women and children on White River, by a lot of fiends under the command of Leschi, Nelson, and others."[40] When a group of Indians attacked the hamlet of Seattle on January 12, 1856, killing two settlers, the *Pioneer and Democrat* blamed Leschi and declared: "There is not a town, settlement or house, this side of the mountains that is safe . . . from attack, destruction, and the massacre of our people!"[41] The newspaper associated Leschi's name with the specter of wholesale slaughter of innocent people, despite the fact that perhaps a dozen homesteaders had been killed and no eyewitnesses had seen Leschi at White River. One Tulalip elder claimed over a century later that Leschi had not killed anyone in Seattle, but that "only he was blamed for it. This is the way it was about the fighting."[42] By early 1856, the *Pioneer and Democrat* admitted that Leschi had "been rendered, perhaps, more notorious in name than in deed." The sensational news coverage made it more likely that Leschi would be named ex post facto as the leader behind any "Indian depredations."[43] The newspaper made Leschi into a terrifying figure by inflating the extent of the fighting and employing stereotypes of Indians as unpredictable and irrational, while characterizing settlers as sympathetic victims.[44]

The *Pioneer and Democrat*'s exaggerated reporting of the hostilities gave events a meaning out of proportion to their scope and length. If the fighting over the winter of 1855–56 rose to the level of war, it was a short and limited one. Only about 300 Natives from the area took up arms, and clashes were brief and sporadic and resulted in few casualties.[45] But the label of "war" carried important implications for Americans' sense of national identity and belonging in the western territory. Over the five-month period of fighting in South Puget Sound, officials' letters and the alarmist stories in the *Pioneer and Democrat* interpreted events as the reaction of a savage people against settlers' superior way of life. This was a well-worn American narrative that justified colonial violence. War with Indians was part of the national myth; conceiving of the violence as an "Indian war" in Puget Sound brought the region into this American narrative. While Nisquallies fought for their own specific, localized reasons, settlers raised on celebratory narratives of pioneering waged a mythical war repeated many times, over the expanse of the continent.[46]

The *Pioneer and Democrat* whipped up panic and escalated the hostilities because an "Indian war" came with the benefit of a story: Indians and Americans would inevitably clash because of their incompatible ways of life, and the superior way of life would emerge victorious. One Olympia volunteer wrote years afterward that the war was caused by Indians' predictable response to "the settlement of the citizens of our country upon soil which the congress . . . declared to be free for settlement and occupancy by virtue of the donation act, and subsequent pre-emption law." He argued that Americans brought legal order to the wilderness and consequently stirred "an ignorant people" to anger. Territorial officials characterized Indian resistance as "treachery," suggesting that Indians did not follow rational rules of war or honor the law as represented by the treaty. In his message to the territorial assembly in December 1855, Mason reported that Indians had gone back on their "solemn pledge" of peace in the treaties and had ambushed "our unoffending citizens."[47] The law was central to justifying settlers' actions. If Indians did not recognize the legitimacy of U.S. sovereignty in the region, it was because of their "savage hatred toward all whites."[48] The label of "Indian war" implied a knee-jerk aboriginal response to "progress" in which non-Indians were blameless.[49]

The term "Indian war" also reveals the contradictions of colonialism: mid-nineteenth-century U.S. officials denied that Indian tribes had the national character to make war but also considered war a legitimate basis for claiming sovereignty over Indian land.[50] The battle over language in the historical record held clear political implications. Ironically, to use the term "war" to describe the hostilities in the region would later become critical to the Nisqually sense of nationhood. The petitioners' argument for Leschi's exoneration, based on his status as an enemy combatant in war, needed the language of war, even if it served non-Indians' purposes to justify colonialism.

American settlers' disagreements over the definition of war foreshadowed a major controversy over the proper operations of law in the territory during and after war. When Stevens returned to Olympia at the completion of his treaty tour in early 1856, he took command of the volunteer forces and directed settlers to gather in blockhouses for protection. Some settlers living in Pierce County—former HBC employees who had taken U.S. citizenship and married Native women—incurred suspicion for refusing to leave their farms and move to the blockhouses.[51] In March 1856, Stevens sent a group of militiamen to arrest the settlers for treason, claiming there was "no such thing . . . as neutrality in an Indian War."[52] However, Stevens had no evidence against them. When the prisoners' lawyer took steps to secure their release, Stevens declared martial law in Pierce County, which closed the courts and held the prisoners without trial. The *Pioneer and Democrat* defended Stevens's declaration as necessary to defeat Leschi and the hostile forces in the region, while a letter printed in the *Puget Sound Courier* criticized Stevens for spitefully pursuing a "rigid persecution" of the territory's citizens to advance his political career.[53] Chief Justice Edward Lander defied the governor and convened a habeas corpus hearing in Steilacoom. Stevens sent militiamen to arrest him from his bench. Lander initially requested protection from army troops but ultimately allowed himself to be arrested after reasoning that an armed confrontation between volunteer and regular soldiers inside a federal courtroom should be avoided. The struggle for authority between federal and territorial forces only narrowly avoided civil war during the martial law incident.

The heated battle over legal rights and governing power continued to play out in the press and in official reports. Pierce County settlers, lawyers, and judges were outraged by what they saw as Olympia's armed invasion of Steilacoom and disruption of the courts on the pretense of military necessity. Members of the bar in the third judicial district sent resolutions condemning Stevens's declaration to the *Puget Sound Courier* and to Secretary of State William Marcy in the hope of federal intervention. The Pierce County lawyers and judges did not succeed in removing Stevens from office, but they did create documentation of Stevens's unauthorized use of law during wartime. Their written protests helped the petitioners in the Historical Court to argue that Stevens was a powerful official who would subvert democracy and civil order to get what he wanted. Although the federal government took no action to rein in the territorial governor, the lawyers of Pierce County ensured that Stevens did not "get away with" an abuse of power in the historical record.[54]

As the fighting in the region quieted, Leschi's case became central to the clash between the territorial governor and the army. In early 1856, U.S. Army general Wool, who commanded operations on the west coast, publicly criticized Stevens's territorial government and accused the local press of exaggerating the dangers Indians posed to settlement in Washington and Oregon. Wool blamed the militia for fomenting Indian anger and called for it to disband. Regular soldiers stationed in the region could manage hostile Indians with leveler heads.[55] Incensed, the *Pioneer and Democrat* charged that "[Wool's] course ha[d] been marked with criminal neglect."[56] The army was supposed to protect American citizens in the federal territory, the newspaper insisted, not abandon them. Stevens responded by directing the militia volunteers in campaigns to finish the war in defiance of the general's orders.

Stevens believed that a truce would not do; settlers had to "bring [hostile Indians] to unconditional surrender" to ensure that the American war met its predetermined conclusion.[57] Stevens and his supporters believed the war should settle a question; like the resolution of a story, the war should gratify the winners with the affirmation that their reason for fighting was right.[58] If white Americans were supposed to be superior and Indians subordinate in the territory, as some American militiamen and settlers expected, the war's end was the plot point that should prove these "facts." It was this appeal to a narrative conclusion with clear winners and losers, in addition to the prospect of political advancement for successful officers, that motivated Stevens and his supporters to prolong the hostilities and punish Leschi afterward.

General Wool, on the other hand, did not have to know Leschi or sympathize with Indians to insist upon an alternative path for U.S. territorial sovereignty in the West. His position suggested that Americans could more effectively promote their interests by making small and feasible accommodations to Native people. Wool voiced an opinion shared by some Pierce County settlers and regular troops that war was a choice, and a costly one at that. The United States could actually increase its power by pursuing diplomatic solutions. According to some federal officials, just because the nation could muster military might was not reason to deploy it. The pro- and anti-Stevens camps focused on Leschi but actually debated how America could reach its goals for territorial expansion most efficiently.

After Leschi and the allied Indian warriors decided to stop fighting and go into hiding, pro- and anti-Stevens factions turned Leschi's fate into a referendum on the proper applications of law. Stevens insisted that the only way to end the war and affirm Indian submission to U.S. authority was to make the Indian war leaders stand trial.[59] Stevens urged hostile Indians to "surrender to the mercy and justice" of territorial officials and offered a $500 reward for Leschi in order to expedite his capture.[60] The governor began a postwar legal process that continued even after he left his western post to serve as territorial delegate to Congress in 1857.[61] One settler argued in a letter to Stevens's successor, Fayette McMullin, who reportedly considered clemency for Leschi, that if Leschi were to walk free it would confirm that General Wool was right and imperil congressional war debt payments. Furthermore, the settler explained, "it is essentially necessary to the safety of our people" that Indians "be taught to fear us."[62] Leschi's murder conviction would exonerate Stevens, the treaties, and the volunteers who had pursued and fought in the war.

On November 17, 1856, Leschi stood before the territory's Third District Court in Steilacoom. His indictment contained inherent contradictions that reveal Indians' ambiguous subject position in territorial law. If Leschi was a murderer, the volunteer soldiers who fought against him were merely a police force and not eligible for veterans' benefits. If Leschi had led a war and was accused of violating international laws of war, the army rather than the territorial courts should have jurisdiction over his case. But given the fact that Colonel Wright offered Leschi protection and General Wool promoted a peaceful resolution to conflict in western Washington, the army was unlikely to pursue a military trial.[63] Pro-Stevens supporters' pragmatic goals led them to contradicting claims that Washington Territory had been in a state of war in 1855 while denying that Leschi's alleged crime was committed during wartime.[64]

From the start of Leschi's first trial in 1856, it was clear that some settlers would support Leschi's acquittal, either out of genuine concern for legal fairness or to challenge Stevens's leadership. Although the court records from the first trial were destroyed by fire in 1859, the *Pioneer and Democrat* reported on the proceedings, and one of the jurors, Ezra Meeker, wrote about the experience nearly fifty years afterward. The newspaper reported Antonio Rabbeson's eyewitness testimony in which he claimed that Leschi stepped from behind a tree and fired on the party on Connell's Prairie.[65] At the conclusion of the testimony, according to Meeker, Judge Chenoweth directed the jury that a defendant could not be held for murder if the killing was an act of war, and a declaration of war could consist of words or actions (and acts of war sometimes preceded a formal declaration). The jurors argued over when the war began and whether Leschi and his troops were "marauders" acting as individuals or as representatives of a nation.[66] The unsettled questions of how to define acts of war and apply law to Indians in wartime led at least two jury members to refuse to find Leschi guilty of murder, and the judge declared a hung jury.

The next month, the territory's judicial districts were redrawn to include Pierce County in the Second District along with Thurston County.

Thus Leschi's indictments were refiled in the Second District on March 9, 1857, and ten days later Leschi stood trial in Olympia. The venue change from Steilacoom to Olympia was a critical blow to Leschi's chances for another split jury. Not only was Olympia the hotbed of pro-Stevens supporters, but the *Pioneer and Democrat* referred to "the notorious Leschi" in a pretrial report—a characterization that could prejudice the local jury pool.[67] Leschi stood before a jury drawn from the *Pioneer and Democrat*'s readership, former volunteer militiamen, and businessmen who benefited from federal contracts and government operations in Olympia. Once again, Rabbeson offered eyewitness testimony, and many of the same witnesses cast doubt on his story. When it came time for the jury to consider the questions in the case, the records are silent on the judge's instructions. There is no existing evidence to suggest that Judge Lander (the same one arrested from his bench by Olympia militiamen) instructed the jury that a wartime killing was not punishable as murder, as Judge Chenoweth had done. The jury quickly returned a unanimous guilty verdict.[68]

Leschi's lawyers moved for a new trial and an arrest of judgment—both of which Lander denied—and then filed a bill of exceptions and petitioned the Territorial Supreme Court for a new trial. The court, which consisted of Judges Lander, Chenoweth, and Obadiah McFadden, met in December 1857 to review the district court decision. The three judges systematically shot down each of the points raised in Leschi's appeal and set Leschi's execution date for January 22, 1858.[69] Justice McFadden addressed the legal contradiction—a civilian court determining the guilt of a war leader—by arguing that the courts were forced to step in out of necessity after the army failed to take appropriate action. McFadden criticized the army for not "taking care" of Leschi during the war with "a summary mode of trial, one in accordance with the practice of government, and in perfect consonance with the rules of international law." McFadden essentially chastised the army for not capturing and executing Leschi in the field, instead leaving the task to the territorial courts.[70] According to the territory's highest court, Leschi's conviction and execution would correct an error by aligning his case with customary practice and the law.

Leschi's journey through the territorial courts was pregnant with meaning for the future character of U.S. legal authority in the territory. Court officials at the time agreed that Leschi's trials represented the best of America's liberal principles and due process: legal procedures that were methodical, divorced from popular passions, fair, and exemplary of U.S.

democracy. McFadden wrote that the fact that Leschi received two trials and an appeal was evidence of the judicial system's impartiality.[71] Those who supported a different vision for American sovereignty in the region argued that Leschi's conviction proved just the opposite. Ironically, Leschi's supporters challenged the legality of the conviction by manipulating the flexible nature of territorial law. One of Leschi's defense attorneys, Frank Clark, in conjunction with military officers from Fort Steilacoom, arranged for the arrest of the Pierce County sheriff who was to carry out Leschi's execution on January 22. The charges were legitimate—selling liquor to Indians—but selectively enforced. The sheriff was detained and was unable to carry out the court's execution order at the scheduled time.[72]

The sheriff's arrest enraged many pro-Stevens settlers, who held so-called indignation meetings in Olympia and Steilacoom to draft resolutions for publication in the *Pioneer and Democrat*. The meetings and public denunciations had little to do with Leschi's life—the secretary who drafted the Steilacoom resolutions was the brother of Ezra Meeker, the juror who had voted for Leschi's acquittal in his first trial.[73] Meeker later claimed that most of the people at the Steilacoom meeting "denounced the persecution of Leschi" but were more offended by the "persistent disregard of the law."[74] Frank Clark's "unauthorized" use of the legal system appeared akin to Stevens's declaration of martial law. Clark was labeled a "knavish pettifogging attorney" in the *Pioneer and Democrat* and hanged in effigy.[75] The territorial legislature called on the court to reschedule Leschi's execution, which was moved to February 19, 1858.

As Leschi's new execution date neared, Clark, August Kautz, and Tolmie (representing Stevens's most vocal critics, Pierce county lawyers, army regulars, and HBC employees, respectively) tried another approach. The trio created an anonymous publication called the *Truth Teller*, printed in Steilacoom for the "dissemination of truth, and the suppression of humbug." First printed on February 3, the *Truth Teller* prominently featured a map of Connell's Prairie drawn to cast doubt upon Rabbeson's testimony and Leschi's murder charge.[76] With the exception of the map, however, much of the material in the issue focused on the public accusations leveled at the men involved in the January 22 incident that saved Leschi from the gallows. The Pierce County sheriff defended himself against the charge that he colluded in his own arrest in order to subvert the will of the courts. The U.S. commissioner who oversaw the sheriff's case wrote that "if there was a plot [to save Leschi] I certainly am the victim. . . . It was a matter

FIGURE 6 A group of historians and researchers examines the site of Leschi's execution near Steilacoom, Washington, ca. 1895. (Washington State Historical Society)

of indifference to me whether Leschi was hanged or no."[77] The *Truth Teller* offered a public record of some settlers' ostensible sympathy for Leschi *and* their respect for proper applications of law in a democracy.[78]

Leschi's supporters fought for his release up to the time of his execution. Lieutenant Colonel Silas Casey refused to allow Leschi's hanging on the "government reserve" of Fort Steilacoom in order to distance the army from the execution it did not condone.[79] Kautz and Clark briefly considered delaying the hanging once again by issuing a writ against the deputy sheriff of Thurston County on the charge that he had no authority to execute Leschi (since the hanging was to take place in Pierce County). In the end, either out of concern for their reputations or resigning themselves to eventual defeat, Kautz and Clark did not carry out the plan. Tolmie, for his part, wrote a letter to Governor McMullin pleading for a last-minute pardon.[80] Leschi was hanged on February 19, 1858, in the territory's first official execution and the only Puget Sound war trial to end in punishment.

The discursive battle over the government's legal actions was not settled with Leschi's death. Non-Indians troubled by the legacy of Leschi's execution made an effort to register their outrage for the records. The second and final issue of the *Truth Teller*, published four days after the hanging, charged that Leschi "was unlawfully executed by a party of hirelings from Olympia under a show of legality from the district court." One particularly pointed statement became highly influential to historians and the petitioners in the Historical Court: "[Leschi] is perhaps the first man every arraigned by the civil courts for an act of war which in truth he was not guilty. Convicted finally by a jury which had perjured him, all clemency was forestalled by remonstrance of a prejudiced people he was at last executed contrary to law. We sincerely hope it may never be cited as precedent."[81] The sentiment of the statement clearly informed the petitioners' argument in the Historical Court: Leschi should not have been judged by a jury of his former enemies after the war because popular prejudice clouded sound legal judgment. Most important, the authors charged that Leschi's conviction and execution chipped away at the moral foundations of law itself and represented a departure from just principles. Although the authors did not save Leschi from the gallows, one historian asserted that the *Truth Teller* at least registered a "moral victory" in the record.[82]

In the 1850s, and for decades afterward, settlers and officials argued about the nature and definitions of war and law in the territory. The debates filled regional archives with a rich documentary record and wealth of personal reminiscences. Ezra Meeker wrote his autobiography alongside Leschi's story in *Pioneer Reminiscences of Puget Sound and the Tragedy of Leschi*, published in 1905.[83] Meeker characterized homesteaders as a noble and dying breed, living relics from a simpler time—in short, like Indians.[84] Meeker observed that "the life, achievements, and fate of Leschi are so intimately connected with those of the pioneers that the history and life struggles of the one cannot well be written without that of the other."[85] His main concern was that "pioneers" received recognition for their role, as Meeker understood it, in creating a civilization in Washington despite unwanted federal intervention and corrupt territorial leadership.[86] Members of the Indian War Veterans Association, meanwhile, organized to preserve volunteers' stories and "remove the stigma cast by Wool," while continuing to call for veterans' benefits. The members recorded their memories as patriotic volunteers fighting to defend their homes and families from merciless Indian attacks.[87]

Despite their different messages, settler reminiscences of the territorial period had much in common. They shared the basic assumption that Indian dispossession was inevitable and American colonization was justified on legal grounds.[88] Settlers recognized the legitimacy of federal laws that granted advantages and dismissed those that limited them in pursuing their interests in the territory. These writers characterized Leschi as either a sympathetic victim or a treacherous savage but agreed that most settlers—the agents of national expansion—were law-abiding and innocent, powerful and good.[89] Territorial settlers debated definitions of war, enemy combatants, and legal rights but did not challenge the justice of colonialism itself.

2004: War and the Historical Court

Meeker wrote in the introduction to *Pioneer Reminiscences of Puget Sound and the Tragedy of Leschi*: "To tell the truth about [Indians] is no more than justice." Although Meeker intended the "truth" to rescue the honor of the "pioneers," one hundred years later the petitioners also equated truth with justice to argue for Leschi's exoneration in the Historical Court.[90] The expert witnesses relied upon a mix of nineteenth-century documents to build their case: government reports, settlers' letters, newspaper reports, public meeting minutes, journals, accounts of the legal proceedings, and other publications. They also used settlers' memoirs penned in the 1890s, because those writings held information about Leschi that was especially helpful to the petitioners' case. Meeker, for example, laid the blame for Leschi's death upon territorial officials, which helped the petitioners build a tidy legal argument but obscured the fact that non-Indians benefited for generations from federal aid and the use of military force against indigenous peoples. The petitioners seemed to accept Meeker's depictions of settlers' innocence as long as the judges admitted that a mistake had been made. In 2007, one of the petitioners' legal advisers said: "It doesn't matter if it's a binding decision or not. Leschi's still dead . . . [but at least] Stevens is discredited."[91] The petitioners used settlers' writings to build an argument in a narrowly defined legalistic case, but the continuities in colonial ideology expressed in these documents remained largely outside of this specific framing.

The Committee to Exonerate Chief Leschi and its legal counsel used the documentary record to develop an argument advocating for the legal status of combatants in U.S. wars, an approach that seemed especially tailored to engage with an on-going debate in the early twenty-first century. In 2003 and 2004, a flurry of books and films from across the political spectrum questioned the so-called War on Terror, especially the U.S. invasion of Iraq in March 2003 and the Bush administration's efforts to justify it.[92] Much like the Puget Sound War in the mid-nineteenth century, U.S. overseas conflicts in the early twenty-first century were arguably an outward manifestation of domestic economic, political, and cultural crisis—"an attempt to manage or defer coming to terms with contradictions besetting the American way of life," as Andrew Bacevich puts it.[93] This context of war and public debate about its righteousness shaped the petitioners' legal arguments and the judges' interpretations of the documentary record related to Leschi. Although the military law experts who testified in the Historical Court did not mention the current wars, one judge recalled afterward that "all of us were aware of what was going on in Iraq and Afghanistan" as they deliberated Leschi's case.[94] Leschi's exoneration offered the judges the opportunity to confirm America's commitment to liberal values of equality and freedom in the midst of an increasingly unpopular war. The judges' decision could help Americans declare the United States as both powerful and good.

The army lawyers' interpretation of Leschi's wartime status as an enemy combatant served as the basis for the petitioners' case and the judges' decision in the Historical Court. The petitioners' argument was especially interesting in light of contemporaneous debates over the legal status of combatants captured in the War on Terror. In the months after the terrorist attacks of September 11, 2001, the United States commenced military operations in Afghanistan and other places in pursuit of members of the al-Qaeda terrorist network. President George W. Bush and military lawyers determined individuals captured in these operations to be *unlawful* enemy combatants because the group was stateless and, according to the United States, waged an illegal war by ignoring international conventions of war. Executive branch lawyers released legal memos justifying detention and torture on legal grounds, despite the fact that international law prohibited such treatment for prisoners of war. President Bush's military order of November 13, 2001, declared that belligerents captured in this conflict could be held indefinitely without legal recourse. If the case advanced to a hearing, the suspects would be tried and sentenced by a special military commission not subject to "the principles of law" generally recognized in U.S. criminal courts. In early 2002, about 500 prisoners were transported to Guantánamo Bay Naval Base.[95] The Central Intelligence Agency, meanwhile, took detainees to detention centers in undisclosed locations around the world, called black sites, to conduct interrogations.[96]

The administration's wartime policy of holding "unlawful combatants" without trial received a great deal of public scrutiny.[97] Just as Nisqually leaders began conversations about exonerating Leschi, half a dozen habeas corpus cases wound their way up to the U.S. Supreme Court. At the same time, in April 2004, *60 Minutes II* broadcast disturbing photographs of abuses at Abu Ghraib prison in Iraq, and the *New Yorker* published the photographs a few days later. The ensuing public horror prompted President Bush to condemn the "disgraceful conduct by a few American troops who dishonored our country and disregarded our values." Those values became the subject of public debate and strengthened the rhetorical impulse toward civil and human rights.[98] By the autumn of 2004, the Supreme Court had rejected sweeping wartime powers claimed by the Bush administration regarding legal rights for enemy combatants.[99] The petitioners thus presented an argument for Leschi's exoneration around an issue of concurrent public concern: U.S. adherence to international laws of war and the legal rights of enemy combatants.

The petitioners' expert witnesses contributed information that would, the petitioners hoped, lead the judges to view Leschi as the leader of a sovereign nation who had had every right to commence war and expect to be released from punishment at the war's end. The first step was to establish that the shooting death of A. B. Moses was a legitimate military action in a war already well under way. Although most settlers and later historians claimed that the ambush of the express party on Connell's Prairie on October 31 signaled the start of the war—and Indians fired the first shots—the petitioners' legal team insisted that the United States had in fact chosen to instigate the war days earlier. John Ladenburg argued that Governor Mason's preemptive decision to bring Leschi to Olympia against his will was an act of war and that Moses's death took place a few days later, when the war was well under way.

In addition to re-characterizing actions as war—and reversing the historical record's narrative of Indian aggression and settler innocence—the petitioners argued that the Nisqually Tribe held sovereign status with the right to commence war. Charles Wilkinson, the expert on Indian law, argued that the treaty confirmed that the United States recognized the national character of the Nisqually Tribe. Furthermore, he pointed out that Chief Justice John Marshall affirmed in his 1832 opinion in *Worcester v. Georgia* that Indian groups constituted separate nations with the right to self-government. Of course, the surviving record of local actions showed that most settlers and several territorial judges only recognized Indians' national character and right to declare legal war when it advanced their pragmatic goals.[100] The respondents' counsel argued that the territory's legal record in fact supported the logic of criminal charges brought against Leschi. Carl Hultman pointed to the trial of another Nisqually war leader,

Wa He Lut, in which the judge determined that Indian tribes did not "have such a national character that they can, at their will, make war, and claim immunity from acts of... murder." Because no state of war could exist between the Nisqually Tribe and the United States, Wa He Lut's actions could only be defined as criminal.[101] Wa He Lut's case illustrated how judges could define Indians so as to make a colonized population subject to U.S. law without the benefit of legal rights. The petitioners asked the judges to address this legal ambiguity by publicly confirming Nisqually nationhood and disavowing the logic that denied its sovereignty.

One of the expert witnesses pointed out that regardless of whether treaties acknowledged tribal sovereignty, Americans considered treaties as binding law—at least for Indians. Kent Richards, Isaac Stevens's biographer, argued that Stevens and others would not have considered Leschi's actions in wartime as justified because he had signed a treaty promising peace. Richards stated that the Nisqually Tribe placed itself under the protection and authority of the United States in the treaty, and thus, according to the views of territorial officials, "the murder of men, women and children at the White River at the end of October and attacks elsewhere [were] indefensible."[102] In Stevens's view, Leschi broke U.S. law by breaching the treaty that bore his mark, and therefore, from territorial officials' perspectives, "inciting war" was a reasonable criminal charge. Richards offered a narrow reading of the treaty and official correspondence to explain Stevens's claim that Indians could be both independent nations and subject to U.S. law. The power to make exceptions when it came to U.S.-Native relations was in fact built into American legal thought and practice.

Although the historical record was a shaky ally when it came to recognition of Nisqually sovereignty, the petitioners turned to documents created by army officials and Ezra Meeker to argue that Leschi should have been given the rights of an enemy combatant after the war. The expert witnesses for the military pointed out that the U.S. Army took the position that once Leschi surrendered, he could not be held on criminal charges. Eugene Ham explained that the army "made formal requests and appealed to the Governor at that time to release Chief Leschi."[103] Richards countered that Stevens may have disagreed with the army's recommendation, but he followed legal conventions in the aftermath of the war. Richards noted that Stevens wanted Indian leaders held responsible for directing a war in which noncombatants were killed, which was consistent with military practice and international law at the time.[104] The historical record from the period was not clear on what constituted the laws of war; if anything, the winners determined which rules to apply depending upon their postwar goals.

The petitioners argued for the continuity of America's good intentions. The army lawyers insisted that Leschi's punishment was inconsistent with American military values. Paul Robson pointed out that international laws of war and sensibilities regarding the legal rights of combatants had evolved since Leschi's time but noted some continuity between the 1850s and 2004. Abraham Lincoln insisted on the codification of laws of war during the Civil War, and after World War II the rights of enemy combatants were extended to fighters who were not members of a state in recognition of nationalist struggles against colonial powers. Article 5 of the 1949 Third Geneva Convention established that reputable tribunals would determine the status of a combatant and whether this combatant was entitled to prisoner of war protections under international laws of war.[105] Robson insisted that the United States has long recognized the customary laws of war, even if these were only recently codified in the international realm.

Although the military experts insisted that the United States has consistently honored these conventions, which helped to convince the judges that Leschi's treatment had been a mistake, this claim was a matter of debate outside of the Historical Court. When alleged combatants were transported to Guantánamo Bay prison, Secretary of Defense Donald Rumsfeld announced that the captives "will be handled not as prisoners of war . . . but as unlawful combatants" who "do not have any rights under the Geneva Convention."[106] President George W. Bush and executive branch lawyers determined the status of those captured in the War on Terror as outside of the tribunal system described in the Geneva Convention. In 2004, the first military commission met to determine the guilt and sentences for detainees. Reporters, lawyers, human rights activists, and military prosecutors raised objections to the commission on the grounds that it followed no previously established rules. Furthermore, the category of "unlawful" combatant, which justified the placement of defendants before the commission in the first place, already presumed the detainees' guilt.[107] The terms "illegal" or "unlawful" enemy combatant had been used in a World War II Supreme Court case but took on more popular usage under President George W. Bush because of the association with the new commission.[108] These contemporary legal debates surrounding this category and whether the United States did, in fact, follow international conventions made the judges attentive to parallels in Leschi's case. When Alexandra Harmon quoted a letter in which Stevens labeled the war "illegal," the word caught the judges' attention. One judge asked Harmon if Stevens had offered a definition for the term "illegal war" (he had not) and whether the words had any meaning to Harmon as a historian (they did not).

The notion of "illegal war" is a contemporary one that had to be read back onto the historical record. When Eugene Ham testified that the army's actions indicated that Leschi was considered a "lawful combatant," Judge Ronald Cox asked Ham to define the term. Ham confirmed that, *depending on the conflict,* a combatant could be either lawful or unlawful. "Someone who behaves in a certain manner that is inconsistent with the law of war," Ham explained, can be considered an unlawful combatant and "loses all the protection, rights that [are] given under the international treaties," such as the Geneva Convention. Captain Robson then stated in his testimony that "the United States has always acknowledged this doctrine of customary international law" that grants rights to *legal* belligerents like Leschi. The military expert witnesses argued that the mistake in Leschi's case was that a combatant had been placed in the wrong category, not that differential legal categories exist even while the United States claims to consistently follow laws of war.

Leschi's name and memory supported the U.S. military in other ways as well, indicating complicated historical entanglements in the region. The Washington State History Museum where the tribunal took place is located less than twenty miles from Joint Base Lewis-McChord (formerly Fort Lewis Army Base and McChord Air Force Base). Justice Alexander had trained at Fort Lewis as a young man and mentioned in the Historical Court his personal experiences with munitions practice on the base's prairies. Generations of soldiers, Native and non-Indian alike, have trained at Fort Lewis for U.S. military missions around the world for most of the twentieth century. At the time of the Historical Court, Fort Lewis was home to three of the army's Stryker Brigades; the first was deployed to Iraq in late 2003. Before their deployment, the soldiers were trained at Leschi Town, the first high-tech urban warfare training facility in the nation, located on the prairie where Leschi had once trained his warriors and where Justice Alexander had practiced military maneuvers.

Leschi Town is a "city" of cinderblocks, wrecked vehicles, and trashed office furnishings surrounded by an open expanse of prairie on one side and dense evergreen forest on the other. Here soldiers secured buildings and cleared out civilians in mock battle situations, sometimes with the help of Iraqi role players. The city is wired with cameras for precise digi-

FIGURE 7 Scene at Leschi Town training facility, Joint Base Lewis-McChord, 2007. (Photo by the author)

tal data capture, which allows trainers to assess soldiers' performances in chaotic battle scenarios.[109] This training in urban warfare took place in buildings labeled "Leschi Town Police Station," "Squalli-absch Farm," and "Nisqually County Municipal."[110] Ham explained that the training facility was named Leschi Town because, according to army regulations, "the person after whom the building is to be named has to be someone who is distinguished or a deceased hero."

The local officials at Fort Lewis who advocated for the commemorative naming took pride in the fact that prominent members of the U.S. Army had condemned Leschi's conviction and execution in the 1850s. Incidentally, in late 2003 and 2004, members of the military lodged objections to the use of torture and the operations of the military commission at Guantánamo. Military lawyers opposed executive branch decisions in defense of laws of war and human rights in the 1850s and in 2004. The U.S. Army won a moral victory in the historical record because 1850s army officials publicly criticized the territorial government's actions toward Leschi. The army lawyers' testimony in the Historical Court and the written record of military objections were crucial to the judges' decision to exonerate

Leschi.[111] In this context, local army officials appropriated Leschi as a symbol for the best American military principles of restraint and humanitarianism, despite the armed forces' powerful capabilities.

The commemorative naming suggests that Leschi also served as a model for soldiers at the base, which represents a conflicting (and conflicted) act of appropriation. Soldiers trained in Leschi Town were expected to carry those values attributed to Leschi—brave defense of one's nation, working for peace even in the midst of war, sacrificing one's life to defend freedom—into U.S. military missions around the world. However, soldiers at the base also learned in their history lectures that settlers in the 1850s thought of Leschi as the "Osama bin Laden of Puget Sound."[112] The lecturer's point in comparing Leschi to the architect of the September 11, 2001 terrorist attacks was perhaps to suggest that as social values evolve, perceptions of "terrorists" change as well.[113] The comparison reveals two crucial continuities in imperialist logic. First, the category of illegal or legal combatant depends upon Americans' assessment of the fighter rather than on universal definitions of conduct or war. Second, this assessment is drawn from culturally specific ideology: resistance to U.S. domination is evidence of an inherently uncivilized nature and is therefore simultaneously subject to and outside of the community of laws.

Thus, Leschi's name was put to work advocating for the moral basis of the same overwhelming military force he battled against in 1855. Even though individuals at Fort Lewis sought to honor and sympathize with Leschi with the commemorative naming—and Nisqually council members and veterans lent their approval and support—the inescapable irony was that (according to many storytellers) Leschi had gone to war against the United States to retain the land on which Leschi Town was built. In a strange twist, Leschi's exoneration could reflect very well on Fort Lewis, celebrate a professional military tradition of respecting and defending laws of war, and confirm the just nature of U.S. military activities around the world in 2004. In the early twenty-first-century political context, the historical record made it possible for both sides in Puget Sound war to present themselves, and each other, as principled fighters.

The controversy over Leschi's conviction among non-Indians speaks to a long-standing ambivalence about the imperial character of American expansion and war. Historian Hubert H. Bancroft wrote in 1886 that the nation was characterized by constant striving to be "both powerful and pure."[114] These twin goals constitute the basis of American exceptionalism, which has often encompassed a claim that the United States is unique among nations because of its superior liberal values of democracy, freedom, and individualism. American statesmen have long maintained that these values represent universal truths and are destined to prevail over others around the world. In this view, U.S. power is the result of superior values.[115] However, U.S. power has also been put to the task of dispossessing others of resources to ensure continued economic growth. Americans wanted Indian land but also wanted to believe that their actions to acquire it were just.[116] In order to have it both ways, to be both powerful and pure, non-Indians consciously wrote and rewrote their histories of war with Indians.

The Historical Court nominally investigated an alleged legal aberration—Leschi's conviction—in order to acknowledge, correct, and ultimately erase a mistake from history. But the United States expanded westward because of, rather than in spite of, such "mistakes." There is little way around it: settler colonialism is premised on acquiring land and dispensing with indigenous people. Settler colonialism is both a structure and a process—a way of seeing, legislating, adjudicating, and justifying the settler colonial state—not an event fixed in time that can be simply corrected or erased.[117] Because liberalism and colonialism in a democratic settler state are woven into the same cloth, one cannot dispense with a single unsightly thread without taking the entire weave into account. The petitioners' legal argument for Leschi's exoneration attempted to change a single moment in history without attending to its effects. It affirmed the continuity of American values without acknowledging how the logic of exceptionalism allows for systematic departures from these ideals. Americans are quick to recognize continuities of liberal ideals but less willing to acknowledge continuities of colonial ideology.

Justice Alexander announced at the conclusion to the tribunal that, although the petitioners posed numerous questions for the judges to consider, they only chose to answer the one regarding Leschi's rights as an enemy combatant. But rather than offering the public a clean vision of history, the Historical Court revealed a messy combination of historical revision, compromise, and avoidance. Leschi was exonerated based in large part on the writings of non-Indians who, with a few exceptions, wanted to celebrate U.S. expansion and defend an ideal of American power and purity. Ironically, Leschi's descendants used these documents to build a case for their interpretation of Leschi's story. But by considering Leschi's case within the narrow frame of U.S. and international law, the ideology of American exceptionalism and the logic of legal exceptions remained unaddressed. The war in Puget Sound extended beyond the exchange of gunfire in 1855 and 1856; battles over the meaning of war, nationhood, sovereignty, and rights under U.S. law are woven into the historical record and retrial for Leschi. As long as Leschi's case is considered an aberration rather than part of a pattern, the war over the meaning of the past will continue to smolder in South Puget Sound.

CHAPTER 3 **Leschi Stories**

Cynthia Iyall, the first Native American representative to take the stand in the Historical Court of Justice, talked about the importance of the exoneration process to the descendants of Chief Leschi. Iyall first named her ancestors back to Leschi's half sister and then pointedly said: "After hearing this story told by our elders with great anger and frustration, we have decided to take one more chance to clarify our history once and for all." Iyall's and the other representatives' goal was to reveal to the public that which Nisquallies had long insisted to be true: Leschi was innocent of murder and had been unjustly convicted. Dorian Sanchez, then chair of the Nisqually tribal council and the next representative to take the stand, presented a tribal council resolution and explained the meaning of Leschi's exoneration to the tribe. Sanchez began with a history of how the tribal members transmitted their knowledge about Leschi across the generations: "We all grew up knowing the story of this great warrior. ... In gathering places on the river and in our houses, we have told and retold the story of Chief Leschi, and our stories have been clouded by other versions of the truth." The representatives all suggested that the source of the story—the elders—proved their special claim to truth in comparison to non-Indian accounts. Sanchez, like Iyall, associated the transmission of memories of Leschi with the intellectual and cultural labor of storytelling. Their testimony shows that Leschi's exoneration would mean more than just clearing Leschi's name; in their eyes it would honor the act of storytelling and the work of elders in preserving the truth over time.[1] Despite the representatives' suggestion to the contrary, the stories about Leschi changed over time and did not remain fully distinct from non-Nisqually accounts. But, significantly, the performance of distinct traditions makes a claim for distinct rights and identity in a liberal multicultural society.[2]

Native stories played an important role in the joint Indian/non-Indian enterprise of the Historical Court. The petitioners included the testimony of Nisqually and Puyallup representatives so that these people could speak for themselves about what they knew to be true, how they came to know it, and what exoneration would mean to them. Leschi's story was a potent reminder of prereservation life, an affirmation of who they were before the pressures of colonialism worked to break them apart and assimilate them. The structure of the symbolic court fulfilled the goals of multiculturalism in which a minority group could be free to interpret the past as its members pleased, independent of Western concepts of objectivity and burdens of proof.[3] As a public history event, the Historical Court of Justice illustrated for the audience the existence of multiple perspectives and competing interpretations. If the sole purpose of the event had been to educate the public about what was known about Leschi by combining epistemological and historical approaches, it was indeed an effective teaching tool.

But the stated purpose of the Historical Court was to *do something*. The petitioners wanted to take action for Leschi, and Justice Gerry Alexander proclaimed that the Historical Court would search for and uncover the truth.[4] These expectations raise a question: What is the role of multiculturalism and alternative narratives in an adversarial system designed to produce a final decision on the truth of a case? Once an apparently authoritative legal decision has been rendered, it is supposed to carry the cultural weight of permanent truth and represent a resolution to disagreement.[5] In its static form, "the law reflects a logic of literacy, of the historical archive rather than of changing historical memory," anthropologist James Clifford notes. "To be successful the trial's result must endure the way a written text endures."[6] The perception of an enduring authoritative decision was part of the appeal for the Nisqually petitioners. They insisted that history books include the court's ruling and had initially hoped that the official legal record might change as well. But unwritten Native stories demonstrate how alternative stories can endure—in fact *must* endure if Native identities are to survive—and maintain dynamism in a way narrow court decisions and published texts cannot. If anything, the history of Native stories about Leschi shows that such storytelling practices will continue, regardless of non-Indian texts, public pronouncements, and legal decisions. Stories are inherently useful, Walter Benjamin claimed, when they offer listeners "less an answer to a question, than a proposal concerning the continuation of a story that is just unfolding."[7] The kind of final decision on the matter that Justice Alexander proposed as the path to historical justice held significance in the Western legal tradition, not in the dynamics of Native oral traditions.

By presenting both the history of Native stories of Leschi and the claims made about and with those stories, I consider how stories enact a kind of historical justice that is culturally situated and constantly evolving. The Native American representatives spoke of a single true history of Leschi that remained distinct from non-Indian understandings as it was transmitted over time. Lushootseed people communicated stories of Leschi over generations to teach correct behavior, explain historical developments and personal experiences, and assert identities. In their testimony in the Historical Court, the representatives affirmed a way of conceiving of the past and locations of truth that differed from and expanded beyond a court judgment. Given the court participants' quest for justice through judicial ruling, the Native Americans' testimony played a paradoxical role in this public process of truth production. Rather than a legal procedure in which the judges sifted through the evidence and weighed competing claims to reveal and proclaim a single truth, the Historical Court presented audiences with the prospect of irreconcilable stories, numerous ways of knowing, and the coexistence of multiple truths. The petitioners hoped the judges would publicly validate the truth in their elders' stories while also illustrating for the audience how the cultural act of storytelling has long endured regardless of the judgments of external authorities. Stories of Leschi would continue to be told in Nisqually families no matter how the judges ruled in the Historical Court, but the court's decision could also potentially shape how the elders spoke of Leschi and how listeners thought about and acted with those stories. Oral tradition and the judges' role in court were both in tension and in dynamic conversation in the Historical Court.

Distinct and Unchanging?
The Dynamics of Native Oral History

Stories of Leschi have been told and retold in Nisqually families, but they also developed as self-consciously distinct from narratives of Leschi that prevailed among non-Indians. In 1966, a retired teacher writing for the *Tacoma News-Tribune* interviewed Nisqually elder Willie Frank and was surprised to hear a story about Leschi that she had not read anywhere before. "Everybody knows about your great Nisqually chief," the interviewer said to Frank, because "history tells us much about him." Frank replied: "No. You can't get much from history. . . . You have to listen to old Indians talk like I did."[8] Frank suggested that the oral tradition was more reliable than published histories, that the elders communicated truths that were absent from non-Indian texts.

Frank's insistence upon a separate Nisqually history of Leschi is also a claim to power. A master narrative is a script in the Enlightenment philosophical tradition that supports the maintenance of dominant groups by casting their experiences and perspectives as universal and normative. Master narratives of history can define and limit acceptable evidence and events and who is entitled to contribute to the creation of the historical record.[9] Frank asserted that Nisqually historians maintain their own stories of Leschi, separate from master narratives, that are based on their distinct experiences and historicity. The histories of Leschi drawn from newspapers, books, archives, and accounts told by non-Indians were, in Frank's estimation, inherently impoverished. The power of counter narrative lies in its ability to deconstruct the master narrative and reveal its limits. If eyewitnesses lied in court testimony, U.S. officials broke laws they were charged to enforce, and history books tell half-truths, then how can written records—and the Enlightenment notion of progressive history—be trusted? Counter narratives reveal other possibilities in human experience as well: time may be cyclical rather than linear, and the past may interact with the present rather than remain separate.

The distinctions between "history" and Nisqually elders' stories ("master narrative" and "counter narrative") have not been as clear as Frank suggested, however, because Native stories have informed and influenced non-Indians' histories (and vice versa) for at least a century.[10] The interview with Willy Frank illustrates how and why narratives of Leschi cannot be categorized as Indian or non-Indian based on content alone. Willy Frank offered his interviewer a story of how Leschi trained his warriors on equestrian maneuvers on the prairie as an example of a Nisqually story not printed in history books. Ironically, Willy Frank's story was then published in the *Tacoma News-Tribune* and informed later historians' published accounts.[11] Furthermore, Willy Frank was not the only person telling the story. A speaker at the Pierce County Historical Society in 1914 claimed that a Hudson's Bay Company (HBC) employee had reported seeing Leschi training his troops on the prairie, and this detail was then reprinted in a 1989 history of the Puget Sound Indian War. Charles Wilkinson printed the same story of Leschi with his troops, told to him by Willy Frank's son Billy, in *Messages from Frank's Landing* in 2000. Billy Frank Jr. also offered the story as an example of a family narrative in a 2004 interview available in audiovisual format on the Washington State Historical Society website.[12] In what sense, then, do Nisqually stories and mainstream "history" remain distinct?

Leschi's story, as presented in recent published accounts and in the Historical Court, reveals a long history of reciprocal influences. Published non-Indian accounts of Leschi have also influenced how Nisquallies talk about Leschi in public. Leschi's headstone bears words written by Ezra Meeker, and Cecelia Carpenter's books draw on Tolmie's and other settlers' accounts. In the Historical Court, Carpenter quoted settlers' descriptions of Leschi to establish his good character. And yet the claim to a separate history, a counter narrative, is important. The social function of Coast Salish stories is to transmit and reflect Coast Salish worldviews, which creates and confirms this group identity. In a society shaped by a history of settler colonialism, it is meaningful when non-Indians recognize Native identity and affirm indigenous claims to authoritative historical knowledge. Nisquallies' ostensibly separate story of Leschi is less about the content of the narrative—which changes over time and reflects reciprocal influences—than it is about the claims to truth, authenticity, and autonomy that a counter narrative can make.

Notably, Leschi's descendants and other elders maintained a master narrative about Leschi as well. Over time, storytellers used particular interpretations of Leschi's life and legacy to pursue contemporary goals. The Historical Court was no different; not all Native stories of Leschi fit into the petitioners' legal strategy, were appropriate for non-Indian audiences, or supported the kind of reading of Leschi's actions that tribal leaders and elders wanted to convey in 2004. Narrative discipline was important to the petitioners' presentation and to tribal goals more broadly. Seven generations after Leschi's death, as tribal leaders struggled to maintain unity and elders worried that the young people seemed more interested in following trends in American culture than tribal traditions, a commonly endorsed story of Leschi as a peaceful, generous, and wise ancestor served an important role in cultural revitalization efforts. And the witnesses' insistence on a single true story of Leschi strategically built the appearance of unity, of a single truth, in the Historical Court.[13]

The realities of memory and storytelling are more nuanced than the Native representatives suggested in their testimony. There are many stories of Leschi told by Coast Salish people over several generations, because individual storytellers remembered or inherited different stories, narrative framing and details changed over time to adapt to social, political, and historical contexts, and the valence and goals of the storyteller shifted according to audience. The multiplicity of stories is also a function and expression of oral history and culture. Each storyteller contributes his or her own voice, so Coast Salish oral histories and texts represent a plurality of subject positions.[14] The storyteller may identify selectively or simultaneously in a specific gendered, class-based, kin-based, moral, political, and/or social world. This Coast Salish multivocality defies composition into a single narrative because it is dynamic, fluid, and episodic rather than fixed, static, and composed of cohering parts.[15] But rather than being a collection of hundreds of isolated pieces, Coast Salish storytellers' common values and experiences lead the stories into convergence. In the moments in which we see narratives intersect and plots overlap—in this case, recounting the life of Leschi—we gain a deeper understanding of Coast Salish history, culture, and sense of justice.[16]

The many Native Puget Sound individuals who have recorded stories of Leschi do not all agree on the details, but they emphasize many of the same lessons: responsibility to others, relationships with spirit helpers, the primacy of Native over U.S. perspectives, and visions for the future. These themes are expressions of what Upper Skagit elder and linguist Vi Hilbert identified as important Lushootseed values that listeners glean from repeated storytellings.[17] Stories that offer the most guidance are those that are locally grounded and culturally specific and that include elements familiar to listeners and their lived experiences.[18] These values, along with the experiences, social positions, and political interests of the storytellers, have been woven into stories of Leschi to create a confluence of historical memory and ancestral wisdom.[19]

South Puget Sound Native people have talked about Leschi's life in episodic pieces to non-Indian anthropologists, historians, and journalists or in their own words to various public audiences for over a century. Because most oral historians recalled or shared only certain portions of Leschi's life, I place these multiple episodes into a narrative sequence to draw attention to common themes and to emphasize these narratives' cooperative construction. Following the narrative of Leschi's life, I will explore one theme unique to Nisqually stories: Leschi's vision of the future, which lived on after his death. I do so to neither validate nor discount this claim, but to consider the function and effect of stories of Leschi as an active force carried through time. Native oral histories are more than the information or lessons they impart. Lushootseed oral traditions foster relationships between the storyteller and the audience (an important function in the Historical Court) and maintain relationships between the individual and collective, the secular and the sacred, the past and the present. Peter Nabokov explains that, rather than seeing history linearly, as is dominant in Western thought, Native oral traditions "maintain that [history] is . . . like a thick rope, a long ladder, or a wide corridor, which also allows for two-way traffic."[20] The stories convey the belief that Leschi's spirit acts in a reciprocal relationship with his descendants: he gave his people wisdom they would need in the future, and his people honor him by telling his story and keeping his name alive.

Leschi's Life in Story

Coast Salish stories of Leschi's birth situate him in a matrix of interconnected people, physical environment, and spirit powers. In Cecelia Carpenter's published account, a spirit power sent an omen to the people on the day of Leschi's birth in January 1808. On that winter night, a star rose over Squally Prairie.[21] Carpenter's reference to the star calls forth other Nisqually stories about stars told for generations and recorded by anthropologists in the late nineteenth century. One story recounts how the Changer had himself come from the realm of the stars, and the other epic details the travails of sisters who married stars and subsequently caused the landscape to be named and occupied by humans.[22] In 2000, Billy Frank Jr. also reflected on the importance of stars, noting that urban development and pollution in South Puget Sound obscured the stars from view. "That's wrong," Frank declared. "Those stars are sovereign. They have a right to be seen."[23] It is important for people to see stars because, in the intellectual traditions of Coast Salish people, they embody active forms of knowledge, not simply its repository.[24] In Carpenter's telling, the star brought the people an important message about a man who would lead the people through great changes in the years to come. Carpenter's version of Leschi's auspicious birth and relationship with powers in the spirit realm dovetails with stories told by other Nisqually elders.[25] As Nabokov explains, "Indian history . . . has always been interpreted by Indian peoples through references to mythic thought. . . . And it always starts with the ground beneath one's feet."[26] The star in Carpenter's story was not simply the messenger, and the prairie was not just the setting.

Together, they created and foretold Leschi's importance, which, in turn, foretold the peoples' survival.

Leschi was raised in the village of Bacalabc at the confluence of the Mashel and Nisqually Rivers (near present-day Eatonville). His father, Wanatco, was a wealthy Nisqually man with many horses, and his mother, Cornezita, was the daughter of a high-ranking Klickitat family, which connected Leschi to relatives and resources across the Cascade Mountains.[27] Because of its location between the Puget Sound peoples and the Naches Pass through the Cascade Mountains, Leschi's bilingual village was closely connected to both Lushootseed and Sahaptin-speaking neighbors and enjoyed an advantageous situation socially, economically, and geographically.[28] Leschi became the headman of Bacalabc, while Quiemuth established a home and ten acres at S'Gukugwas near the source of Muck Creek. As adults, both brothers likely gathered for ceremonies and other social interactions at the winter village called Yll-whaltz, located on the prairie near the creek.[29]

Leschi inherited his *siab* title—a distinction of noble class—and his family wealth came mainly from horses. Leschi was known to have an impressive herd.[30] Like other siab, Leschi owned at least one slave, a gift from his father-in-law, and he had three wives by 1854. Leschi's third wife, Mary, later said that she married him because he provided her with many gifts and was "rich and had lots of horses."[31] Because high-class marriages brought together families from different villages and even language groups, Leschi's multiple marriages illuminate his high esteem and influence among a larger network of Northwest Native peoples.[32]

Prestige was not considered a mark of individual initiative but rather evidence of one's proper actions in a constellation of relationships. In Nisqually communities, humans and spirit powers entered into reciprocal relationships in which the human would agree to certain actions (such as performing a dance or song) and receive certain powers in return. The ability to acquire wealth was one of the powers provided by some spirit helpers. Leschi's spirit helper was said to be his horse and the horse of his third wife, which explains both his wealth in horses and his later abilities as war leader. High-status Coast Salish individuals were also obligated to provide generously for kin and were expected to earn villagers' respect and admiration by giving away property to others in a ceremonial giveaway, or potlatch.[33] Connie McCloud said of Leschi in the Historical Court: "In order to stand as a chief, he had to be able to take care of his family, his own people." Leschi's wealth meant he was in a better position to fulfill his responsibilities and to extend his influence beyond his village. These qualities endeared him to villagers and siab families of the region, who looked to him as an arbiter in disputes between villages.[34]

When the HBC built Fort Nisqually in 1833, Leschi and Quiemuth readily worked with the traders to acquire status items that attested to their prestige.[35] Mary described how Leschi "would take a horse to the Fort and sell it and bring home a lot of things. We always lived well."[36] Some HBC trade goods were desirable not for their inherent value or monetary equivalent but because the items symbolized personal relationships and one's ability to establish more such desirable relationships.[37] As a few American settlers ventured into Nisqually territory in the 1840s and American troops established Fort Steilacoom in 1849, Leschi and Quiemuth continued to reach out to the newcomers. Leschi and Quiemuth attempted to bring the newcomers into social affiliation through marriage—a Coast Salish practice that established relationships to repair bad feelings, smooth out tensions, or commit to peaceful cooperation.[38] Recognizing the army personnel as men of authority, Quiemuth married his daughter "Kitty" to Lieutenant August Kautz, and Leschi's daughter Kalakala married settler Charles Eaton.[39] Leschi's wealth and status represented his careful attention to relationships with family, spirit powers, and outsiders. To Nisqually storytellers, the details in Leschi's story demonstrated compassion, responsibility to others, and initiative without the stain of personal interest or greed.

Native accounts of Leschi's actions in the Medicine Creek Treaty council and the ensuing war modeled how one might use traditional values and expectations to navigate changes while asserting the primacy of indigenous over U.S. perspectives. Nisqually historians note that Leschi constantly attempted to enact Nisqually values in his dealings with Americans. Leschi had been cooperative with the newcomers, giving generously and making few demands. Leschi entered into relations with U.S. settlers and officials as a peace negotiator, a man who brought calm siab sensibilities to an increasingly tense situation. Carpenter's history leading up to the Medicine Creek Treaty focuses on both settlers' bad behavior and encroaching government authority over the Nisqually Tribe and its land.[40] Nisquallies claim that Leschi's efforts to maintain peace broke down only when Americans made threats to move them.

Nisqually depictions of Leschi as an arbiter differ considerably from many American narratives that assume Indians and whites would inevitably clash in a "race war" instigated by Native peoples' stubborn refusal to give up their way of life.[41] On the contrary, Willy Frank told his children in the mid-twentieth century, it was the Europeans and their descendants who clung tightly and conceitedly to their own ways in a new place.[42] U.S. settlers' and officials' poor manners and uncompromising stance fostered bad feelings and distrust among Native people, who lived with different expectations of moral behavior. In this counter narrative, Leschi's role as a peaceful arbiter served to highlight U.S. officials' rude behavior and improper demands. More than that, it also represented Nisqually culture as dynamic, progressive, and modern: Leschi was willing to consider new viewpoints and make adaptations, while representatives of the United States were closed-minded and dogmatically held to their religious and economic traditions.

Native people maintain that Leschi distinguished himself at the Medicine Creek Treaty council by taking issue with the U.S. government's demands for the best land in the area. Billy Frank Jr. explained in the Historical Court that Leschi realized Americans wanted to move them from the prairie. "That's where our medicine was," Frank said, alluding to the significance of the prairie as a sentient place of resources and spirit agents.[43] To Frank, such a loss would mean the Nisqually would sacrifice everything. But other stories indicate that not all of the headmen protested the treaty because the proposed reservations did not threaten their resources to the same extent. Informants told geographer T. T. Waterman in the early twentieth century that the "saltwater" people in villages near Puget Sound and the "freshwater" people in villages farther upriver considered themselves and their interests to be quite different from each other.[44] Some early twentieth-century anthropologists, following their informants' linguistic and cultural clues, even identified a "band of Mashel or upper Nisqually River people" as a separate tribal group from the Nisqually people downstream, although a Nisqually informant denied this distinction in 1963.[45]

The different social and economic orientations of the saltwater villages and the prairie villages in the 1850s contributed to different views of the reservation proposed in the treaty. The small beachfront reservation proposed in the Medicine Creek Treaty did not significantly affect the saltwater villagers adversely because they traded and socialized with other Puget Sound peoples. But the inland villagers would be expected to leave their homes and face isolation from eastern kin and trade networks.[46] Leschi's inland village was farthest from the proposed reservation site, and moving would endanger his family's access to inherited land and resources, and take them far from Klickitat relatives.[47] Despite the fact that there were far more saltwater villages near the mouth of the Nisqually River than upriver villages in 1854, men from the prairie villages were most prominent in the treaty negotiations because of the relationships the headmen had fostered with William Tolmie, who had in turn nominated certain headmen for the treaty negotiations.[48] Not surprisingly, a small faction of headmen supported the treaty terms, while others who owned horses or held eastern kin connections opposed them.[49]

Leschi had a great deal to lose from the proposed reservation, but Nisqually historians do not speak of Leschi as following personal interests at the Medicine Creek Treaty council. Rather, Leschi observed proper protocol by defying the reservation terms. High-class families had to safeguard their kinship property from incursion because so many others depended upon them. Mary recounted that once, while she was traveling with her husband through the mountains, Leschi found gold in a crevasse where he was searching for water. He showed her the gold but kept the discovery quiet. Leschi's widow claimed at the turn of the twentieth century that she did not remember the location and that "Leschi in his lifetime never would divulge the secret as to the location—only said he found it in the mountains."[50] Although Mary did not elaborate on the meaning or significance of this find, the story of Leschi's gold suggests that spirit helpers in the mountain chose to impart special knowledge to Leschi, who, in turn, would have a responsibility to protect access to such sites of power.[51] Leschi may have been motivated to protect his families' resources and his own sources of wealth in the treaty negotiations, but in Nisqually stories, his interests were inseparable from the well-being of those socially, economically, and spiritually affiliated with him.

By the 1890s, some of the divided parties in the treaty attempted to reconcile their stories of Leschi. Luke (lu′kʷ), who reportedly came from the same upriver village as Leschi, held firm to his opinion of saltwater headmen. He told amateur ethnographer James Wickersham that Leschi and Quiemuth had refused to sign the treaty and had left the council. After they left, the saltwater headmen agreed to the treaty because they "held no property, no horses," and could be easily persuaded to "live the balance of their days either on clams, or at the mercy of the white man."[52] The prairie village leaders, Luke implied, were wealthy and unwilling to bow to the Americans' demands, while the saltwater headmen were a pathetic lot. John Hiaton, the headman of a saltwater village who was known to have supported the treaty and opposed Leschi, claimed in the 1890s that he had also decided against signing. Hiaton insisted that, like Leschi's, his own mark was forged and that one settler-turned-official at the council threatened even the Indians who initially supported the treaty by saying that he would sign for them if they refused.[53]

Although Hiaton had disagreed with Leschi at the treaty council, he had apparently changed his mind over the years and had even given a speech to commemorate Leschi in 1895. It is unclear what motivated Hiaton; perhaps he came to appreciate Leschi's decision, or he recognized that a story of principled resistance had acquired social currency. Either way, after years of broken promises, Hiaton's charge of Americans' shady treaty dealings was a believable claim in the 1890s. Leschi could serve as a shared icon of general Indian defiance and form the basis of a narrative to counter the one about U.S. benevolent domination. This sense of unified support for Leschi's actions at the treaty council remained a feature of stories of Leschi throughout the twentieth century. "Basically, Leschi just said, 'We're not moving,'" Billy Frank Jr. explained in 2000.[54] The "we" in Leschi's story expanded to include those who identified with his principles, if not his demands for specific resources.

Stories about the war of 1855–56, like those regarding the treaty, reflect Native values, specific subject positions, and historical experiences over time. In his late 1990s interviews with Billy Frank Jr., Charles Wilkinson asked the Nisqually activist what he thought when he heard people speak of the 1855–56 conflict. Without pause, Frank answered: "The Leschi War."[55] Narratives of the Leschi War have some points of comparison with Coast Salish stories of a mid-1800s maritime battle at Maple Bay. Narratives of the battle between affiliated Southern Coast Salish tribes and the Kwakwaka'waka Lekwiltok on Vancouver Island paralleled mythic-time stories about the creation of the moral world. The Coast Salish, who sought retribution for years of Lekwiltok raiding, told stories of the battle in terms that conveyed their view that supernatural justice was brought to bear against an enemy to establish order and make the world right again.[56] This sense of justice, of bringing the world back to moral order, permeated Coast Salish narratives of the Leschi War and, notably, the petitioners' argument for Leschi's exoneration in 2004. Not all Coast Salish narratives of the war were included in the Historical Court, however. Some would likely have worked against public sympathy for Leschi.

One of the most comprehensive early accounts of the war was told by Frank Allen, a Skokomish Indian, to anthropologist William Elmendorf in 1940. His narrative was markedly different from previously published accounts and more recent Nisqually renderings. Born around 1858, Allen grew up hearing about Leschi's war from Luke and his great uncle Wa He Lut. Allen's account was shaped by the storytellers who knew Leschi, as well as by the events that affected Native peoples around South Puget Sound in Allen's lifetime.[57] Although descended from a Nisqually family, Allen was raised in a Skokomish community. His background is not unique among Native people of South Puget Sound, who carried a fluid notion of tribal identity. Allen's Skokomish affiliation may have resulted as much from U.S. tribal enrollment rules and allotment policies as kinship connections.[58] Allen's account offers an expanded perspective on Leschi's story from outside of the current Nisqually Tribe. It also illustrates a dynamic function of collective memory: as values and goals change, some interpretations of the past gain or lose relevance.[59] Allen's depiction of Leschi in wartime was not repeated in Carpenter's published history of the tribe, *The Nisqually, My People*, and differed from the image presented by the petitioners in the Historical Court.

Allen explained that the war began not because of the Medicine Creek Treaty, but rather as a response to settlers' violent attack. According to Allen, Leschi told his Yakama allies that he decided to go to war for reasons close to home: "'I was out on the bay fishing and they burned my village dIsqʷaʼlˑɛ. . . . That's why I'm going to fight!'"[60] Allen's reference to burning villages reflects a documented method settlers employed to destroy Indian improvements in order to claim their land.[61] Allen's account presents Leschi as a fiery warrior who sought revenge for the destruction of his village, not a peaceful arbiter or principled chief who defended all Nisqually people. Allen's perspective reflected a nineteenth-century construction of Indian identity and political organization that had changed rapidly during his lifetime. Coast Salish people increasingly identified as members of a tribe, rather than with families and villages, by the time of Allen's telling in the mid-twentieth century.[62] Allen's narrative explained the act of burning down a village and displacing family members as a deeply personal attack—one which a headman such as Leschi was expected to answer. But it was also a political, cultural, and social attack. The village was a symbol for a way of organizing Southern Coast Salish people and resources with a cultural and political logic. In Allen's telling, Leschi went to war to defend Native peoples' individual rights to property and to organize into autonomous villages—a particular concern following the U.S. reservation policy and civilizing programs of Allen's generation.

Leschi's story, as told by Allen, expanded outward as a way for Natives around the region to protest settler and government aggression against their families and the reordering of their sociopolitical worlds. Other non-Nisquallies also saw Leschi through their own interpretive frameworks shaped by historical experiences. After watching Leschi's exoneration in the 2004 Historical Court, one central Puget Sound elder was reminded of her family's forced relocation to the Lummi reservation when she was a young girl. The woman told of departing from her home in a canoe and how, turning around to take a final look, she saw her village burning. The elder associated her family's move with Leschi's resistance to reservations and explained that Leschi's exoneration marked a time of healing from the trauma of relocation and loss.[63] The motif of burning villages exemplifies how various Coast Salish families' experiences with colonialism converged in and found expression through Leschi's story, even if they fell outside of the petitioners' narrative in the Historical Court.

Allen's account of Leschi's actions during wartime, compared with later Nisqually narratives, illustrates the situational use of stories. Some Nisqually stories of Leschi's wartime decisions reflect Coast Salish siab sensibilities while also dovetailing with Western definitions of "civilized" war leadership. In some tellings, Leschi's wartime actions modeled those of a high-class, compassionate, and peace-oriented leader who was not responsible for the killings of U.S. civilians in the war. Wa He Lut reported in the 1890s that Leschi insisted his fighters spare women and children.[64] Both Nisqually historian Cecelia Carpenter and Tulalip elder Ruth Shelton asserted that Leschi did not order the attack on civilians in the siege on Seattle in 1856 and criticized U.S. chroniclers for blaming Leschi for the deed.[65] In her testimony in the Historical Court, Carpenter emphasized that Leschi continually made appeals for a peaceful resolution to the war, but that, after failing to broker peace, he fled to the mountains to avoid further conflict. This peace-seeking behavior was consistent with many other Nisqually descriptions of Leschi and follows Coast Salish expectations for siab men. Notably, non-Indians would also find such an image of Leschi appealing and sympathetic. These stories of Leschi as a reluctant warrior could be strategically mobilized to support Leschi's exoneration in the Historical Court. In her testimony, Carpenter described Leschi as a peaceful arbiter who defended human dignity, which supported the petitioners' argument that the label of "murderer" had been unjustly applied.

However, Allen's account, handed down from warriors and their male descendants, characterized Leschi as a calculating tactician and fierce fighter. According to Allen, Leschi traveled far beyond South Puget Sound and led a force that terrorized most of western Washington: "They went . . . all over [and] wherever they found white people they slaughtered them. And when they cleaned out all the white people there they came back and started in on the white settlers on the Sound."[66] Allen attached regional significance to Leschi's actions. As historian Alexander Olson observed, "Allen's Leschi attacked the entire enterprise of American settlement, reclaiming the geography of Puget Sound piece by piece."[67] In so doing, Leschi became an icon of regional Native resistance—a development that emerged only after the treaty period when diverse Native groups suffered similar attacks on their lands and sovereignty. In Allen's 1940 telling, Leschi was a hero not just to the interests of prairie villagers along the Nisqually River, but to Native people of the entire western Washington region.

After sweeping Puget Sound of settlers, Allen said, Leschi led his men in a ten-day battle against the army and "slaughtered them," reporting that even though Leschi and his men were outmanned and outgunned in this battle, "none of the Indians had been killed yet, but they had killed lots of soldiers. There were only . . . ten warriors against all these soldiers." Allen credited the valor of Nisqually warriors and emphasized the contributions of their spirit helpers. Luke, for example, was said to have been shot many times, but the bullets could not kill him because of his spirit helper. The army sent reinforcements from Fort Steilacoom, but the U.S. soldiers gave up the war, exasperated: "You can't kill those Indians! You can't see them. Where are they?"[68] Allen's narrative rendered U.S. soldiers weak and confused before the skills and spirit helpers of the Coast Salish warriors.

Allen's narrative is markedly different from accounts of the fighting offered by American forces afterward. In 1904, the *Seattle Post-Intelligencer* published a speech attributed to Leschi but penned by army official Benjamin Shaw in which Leschi supposedly admitted that the battles did not go well: "The Indians did not keep in order like the soldiers and . . . had to resort to ambush and seek the cover of trees, logs and everything that would hide them from the bullets."[69] Shaw's memory of the speech is suspect, to say the least, and demonstrates what Allen remembered *against*. While Allen's account emphasized the protection of spirit helpers, Shaw characterized the Nisqually warriors as weak and vulnerable. In Allen's story, the Nisqually warriors were all but invincible, but Shaw depicted Leschi as an ineffectual leader at the helm of undisciplined troops. According to Shaw, Leschi lamented the war as an impossible cause with an inevitable conclusion: "I could not gain anything by going to war with the United States, but would be beaten and humbled, and would have to hide like a wild beast in the end."[70] Allen's narrative directly challenged this popular American narrative of inevitable Indian defeat. As may be expected, the narrative that Allen repeated from Wa He Lut is the proud boasting of a war veteran who was far from "beaten and humbled."[71]

The war did turn sour for Leschi, but, according to Allen, it was not because of superior U.S. military power or the inevitable dominance of American civilization. Allen claimed that the Snoqualmie leader Patkanim, who allied with the United States in exchange for blankets and other status goods, was the only force capable of defeating Nisqually fighters. Patkanim told Leschi he wished to join him but turned and attacked the Nisqually warriors instead. Leschi and his men escaped with a single casualty but had to hide in the woods.[72] Notably, in Allen's narrative it was the Snoqualmie scouts, not the U.S. Army, that sent the Nisqually fighters into hiding. In fact, in Allen's narrative, the U.S. Army was practically irrelevant. He situated the "real" battle in terms of Native justice in which older animosities between the Nisqually and the Snoqualmie were the source of the violence between them.[73] Although some Nisqually histories describe the Snoqualmie treachery with bitterness, this story was not recounted in the Historical Court. Historical intertribal grudges served no productive purpose in a review of Leschi's legal case. The petitioners wished to focus their case on the relationship between the United States and Leschi, because, ultimately, they demanded justice from representatives of the United States.

According to Native accounts, territorial officials were able to bring Leschi out from hiding only when Leschi's nephew Sluggia betrayed his uncle and delivered him to territorial government custody.[74] Individual storytellers ascribed different motivations to Sluggia. Wa He Lut maintained that Sluggia resented his uncle for disallowing indiscriminate slaughter of settlers in the war. Cynthia Iyall heard from her elders that Sluggia was in love with Leschi's youngest wife, Mary, and was consumed by jealousy.[75] Allen recalled that Sluggia was enticed by the reward of blankets to "sell" his uncle. Despite differences in the details, Native storytellers all agreed that Sluggia acted out of greedy self-interest and that he got what he deserved when Wa He Lut killed him to avenge Leschi. To Coast Salish people, the story of Sluggia served as a cautionary tale about shameful personal shortcomings.[76] In the Historical Court, however, Carpenter described Sluggia's actions to call attention to Americans' empty promises. In her testimony, Carpenter recounted that Leschi was "tricked by his nephew, who was promised Leschi would have a fair hearing." She characterized Sluggia as naive, and himself betrayed by the territorial government's unfair legal treatment of Leschi. Sluggia's actions could be strategically framed to emphasize the moral failings of U.S. authorities, who made promises they did not keep—a subtle way to convince the judges to exonerate Leschi from an unfair conviction.[77]

Native stories told to non-Indians or in public gatherings do not provide much detail on Leschi's sixteen-month imprisonment and court trials—the portions of Leschi's story that captured the most interest in non-Indian historical narratives. In Native stories of Leschi's life, what mattered most were his final words of wisdom to his people presented just before he died. Billy Frank Jr. offered a distinct version of Leschi's last speech in 2004: "Whatever the future holds, do not forget who you are. Teach your children, teach your children's children, and then teach their children also. Teach them the pride of a great people."[78] Many elders recounted the scene of the hanging in the bowl-shaped prairie as Indians played drums from a distance.[79] But, according to Frank, Leschi looked to the future and denied that his death was an ending.

Leschi's supposed last words also established a counter narrative to non-Indian accounts. A week after his execution, the *Pioneer and Democrat* printed an account that probably came from a French Catholic missionary who joined Leschi on the scaffold to encourage him to repent. In his narrative, the missionary focused on Leschi's last words as a measure of his successful conversion work: "In his last moment, he cried out, 'I pardon everyone!' and that is truly Christian. But, unfortunately, he added one exception, which distressed me a lot." The newspaper printed a similar version in which Leschi announced in Chinook jargon that "he would soon meet his maker—that he had made peace with God and desired to live no longer—that he bore malice to none, save one man."[80] The notorious exception was presumably Michael Simmons, the treaty adviser and Indian agent whom Leschi reportedly blamed for the war.[81] The newspaper left out the missionary's reference to Leschi's forgiveness, which conveyed the uncomfortable suggestion that Americans had made a mistake. While Frank's account described Leschi as concerned primarily with inspiring his people in the future, the missionary's story implied that Leschi had converted and was resigned to his death. The first story imbued Leschi with energy and vision, while the missionary and newspaper painted Leschi as a defeated and humbled man. Frank's story helped the listener to imagine how Leschi's spirit could continue to live on through his people, while the missionary's, framed in Catholic theology, inspired an image of Leschi's spirit departing from this world. As time went on, settler narratives of Leschi's last words grew more creative and focused on the settlers themselves. In "the last talk Leschi made to his people," one elderly settler wrote in 1930, Leschi "pleaded with them to be at peace with the white people and to fight no more."[82] Leschi's supposed overture for peace appeared to bring a tidy conclusion to the war and accepted that Indians were solely responsible for violence. In non-Indian accounts, Leschi's last words could be used to celebrate simultaneously the Indian man and the moral superiority of the colonial project in the region. The settler's account was a romantically tragic ending to a doomed fight.

Perhaps in response to such a narrative, one Southern Coast Salish historian framed Leschi's execution as representative of the many legal injustices Native fighters endured after the war that non-Indians had failed to acknowledge. Leschi's grandnephew, Henry Sicade, told a biographer in 1936 that because Leschi's hanging took place long after the fighting had ended, his death merely satisfied white settlers' calls for revenge. In Sicade's estimation, Leschi's execution was representative of Indians' poor treatment in an unfair legal system. "Indians suspected of taking part in the uprisings of 1855–56 were usually tried and put to death by prejudiced white courts of justice," wrote Sicade's biographer. "Very few Indians were ever given a chance to defend themselves in the makeshift courts."[83] In fact, other war leaders did stand trial, but Leschi was the only warrior of 1855–56 to be executed following conviction in Washington territorial courts. Yet Sicade understood Leschi's conviction as part of a larger pattern and persistent problem in the period. Sicade likely drew this conclusion based on personal experience negotiating with state courts; he served on both the Puyallup tribal council and the Fife city council and held positions in the tribal police and judicial systems.[84]

The contemporaneous story that Frank Allen told about Leschi's death in 1940, however, refused to accept U.S. control over Leschi's fate on the day of his death. According to Allen, the territorial courts carried little authority, and Leschi, with the aid of his spirit helpers and loyal friends, outsmarted the white settlers who called for his head. Allen recounted how a mob of whites came to the jail in search of the famous prisoner and how Leschi's spirit helper warned him that they would try to kill him. Allen did not specify whether the "mob" was composed of vigilantes defying the law or territorial officials planning to enforce it. Either way, Allen's characterization of the "mob" reinforced his perception that territorial law was not legitimate. Allen explained that Leschi responded to the warning by instructing Luke and Wa He Lut to "loosen the rope from my neck" after the hanging and "put me on my horse and take me home quick! I am not going to die." As directed, Leschi's lieutenants removed his body from the scaffold and rushed it home, where he breathed again. But three or four shaman conspired to kill Leschi's power, lest he resume the war and cause more hardships. "Those doctors chased that power of Leschi's until they caught him . . . and Leschi was gone," Allen said.[85] Stories of spirit powers have fallen from favor among later generations, or at least the topic has been avoided when speaking to non-Indians, for understandable fear of misinterpretation, but in Allen's time these lessons were important for making sense of Leschi's death.[86] In Allen's narrative, spirits fought one another to restore balance to the world in the aftermath of war. Americans' laws and deeds were irrelevant. While settlers alternately enforced and subverted their own legal standards, spirit helpers intelligently and independently ordered relationships and events.[87] Allen's narrative served as a reminder that Leschi was an important figure primarily because of his spirit power; his relationships within an active moral universe gave him some measure of control over his fate, but spirit powers also have an independent will.

Leschi's Vision in Action

Leschi's legacy, as interpreted by several individuals, was his vision of the future that he asked to be carried from generation to generation. Billy Frank Jr. explained that Leschi "could see what was going to happen to us and it happened. Just like he said. He had a vision of that."[88] James McCloud described Leschi as "brilliant" for giving his people the tools they needed to survive the difficulties he foresaw for them. McCloud heard from his elders that Leschi told his people the challenges would be great, but he reassured them that "I'll always be here for you." McCloud described Leschi's story as his gift to the future that continues on: "It isn't like he's gone."[89] Those who transmitted histories of Leschi were participants in and creators of a social world built through reciprocal actions between generations across time. Some Native storytellers consciously took on the responsibility of keeping his name alive by living by the ancestors' lessons. Young people received direction and hope from these stories and honored those gifts by passing them on in turn. In this way, some Native storytellers understand Leschi as an active force in their lives. As anthropologist Frederica de Laguna explained, "Every people live their own myths. . . . Their conduct in the present reflects what they believe their past to have been, since that past, as well as the present and the future, are aspects of the 'destiny' in which they exhibit themselves as they think they really are."[90] These storytellers re-created Leschi in their present to explain who they believed themselves to be, which was exactly what Leschi foresaw for them.

The last direct Nisqually descendant of Quiemuth was Sherman Leschi, a man who Cynthia Iyall claimed was profoundly shaped by his namesake. Up until his death in 2002, Sherman took special care of Leschi's memory—a responsibility he had inherited from Leschi's nephew George, who had taken the Leschi name to honor his uncle.[91] According to Iyall, the descendants of George Leschi "worked very hard in keeping the Leschi name and the Leschi history alive."[92] Sherman Leschi's responsibility was great, for names are considered family property. "Each name is a possession to be respected and treasured," Dewey Mitchell (Upper Skagit) explained. A name is considered a living identity that has the power to shape the lives of those who acquire it. At the end of a Lushootseed naming ceremony, Mitchell wrote, "We are gently advised and cautioned to carry and wear our names with the dignity and respect that our ancestors would naturally expect."[93] Sherman told Iyall that he had "wild teenage years" but realized early on in his adulthood that he needed to reform his ways to "protect the name and present it well." Sherman recognized the responsibility that fell upon him with Leschi's name, and thereafter he led what Iyall characterized as a straight and sober life as a result.[94]

Other tribal elders credit Leschi for sustaining them as they worked to bring their understanding of Leschi's vision into reality. Elders believed that the treaty-era leaders' names could help to educate younger generations about Southern Coast Salish ways. In the mid-1970s, Nisqually elders and activists founded two schools to serve tribal communities: Chief Leschi and Wa He Lut. Chief Leschi Schools in the Puyallup Valley offer Lushootseed language instruction and promote culturally based educational programs. Wa He Lut, located near Frank's Landing, features a portrait of Leschi and a history of the Nisqually watershed in which the school is located.[95] The tribal leaders of the 1970s hoped that the honorific naming would orient Southern Coast Salish children toward core values and practices. As Sherman Leschi came to the last years of his life, he told Iyall that Leschi was particularly concerned for the youth of the seventh generation. Leschi "wanted the youth to bring back the culture and be proud of who they are," Sherman explained to Iyall. Part of the responsibility of carrying the name was teaching younger generations to feel the same gratitude and sense of responsibility.

With this concern for the future and his responsibilities to the past prominent in his mind, Sherman told Iyall to "do something about Leschi." Iyall recounted an initial period of self-doubt after Sherman's death but was reassured one spring afternoon on a walk in the woods, when an owl landed on a branch right before her face. She walked further and the owl followed her, landing again on a branch above her and meeting her eyes. Iyall understood the owl to carry a message from Sherman and other Nisqually ancestors: "You've been given something to do. Do it. We will be with you."[96] Iyall was open to this message because she had grown up with stories of ancestors intervening in the world and an understanding that reciprocal relationships could operate cyclically in time. By pursuing exoneration for Leschi, Iyall would be fulfilling a responsibility to her family and the Nisqually Tribe. Iyall explained in an interview that the Historical Court was meant "to honor the work [the elders] did to continue the development of the tribe. It is to honor the legacy they have left for future generations and ours."[97]

The Historical Court

Although many historians contributed to the stories of Leschi's life as recounted above, the petitioners in the Historical Court did not focus on the dynamism of oral tradition. Rather, they explained the Nisqually understanding of Leschi's vision as an active (and cooperatively realized) force through time: those who told his story helped to create the future that he had foretold before his death. Some of the petitioners explained that Leschi's spirit became present when they worked to bring his vision into existence, and Leschi knew the Historical Court was going to happen. Iyall had been told that "one day, the spirit of Leschi would return when all of the people were able to get together again in good times," and Frank similarly reported that Leschi promised his spirit would be there when the people celebrated together with great joy.[98] In a reciprocal relationship, each party must fulfill its own responsibilities; Iyall understood that it was her job to create the Historical Court in order to fulfill Leschi's vision.

The Native American representatives gave testimony not only to inform the judges and non-Indian audiences about what they knew of Leschi's history. They also modeled storytelling as a ritual act. Dorian Sanchez took the stand to do the very thing he described: retell the story of Leschi even in the midst of other versions. Iyall opined before the Historical Court convened that her priority was that Leschi be "correctly" portrayed so that Nisqually children "can inherit and feel the strength, pride, tenacity and intelligence that Leschi left us."[99] The Historical Court could be imagined as a space of cultural reproduction, where Native people could learn about Leschi while doing the very things he foresaw for the future and maintaining continuity with the oral traditions of the past.

In the case of the Historical Court, Native children witnessed tribal leaders claiming an identity and way of knowing apart from the dominant society and the American legal system. With the judges' decision to exonerate Leschi, they also saw an important public affirmation of Native views of history. Dorian Sanchez stated in his testimony that wide public recognition of its stories enhanced and contributed to tribal resilience: "As we celebrate the vision of our elders and words of the treaty that gives us strength, we now can also celebrate that the world knows the name Leschi as we know it—warrior, leader, hero, and innocent." Andreya Squally, a seventeen-year-old high school student who had argued with classmates over the fairness of Leschi's conviction, reflected afterward that the event made her happy because it validated what she had heard from her elders to be true. "[Classmates] said [Leschi's conviction] was right because it was in the history book," Squally said. "Now they have to change the history books."[100] The persistent Native claim to a separate history is important for surviving colonialism as a distinct people with a shared past. "One of the most powerful tools of colonialism is making children ashamed of their parents," writes United Nations diplomat Erica-Irene Daes. "Power can never completely crush a people who cherish their heritage."[101] Squally witnessed an event in which representatives of the state affirmed that her elders were right. Significantly, she expected the "history books," representing the master narrative, to change as a result. The consciously cultivated claim to a counter narrative shaped how Native people "read" the Historical Court as a ritual act and defined historical justice.

Some Native people reported a sense of empowerment following Leschi's exoneration, because what had seemed impossible before—the state acknowledging a mistake—had finally happened, which opened up new possibilities.[102] People could tell their stories of the past and demand public recognition. What was once a burden of keeping and transmitting painful stories could transform into an empowering tool with which to fight oppression and shame. The ethic of reciprocity was built into this hope for the future. Leschi was the inspiring visionary, but subsequent generations did important work by retelling his story: they created the tribe, they built a sense of group identity, and they tied the past to the present and future. The Leschi story is a collective act of creation and re-creation that is, at its core, hopeful.

How can counter narrative—or the *claim* to a different narrative—produce a sense of historical justice in this quasi-legal context? Alternative narratives have the potential to alter social relations and reconfigure power by deviating from the plot expected in the master narrative.[103] The particulars of Leschi's story as told by Native elders did not necessarily deviate from expectations. Rather, the Native representatives' act of testifying about Leschi and the ways they came to know about him reveals this deviation from the plot—and their resistance to domination. The representatives in the Historical Court countered an expectation of Indians' disappearance. Cecelia Carpenter distilled the significance of the Historical Court down to one idea: it was a way of proving that Indians are still here.[104] Not only did they conceive of Leschi's vision as a continuing force in the world, but the representatives also demonstrated that they resisted assimilation and retained the power to shape their own future. In so doing, they suggested an alternative conceptualization of historical justice. Rather than being an act of compassion from the state, Leschi's exoneration represented confirmation of continuing Nisqually ways. After the judges declared Leschi exonerated, Carpenter mused: "I think [Leschi's] watching from up above and he's clapping his hands and saying, 'Well, you finally did it.'" Cynthia Iyall, meanwhile, saw the exoneration as an accomplishment that contributed to the future and refashioned *written* histories: "We will be able to add a chapter or a paragraph to every story that is out there," she told a *New York Times* reporter. "A correct ending to *every* story, added in 2004."[105]

CHAPTER 4 **The Leschi Message**

On the witness stand in the Historical Court of Justice, Billy Frank Jr. drew a direct connection between Leschi's actions in the 1850s and the work of Nisqually leaders and elders in 2004. "If Leschi was alive today," he told the judges and audience, "he'd be doing what we do as Indian people—teaching our language, our culture and way of life, praying and doing our ceremonies." Frank discursively collapsed the time between 1854 and 2004, interweaving the past into the present, blurring the distinction between Leschi and contemporary Indian people, and emphasizing historical continuity. Frank and the other Native American representatives in the Historical Court situated Leschi in both Nisqually history and contemporary politics and, most important, claimed the authority to interpret Leschi's actions and legacy on their own terms. The history of public commemorations for Leschi, including the Historical Court, shows that Nisqually leaders have long sought interpretive control over Leschi's representation as a way to advance the tribe's interests and, at times, their political and cultural survival.

Reflecting on his own life's work as a fishing rights activist, Frank said that he tried to live in a way that would "take the Leschi message forward" in two ways: taking it forward in time to maintain historical continuity with the past, and advancing knowledge of the tribe's history by presenting his personal knowledge and experiences to listening audiences. Frank's testimony about Leschi accomplished important memory work because of, and in spite of, the history of colonialism in South Puget Sound. Frank made the past inseparable from perceptions of the present and gathered together moments spanning 150 years of Nisqually history and contracted them into a single message.[1] He interpreted the message to mean that the Nisqually way compelled them to cooperate with non-Nisquallies when possible but also to fight to defend the homeland, resources, and autonomy if threatened. Frank claimed that Leschi modeled a principled defense of Nisqually self-determination—the sovereign right of the autonomous Indian nation to shape its present and future.

Frank's testimony wove together memory and political-cultural aims, simultaneously commemorating Leschi as a historical actor and claiming him as a mythic figure for political purposes.[2] His testimony implies that whoever "owns" Leschi's memory has an opportunity to define political rights and exercise political power. The Historical Court functioned as an educational and commemorative event, and was therefore a political arena in which Billy Frank Jr. and the other Southern Coast Salish representatives worked to define and control "the Leschi message" as part of a larger process of asserting self-determination. Frank's discursive collapse of time encouraged Historical Court audiences to think of Leschi as a political actor and a representative for a collective group (rather than a singular wronged individual) and, perhaps for the first time, consider the political legacy of Leschi's choices.

Frank's framing of Leschi's story was both inspired by and intended to inspire tribal elders and leaders. His testimony was backward-looking, but also functioned to create a future for the tribe free from the struggles of the past; to refashion historical narratives to emphasize tribal autonomy is to challenge existing structures of political power in a settler state and build new possibilities.[3] Similarly, at moments of tribal crisis from the 1870s through the twentieth century, tribal leaders revised and reinterpreted the Leschi message as they worked to protect their visions for self-determination. Leschi could stand as an example for cooperation and goodwill or as a model of resistance (or a threat), depending upon the political, economic, and social context in which his name was invoked. Three eras of tribal crisis and commemoration—the 1870s to the 1920s, 1917–18, and the 1940s to the 1970s—illustrate the political stakes involved in such memory work. The Historical Court was made possible because of this history. But rather than a culminating moment, the Historical Court represents another development in an ongoing Southern Coast Salish expression of collective autonomy and demand for full self-determination.

The way that Nisquallies interpreted Leschi's actions in relation to the 1854 Medicine Creek Treaty illustrates the entanglements of politics, memory, and changing U.S. Indian policy over more than a century. Native claims about the treaty and Leschi were inseparable, evolving together through shifting Native/non-Indian relations and with the pendulum swings of U.S. Indian policy. Across the Northwest, Isaac I. Stevens's treaties hold legal force and have played (and continue to play) a significant role in legal contests.⁴ The fact that Puget Sound Indians have long used treaties in public contests shows treaties to be living documents whose significance goes beyond the ostensible original intent of the signers and specific circumstances of the 1850s.⁵ Parties to treaties continue to interpret their meaning because social mores, technology, markets, and other conditions change over time. Indian peoples and the United States must reinterpret the terms of their relationship in the context of these changes because they signed a treaty that remains in force, and treaties are often the legal battleground on which local contests between Indians and neighboring non-Indians take place. Nisqually leaders maintained continuities in the Leschi message in a way that parallels the political and historical continuities in treaties.

Today, Native American tribes look to their treaties as the law of the land that guarantees certain rights in a binding political compact with the United States. Although many Northwest tribes now consider their treaties central to their efforts to protect their cultural activities and resources, such respect for treaties was not always the case. Coast Salish groups came to embrace the political designations of "tribe" and "nation" as an adaptation to an American legal system that assumed the existence of discrete tribes as described in the treaties. By the end of the nineteenth century, some Native people of Puget Sound began to self-identify more strongly with a tribe or reservation than with family or social class and increasingly thought of their rights as originating in treaties. Accordingly, Nisqually political identity aligned more closely with the Medicine Creek Treaty as time went on. Rapidly shifting and contradictory government Indian policies also prompted Indians and their supporters to reappraise the legal utility of Pacific Northwest treaties. The twists of policy explain why, by the end of the twentieth century, treaty rights advocates turned to the inconsistent argument that the United States erred both by imposing unfair treaties and by breaking them.⁶ The memorializing process in which Leschi was remade from the headman of a high-class family into a tribal icon parallels the historical process in which Nisquallies embraced the treaty, once considered by many as a means of oppression, as a way to secure rights.

From the end of the treaty period through the twentieth century, Nisquallies faced three major challenges to their culture and political autonomy: the U.S. "civilizing" mission of the 1870s to the 1920s, which threatened tribal identity, knowledge, and lands; a 1918 Pierce County land condemnation, which caused great suffering and land loss; and the state's sustained harassment of Indian fishermen from the 1940s through the 1970s, which jeopardized the tribe's crucial resources and livelihoods. In response to these crises, Nisqually elders and activists connected memories of Leschi to the rights reserved in the Medicine Creek Treaty. Commemorations for Leschi offered opportunities for Indians and non-Indians to redefine their relationships to one another and reinterpret the meaning of the treaty they share. Tribal leaders long used non-Indian interest in Leschi as a way to bring attention to Nisqually self-determination and treaty rights when other public channels were closed to them. By 2004, as Frank's testimony demonstrates, the treaty and memories of Leschi were mutually constitutive. Native leaders connected Leschi's exoneration to an affirmation of Nisqually self-determination and claimed that their struggles to defend the treaty (which Leschi allegedly refused to sign) honored the "Leschi message."[7]

1854: Medicine Creek Treaty

In 1854, in preparation for the first of his treaty councils, Isaac Stevens sought to identify Indian leaders who could act as representatives for the anticipated land cession. American settler Michael T. Simmons recommended Quiemuth and Leschi for the roles because they had provided assistance to settlers for a decade. William Tolmie also nominated the men based on his positive social and economic interactions with them, declaring them "the two best men amongst the Nisquallies."[8] Leschi's relationship to British traders and American settlers helped Leschi over time to acquire status among his own people. Billy Frank Jr. stated in 2004 that Leschi had a peaceful and cooperative nature that gained him "a lot of white friends."[9]

In accordance with the recommendations, Stevens conferred the titles of chief and sub-chief upon Quiemuth and Leschi, respectively. These titles reflected American perceptions of centralized leadership as well as the Coast Salish political economy in which high status strengthened a headman's influence. Although Nisqually political identity centered on the household and village community in the nineteenth century, the headmen from each village occasionally gathered in a general council to discuss matters of mutual concern. In times of crisis, villages allied with one another, and an individual from the upper class who exercised influence in villages other than his own could rise as leader.[10] In 2004, Cynthia Iyall embraced the title of chief assigned to Leschi, asserting that the Nisqually people selected Leschi as chief independent of Stevens's appointment. He had distinguished himself as a fair arbiter in past disputes and therefore garnered the authority to negotiate the treaty as a chief.[11]

When Leschi received his appointment of sub-chief from the U.S. officials, the nearby villagers apparently accepted his leadership, although his status as a high-class arbiter was at odds with expectations for a "chief" representing and advocating for one side in a political negotiation. Ideally, upper-class Coast Salish men were to be gentle and gracious and conduct themselves so as to avoid conflict. But a chief in formal negotiations with whites would be expected to take an uncompromising stand for the peoples' interests.[12] In the treaty council on Medicine Creek in 1854, Leschi was one among dozens of men from the region who weighed the U.S. officials' proposal against expectations arising from their class identity and family and village loyalties. Should the upper-class headmen protect their families' favored access to the watershed's resources and sacrifice some land to homesteaders or resolve to keep all of the land and risk bad relations with whites? How could they maintain their wealth and fulfill the many obligations of their high status?

On a rainy Christmas day, Stevens presented the predrawn treaty terms to the gathered headmen through an interpreter whom he instructed to speak only in Chinook jargon, a crude trade language.[13] Despite the challenges the treaty posed to the newly appointed chiefs, the council began on a familiar note: Stevens distributed gifts to the headmen to honor their status. The headmen knew it was bad manners to speak unfavorably of the host of a give-away and dangerous to criticize a nonrelative.[14] The thirteen articles of the treaty called for peace between the treating members and defined the relationship between the parties. The Indians would cede land in exchange for annuity payments for twenty years and services at a central agency, including a school and carpenter shop. For Native headmen accustomed to economic relationships with non-Indians, the promise of learning English and receiving services might have held great appeal; education in the newcomers' ways meant they could carve out a competitive place for themselves and their children in a changing marketplace.[15] Article III also gave the Native leaders reasons for satisfaction, for it assured the rights of hunting, gathering, and "taking fish at all usual and accustomed grounds and stations . . . in common with all Citizens of the Territory."[16]

Some aspects might have been appealing, but other articles of the treaty gave the headmen various reasons for concern. Article XI stipulated that all slaves held by the tribes be freed—a requirement that affected some headmen more than others. Nisqually villages had proportionately higher slave populations than the other signatory tribes and bands.[17] Other aspects of the treaty impacted the Nisqually headmen more directly as well. The article assuring the rights to hunting, gathering, and horse pasturing stipulated that these activities were limited to "open and unclaimed lands."[18] High-class families expected newcomers to ask their permission before accessing the village's territory, but this article—assuming the nuances were adequately explained to the headmen using the very limited trade jargon—undercut their prerogative to control access to regional resources. Furthermore, the headmen's source of wealth could be threatened. The Americans' intention with the treaty was to secure the best farmland and pastureland for settlers. As farmers and horse owners, Leschi and Quiemuth lived and prospered on the same arable prairieland most coveted by American settlers.[19] The treaty presented the possibility that settlers would take homesteads on Leschi's and Quiemuth's fields and that the brothers would have to find room for their herds on the "unclaimed" scraps. Assuming the Native leaders did receive a satisfactory translation of the wording, they could have seen how this article specifically threatened the headmen's ability to control access to the region's resources and compromised their wealth and status as the owners of large horse herds.

Finally, Stevens proposed a reservation for the Nisqually Tribe that was small and almost entirely made up of heavily forested steep hillside and marshy saltwater shore. To Nisquallies in upriver and foothills villages, this plan understandably held little appeal. Tolmie wrote in 1858 that "Leschi . . . protested vehemently [at the treaty council] against the reservation originally appointed for the Nisquallies."[20] Some Nisqually oral histories maintained that Leschi demanded prairieland on the reservation for his horses, but when Stevens refused to negotiate, Leschi threatened war and left the treaty grounds without signing. According to most available sources, Leschi surmised that the small reservation was only the first step in the U.S. government's plan to remove the Nisquallies to a more distant reserve.[21]

Leschi reportedly broke from custom by showing anger and making demands about the reservation—behavior usually unbecoming of his status. Leschi had become wealthy in part because of his connections to white traders and settlers, yet those connections brought him to negotiate a treaty that threatened his livelihood and status and his ability to meet his obligations to others. Although Leschi initially attempted to cooperate and compromise over the reservation land, perhaps in an attempt to arbitrate between settlers' and the headmen's competing interests, in the end he refused to accept Stevens's demands. Ironically, U.S. officials helped to make Leschi into a Native icon by pushing him away from his practiced role as a peacemaker and into a position of fighting and resisting U.S. pressures.

The "Leschi War" was controversial among Southern Coast Salish villagers who variously chose to join the Nisqually leader, remain neutral, or ally with the United States. Invariably, the fighting in late 1855 and early 1856 caused major disruptions for the region's Native communities. Some family groups took their chances and camped in the foothills along the rivers, while others declared themselves "friendly" to the United States and were forcibly removed to island camps in Puget Sound to live under armed supervision. In January 1856, Leschi traveled to the island camp of Fox Island, near Steilacoom, to speak with the Indian agent, John Swan, in an apparent effort to negotiate peace terms. Leschi reportedly told Swan that he wanted to stop fighting and draw up a new treaty with fair-minded men. "All he wanted was enough land to raise a few potatoes," Swan related to the press.[22] In August 1856, Stevens called a council on Fox Island with the "friendly" Puget Sound Indians in order to change the reservation boundaries outlined in the Medicine Creek Treaty. Governor Stevens insisted that he came before them in the spirit of the treaty, which called for reservations that met with their satisfaction, and not because Leschi's war had forced him to the table. Stevens repeatedly insisted that Leschi started the war unnecessarily because Stevens had always planned to change the reservation boundaries. Whatever Stevens's motivation, the outcome of the Fox Island council was an anomaly. Although most Indian tribes that fought the United States over treaty terms ended up settling for less with new treaties, the Indian signatories of the Medicine Creek Treaty did not share this fate.[23] The Nisqually and Puyallup people asked for and received enlarged reservations along the lines demanded by their headmen at the original treaty council. The new Nisqually reservation quadrupled in size to 4,700 acres, straddled the Nisqually River, and included the expansive prairieland around Muck Creek, where several of the largest inland villages and winter longhouses were located.[24]

Over the long twentieth century, Native people increasingly celebrated Leschi as the defender of the Medicine Creek Treaty and the peoples' land, and few repeat the claims Stevens made in the Fox Island council. Cecelia Carpenter explained the increased reservation size as the result of Leschi's decision to fight; she asserted that Stevens assented to the new reservation to end the war and that Nisquallies owed their reservation to Leschi.[25] Scholars of collective memory argue that people acquire, situate, and recall memories within a group context. Memories are located within the mental and material spaces of the group.[26] The prairie land and upland waterways Leschi was credited with defending provided the space in which Nisqually identity and political survival could be confirmed and transmitted across generations.

The "Civilizing Mission": 1870s–1920s

In the years following the treaty and war, tribal identities or affiliations remained fluid and Indian agents were largely unsuccessful at keeping Indians in regular residence on a single reservation. But in the two decades after the Civil War, the settler population west of the Cascades quadrupled. Many Natives returned from their seasonal work travels to find their homes burned or their fields claimed as part of a settler's homestead.[27] At the same time, federal Indian policy shifted to pursue the contradictory goals of quarantining Indians on reservations and assimilating them into American society. Through a number of intrusive programs, the government "civilizing" campaign sought to destroy tribal cultures and foster American-style dress, religion, and relations among the Native "pupils." Native people responded to these upheavals in multiple ways. Notably, some chose to engage with U.S. courts, journalists, and commemorative practices on terms that emphasized treaty rights and historical continuities.

The U.S. government's assimilation program had two major thrusts: to break down tribes and to create American citizens by resocializing and reeducating Indians. The government opened an Indian boarding school on the Puyallup reservation in 1860, and a Catholic school opened close by in 1888. Agents pressured Indian parents to send their children to residential schools for instruction and industrial training. The Lushootseed language was banned there, and Leschi's grandnephew, Henry Sicade, who attended the government school in the 1870s, recalled severe punishments—whippings and jail—for minor infractions such as catching and cooking fish when the boys were hungry.[28] James McCloud, an elder who listened to his grandparents talk about the schools, said that they "lost a lot of relatives, a lot of friends—a very traumatic time." The most significant outcome of the compulsory schooling was a generation of Nisqually people literate in English but wary of speaking about their history and customs for fear of punishment or shame.[29]

The new Indian policy also aimed to disassemble tribal affiliations by dispensing with communally held land. Acting on the recommendation of the superintendent of Indian Affairs, surveyors arrived on the Nisqually reservation in the early 1870s to create forty-acre agricultural plots, as stipulated in the 1854 treaty. This individualization of reserved land soon became federal policy; in 1887 Congress passed the General Allotment Act on the conviction that altering Indians' traditional property relations and economic practices would help them to become self-sufficient and, in combination with education, create "civilized" people ready for assimilation into American society. The authors of the law assumed individual allotments would teach Indians the value of private property, although the government held the title in trust. The law provided a general and conditional plan for enfranchisement as well: Indians who farmed allotments and adopted "higher" standards of behavior could apply for U.S. citizenship. Three years before the General Allotment Act was implemented nationally, eighty-two Nisqually individuals acquired patents for thirty allotments.[30]

Developers in the growing city of Tacoma eyed the nearby Puyallup lands and in 1890 pressured Congress to institute a legal process to buy Puyallup allotments. In due course, Washington State's congressional delegation introduced legislation to terminate the Indians' trust titles on their allotted land, and Congress opened up direct land sales by Puyallup allottees in 1903.[31] The Puyallup Tribe retained only a remnant of its original holdings, and the Nisqually reservation, although it retained immunity from taxation, suffered similar "checker-boarding" due to land sales throughout the century.[32] The results of the policy of allotment and the subsequent land sales were devastating for the Puyallup Tribe and others across the West, representing a massive legal dispossession of reserved Indian land.[33]

Some Washington tribes turned to the courts to sue for treaty rights and challenge land loss, with mixed results.[34] Although some courts ruled in favor of Indian treaty rights, the press and some judges insisted that Indians had been assimilated and could no longer claim a separate political identity. James Goudy (Puyallup-Skagit) brought a suit against Pierce County in 1906 to challenge the state's taxation of Puyallup allotment land because it forced many tribal members to sell their plots. The Washington Supreme Court found against Goudy on the grounds that Puyallups had become U.S. citizens when they took allotments and were therefore subject to state laws.[35] The editor of the *Seattle Post-Intelligencer* opined in 1904: "Everything that points out to them that they have no special rights and no special privileges different from [other] inhabitants of the state is a good thing for the Indians."[36] Yet the preponderance of treaty rights cases in Washington in this period illustrates that Native people had begun to seize on their treaties to argue just the opposite.[37] Amid the flurry of treaty rights court cases and Americans' "civilizing" zeal, many Nisqually people made great efforts to continue their language, ceremonies, and competitions out of sight of the Indian agents, and persisted in hunting, gathering berries, and fishing in the watershed.[38]

In the 1890s, non-Indian interest in Leschi offered Nisqually people a rare opportunity to speak publicly about their history and openly exhibit their traditions. As the first American immigrants to the region passed away in greater numbers, newspapers published the surviving settlers' memories of the territorial period and exciting Indian encounters. Although reservation agents and missionaries avoided discussions of the treaty period and tribal ways, the non-Indian "pioneer" generation relished these topics and insisted on public commemorations. For older Southern Coast Salish people, sharing their memories of Leschi with settlers intent on publishing them provided rare access to a wide reading audience. Older Indians could reminisce along with the settlers at a time when most agents discouraged the transmission of tribal histories. Furthermore, settler reminiscences offered an opportunity to educate non-Indians about the Medicine Creek Treaty and the tribe's separate political status when the courts largely refused to support this claim.

In the 1890s, Ezra Meeker conducted interviews with longtime settlers and Natives for his book, *Pioneer Reminiscences of Puget Sound and the Tragedy of Leschi*.[39] Meeker was especially interested in accounts of the treaty council, which set the stage for his narrative of Leschi's execution. Chief John Steilacoom met Meeker on the Nisqually Delta to reenact the exchange between Leschi and Stevens at the council. First, Steilacoom played the role of Leschi and gave a fiery speech in Lushootseed, then he pantomimed Stevens acting the bully, and finally he turned back to Leschi to storm off the council grounds without signing the treaty.[40] Meeker supplemented his description of this performance with the testimony of headman John Hiaton and witnesses "Old Pa-al-la" and Luke, who agreed that Leschi not only refused to sign but also threatened Stevens with war.[41]

Through their contributions to Meeker's work, Native informants helped to shape popular perceptions of Leschi and initiated discourse about the conditions at the treaty councils. Ironically, these Native informants focused on Leschi's refusal to sign the treaty, suggesting the flawed nature of the document, at a time when several tribes were fighting for more expansive readings of their treaties in state and federal courts. Perhaps the informants hoped to show that the treaty process had been unfair, which might encourage more sympathetic court decisions of treaty rights.

The tribe also held a reburial ceremony for Leschi and Quiemuth in 1895, which appealed to old settlers' commemorative interests. Leschi's remains had to be removed from the original burial site after surveyors, in the course of delineating separate allotments, determined that the cemetery was outside the reservation boundary. On the first day of the event, Leschi and his brother were reinterred in a wooded glade on the Nisqually Prairie, and the next day, July 4, was filled with socializing, feasting, games, and competitions. Newspapers reported that the event was of particular interest to old settlers, for Leschi had many non-Indians friends who wished to witness the service.[42] The ceremony gave local newspapers the chance to highlight an Indian "pageant" for curious readers, Meeker could publicize his book, and "pioneers" could discuss the old days and reconfirm a sense of group identity. The event also represented an unprecedented opportunity for Nisquallies to dance and sing without government intrusion and to talk about their leaders' political concerns to the press. Just three years earlier, in 1892, the commissioner of Indian Affairs had declared certain Indian gatherings and cultural practices, such as songs and dances, to be punishable as criminal offenses.[43] The reburial right before the Fourth of July provided a cover for Native people of South Puget Sound to conduct the reburial ceremonies required of the high-status leader and helped to foster a sense of tribal unity and shared purpose without incurring suspicion from the Indian agent.[44] In addition, tribal leaders advanced a public relations strategy by inviting non-Indian journalists and local elites to view a nonthreatening Coast Salish cultural activity that invoked their sympathy and goodwill.

The proceedings reflected a long Coast Salish tradition of engaging outsiders in tribal events using important cultural settings and symbols. At such open gatherings, honored guests from outside of the community were expected to witness orations on topics of tribal concern with the assumption that they would repay their generous hosts by reporting the content of these messages upon their return home. Although this tradition once took place in winter houses and on ceremonial occasions (particularly a potlatch), after government officials discouraged such gatherings, Leschi's reburial event provided an occasion for Coast Salish leaders to adapt a familiar political strategy to changing circumstances.[45] On the first day, in a ceremony directed by an individual with special spirit powers, the leaders' bones were removed from their graves, rewrapped, and marched to the reservation Presbyterian Church for the memorial service.[46] That same day, the Northern Pacific Railway ran an excursion train from Tacoma to Nisqually for about forty white spectators, who were then escorted to the church by Indian men driving buggies and wagons. Two Puyallup men reportedly served on a security detail to ensure that the non-Indians did not encounter "disorder" as they moved past hundreds of tents erected by Indian visitors who had traveled from around the Sound for the Fourth of July events.[47] The church services were conducted in Lushootseed and offered a glimpse into the Nisqually Tribe's political dynamics. On the one hand, Leschi's lieutenants and medicine men watched over his remains and conducted important ceremonies. On the other hand, a new generation of tribal leadership—in most cases men educated in boarding schools—cooperated with local journalists to foster a positive image of the tribe. This public relations work was especially important to counteract the many newspaper accounts of Indian treaty rights cases that encouraged readers to see tribes as antagonistic and a threat to non-Indians' control over local resources.[48]

The ceremony began with a few words by Henry Martin, Leschi's cousin. Martin had attended boarding school in Oregon but returned to the area as an adult and occasionally worked as an interpreter.[49] His speech was followed by a number of others, although only George Leschi, Quiemuth's son, was quoted at length in the newspaper. George Leschi's speech honored Leschi's memory with a history lesson and an interpretation of the Leschi message. "The white men wanted our lands and tried to move our people to the salt water," George Leschi stated. Leschi had not wanted to go to war but felt he had no choice: "He only wanted to keep the governor from sending him and our people away from our homes . . . [Leschi] died to save our reservation lands for us."[50] Although the journalists did not record all of the speeches, the most detailed account, printed in the *Tacoma Ledger*, stated: "The character of Leschi was highly eulogized and his constant advocacy of the rights of his people against the encroachments of the whites commented upon at length."[51] To the Nisqually speakers, Leschi's life and death contained a political lesson. They understood Leschi's example as working for peaceful coexistence but fighting when necessary; this served as inspiration and a source of strength to a new generation facing similar challenges in the allotment period.

After the service, the mourners walked the four miles to the cemetery site in a procession nearly a mile long.[52] The new burial ground was situated in an oak grove on the edge of the prairie near Muck Creek. At the gravesite, John Hiaton, a headman who had petitioned for Leschi's pardon in 1858 and served as a leader and spokesman for the tribe in the difficult years following the war, made a final speech to conclude the service. He then suggested that the Indians reconvene after the white people had gone so they could conduct a private ceremony—a request apparently granted.[53] But before the journalists departed, Leschi's lieutenants, descendants, and medicine men gathered together for a photograph. Standing in a line, Bill Quiemuth, Luke, George Leschi, Wa He Lut, and Steilacoom look mournful yet dignified.[54] These men represent both the older and the younger generations, and as James McCloud explained in 2004, these men "kept a lot of responsibility" during the difficult time.[55] The elders' responsibilities were indeed complex. Elders sought to educate Nisqually youth about their history at a time when the children faced punishment in boarding school for exhibiting linguistic, cultural, or historical knowledge of the old ways. In addition, elders and younger leaders had to negotiate non-Indian curiosity and determine how and to what extent to share Leschi with non-Nisqually publics. As Puget Sound Indians increasingly turned to the courts to demand treaty rights, non-Indians' sympathy was also important. Nisqually leaders followed a strategy of limited cooperation; sharing their icon with settlers and the press meant that they could empower outsiders to spread their views while gathering together and conducting ceremonies that built a sense of Nisqually collective identity and a shared history.

Nisqually leaders' attempts to speak for themselves in circumscribed conditions had mixed results. Academics and some former territorial officials attacked Meeker's book, and especially the charge that Leschi's mark on the treaty was forged, claiming Indians were unreliable witnesses and oral history an inferior form of historical evidence. The newspaper coverage of the 1895 reburial was sometimes disrespectful, with one account providing lurid details about Quiemuth's remains and characterizing Native peoples' expressions of grief at the service as exotic curiosities.[56] But the newspaper accounts and settler reminiscences also quoted George Leschi, Luke, Steilacoom, and others as they gave their own versions of

FIGURE 8 Tribal members and relatives gather for Leschi's reburial ceremony on the Nisqually reservation, 1895. Left to right: Bill Quiemuth, Luke, George Leschi, Wa He Lut, and Old Steilacoom. (Washington State Historical Society)

the past printed nowhere else. The reburial event brought together Native people from around South Puget Sound and afforded an opportunity for old friends to meet, dance, compete, and sing. Newspapers called it the "greatest gathering of Indians held in the Northwest in years" with "fully a thousand Indians" in attendance, defying all expectations of Indian disappearance.[57] Leschi's reburial and commemoration provided a rare opportunity to affirm Indian identity and tribal autonomy when U.S. policy worked to dismantle it.

Fort Lewis: 1917–1918

Sixty years after Leschi's remains were first interred and twenty-five years after the Fourth of July reburial ceremony, Nisquallies once again faced the prospect of moving Leschi's body when they lost access to the prairie. Leschi's repeated burials signaled the tribes' incremental land loss over the span of a few generations, but the reinterments also functioned as moments of memorialization. Once again, tribal members were prompted to consider Leschi's significance in the midst of land loss, and older generations who likely had attended the previous burial could provide younger members with memories of continuity in the face of immense disruptions to tribal life. In 1917, it was the U.S. Army, not settlers or land speculators, who looked longingly at a portion of Nisqually reserved land. The prairie on which Leschi was buried was not just any stretch of land—it stood at the heart of Nisqually economic, social, and religious activities. There women harvested edible roots, berries, and grasses for baskets, and men and women conducted vision quests and visited sacred sites. Most Nisqually allottees lived on or near this prairie because it offered a freshwater spring, a great winter chum salmon run, and some of the best agricultural soil on the Nisqually reservation.[58] The prairie was also important for community social functions because the Catholic and Presbyterian churches and numerous cemeteries and historic village sites had been constructed there.[59]

In the early 1910s, the U.S. military began leasing thousands of acres in Pierce County, including the prairieland of the Nisqually reservation, for munitions firing practice. When the United States entered World War I in 1917 and the drills increased, the army general claimed that he could not ensure the safety of civilians who lived nearby unless they were removed during practice hours.[60] The best long-term solution, as far as the army was concerned, was to secure unfettered access to this training ground during wartime. The Nisqually people and other homesteaders would have to be permanently evicted.

The military moved swiftly to claim the land with the enthusiastic support of Pierce County administrators and some powerful residents. Tacoma merchants and builders could benefit from their proximity to the base and the soldiers stationed there. In 1917, Pierce County voters overwhelmingly passed a twenty-year bond to purchase 70,000 acres of land—including 3,200 acres of the Nisqually reservation—and donate it to the army for military training. Many of the voters likely thought they were doing their patriotic duty to help their country in wartime, even if it meant forcing hundreds of their neighbors to sacrifice their homes.[61] The bond meant the county had a way to pay private landowners for their land, but Indian allotments were federal trust land. The county used an eminent domain law to purchase allotments for below-market prices, condemn the homes of Indians protected by treaty and managed by the Department of the Interior, and donate the land at reduced value to the Department of War. Pierce County's Condemnation Board based its authority on a 1901 statute, which held that land allotted in severalty could be condemned for any public purpose under the laws of the state. The board considered Indian allotments private property, but the federal government held title to these plots and, by federal law, only an act of Congress could authorize the sale. However, federal authorities did not stop this dispossession of their Indian wards by popular vote and essentially allowed a small group of county board members to abrogate a treaty. "The Bureau [of Indian Affairs] stood there and didn't do a damn thing about it," former tribal chair Georgiana Kautz said in 2010. "No one did."[62] The condemnation represented a major breakdown in the trust relationship between the United States and the tribe.

In anticipation of the condemnation proceedings, the superintendent at the Cushman Indian School wrote to the commissioner of Indian Affairs in 1917 to warn that removing Nisqually allottees would "cause violent opposition on the part of the Indians," who were well aware of their treaty rights.[63] Even so, the Department of the Interior was slow to act on behalf of its wards, later claiming that the department was not notified when the county commenced condemnation proceedings in 1918. Rather than delay or challenge the proceedings, federal authorities sent weak legal representation to protect the Indians' interests. The assistant U.S. attorney assigned to advocate for Indian allottees in negotiations between the army, county, and Indian Bureau appraisal boards appeared to favor the lowest assessments. As a later investigation uncovered, the attorney overlooked improvements and other qualities of the reserved Indian land that added significant value, such as freshwater springs, treaty fishing rights, and tax-exempt status. Leschi's grandnephew, Henry Sicade, was one of the appraisers sent to arbitrate the valuation of condemned land and delivered estimates on nine sections of land and water systems transferred to Pierce County. The attorney ultimately agreed with the county appraisals and accepted payment to the Indian allottees that was far below market value for their lands. On average, non-Indian landowners who hired private lawyers received significantly higher out-of-court compensation packages for their lands. The compromise for allotted lands was hastily reached, according to an Interior Department investigation, "in view of immediate war necessity" and with the expectation that the displaced Nisqually families would be further compensated for moving expenses at a later time.[64] The condemnation was not only an improper seizure of federal trust land through county channels but also, as Cecelia Carpenter put it, "an unacknowledged transfer of wealth from one nation to another."[65] The allottees were forced to vacate their homes within two weeks when the final adjustment of land values was announced in April 1918.[66] Some displaced families sought housing with relatives on other reservations, but others were forced to take refuge in makeshift shelters in the woods.[67]

The results were socially, politically, and economically catastrophic for the Nisqually community. Tribal functions were severely disrupted when most of the homes, six cemeteries, two churches, and tribal headquarters were lost in the condemnation. Three-fourths of the tribe was displaced, and communal meeting places were simply closed without a plan for their relocation.[68] Plans for the displaced Nisqually allottees were hastily drawn at best. If the compensation turned out to be insufficient to cover the costs of moving and purchasing new land, the Indians had to go through the lengthy process of requesting a supplement from Congress.[69] Over a year after the condemnation, the official in charge of finding replacement land for the ousted families had met with little success.[70]

A new generation of Nisqually leadership, led by boarding school–educated young men, struggled to hold the people together through this displacement. Henry Martin's nephew, Peter Kalama, inherited his uncle's allotment and responsibilities and would oversee another of Leschi's reburials.[71] The Martin allotment contained an old mill with workers' barracks, and Kalama opened this shelter to older relatives displaced by the condemnation and fed many people from his garden.[72] Kalama used the English language skills he had acquired at boarding school to implore the government to return the condemned land. His tactic was to express concern for U.S. national interests in the spirit of cooperation. In October 1918, Kalama sent a petition to the Indian Department and the Department of the Interior in which he diplomatically acknowledged that exigencies of of war called for the land seizure but argued that the lands should be returned to the Nisqually families at the war's conclusion. Kalama explained that he had done his best to care for the sick and the old of the tribe, but some Indians who were "blind, aged, and decrepit" were living in "old leaky shacks and tents" along the Nisqually River and it would be an "act of mercy and justice" if the petition were granted.[73] Given few alternatives, Kalama attempted to cooperate with U.S. officials and go through proper political channels to secure some relief.

In response to Kalama's overtures, the Indian Department led investigations and issued reports and recommendations on the matter. The 1920 Indian Department report on the condition of the Nisqually allottees recorded the Nisqually people's many grievances but did not advise that the condemned land be restored to them. Instead, the tone was dismissive:

"We can not expect contentment in their new homes, especially among the older people, who will never cease to long for their old homes, around which center a lifetime of intimate memories and affections."[74] Investigators acknowledged the significant link between the land and historical memory. However, the report suggested that the solution was simply to wait until the older generation and their memories had died and the younger people had been assimilated. The Indian Department presumably saw no need to plan for the future survival of the tribe and, consequently, did not consider the possibility that attachment to the tribal homeland would be transmitted across generations. The government report reveals how memory linked to politics: if the old peoples' memories died, the United States could eventually secure the land, but as long as these memories survived, the complaints against the government—and contests over the land—would continue. After the conclusion of World War I, Fort Lewis increased in size and troops continued to fire munitions over the remaining reservation land. But Kalama doggedly persisted in his letter-writing campaign and eventually did help to secure a sizable congressional payment for the relocation expenses. The families accepted the money as compensation for their property, but refused to recognize the transfer of ownership over the reserved land. One longtime employee of the Nisqually Tribe said recently that "the Indian reservation still exists" on the prairie because Congress never explicitly approved of the condemnation (although it did implicitly lend approval by offering monetary compensation).[75] The tribal members' attachment to the condemned land persisted for generations after condemnation—in part through stories of Leschi's efforts to retain it.

With the exception of the Indian Department investigations, the plight of the displaced Nisqually families attracted little public concern. In those circumstances, anthropologists and researchers interested in Indian "folklore" represented the same limited potential for public attention as had the "pioneer" reminiscences a generation earlier. In the spring of 1917, Arthur Ballard, a field researcher from the Smithsonian Institution, sought to talk with one of the last surviving Nisqually veterans of the Puget Sound Indian War. When he finally tracked down Charlie Martin, "Nisqually Charlie," with the help of Puyallup interpreter James Goudy, Ballard was shocked to find him living in a "rude shelter."[76] Charlie and his wife, like many other Nisqually allottees, had struggled to survive when they were forced from their homes. "At first view, the premises seemed unoccupied," Ballard recalled, "but as my interpreter disturbed the bedding spread upon the ground two pitiful creatures rose to a sitting position."[77] Ballard took a photograph of Charlie and his wife, disheveled and groggy from their disturbed slumber.[78] While Ballard astutely observed that it was a "singularly inopportune" moment to conduct research, he could not help himself. He did not record the questions he asked of Charlie, but Charlie's monologue, filtered through Goudy's translation and Ballard's reconstructed notes, fixed squarely on Leschi and the Medicine Creek Treaty.

As a participant in the treaty council, Charlie recounted that "Governor Stevens tried to get us Indians to agree to be moved." When they realized that Stevens refused to compromise, Charlie recalled, "Leschi and his brothers and the other chiefs, I with them, got up and left. Leschi did not sign the treaty and Quiemuth did not." They would not agree to the possibility of losing their land. In sum: "The reason we fought was that we did not wish to be moved from our homes down to the bluff by the bay." The sad irony of Charlie's current situation may have been lost on Ballard, but Charlie kept the treaty at the forefront of his thoughts. Charlie insisted that he had fought in a war to keep his home on the prairie in 1855, yet the army had ultimately succeeded in taking this land through legal channels. Ballard did not publish what he learned about the hardships facing displaced Nisquallies in the condemnation, but his photograph and notes would be entered as evidence in a treaty claims case nearly forty years later.[79]

Shared interest in Leschi facilitated other connections between Nisquallies and non-Indians at this time, with equally ambiguous results. In addition to the living allottees, the remains of 162 people, including Leschi, had to be relocated due to the condemnation.[80] The tribe petitioned Congress for funds to transfer the remains to a new cemetery, but they did not receive the money until 1929.[81] For twelve years following the condemnation, Nisqually leaders scrambled to find land for a new cemetery without sufficient government appropriations. Although affordable land was rare, grave protection was a pressing matter for the Nisqually people. To abandon the cemeteries off the reservation was not an option, for Nisqually people needed to visit and protect their ancestors' graves from intrusion.[82] White collectors prized the "flattened" skulls of high-status Salish individuals like Leschi, and anthropologists routinely sent Nisqually remains to the Smithsonian Institution for study, including a cranium falsely labeled as Leschi's.[83] One old settler claimed in a public speech that he had unearthed and opened Leschi's casket in 1879 and reported to his audience on the silk shrouds and tin vessels that allegedly adorned Leschi's body.[84] Such lurid details no doubt tempted relic hunters to search for souvenirs. During a period of displacement, the prospect of reburying the ancestors also prompted Nisquallies to reflect on and reconsider their shared history in relation to contemporary political challenges.

As a testament to his honored status, Leschi's body was among the first to be moved in the spring of 1918, despite the fact that Nisquallies had not yet located affordable land to serve as the new tribal cemetery. Several years earlier, the Puyallup tribal council (which included Henry Sicade) had set aside funds to be used for a cemetery on reserved tribal land adjacent to the Cushman Indian School. Leschi's daughter married an employee at the school, and although an off-reservation burial was not ideal, she was able to secure a plot for Leschi's remains at the cemetery there.[85] This 1918 reburial was a far cry from the two-day ceremony and gathering in 1895 — a reflection of the government's pointed efforts to dismantle and disperse the tribe. "Today several of us volunteered to remove the remains of Leschi from Squally to Puyallup Indian Cemetery," Henry Sicade wrote to Ezra Meeker on April 29. Perhaps with the unfulfilled hope that the sympathetic old settler might bring the issue to public attention, Sicade explained that the event was rushed because of the Pierce County condemnation.

Although a large reburial ceremony was not possible under the circumstances, Sicade appealed to Meeker for ways to commemorate their leader. Sicade suggested that the two launch a cooperative venture: "What do you think of the idea of getting public subscriptions . . . to erect a monument to Leschi's memory?" Sicade reminded Meeker of their common interest in educating the public about territorial history and that Leschi's grave was now in Puyallup, their shared home. Sicade diplomatically suggested that older Indians could solicit subscriptions from citizens, and Meeker could help to write the monument inscription. Perhaps Sicade reasoned that publicly commemorating Leschi would draw attention to the displaced Nisquallies' plight and bring support for their rights. Meeker's letter books do not record a response to Sicade. No monument was erected to Leschi in the years following this letter, and the newspapers did not record a public ceremony conducted over Leschi's remains at the time of his reinterment. Public memory at the time deeply favored settlers' perspectives. In the years immediately following Sicade's request, the Washington State Historical Society erected two monuments to Americans killed by Indians in the 1855–56 war, one of which was dedicated to the militiamen Leschi allegedly killed on Connell's Prairie.[86]

Leschi had to wait over ten years for a headstone, but the inscription

FIGURE 9 Leschi's headstone in the Puyallup tribal cemetery, 2011. (Photo by author)

does suggest some collaboration with Meeker. The front of the stone tablet states the dates of his life and the title "Chief Leschi, an arbitrator of his people." On the back is a short narrative:

> Leschi, judicially murdered February 19, 1858, owing to misunderstanding growing out of treaty of 1854–55 and war of 1855 and 1856. Serving his people by his death, sacrificed to a principle. A martyr to liberty, honor, and the rights of people and his Native land. Erected by those he died to serve, 1929.

The words were inspired by, and largely drawn from, *Pioneer Reminiscences of Puget Sound and the Tragedy of Leschi*. Meeker had written that Leschi was "judicially murdered" and was a "sacrifice to a principle, a martyr to a cause, and a savior of his people" because he suffered so that his people had a place to live.[87] Meeker also printed an interview with the hangman, who reported that Leschi's last words on the scaffold indicated that the evidence against him was false but that, like Christ, he would die for his people.[88]

The fact that the words were drawn from a white writer may lead people to see Leschi as merely a vessel for non-Indian sentiments and concerns. However, this assumption obscures Native peoples' voices and memorial practices, which maintained Leschi as representative of historical and cultural experiences, as well as a symbol for the tribe's dynamic political goals.[89] Leschi's headstone title of "arbitrator" can be found in Meeker's book, but the source can be tracked back to Nisquallies. Meeker published a letter by Tolmie in which he explained that Leschi was "respected by his tribe and often referred to as an arbitrator in their disputes."[90] Leschi's life story was rendered in religious, liberal, and political tones on the headstone as well. The word "martyr" reflected the significant influence of the Catholic Church on Nisqually life, which sent missionaries among them in the early 1840s and opened a boarding school north of the Puyallup agency in 1888. At the 1895 reburial church service, George Leschi, too, expressed the notion that Leschi sacrificed his life to save the tribe's reserved lands.[91] The concept of "liberty," an Enlightenment notion that referenced America's own founding principles, was appropriated to describe Nisqually nationhood a few years after some Nisqually leaders had successfully lobbied in Washington D.C., for U.S. citizenship for all Indians.[92] The words "treaty," "war," and "rights" all carry political weight and commemorate Leschi as a defender of Nisqually sovereignty. The "judicially murdered" quote indicted the territorial court as the true murderer, thus questioning the authority of the U.S. legal system to judge Leschi's political actions. The headstone is equivocal about the treaty, however, only offering that there was a "misunderstanding" over the treaty without additional detail. The memories of the treaty were perhaps too complex to convey on a headstone, for Nisquallies did not interpret Leschi's actions strictly as defending the treaty or as rejecting many of the rights it promised. At a time when the tribe was weathering acute challenges to its survival, Leschi's headstone represented an act of commemoration that communicated tribal principles adapted to meet contemporary challenges.

Fish Wars and Treaty Rights, 1940s–1970s

For several decades following the Fort Lewis land seizure, the Nisqually Tribe struggled to survive politically. "If anything was done to kill a tribe," Carpenter declared of the Fort Lewis condemnations, "this was it!!"[93] The effects of the condemnation caused the tribe to fall into a low period of political organization from the 1920s through the 1950s. Families displaced in the condemnation lost their tax-exempt land and, priced out of most nearby lands, moved to other reservations or, as Carpenter put it, "were lost in white towns and cities."[94] The tribal council struggled to maintain coherence amid the upheavals, and shifts in Indian policy exacerbated family rifts over tribal enrollment. By the 1940s, the voting membership of the tribe had dropped to about sixty members—a size so small that it was rendered politically weak and fractured.[95]

During this crisis of tribal fragmentation, Nisqually elders strived for coherence of purpose by remembering Leschi. Carpenter recalled from her childhood in the 1930s and 1940s that her Nisqually mother, who would often tell her about Leschi's defense of Nisqually rights, would firmly instruct her daughter: "And don't you forget it!" At a time when public commemorations ceased, private family memories persisted. Carpenter's mother was so insistent in her instruction because her stories were the only defense against the government's institutionalized efforts, such as boarding schools and legal condemnation, to break collective memory. Carpenter grew more appreciative of Leschi as she learned more about the tribe's struggles in the twentieth century. She wrote: "By the time I was six years old, Chief Leschi was my hero . . . I realized that the very land that Leschi had died for had been condemned in 1918."[96] The elders encouraged the younger generation to think about Leschi's actions not in the context of his time but as an icon for a principle, a way of framing the meaning of events in the near-past and the present.

Another important moment for memory work came in the early 1950s, when the Nisqually Tribe filed a claim for compensation for broken treaty agreements in the Indian Claims Commission (ICC).[97] Congress created the ICC, partially in response to lobbying from a national Indian organization, to hear and rule on claims made by tribes against the United States.[98] Cynthia Iyall, the current tribal chairwoman, recalled listening to the people of her grandparents' generation talk about Leschi during this time. Paul Leschi, a grandnephew of Leschi and a vice chairman of the tribe through the 1940s and the ICC case of the 1950s, talked with Ida Iyall (Cynthia's great-grandmother) about "getting some kind of action taken" on behalf of Leschi.[99] Although the ICC procedures suggested that the U.S. government might be ready to acknowledge Indian grievances and make amends, Ida Iyall and Paul Leschi had no clear political or legal path by which to contest Leschi's conviction. The elders did not have strong English language skills or powerful non-Indian allies and stood little chance of pushing for Leschi's exoneration during the nadir of Nisqually political power in the 1950s. But, significantly, Paul thought of Leschi at the same time as he testified for the ICC and about what his elders had told him about the treaty. This suggests a collapsing of time, a distillation of history: the tribe's responses to the government's broken promises throughout the previous century were reenactments of Leschi's confrontation with U.S. agents in the 1850s. Each successive challenge to the tribe reminded Nisquallies that Leschi provided an example to follow. This memory work accomplished more than just eliciting a commemorative impulse—it inspired demands. The elders' discussions of Leschi and painful losses in the tribe's history planted a sense of responsibility in the younger generations to take action for both treaty rights and Leschi. They modeled for Cynthia Iyall—a future political leader—the importance of preserving historical memory as a way of facilitating political rights.

The 1960s and 1970s political resurgence of Puget Sound tribes was built from a foundation established by the previous generation as Natives learned how to navigate the U.S. political system. This political resurgence was long in the making and reflected internal tribal conflict, reorganization, and consolidation as much as a response to outside pressures.[100] In part because of the Nisqually diaspora produced by allotment and condemnation in the first quarter of the twentieth century, Leschi became a regional icon by the second half. In addition to Leschi's descendants who remained on the reservation or purchased land nearby, many Native people around South Puget Sound identified as "the people of Chief Leschi."[101] Eventually, it was through defending treaty fishing rights that the people of Chief Leschi regrouped with a shared sense of identity and purpose.

When Pierce County redrew the boundaries of Nisqually land after the condemnation, the Nisqually River became the site of clashes over shared resources. A 1919 Indian Department report stated that the Indian fisherman who returned to their usual fishing stations on the Nisqually River after the condemnation "are likely to be molested by the authorities and other citizens, as has been the case on other reservations where the river was the boundary."[102] The condemnation coincided with increasingly restrictive state game and fish policies and taxation regimes. Washington State fish wardens began to arrest Puget Sound Indians in the 1920s for defying state laws against gillnet fishing.[103] In 1937, Peter Kalama filed a bill of complaint as the first step in initiating a lawsuit against the state on this issue, but the judge threw it out. The fishermen successfully obtained a federal court injunction against state interference with their fishing, but the state continued to arrest Indian fishermen.[104] Billy Frank Jr. recalled the harassment he and other fishermen regularly endured, from having nets confiscated to being chased and tear-gassed, tackled, and dragged to jail.[105] The legislature and game wardens ignored the 1942 Washington State Supreme Court ruling in *Tulee v. Washington*, which declared enrolled tribal members to be exempt from state licensing requirements, and proceeded to impose additional conservation regulations upon Indian fishermen.[106] The State of Washington insisted that Indians had no "special privileges" above those of other state citizens.[107] Although the Nisqually Tribe was politically disorganized and divided at the time, its shared persecution by state game officials led members to rally around their treaty fishing rights. Of course, those rights would not have mattered if the elders had not transmitted memories connecting Coast Salish identity to fishing and imparted a sense of responsibility in the younger generation to maintain that connection for the future.

Frustrated with state courts but hopeful that the federal judiciary would honor their treaty rights if forced to take action, several Indian fishermen turned away from cooperation and toward open defiance. Inspired by the sit-ins across the U.S. South to challenge Jim Crow segregation, Native fishermen-turned-radical activists and their allies staged "fish-ins" to protest what they believed to be unfair state persecution. In the spring of 1964, Puget Sound Indian activists gathered at Frank's Landing, the boat launch area Willy Frank purchased near the mouth of the river after his Pierce County allotment had been condemned.[108] From here, the activists called the press and the game wardens and went fishing. The newspaper images of young Native people—some girls as young as twelve—being roughly handled and arrested for fishing elicited national sympathy.[109] Although the fish-ins earned national support, Indian fishing rights remained a highly contentious local issue. As the activists' tactics grew increasingly militant (which brought increasingly harsh police crackdowns in response), some Indians were fearful of the negative reactions the activism would provoke from non-Indian neighbors. The official Nisqually government (recognized by the Bureau of Indian Affairs) distanced itself from the activists and hoped to find a solution through established channels.[110]

It was within the context of local Indian fishing rights activism and heightened awareness of racial tensions nationwide that the Pierce County Pioneer and Historical Association decided to dedicate a stone memorial to Leschi in the spirit of cooperation. The memorial, unveiled on April 15, 1964, at Thunderbird Plaza in the suburban town of Lakewood, marked the approximate location of Leschi's hanging. This memorial took the form

FIGURE 10 Front view of memorial stone near the site of Leschi's execution, Lakewood, Washington, 2011. (Photo by author)

of a gray boulder, not a Roman obelisk or Greek temple more typical of memorials in the United States that invoke the accomplishments of past civilizations.[111] Rather, the boulder linked the Indian man to primordial nature, unformed by culture and silently enduring. Situated on a small grass patch between an expansive parking lot and strip mall storefronts, the memorial referenced the "premodern" natural elements of the area that lay *below* the asphalt and *before* the post–World War II population explosion in South Puget Sound. The purpose of a memorial is to commemorate the dead, mark an ending, and explain the principles for which the life was sacrificed.[112] However, this commemoration largely ignored living Indians and their concerns and emptied Leschi's memory of political meaning.

According to the *Tacoma News-Tribune*, the words on the memorial were "bitter" and invoked the spirit of Leschi.[113] The inscription reads: "Leschi, Chief of the Nisquallies, martyr to the vengeance of the unforgiving white man, was hanged 300 yards S.E. from here." The words were drawn from the writing of Major Granville O. Haller, a "defender of Leschi" in the decades after his death.[114] Notwithstanding his language, Haller's intention was not to indict white people in general, as Haller knew that Leschi had non-Indian friends who had worked for his pardon.[115] In stark contrast to the inscription on Leschi's headstone erected thirty-five years earlier, the memorial does not include the words "rights" and "treaty" nor refer to the Nisqually people beyond Leschi's title as "chief" of the tribe. The inscription isolated Leschi from his cultural, legal, and political context and painted Leschi as a singular passive victim. The inscription makes no reference to what Leschi may have done to provoke vengeance or the significant impact of his actions on Nisqually people.[116] The memorial was not really about Leschi and his acts of defiance but rather about white people and their acts of domination.[117]

By indicting "the white man" for irrational and unfair behavior on the inscription, the association members employed a discourse of conciliation.[118] Notably, the memorial was dedicated during a period of strengthening rights-based social movements; it was not just a material reflection of changing social ideologies but also an enactment of the kind of social change the association members hoped to bring about.[119] The association members wanted to end racial prejudice and focused on Leschi to signal their commitment to the project while encouraging a similar transformation among the viewers. The memorial's wording condemned racism of the past in order to exhibit the association members' own progressive social values in 1964. But this was a self-referential exercise in remembering that removed the agency of actors who fought against prejudice.[120] The memorial was not one the Nisquallies had requested. Carpenter dismissed the memorial altogether, saying that those who created it "didn't care about Indians."[121]

The newspapers reporting on the memorial dedication printed photographs of Indian people in attendance but mainly quoted non-Indian speakers. Della Gould Emmons, author of a historical novel about Leschi, gave a speech at the Pioneer Association luncheon earlier in the day. The *Tacoma News-Tribune* reported that Emmons focused her comments on the Medicine Creek Treaty. The size of the reservation was inadequate, Emmons conceded, but she declared that the worst part of the treaty was the clause that reserved to Indians the right to fish in "usual and accustomed grounds . . . in common with all citizens of the territory." She implored her audience: "What chance did these poor Indians have in signing such a treaty? None."[122] Emmons's interpretation of the treaty clause was the same as the state courts': Indians had no "special" rights to fish not enjoyed by any other state citizen. To South Puget Sound Indian fishermen, however, the treaty clause was not as problematic as the state's interpretation of it and the federal government's refusal to honor it. Significantly, Emmons suggested that the treaty was only the first blow dealt the Nisqually and that Leschi's hanging should be understood as part of a longer story of the victimization of these "poor Indians." This narrative contradicted Nisqually memories insisting that Leschi objected to the treaty on the matter of land, not fishing rights, and that, rather than symbolizing victimization, Leschi had left a legacy of defiance.

Bruce Le Roy, director of the Washington State Historical Society, explained at the unveiling that the dignity of Leschi's death provided a lesson for cooperation. By forgiving those who convicted him and called for his execution, Le Roy announced that Leschi serves as "a symbol of the brotherhood of man."[123] Le Roy's appeal to peace was understandable in that politically tumultuous moment, when many authorities were particularly anxious about youth activism. His speech attempted to turn the terms of engagement back to cooperation at a time when some Native people felt that they had been pushed to the point of resistance.

To Native activists, the memorial served to depoliticize and tidy up U.S.-Indian relations just when the activists demanded change. Although sympathetic to Indians, the memorial was out of step with the activists' political message about fishing rights. One of the audience members at the ceremony, Janet McCloud, sought out journalists' attention to counter the memorial planners' message of victimization and conciliation. The Nisqually activist brought a group of Indian children dressed in regalia to the event, including one boy holding a stick from which an effigy of Stevens dangled.[124] McCloud reportedly stayed "on the sidelines" during the ceremony, standing with her husband and "several other Indian fishermen who had been in jail." When a journalist asked McCloud what she thought, she criticized the association for not including Nisqually people and said: "I think this is silly when the Nisqually are still fighting for their rights."[125] McCloud objected that the memorial focused on the past without referencing contemporary treaty rights. More to the point, she expressed frustration that Leschi had been used for non-Indians' political purposes rather than her own. A week after the memorial dedication, the Survival of the American Indian Association, of which Janet McCloud was president, announced its intention to stage another fish-in.[126]

The 1964 memorial dedication illustrated one of the possible results when non-Indians appropriated Leschi and interpreted his story according to their own concerns. Unlike the commemorative moments surrounding Leschi's reburials, in this context Nisqually people could not control the political message with which his life and death were associated. The public sympathy that the Native fishermen sought through principled lawbreaking inspired other activists to appropriate Leschi for an array of 1960s causes. For example, in 1968, students blocked off the west entrance to the University of Washington campus in Seattle, declaring the spot as the "People's Republic of Leschi."[127] The crowd was dispersed quickly with tear gas, and the event was lost among the multitude of militant student protests; the honorific naming suggests, though, that students saw Leschi as a symbol of defiance of government authority. McCloud and other fishing rights activists wanted the federal government to intervene to protect their rights, but the name of the protest space—the People's Republic—suggested political autonomy hinged on breaking free of government intervention. In the midst of more dominant discourses about civil rights and third world decolonization, Native activists in the region and across the country struggled to articulate a unique definition of tribal nationalism that combined federal responsibilities with Indian self-determination. The various popular appropriations of Leschi offered Native people support as U.S. citizens who deserved civil rights or as colonized people who should be "left alone." They did not support the activists' more complex political demand that the federal government should be forced to honor the promises it made in treaties by supplying resources to tribes with which they could secure self-determination.[128] In this period, South Puget Sound Native activists faced a paradoxical and familiar trade-off: in exchange for sharing Leschi and gaining public sympathy and a space to speak, Nisquallies lost interpretive control over their icon and public focus on the specific concerns to which they hoped to bring attention.

The fish-in activists did finally receive the federal intervention they sought. In response to the increasingly worrisome tensions in the region, the federal government announced that it would act as a trustee for seven tribes party to the 1854 and 1855 Puget Sound treaties. In 1970, Justice Department lawyers sued state fishery agencies in federal district court in Tacoma, arguing for a more expansive reading of the fishing rights clause. The case went before Judge George Boldt, who ruled in *United States v. Washington* (1974) that the plaintiff tribes had a right to take half of the harvestable salmon in each year's run.[129] This landmark ruling, affirmed by the Supreme Court in 1979, was instrumental in refiguring the relationship of Indian nations, the federal government, and states in regard to fishing rights. The case affirmed that the fishing rights clause in the treaty meant the state could no longer impose regulations that impinged on Indians' right to take their share of salmon. Indian treaties, in this case, trumped state law. As a result of this legal decision, some of the rifts between militant fishing rights activists and official tribal leadership began to close, but they have not disappeared. One former Nisqually chairwoman recently said of the radical activist Billy Frank Jr.: "There's some people that don't support him, but not that many. He'll go down in history ... like our Chief Leschi."[130] Leschi offered a framework for understanding an array of political strategies Nisqually individuals have used to protect the peoples' resources—even if not everyone agreed with those choices at the time.

The court ruling confirmed that the tribe had a right to a portion of river fish and an expanded role in salmon population maintenance, which signaled to tribal leadership, official and not official alike, that the time for civil disobedience had passed. The tribe worked through legal and legislative channels to uphold and implement the Boldt decision, mitigate the impacts of upriver dams on the Nisqually River, and address other environmental concerns.[131] No longer forced to simply respond to the effects of environmental degradation in the Nisqually watershed, the tribe could begin to build cooperative partnerships and negotiate compacts with timber companies, state fisheries, Fort Lewis, and farmers to protect the resources it shares. Billy Frank Jr., longtime chair of the Northwest Indian Fisheries Commission, which manages these relations, claimed that such peaceful collaboration was all Leschi ever wanted.[132] This was Leschi's message in action. On the stand in the Historical Court, Frank once again connected Leschi to a sense of cooperation and affirmation of treaty rights: "30 years ago, that great [Boldt] decision ... came about through ... Chief Leschi and the United States government. ... We only carry that message as we travel today." Frank read Leschi's presence into the Medicine Creek Treaty, intertwining the meaning of the treaty as a living document with the continuation of the Leschi message. The treaty and Leschi both established a framework for Nisqually-U.S. relations in the 1850s that continued to evolve and shape interactions over the years. Ironically, Frank suggested that the treaty that Leschi allegedly refused to sign carried his influence 120 years later.

The Historical Court: 2001–2004

Following the U.S. Supreme Court's affirmation of the *United States v. Washington* decision, public opinion regarding treaty rights grew generally more sympathetic to Indians.[133] Even in these circumstances, Carpenter insisted that the tribe proceed with caution when it came to commemorating Leschi. She noted at least two prior attempts to pardon Leschi by individuals who had neither the knowledge nor the authority to do so. "One gentleman from the fisheries came to us and suggested we clear his name," Carpenter recalled. The other was an older woman, a direct descendant of Leschi, who had apparently been influenced by a reporter to demand a pardon. Carpenter was suspicious not only because the woman seemed to take a reporter's advice, but also because the woman knew little about her lineage except that she could trace it back to the tribal icon.[134] Carpenter opposed both initiatives because she believed a pardon would only maintain the notion that Leschi was guilty of murder.[135] Carpenter identified "outsiders" as problematic because they did not know their history. If they understood the stakes involved, Carpenter implied, these individuals would have wanted more than a pardon for Leschi.

The process that culminated in the Historical Court had to be initiated by someone who carried a sense of responsibility for continuing the Leschi message. In 2001, Sherman Leschi, the last of Leschi's descendants on the Nisqually reservation, told Cynthia Iyall to "take care of Leschi."[136] Iyall held meetings at the Nisqually reservation to make sure that she had the blessing of the tribe to take action, since, as Carpenter put it, "Leschi belongs to all of us."[137] Iyall and Carpenter then chose the "outsiders" who could support their effort to exonerate Leschi. At the state museum in Tacoma, curators were developing an exhibition on Washington treaties, and the museum director offered to host the exoneration in the auditorium as an appropriate accompaniment to the exhibit.[138] The sesquicentennial of the 1854 Medicine Creek Treaty was an important factor for Carpenter and Iyall's goal of building collaborative relationships and securing non-Indian support for the retrial.

The Historical Court provided another moment, like many over the previous century, in which Native people talked about Leschi in relation to the tribe's past struggles and future hopes. In the months before the exoneration, Iyall reflected on the different ways non-Indians and Nisquallies thought about Leschi and experienced the impact of his death. In February 2004, she told a journalist that public audiences and judges "have gotten past the emotion of the moment, and can look at it in a factual, historical way."[139] However, Nisqually elders remained deeply affected by Leschi's story: "You could see the pain in their faces. You could see the anger," she told one reporter.[140] In the Historical Court, Puyallup tribal representative

Connie McCloud testified about Leschi in terms of Puget Sound tribes' shared hardships and resilience:

> Hundreds of people gathered to witness what happened at the time of his murder. Our chiefs understood that this was going to be a time of great change and a time that would affect our people on into the future. Our people have suffered generation after generations of multiple trauma and wounds. . . . By law we could [once] no longer speak our traditional languages [because of] the forced removal of our children to boarding schools when we were moved to reservations. . . . We look to that leadership and understand that today we have the opportunity to continue by law our own traditional practices . . . to be able to practice our own traditional religion. . . . We can speak in our own language. . . . What has happened to us in this 150 years has allowed us to continue to be here today, to witness.

Although McCloud did not claim Leschi—Carpenter in particular thought it improper for Puyallups to do so—she did link the 1850s leaders' example to the peoples' cultural revitalization following years of struggle.[141] This was also a discursive collapsing of time in which McCloud implored the audience to see the survival of Indian people and their traditions as confirmation of the treaty period leadership at work in the present.

Likewise, Billy Frank Jr. provided a distilled political history of the tribe but placed Leschi at its center: "The reason that Leschi walked away [from the treaty] was because again the people of this country represented by the United States broke another word. They tried to move us [from the prairie]." If Leschi had been alive during the Pierce County condemnation proceedings, Frank asserted, "he would have fought for that land like we did at that time." The same was true of the fishing rights battle. Frank characterized the tribe's political tactics as inspired by Leschi but shaped by the vacillations of Indian policy: "If you back us into a corner, we will fight [by] whatever means we have. We use the news media. We use our people. We use our neighbors. We do whatever we have to do. We use the justice of our country, because we stand on that justice and on that Constitution of our country. That's been proven." Frank went on to say that he welcomed the new century because the courts now protected the open expression of Indian ways and there was hope that the treaties would only get stronger. It is telling that in the course of defining Nisqually self-determination for the audience, Frank invoked the tribe's history and Leschi's example. It is this combination that characterizes the "Leschi message" as crafted by Nisquallies over the course of the century.

Maintaining control over the use of Leschi's message was a part of each significant Nisqually treaty rights battle in the twentieth century. Ironically, even when Nisquallies lost interpretive power over public memorials to Leschi, they could appropriate non-Indian productions as part of the Leschi message. The Lakewood memorial, for instance, was churned into Nisqually historical memory-making in more private ways. Cynthia Iyall first visited the memorial with Sherman Leschi shortly before he died to discuss the work to be done.[142] On the witness stand in the Historical Court, Frank recalled visiting the site of the hanging with his father and listening there to stories about Leschi. As an adult, he made regular visits to the Lakewood memorial as an occasion to educate younger Nisquallies. "We teach about our leader being hung by this society," Frank explained, but he also added, "I don't think the Steilacoom people are proud to be a part of that hanging, from what they tell me." He saw hope for future cooperation in the conciliatory message of the memorial. Reaching out to others, building collaborations, working together, arbitrating—according to Frank, this approach to dealing with non-Indians was now the best way to protect Nisqually ways, and that is the Leschi message.

CHAPTER 5 **Performing Justice**

On December 10, 2004, the basement auditorium of the Washington State Historical Society took on the theatrical accoutrements of a courtroom. The judges, witnesses, and lawyers played their parts in appropriate dress. A panel of seven robed judges sat at the makeshift bench, and the legal teams for the petitioners and the respondents sat at tables. Some witnesses sported suit jackets, while others wore formal Coast Salish regalia. The auditorium space was clearly demarcated by legal authority. The judges' bench stood at the center, the lawyers' desks were off to the sides, the witness podium jutted out from the bench, and the public audience filled the auditorium to the back walls. The participants went through all the motions appropriate to and expected of a court setting: the witnesses were sworn in en masse, the justices and legal counsel used specialized language, and a support cast of court officials and videographers told people where to sit and when to speak. The Historical Court represented a performance of legality, even if the court's ruling carried no legal significance.

Legality permeates American life, so it is not surprising that Leschi's story was framed as a legal problem suited for a courtroom. The performances in the Historical Court reflected both the pervasiveness of legality in American culture and the way people understand themselves and their rights in a liberal democracy.[1] When the Nisqually petitioners performed in the court, they affirmed the authority of the American courtroom in order to demonstrate how that authority could be directed toward Natives' interests. Lawyers and judges also performed legality in order to affirm Western law as an inherently just institution.[2] Native peoples and legal professionals invoked the law and affirmed state power in pursuit of different goals. Even though the court's findings would be symbolic, the judges' decision gained legitimacy in the eyes of Indians and non-Indians alike by playing on popular associations between courtroom space and ideals of truth, fairness, and authority. This performance of legality had poten-

FIGURE 11 Panel of judges listening to testimony in the Historical Court, 2004. Left to right: Karen Seinfeld, Susan Owens, Gerry Alexander, Ronald Cox, Daniel Berschauer, and Theresa Pouley (not pictured: Donald Thompson). (Washington State Historical Society)

tial for a radical *redefinition*: the historical record could point to Leschi's innocence rather than guilt; the courts could be revealed as fallible institutions that have supported white privilege; and Indians' historical rights claims could be shown as righteous and legitimate rather than dismissed as anachronistic appeals for "special" rights. However, this potential for change was stymied by the orientation and procedural restraints of the court. Law draws its legitimacy from so-called universal principles of fairness and equality, which could not be challenged without endangering the court's authority.

The Historical Court was not exactly what the Nisqually petitioners had envisioned when they began the process of seeking Leschi's exoneration. At first the Committee to Exonerate Chief Leschi had reasoned that the judicial model was an apt answer to its specific complaint that Leschi had been wrongly convicted. But, as the previous chapters have shown, Nisquallies had long engaged with American courts and the outcome had not always been what they wanted. In this case, by settling for a symbolic court, the petitioners acquiesced to some of the limits and exclusions of

U.S. law. Even so, the Nisqually petitioners accepted that a symbolic exoneration amounted to a public acknowledgment that the territorial court had made a mistake. It was at least a step toward their vision of justice.[3] As Cecelia Carpenter reflected on the Historical Court in 2007, "A lot was left undone," but the important thing was that "we got Leschi exonerated."[4] The petitioners adjusted their goals to what they could realistically achieve, but they were forced to abandon some of the court's radical potential for redefinition in the process.

The State of Washington, represented by supreme court justices and legislators, supported the liberal tenets of equality by reexamining Leschi's murder case and offering an apology. They did not, however, address one of the issues that allowed for Leschi's conviction in the first place: legal decisions that maintain and justify U.S. power to dispossess others by blurring national interest with universal liberal values. To address a systematic legal failing would have meant acknowledging that the government of the State of Washington does not have the authority to arbitrate in Indian affairs, that the United States has failed to recognize and act according to international laws of war, and that the United States created its own legal authority to justify the dispossession of Native land.[5] The petitioners certainly understood the limits of what they could accomplish in this context. Dorian Sanchez added at the end of his testimony: "I cannot express my feelings toward Leschi, [nor] of all the Indians of the past who have suffered injustice in white courts." The courtroom was invoked for its legal symbolism, its power to define justice, and its ability to exhibit legal authority, but it also reserved authority in the same system that legally justified Leschi's conviction and rendered an official (that is, actual) exoneration impossible.

For indigenous people in the United States, courts represent both a powerful colonial technology of dispossession and a promising liberal institution capable of protecting treaty rights and affirming self-determination. Scholars of legal history and aboriginal land claims have pointed out that legality has a malleable quality that renders it open to appropriation.[6] Law in settler societies was and continues to be an instrument of colonization, but indigenous peoples have long contested and shaped legality in local places and used legal practice for decolonization in claims cases.[7] The Historical Court offers insight into this seemingly paradoxical problem for indigenous people in a colonial context: Nisqually people used the symbolic court as a means of redress for what they believed to be an injustice perpetrated by a real court. This chapter situates the Historical Court within legal discourse and performance in order to assess both its radical potential and its conservative undercurrents. Legal performance allowed the petitioners to make a claim for Nisqually sovereignty, but the unofficial nature of the court also worked against an expansion of rights through which sovereignty could be exercised.

Choosing the Court

The tortuous negotiations that went into the creation of the Historical Court reveal Americans' deep faith in the liberal institution as well as ambivalence (among non-Indians and Natives alike) about how indigenous peoples' historical claims might fit within or challenge the law. Cynthia Iyall encountered understandably mixed feelings when she first introduced the idea of legal redress for Leschi in tribal council meetings in 2002. "People on the tribal side knew that [Leschi] never should have been tried in the first place," Iyall recalled, but some members resisted her plan because "people don't trust the courts."[8] The courts had not consistently protected Nisqually treaty rights and expressions of tribal cultural identity. But perhaps Leschi, as a single individual involved in a discrete legal case, would fare better in court. Following six months of council meetings and discussions with tribal elders, Iyall came to the conclusion that a legal route was the appropriate one and received tribal council endorsement.[9]

Soon afterward, Cynthia Iyall, Cecelia Carpenter, and Melissa Parr organized as the Committee to Exonerate Chief Leschi with three main goals: judicial exoneration, a correction of the historical record, and an apology from the State of Washington to the people of Chief Leschi.[10] The second and third goals, which are political in nature, turned out to be relatively quick to attain because of the supportive political climate in Washington in the early 2000s. The first goal, which is legal, was more difficult because of the bureaucratic and technical rules that make change more difficult.

Native nations must make claims against the United States from a less powerful position, so they may resort to "soft power" mechanisms and moral arguments that stir the conscience and evoke sympathy. This tactic gains purchase in human rights systems and political gestures like state apologies, but questions of morality are more complicated when it comes to positive law and the common law tradition. We often think of positive law—that is, law originating from human practice as opposed to natural law originating from God—as a coherent system of enduring principles and procedures designed to limit the influence of social, political, and emotional concerns in legal decisions. In the United States, the common law judicial task is to both reflect society's moral norms and bring underlying principles to light while mitigating exceptions and anomalies.[11] Most Americans understand the system to be fair if everyone respects the procedural safeguards built into law, which ideally lead to equal treatment for all members of society.[12] Law in large part gains its legitimacy from the perception that it is rational, above the chaos of politics and passions.[13] This legitimacy is precisely what made exoneration for Leschi appealing to the committee and precisely what made it difficult for them to access.

The committee members were not legal professionals, but they felt confident in the existing evidence and the righteousness of their cause. For this reason, Carpenter insisted the group seek out a legal reversal of Leschi's conviction in federal or state court rather than settle for a political solution like a pardon.[14] In consultation with lawyers, the committee found that their greatest challenge would be the law itself because of the procedural issues their case presented. The witnesses and defendant were long dead, the window for timely appeals had passed, the evidence was questionable because the court transcript from Leschi's first trial had been destroyed, and an unknown amount of other evidence had been lost over time. Even the legal body that decided Leschi's case was gone—the territorial court ceased to exist when Washington became a state in 1889.[15] The case presented challenges, to be sure, but they decided to move forward nevertheless.

The committee members weighed their options for an appropriate venue. Federal court represented the logical choice for two reasons: tribal leaders and lawyers insisted the Nisqually Tribe negotiate in a nation-to-nation relationship with the United States to emphasize its sovereign status and because the territorial court that convicted Leschi was a federal entity. The committee and its legal counsel soon realized, however, that the cost and time required to prepare a case for federal court and lobby for its importance was daunting and possibly prohibitively expensive.[16] It was a small tribe with limited resources, and the Nisquallies and their legal counsel recognized that the price of federal court was simply too high. State court seemed the next place to turn. One important ally, Pierce County executive John Ladenburg, urged the group to keep the matter local, arguing that people living in the region bore the responsibility for correcting the injustice against Leschi.[17] Although the territorial court that convicted Leschi was a federal entity, Washingtonians trace their state and local histories to the territorial era. Leschi's case was tied to the state by memory and place, not jurisdiction.

The committee's legal counsel noted with hope that the Washington State Supreme Court seemed prepared to address social issues of historical concern. In 2001, the court responded to a petition from the University of Washington law school and the state bar association to revisit the case of Takuji Yamashita, a Japanese man barred from practicing law in Washington in 1902 on account of his race. The supreme court posthumously admitted Yamashita to the bar, and Chief Justice Gerry Alexander stated that it was "important to symbolically right this wrong."[18] According to Robert Anderson, a University of Washington law professor who offered legal advice to the committee, Leschi's court proceeding was modeled on Yamashita's case.[19]

The committee did not initially appeal directly to the State Supreme Court, however. Instead, they chose to build political will for their cause. In September 2003, the committee began to reach out to state legislators, lawyers, and journalists to pursue an apology and correction of the record.[20] The committee and its legal counsel found that the process progressed quickly at the local level with the help of powerful and well-placed allies.[21] Iyall took a resolution drafted by the tribe's lawyers to her state senator, Democrat Marilyn Rasmussen of Eatonville, who, much to Iyall's surprise, was a self-declared "Leschi fan."[22] She agreed with Iyall that the state legislature should initiate discussion about Leschi, but it was ultimately up to the judicial branch to find a resolution to the historical matter. "We really need to have the records expunged and have the issue brought up before the Supreme Court," Rasmussen told the *Seattle Post-Intelligencer*. "We're talking about history and righting a wrong. It would have been easier to make a resolution, but that wouldn't have changed history."[23]

Rasmussen's comment suggests that although the legislature had to take responsibility for the institution's past role in Leschi's execution, only a court decision could "change history." But how does expunging the record change history any more than an apology or resolution? Leschi cannot be brought back from the dead, and the fact of his conviction could not be wiped from the minds of generations of Washingtonians. Leschi's conviction was reported for over a century in thousands of history books. Collecting and reprinting them all would be out of the question. Rasmussen assumed that expunging the record would address its *effect* in the present. Of course concrete legislative actions—fully within the legislature's power—could also address Nisquallies' present circumstances. But Rasmussen's statement sent the message that the courts were endowed with the special authority (and responsibility) to address Leschi's case. Within this appeal to legality we can see how and why soft power moral demands and human rights claims that fall outside of common law nevertheless turn to judicial formats and procedures for resolution. As legal historian Christopher Tomlins explains, "in situations of extreme fluidity" in American history, people looked to legality to structure a new social order and then relied upon law's institutional technology to give the order real effect.[24] As state representatives began to venture into the uncertainty of revising and reckoning with the past, legality seemed to offer a roadmap, and the courts a mechanism, for changing history and creating a more just society.

Rasmussen agreed to present Iyall's resolution before the Judicial Committee and get the process started in time for the next legislative term.[25] The first Senate Joint Memorial, read in February 2004 after some revisions in committee, laid out the historical events based on Carpenter's records, characterized Leschi's trials and execution as an injustice, and urged school districts throughout the state to adopt history texts that "accurately and fairly" presented Leschi's life and conviction.[26] The memorialists acknowledged the legislative body's role in Leschi's case—the territorial legislature ordered the supreme court to schedule Leschi's execution—and therefore concluded: "like Takuji Yamashita, Chief Leschi was the victim of discrimination . . . being executed because he was non-Caucasian." The memorial recounted what amounted to legal errors in Leschi's case and encouraged the state courts to also take responsibility: "Your memorialists respectfully pray that the Supreme Court of the State of Washington use its inherent power of providing justice to vacate the conviction of Chief Leschi and depublish the record in his case. . . . Your memorialists further pray that . . . the commitment to a legal system under which a fair trial is the right of everyone regardless of race or creed be reaffirmed."[27] The memorial challenged the Washington State Supreme Court to use its "inherent authority" to live up to its liberal principles.

The resolution reflected a relatively recent sympathy for Indians, which was connected to urban northwesterners' environmental and social concerns. In the Tacoma area, several non-Indian writers had taken Leschi as their heroic subject, including one popular 1960 poem that reimagined Leschi's execution as a poignant warning to non-Indians about the dangers of racism, capitalism, and environmental degradation.[28] Throughout the "fish-ins" of the late 1960s and early 1970s, Native people of the region appealed to and received a great deal of public sympathy in urban areas. In

Seattle, churches, civil rights organizations, and other groups were crucial in garnering wider support for fishing rights. The ruling in *United States v. Washington* was lauded around Puget Sound (with the notable and vocal exception of commercial and sport fishermen and in rural areas) as both a human rights and a conservation victory. Non-Indian sympathy for the region's Native people grew in the decades following the court decision. In the 1980s, Seattle-area churches issued a formal apology for acts of cultural genocide and religious oppression against Native people and conservation groups praised tribal environmental stewardship.[29] This public sympathy should not be overstated and can be countered by examples of anti-Indian vitriol. For example, in 1978 one congressional representative from Washington introduced a bill to allow the president to unilaterally abrogate treaties with Indians and to terminate the trust relationship between the federal government and tribes. In 1984, non-Indian organizations placed an initiative on the election ballot to end treaty rights, which passed.[30] Nevertheless, the tide slowly shifted. In the thirty years leading up to the Senate memorial for Leschi, Billy Frank Jr. worked to foster cooperative relationships with regional and local officials, organizations, and publics and build a positive reputation for tribes. The Nisqually Tribe, and especially Billy Frank Jr., gained national recognition for salmon restoration and natural resource management efforts in a state particularly concerned about environmental issues.[31] The exoneration committee and its counsel pursued a strategy of fostering local political will because the progressive culture in urban western Washington in the early 2000s offered such promise.[32]

The committee's efforts may have also benefited from a regional sympathy for warriors. South Puget Sound is home to a sizable military population stationed at Joint Base Lewis-McChord. In 2003, the United States entered into war in Iraq, and many soldiers trained on the base deployed that year. American soldiers and veterans may have recognized themselves and their concerns in the resolution for Leschi, which pledged public support to a principled warrior who fought to defend his people. The deployments in the region in 2003 and 2004 created a swell of patriotism around what President George W. Bush described as the U.S. military effort to "make [Iraq's] people free."[33] Legal scholar Roy Brooks argues that "the most significant advancements in racial progress have come during times of major war," which set the stage for a "moral apology" for historic inequalities. In times of war, patriotism is strengthened by claims to loving one's country because it is virtuous. Making amends for past national injustices means recovering a measure of moral capital and shoring up the domestic perception of a shared sense of human rights.[34] Perhaps the local deployments and news reports from around the world helped to convince legislators to support a memorial that celebrated the warrior ideal and the liberal democratic principles that set the United States apart from other governing regimes.

The legislative resolution also reflected a decade-old national trend toward multiculturalism—that is, policies that seek to accommodate group differences and maintain social cohesion in a culturally diverse democracy. Classical liberal thought supports the view that all individuals (but not necessarily all cultures) are equal and as such are deserving of equal consideration and respect. Those who support this view argue that to treat people equally is to treat them the same.[35] The Washington resolution affirmed that the court—as a liberal institution—should endeavor to treat Leschi (as an individual member of a minority group) equally under the law. In doing so, the state could return to the ideal of neutrality—recognizing no inherent moral differences among individuals. But the memorial also asked that the state courts take specific action for the Nisqually petitioners, which supports multiculturalists' belief that treating members of minority groups with equal consideration will sometimes mean accommodating differences. The memorial supported the view that, in Leschi's case, the courts had violated the principle of neutrality by favoring one segment of society in 1857. Positive action, such as rewriting state history texts, should be taken to ensure that racial minorities would not be treated unequally in the future as a result.[36]

Even multiculturalists' efforts to dislodge Euro-American ethnocentrism, however, may reaffirm American liberal ideology to the exclusion of other ways of knowing. By drawing a parallel with the Yamashita case, the resolution ignored the political and historical elements specific to indigenous claims. Non-Indians may see race as an explanation for inequality in society, but Native peoples do not describe themselves and their histories exclusively through this language.[37] Furthermore, settlers might have invoked the concept of race in order to claim land belonging to Native peoples, but focusing solely on settlers' ideological rationales obscures the political act of dispossession at work.[38] While the legislature's resolution acknowledged that Leschi had been a leader of the Nisqually people and party to the Medicine Creek Treaty, the authors interpreted the injustice as bias against an individual based on race or creed, not in terms of his political status or his specific resistance to land loss.

The resolution can also be understood in an international law context as one of numerous recent initiatives to adopt the discourse of human rights by expressing sympathy for Leschi, describing him as a victim, and affirming the universal right to a fair trial. Critics note the purposefully constructed apolitical posture of human rights discourse, which centers on pain and suffering rather than a more comprehensive political discourse such as self-determination and redistribution.[39] The memorial's wording reflects this concern for apolitical posturing by focusing on morality. In this case, the state took on moral responsibilities for correct behavior usually attributed to individuals. The Washington legislature made a public pronouncement of regret and atonement in a process of moral self-definition.[40] By declaring the state's sympathy for Leschi and regret for a predecessor's discrimination against a member of a minority group, the legislature announced the state's redemption—or at least the legislature's. The resolution framed Leschi's story in the human rights discourse that permeates the international realm and encouraged the Washington Supreme Court to similarly act as a moral entity to redeem itself.

But just because the legislature was prepared to promote multiculturalism and human rights discourse did not mean the Washington Supreme Court was poised to follow. After all, the legislature did not have the authority to determine which case the court should address and how the judges should rule.[41] Two resolutions by the House and Senate followed the memorial, but the Senate Rules Committee wrestled over wording that the court might find objectionable. The final resolutions in March 2004 removed reference to the Yamashita case and wording directing the court toward a particular finding, only expressing "hope that the Nisqually Tribe is successful in its efforts to right a gross injustice" in the Washington Supreme Court.[42] Although the joint session of the legislature recessed before a final vote could pass the resolution, the political will was on the committee's side, and it considered the resolution a success.[43] The legislature's request for judicial review of a long-closed case was unprecedented. "I haven't seen anything like this," Chief Justice Alexander told a reporter in response to news of the joint resolution.[44] This legislative victory meant the Committee to Exonerate Chief Leschi had reached two of its goals: an apology and a plan to revise school history books. "It's a huge victory and a great start to getting this completed," Iyall told a reporter for the *Tacoma News-Tribune*.[45] The resolution represented an official ratification of a new historical narrative. Beyond the immediate significance to the committee's three-part goal, the resolution offered a larger public affirmation of the righteousness of indigenous rights claims.[46]

Legal Rules and Procedural Restraints

The Committee to Exonerate Chief Leschi held firm to its faith in the authority of law to change history. It and state legislators continued to press the Washington Supreme Court to take action. In March 2004, several legislators sent a letter to Chief Justice Alexander formally requesting that the court examine the circumstances of Leschi's case and, if the case fell within its jurisdiction, to "vacate the conviction of Chief Leschi and depublish the record in his case."[47] The legislators hoped that the court, through its rigid structures and procedures, could "order" historical memory and therefore address one of the impacts of colonialism in the present.[48] The same tool settlers used to bring "rationality" to South Puget Sound during Washington's territorial period could also help indigenous people advance claims in new political terrain in the twenty-first century.

The justices of the Washington Supreme Court did not necessarily appreciate the committee's and legislators' assertions about legality, however. Alexander found the directive from the legislature to be inappropriate and a violation of the state's separation of powers. Alexander responded that the court was willing to review any petition filed directly by a party to the litigation, but had received no such petition, and the joint resolution hardly counted as such. As an elected judge, Alexander would open himself to charges of judicial activism if he convened a special court or made an exception—possibly for political reasons—rather than simply responded to petitions brought directly before him by aggrieved parties with standing.[49] In an effort to maintain a sense of fairness and because his authority would not be recognized otherwise, Alexander insisted on respecting the procedural constraints applicable to all citizens.

In addition to the unprecedented origin of the request, Alexander found serious legal issues with the case. First was the question of jurisdiction, which had not been an issue in the Yamashita case. The Congressional Enabling Act, which had created the State of Washington in 1889, provided that only cases still active could be reopened by the State Supreme Court.[50] Cases like Leschi's that had been finally adjudicated years earlier presumably could not. The record from the territorial period was legally untouchable. Congress wiped the slate clean with statehood even though the territorial court's decisions would continue to be published. Alexander also noted that the court would need petitioners with legal standing to seek relief in a proceeding in which the defendant was deceased. Alexander had not yet received a petition and was not at all sure who the respondent should be. The state? The courts? Proxies for the 1857 judges? The question of respondent was crucial, Alexander explained, "since a hallmark of American jurisprudence is that the truth is best ascertained when a case is presented to the court in an adversarial setting." Clearly, Alexander was not interested in convening a show trial in which the outcome was predetermined, as the legislature seemed to expect. No matter the political momentum behind it, Alexander insisted that an official decision was not possible.[51]

Cynthia Iyall then stepped forward to negotiate directly with the court. A week after Alexander's response, she requested a meeting between the court justices and the Committee to Exonerate Chief Leschi.[52] After some discussion among the justices, only Alexander and Susan Owens decided to meet with Iyall and pursue possible action for Leschi. In the meeting, Alexander repeated his resistance to Leschi's case because of the technical issues and because he perceived that bypassing legal structures or making an exception for a single case was unfair and would injure the authority of the court. Ironically, it was the court's insistence on abiding by procedural rules that made the court attractive to Leschi's descendants in the first place. Alexander's conservative stance accomplished more than protecting the integrity of the legal system or the justices' positions of authority, however. Alexander's insistence on procedural rules meant he could avoid publicly criticizing his predecessors. Yet an acknowledgment of a legal mistake was exactly what the committee wanted. Carpenter, in particular, argued against anything less than an official legal action, but the committee had come up against the limits for an indigenous historical claim in the U.S. legal system.[53]

Alternative Court

Finally the group agreed that what mattered was, in legal counselor Tina Kuckkahn's words, "justice, not law," and that a compromise could be reached outside of formal legal channels in an alternative symbolic court. This compromise separated the principle of justice (clearing Leschi's name) from its administration (actual exoneration).[54] "We began to talk about it from a completely different perspective," Kuckkahn recalled. "We knew we were creating something completely different and unprecedented and we had to talk about what that would mean."[55] Carpenter remained skeptical. Relegating the matter to a quasi-legal court stripped the case of its legal merit and departed from the committee's goal of expunging the legal record.

The committee took several months to consider the implications of a historical court weighed against the realities they faced if they continued to press the matter in state or federal courts. In July 2004, Iyall finally decided to pursue the historical court idea and began meetings with Alexander and her allies to determine the witnesses, venue, and timing.[56] It was a difficult compromise for Carpenter to accept. Nevertheless, the committee and its allies embraced the symbolic court as an opportunity. Nisqually legal counsel Thor Hoyte recalled two years afterward that the most important hurdle to exoneration was getting Alexander to agree to pursue the case. Once that happened, the group was free to tell the Nisqually side of the story.[57] Kuckkahn explained that because the group was not bound by official rules, they had the freedom to determine who could contribute to and adjudicate the case.[58] That a historical court offered a public decision without the expensive, time-consuming, and potentially harmful outcomes of federal litigation for the tribe added to its appeal.

The creation of the Historical Court reveals the symbolic power of law as well as the colonial and decolonizing potential of that liberal institution. Indigenous peoples' desire for change is rooted in their struggles against the persistent logic of colonialism that subjugated them and disregarded their experiences.[59] Attending to these grievances requires examining historical events and their effects, yet U.S. common law is built on technical rules that not only fail to consider the colonial force that created them but also, in some ways, reaffirm the colonial condition for indigenous people. The shifts in jurisdiction that moved Leschi's case from one district to another and from federal to state purview took place according to the growth and patterns of white settlement while indigenous people were unenfranchised. Late nineteenth-century government policies forced Nisquallies into ward status, which prevented them from making legal challenges on Leschi's case until long after the statute of limitations had expired. By the time Leschi's descendants demanded legal redress, they had to explain the basis of their legal standing to bring a claim for a deceased individual. But how could the petitioners prove harm resulting from Leschi's conviction? Such a claim could work against Nisqually interests in two ways. First, arguing for cross-generational harm comes with the danger of essentializing Nisqually people as damaged and their cultural transmission across generations—storytelling—as pathological. Second, allowing non-Indian judges to determine the definition and extent of harm opens the possibility for significant non-Indian intrusions, scrutiny, and knowledge-claims—all of which contributed to Nisquallies' suffering in the first place.[60] More than just legal technicalities obstructed an official exoneration. The history of colonialism and the disempowered status of Native petitioners in the court system also worked against their interests.

Procedural restraints simultaneously naturalized colonialism and provided the court with its authority and air of impartiality that led the committee to accept the quasi-legal format. In Alexander's formulation, the Washington Supreme Court could only maintain fairness by enforcing legal standards that precluded Leschi's descendants from receiving an actual trial. The liberal ideal of equality meant Leschi's descendants had no right to special treatment under the law. And yet the moral appeal of justice compelled two members of the court to consider a new way to address the Nisqually claim. The symbolic court would maintain the perception that courts were the source of both authority *and* justice. The decision would draw its legitimacy not from law, but from public perception of the legal authority that performances in the Historical Court helped to create.

The Nisqually petitioners' drive toward judicial redress and their eventual compromise for a symbolic court offer insight into the ironies of Native Americans' exceptional status—their "postcolonial condition." As political scientist Duncan Ivison explains, "The 'postcolonial condition' is one in which the legacy of colonialism—practically, historically and theoretically—is ever-present, even in the attempt to think beyond it."[61] Recognizing the limitations of their case, the petitioners agreed to a quasi-legal court because of the symbolic power of law. For colonized subjects, law often seems the only means at hand to resist inequality because it is a part of the technology of rule under which the conditions of inequality were created.[62] The Historical Court set a limit to the ways in which the aggrieved descendants of Leschi could define and seek justice for Leschi, but it also embodied some of the transformational potential of indigenous claims using legal discourse.

Antecedents and Models

Although the Historical Court was a novel creation shaped by local circumstances, the format borrowed from a number of antecedents. The Historical Court was not an appellate court in a state-run legal system, nor was it an open forum to express grievances like the testimony in a truth and reconciliation commission (TRC), nor did it identify a guilty party for punishment like a tribunal.[63] Although the Washington State legislature officially sanctioned the inquiry into Leschi's case in early 2004, the findings of the Historical Court would neither be legally binding nor recommend future action. But like other tribunals and courts, the Historical Court created an adversarial atmosphere to give the decision public legitimacy. Indeed, the contemporary tribunal process is part of a long indigenous tradition of judicial action. For several Maori communities, for example, their appearance before the Waitangi Tribunal in New Zealand was a reenactment of the deeds of their ancestors, who made numerous demands upon the British Crown for their treaty rights over a 150-year period.[64] Similarly, the Historical Court was built on a foundation of Nisqually engagements with U.S. courts. It also fit within a tradition of protest in the courts that maintained the legal stature of the tribe as a separate nation in relation to the U.S. and Washington State governments. The notable difference between those previous legal performances and the Historical Court was that Nisqually people could negotiate over the details and hope to present testimony that would rewrite one facet of the history of the region.

In this respect, the Historical Court also exhibited aspects of a TRC, a human rights remedy primarily concerned with collecting testimony rather than following judicial rules, entering written evidence, cross-examining witnesses, or other efforts to identify falsehood.[65] Testimony is foundational to the TRC, for it is through victim testimony that public audiences come to acknowledge and confront the undeniable truth of state-sponsored injustice and rewrite national histories. In these contexts, testimony from victims of state violence is a form of redress, in and of itself.[66] Even when reparations or other tangible amends are not possible, the ability to testify—to put into narrative a deep or generational pain before a public audience—is an important outcome, if the only one. Victims' public testimony has the potential to engender a political response by placing demands upon the audience to restore social harmony.[67]

The Committee to Exonerate Chief Leschi and its allies designed the Historical Court to allow Nisqually petitioners to speak for themselves, on their own terms. This was a different purpose from the original plan of simply gaining a legal judgment, but one made possible because of the flexible format of the symbolic court. As Carl Hultman explained, the Historical Court combined the rigid elements of a court of law with the more historical (and flexible) elements of a court of equity. The Native American representatives offered themselves as both injured parties and survivors to highlight the impact of Leschi's conviction from the unbroken past and to demand a just ruling.[68] As Chapter 3 explains, Coast Salish stories about Leschi, handed down through families, were meant by their very existence as testimony to the power of oral tradition to carry truth over time. Testimony from nonexperts was an important feature of the Historical Court as well, because judges have, at times, refused to allow oral history offered by tribal elders.[69] Furthermore, when Connie McCloud explained how South Puget Sound Native peoples had survived "generations of traumas," she gave voice to ongoing collective pain that was outside of the bounds of Leschi's narrowly defined legal case. The Historical Court planners borrowed from an international human rights discourse that emphasized testimony as truth telling and healing. This discourse is controversial among indigenous scholars, however, who warn that testimony of suffering, if not answered by a commitment to dismantle mechanisms of injustice, represents assimilation into the same liberal system that maintains colonial power.[70]

In addition to TRCs, some indigenous peoples have turned to symbolic courts as a way to voice protest by creating a public record of indigenous perspectives that show they continue to resist domination.[71] Furthermore, the court format creates a space for rights claims in a way that is acceptable and recognizable to the dominant society, which is most comfortable with legal discourse.[72] In October 1992, activists and scholars convened the International Tribunal on Indigenous Peoples and Oppressed Nations in the United States to put the U.S. government on trial for ongoing human rights abuses. The tribunal found the United States guilty of genocide and recommended that the world community condemn the federal government as an international criminal organization.[73] A year later, the People's International Tribunal convened in Hawai'i with the purposes of reaching findings of fact and conclusions of law and offering recommendations to redress grievances among the Kanaka Maoli.[74] In both cases, the decisions and recommendations were symbolic, but the main purpose was to educate the public about U.S. history and create a venue for indigenous truth claims.[75] The court model was crucial to this protest because the form of the liberal institution has such wide public recognition. Spontaneous or uncontrolled public protests may appear dangerous and draw condemnation for upsetting public order, but these tribunals create a controlled presentation of indigenous peoples' grievances that is recognizable and palatable to audiences that associate courtrooms with respect for law and order.[76]

The recent growth in tribunals suggests that indigenous peoples' calls for justice have begun to evolve from public acts of mass protest and civil disobedience (associated with the American Indian Movement in the 1960s and 1970s) into appropriations of the colonizers' legal system as a form of empowerment. The fact that symbolic courts have no legal standing or enforcement mechanism is a considerable limitation—as the Hawaiian petitioners found in 2009 when a U.S. Supreme Court ruling determined that Hawai'i's state sovereignty trumped the report's recommendations.[77] As the Committee to Exonerate Chief Leschi also discovered, political will and legislative support are important, but public sympathy did not lead to an actual court decision with legal significance.

The committee did not demand expanded rights or redress, and this was an important ingredient to its successes in 2004. As the committee gathered allies, the members focused specifically on Leschi's 1857 murder conviction so that their agenda appeared purely legal and historical rather than political. The all-female committee presented a nonthreatening appeal for justice that was a far cry from the images of militant male American Indian Movement activists. Gerry Alexander recalled that his first experience with Indian law was, as a young judge in Olympia in the 1970s, watching Indian treaty fishing rights activists stage a public display on the capitol grounds. Although he respected their right to assemble and protest, Alexander was not supportive of the politicization of an issue he believed to be legal in nature.[78] In 2003 and 2004, Iyall and Carpenter spoke publicly on the moral issues of justice and of honoring Leschi, not of political imperatives of Nisqually sovereignty. Like many female Indian activists, Iyall and Carpenter engaged in behind-the-scenes coalition building, educational initiatives, and grassroots organizing. Their approach encouraged cooperation from the legal community by appealing to a shared respect for the courtroom and human rights. The committee's strategy, which built support for multiculturalism and made an emotional appeal for the principle of justice, demonstrates savvy engagement with liberal traditions and international human rights discourse. Their approach also reveals the limits to liberalism and Americans' willingness to engage with the past. Acting according to most conventions of legality created a boundary around Leschi's case: a retrial could affirm the liberal principle of individual equality but avoid larger discussions about the roots of ongoing indigenous political claims. Legal discourse affirmed the legitimacy of American institutions, but acknowledging the violence of settler colonialism, government policies of ethnocide, and systematic denial of indigenous sovereignty questioned that legitimacy and therefore was not featured in the planning phase.

Thus, the creation of the Historical Court represented both a painful compromise and an opportunity for the indigenous petitioners—a situation that reveals an unresolved tension in liberalism. Critical legal studies scholars view the law as a mode of governance with an internal logic that supports the interests of the powerful while resolutely resisting change from within.[79] This inherent conservatism safeguards against the overt political use of the courts, even though courts often offer the most fruitful avenue for securing expanded political rights for members of minority groups. Minority groups must declare themselves a part of and invested in the very system they seek to reform. Groups and individuals victimized by the operations of a legal regime must affirm the regime's legitimate right to rule. After all, if the law had no authority, neither would symbolic court rulings such as Leschi's exoneration.

A similar paradox emerged in the Waitangi Tribunal, when New Zealand reviewed its own wrongdoing toward indigenous people. The Waitangi Tribunal report attempted to show that the state had made a mistake but could not offer redress without undercutting the state's authority on which the tribunal relied to implement its recommendations. The tribunal ultimately addressed this paradox by condemning the results of colonialism while maintaining that colonialism could have been better managed, specifically through the establishment of Maori political power to smooth the process.[80] The petitioners in the Historical Court, because of the narrow legal focus of the case, achieved neither a public condemnation of colonialism nor an expansion of Nisqually political power in the region. Instead, the petitioners' legal counsel argued that a decision to exonerate Leschi would follow the law with fidelity and support the court's true values.

Using the Law?

The petitioners' legal team recognized that the committee wished to prove Leschi's innocence but chose to make its case for exoneration based on arguments of law that made the question of Leschi's part in the alleged murder irrelevant. John Ladenburg, the petitioners' counsel, informed the petitioners that August Kautz's map could not serve as the basis for Leschi's exoneration. A legal case built solely on archival evidence would quickly falter in an adversarial environment; the respondents could easily claim that insufficient evidence remains after 150 years on which to prove or disprove its reliability. This was an astute assessment, for the respondents' counsel did make such an argument. Ladenburg thought the petitioners' case should be built primarily on a legal argument: Leschi was an enemy combatant who should not have stood trial for a killing committed during a time of war.[81] The lawyers' legal performances all but announced that questions of fact (whether Leschi did or did not kill Moses) would be subordinate to questions of law. Yet this was a necessary compromise to counter the respondents' claim and establish a convincing case for the judges.

Thus, the petitioners' legal counsel, not the committee members, articulated an argument that explicitly linked Leschi's exoneration to tribal sovereignty. Charles Wilkinson testified that the Medicine Creek Treaty acknowledged Nisqually sovereignty and thus militiaman A. B. Moses's death was the result of war between nations. Captain Eugene Ham supported Wilkinson with evidence that the army defined the fighting between Nisquallies and U.S. soldiers in 1855 as a war and considered Leschi a lawful combatant. The petitioners' case rested on the legal assumption of Nisqually nationhood and sovereign right to declare and commence war, and it thus offered a more politically urgent message than the Committee to Exonerate Chief Leschi had planned. Carpenter was convinced that the simple truth was that Leschi had not killed A. B. Moses on Connell's Prairie in 1855. She later said that tribal sovereignty played no role in her decision to press for Leschi's exoneration, yet tribal sovereignty was the basis on which the petitioners' counsel built its legal case and a major consideration in the justices' ruling.[82]

After the closing statements in the Historical Court, the panel of judges had moral, historical, and legal issues to consider: the Native American representatives testified to their knowledge of Leschi and his meaning to them; historians laid out their interpretations of events based on documentary evidence; military lawyers explained how the U.S. Army categorized Leschi at the time and today; and the legal counsel for both sides made their cases based on a defense of the rule of law. The Historical Court had partially revised the historical narrative by presenting this testimony in a public forum, but it was ultimately up to the judges to proclaim what the law (and a moral society by extension) should make of this history.

The justices in the Historical Court could determine the criteria of "fact" as well as "law" to be applied in the case. Technically, as the state's respondent counsel pointed out, the presence of what appears by today's standards to be gross injustices in Leschi's trial were in fact legal in 1857. The justices in the Historical Court therefore chose which standards of law to apply in the case, as well as the criteria for determining historical facts.[83] The judge has a privileged place within the common law conception, legal theorist Roger Cotterrell explains, because he or she "expresses the essence of the community's moral experience" by distilling it in the form of a decision that both satisfies the community's sense of justice and appears "rational, principled, and consistent."[84] To Justice Alexander, the authority of the judge to make these determinations was one of the hallmarks of an adversarial setting and an expression of the moral logic of the law itself.

The Historical Court was a space in which different ways of knowing history could be shared, but the participants did not necessarily develop a shared approach for defining truth and justice. This fact was borne out in the judges' different treatment of expert witnesses and Native American representatives. The expert witnesses fielded questions about law, the content of written records, and their interpretations of certain events. But, tellingly, the judges and the respondents' lawyers did not ask follow-up questions of the Native American representatives. When Justice Alexander declared the court's decision, he pointed to legal rules as the basis for the ruling. The judges operated in a Western legal fact-finding, truth-seeking tradition, which did not need to account for other ways of knowing. Other histories could exist in the multicultural space of the Historical Court, but they were not included within the framework of a Western legal tradition. The representatives may have presented the judges with a *moral* case for exoneration, but if the basis of the judges' decision is indicative, the legal framework was not noticeably altered as a result of the representatives' testimony. The different conceptions of history and time operating in the court challenged the quest for a single, collective sense of justice in an adversarial setting.

However, the participants productively wrestled with how these different conceptions of history and time might coexist. Unable to develop an approach to the search for legal fact that included Native ways of knowing, the judges chose not to assess Native stories according to Western rules of evidence or definitions of truth. Oftentimes, when historians and lawyers measured the veracity of Native stories by the yardstick of Western truths, these stories not surprisingly came up short. The representatives who testified were not concerned with precise facts and dates and painted idealized images of Leschi as an honored predecessor.[85] Rather than interrogating

FIGURE 12 Respondents' counsel Carl Hultman questions expert witness Alexandra Harmon as the audience and petitioners' legal team looks on (left to right: Alexandra Harmon, Connie McCloud, Tina Kuckkahn, John Ladenburg, Robert Anderson, Thor Hoyte, Bill Tobin, and Carl Hultman). (Washington State Historical Society)

these witnesses, Justice Alexander simply acknowledged them at the end of the event, saying that their contribution was "interesting" and educational for all Washingtonians. The judges made room for the Native American representatives' testimony in the tribunal but avoided categorizing or placing the testimony into a prescriptive role in the search for truth.

The reality of the judges' autonomous power became clear to the Native petitioners as they waited in anxious anticipation for the judges' decision. "You just don't know what goes on behind closed doors," Kuckkahn recalled, thinking of how Alexander had resisted the idea of exoneration at the beginning. Iyall feared that the judges would humiliate her in front of the people who had placed so much trust in her judgment: "I took a huge gamble in front of 600 tribal members to throw that back out in public again. It could have gone the other way. It wasn't a give-me."[86] The performance of law—especially the authority of the judges to determine "truth" as the Nisqually petitioners looked on—gave the event its legitimacy, but it also revealed the limits to Nisqually power. Leschi's descendants had to rely upon representatives of the state courts to recognize their predecessors' wrongdoing in order to exonerate Leschi.

When the court reconvened, Alexander announced the court's decision to symbolically exonerate Leschi. Unlike truly adversarial trials, in this case both the petitioners and the respondents applauded the verdict.[87] Although the spectators and lawyers appeared to agree with the court's conclusion, the justices' proclamation belied the compromises that made Leschi's exoneration possible. Carpenter told a journalist afterward: "It doesn't change the legal record. This was really a way for white people, for the state of Washington, to say, 'We're sorry.' I accept that. It's the best we can do."[88] It was what was possible on the terms on which the petitioners and justices could agree.

Legal performances in the court made it possible to hold a public conversation about history and a redefinition of society as compassionate and principled.[89] Carpenter's comment tellingly alludes to a different perspective on what the legal performance of the Historical Court generated. Although Ladenburg argued in his closing statement that the Historical Court held the unique authority to *give* justice *to* Leschi—"restore his good name"—Carpenter characterized the Historical Court as a way of giving "white people" and the state a way to come to terms with the past. If we consider "historical justice" as a gift to be given, Carpenter suggested that it was Leschi's descendants who gifted non-Indians with peace and healing—not the other way around. Public judicial events present a kind of ritual of confession-conversion that allows perpetrators to reveal publicly their own burden of guilt and thus be made into one of the victims.[90] In accepting the blame for Leschi's unjust conviction, "society" could free itself from what Ladenburg called the "black mark on the history of the state of Washington, on Pierce County, on Thurston County, on the legislature, the Supreme Court and the governor."[91] Carpenter read the decision and the process of confession-conversion as an apology, but she may have been wrong. Alexander gave no indication that he intended the exoneration to serve as an apology. In fact, the court decision sidestepped an assignment of guilt for the error of Leschi's conviction. Admitting that "mistakes were made" is not the same as taking responsibility, which is a vital component of apology.

The symbolic court opened an opportunity for Leschi's descendants to tell their stories and for the legal community to affirm public morality and build a teleological narrative of law moving ever closer to perfect justice. Through this legal performance, it was not Leschi—or not *only*

Leschi—who was redeemed; the American legal system won a moral victory without giving up authority. The Washington Supreme Court did not address Leschi's case in official chambers, and the territorial court's ruling remained untouched. Even though the Historical Court represented a collaborative effort among the state legislature, courts, and a federally recognized tribe, only the latter party had to compromise in pursuit of justice. For this reason, some indigenous rights scholars and activists insist that symbolic courts and tribunals demand sacrifices of Native autonomy that render these forums not only ineffectual but also self-defeating. Gerald Taiaiake Alfred insists that "it is impossible either to transform the colonial society from within colonial institutions or to achieve justice and peaceful coexistence without fundamentally transforming the institutions of the colonial society themselves." According to Alfred, if Native American leaders continue to find satisfaction in symbolic gestures, they participate in their own assimilation.[92] Certainly, Nisqually tribal leaders insist on self-determination, but what choice does a small tribe have to press claims if state institutions are not compelled to transform from within? As tribal attorney Thor Hoyte said afterward, the Committee to Exonerate Chief Leschi did not choose a symbolic over an official court or state over federal court; they chose the only opportunity to approximate justice available to them.[93] It was a much better solution than doing nothing at all.

Though the exoneration did not change the legal record, the testimony in the Historical Court was not insignificant.[94] Symbolic acts that press the state to reassess public morality and discuss the nature of human rights can have important consequences. Committee member Melissa Parr reflected later: "People will be thinking and writing about social justice because of what we did. I was honored to be a part of it."[95] Over time, symbolic actions can influence public thought and morality. That the Historical Court came about at all illustrates the ways Nisqually petitioners had to compromise in their quest for justice but also shows the ways Native activists adapt the tools of the colonizer for their own benefit. The multivalent language of law in settler colonial contexts illustrates the flexible nature of legal discourse in equal measure to its built-in resistance to change.[96] The Historical Court revealed the opportunities and limitations facing indigenous people seeking redress without assimilation and historical revision without political capitulation.

CHAPTER 6 **Haunting**

"You know how certain things go on in life and you kind of know that they happened, but it's still sort of untouched?" asked Peggy McCloud, a teacher and cultural programs coordinator at Chief Leschi Elementary School, when I interviewed her in 2007. "It's kind of like the unspoken topic," she continued, "like the white elephant in the room." The topic McCloud was referring to was not Leschi's case, but rather his brother Quiemuth's.[1] As she discussed the impact of the Historical Court on the students and the school's curriculum, she noted Quiemuth's absence in the court proceedings. "I can't believe [it] wasn't brought up," she mused, considering how much the elders talk about him. She concluded, "I think at the state level they haven't really acknowledged that he was killed."[2] What McCloud described was a "haunting," a particular way of knowing what has happened even as it appears not to be there at all. The ghost of Quiemuth was at the center of the unsettling negotiation between what was known about the past and what was acknowledged in the Historical Court.[3]

U.S. citizens killed both brothers after the war—territorial officials hanged Leschi in 1858 and anonymous vigilantes shot and stabbed Quiemuth in 1856—yet Leschi's fame grew over the next century, culminating in his symbolic exoneration, while his older brother nearly disappeared from popular memory and history. As McCloud insisted, Nisqually and Puyallup elders continue to remember Quiemuth and consider ways to seek restitution on his behalf.[4] But unlike Leschi, Quiemuth was never tried and convicted. The Historical Court could review and assess due process in Leschi's 1857 trial and, in so doing, acknowledge Leschi's conviction and execution to be mistakes. But Quiemuth's death took place outside of the courts and the light of day, in predawn darkness that concealed the killers' identities. His assassination was extralegal and embarrassing; his death challenged most celebratory narratives of pioneer honor, the in-

FIGURE 13 Portrait of Quiemuth sketched by unknown artist, n.d. (Washington State Historical Society)

herent justice of legal institutions, and the inevitability of a state-centered legal order. Leschi's case demonstrated that the state (that is, U.S. and territorial officials) controlled the characterization of violence on the "frontier." But Quiemuth's story illuminates the messy and contested shift from legal pluralism and syncretism to state-centered law in territorial Washington.[5] In the Historical Court, Leschi's exoneration depended upon the legitimacy, dominance, and universality of the U.S. legal order, but the context of Quiemuth's death threw these notions into doubt. Quiemuth's story directs attention to the hauntings that are dismissed, the historical understandings that are avoided, and the deeply imbedded pain that is ignored by locating "historical justice" in due process.

Leschi's 1850s trials and his 2004 exoneration were marked by a heavy emphasis on due process.[6] And yet, the transformation from a plural legal order to one dominated by the state was highly contested. Residents of South Puget Sound did not agree on the legitimacy of federal law or the notion of due process on which it rested. To some settlers, territorial law represented a corrupt and unwanted incursion into local affairs. Territorial officials, however, hoped to validate the state-centered legal order through the trials of Indian leaders. Leschi's was one of several postwar murder trials of Indian leaders and the only one to end in execution.[7] Historian Brad Asher notes that Washington's territorial courts acquitted Indian defendants at relatively high rates, and Leschi stands out as a notable exception.⁸ Some settlers saw the acquittals of Indian defendants as damaging to the project of settler colonialism in South Puget Sound, and rejected the authority of federal institutions. Indigenous people, meanwhile, attempted to fit the new legal order into their own framework and variously pushed against and engaged with U.S. legal institutions. Imperial powers across the world in the mid-nineteenth century experienced similar jurisdictional jockeying and disputes in the process of instituting state law in colonial settings. The shift from legal plurality to state legal hegemony ultimately came about because of the uncertain legal standing of the colony's marginalized indigenous population.⁹ Both Leschi and Quiemuth played roles in this transformation in Washington in the 1850s. In 2004, Leschi's exoneration supported the legitimacy of state-centered legal order, and Quiemuth's absence obscured the judicial uncertainty that came before.

By acknowledging hauntings in the historical record and Historical Court, we can see how some notions of law and justice come to dominate others. That due process and the legitimacy of federal courts were matters of debate in the 1850s was not mentioned in the Historical Court. Indeed, the 2004 court took for granted that territorial law was simply applied to Leschi and did not consider that it was constituted through Leschi's case. After his death, memories of Leschi's legal drama, shored up by the power of legal discourse, obscured the existence of Native law and the conflicts over legal plurality in the territory. Historian Sidney Harring details how "U.S. legal institutions attempted to bury tribal law" and largely succeeded after the 1880s.¹⁰ State officials and institutions not only dominated other types of law but also cultivated authority to set rules that redirected debate away from plurality and fairness in colonial settings and toward due process.¹¹ The Historical Court focused on due process and jurisdiction, not on the contested nature of law in the 1850s and the potential for legal pluralism today.

The Historical Court illustrates the power of legal discourse to simultaneously invoke and ignore the contests that create law, to acknowledge some kinds of colonial violence while silencing others. Quiemuth's persistent haunting brings to the surface that which goes unspoken, illuminating a symptom of what is missing.¹² Quiemuth stands as a sign of the place of indigenous peoples in narratives of U.S. history: at once ever-present and invisible, invoked only to bring attention to absence and disappearance. And although an Indian ghost is by now a cliché in American literature—an expression of settler guilt and anxiety—Quiemuth is more than a metaphor. His life and death helped to shape events and ideas about territorial law and form part of an ongoing Native struggle for recognition, autonomy, and respect. As several scholars have shown, ghosts are political.[13] In the course of remembering Leschi, the Historical Court ignored Quiemuth. As Andreas Huyssen writes, "Inevitably, every act of memory carries with it a dimension of betrayal, forgetting, and absence."[14] Quiemuth's haunting reveals the limits to historical reckoning in a Western courtroom because due process and memory are entangled.

Quiemuth's Story

According to non-Indian friends, Leschi and Quiemuth were "inseparable." Both traded with the Hudson's Bay Company (HBC), guided American homesteaders, farmed and raised horses, and enjoyed high status among Nisqually villagers. In the last years of his life, the quieter and more reserved Quiemuth played a prominent political role in tribal history that followed the contours of his younger brother's experiences. Governor Stevens appointed Quiemuth as chief for the Medicine Creek Treaty negotiations in 1854, although Leschi may have been more vocal at the treaty council.[15] Quiemuth apparently remained on friendly terms with American officials and settlers after the treaty, and found some advantage in his social connections with the newcomers.[16] In the tense days before the war in 1855, Acting Governor Charles Mason requested that the brothers prove their peaceful intentions, and it may have been Quiemuth rather than Leschi who traveled to Olympia to reassure the governor. When Mason deployed a group of rangers to bring them to the capital, both men fled; Quiemuth reportedly dropped his plow in his field to quickly conceal his family in the nearby woods.[17] Dr. William Tolmie reflected later: "Neither Leschi nor Quyeimal [Quiemuth] would have taken up arms, unless virtually driven from their homes, as they were."[18]

Among the rangers sent to retrieve the brothers was James McAllister, a longtime Nisqually Delta settler. McAllister had maintained friendly relations with Leschi and Quiemuth, but in the fall of 1855 he contributed to an already unstable situation by reporting to Mason that Leschi was planning an attack and encouraged the governor to detain the Nisqually leader.[19] A few days after writing the letter, McAllister and a settler named Michael Connell were killed while on a reconnaissance mission to locate Leschi's and Quiemuth's camp. The only surviving witness to McAllister's death (besides the shooters) was the ranger's Indian guide, but the newspapers considered Indian testimony unreliable. Instead, the newspapers printed other rangers' panicked and contradictory reports of the attack, along with their speculations about the responsible party. The published accounts variously identified McAllister's killer as the unnamed surviving guide, Stahi, Too-a-pi-ti, or Leschi. One ranger later claimed that McAllister's son James, who was nine years old at the time, reported to Fort Steilacoom that troops under Quiemuth's command had killed his father.[20] In the war, Quiemuth stood out as an able tactician, while Leschi was the gifted orator who, settlers especially feared, would convince Native people to ally and push white settlers from the area.[21] After the war, Stevens insisted the Native leaders surrender to territorial officials; Leschi was turned over to government custody on November 12, 1856, while Quiemuth remained in hiding. Leschi would be charged for killing a specific militiaman in an ambush, but Quiemuth was not officially charged with McAllister's murder and the ranger's case never achieved legal resolution. Despite the tangle of rumors surrounding McAllister's death, or perhaps because of them, settlers exacted extralegal retribution on Quiemuth and other Indian suspects for years to come.

Although Leschi's first trial would take place within days of his capture, a posse of settlers was determined to kill Leschi even before he could enter the territorial court system. Governor Stevens's young son Hazard wrote about the scene of Leschi's imprisonment at Olympia the day after he was taken into custody: "Leschi is now at Olympia at our house.... When the people heard of his arrival they were bound to kill him. To prevent this father had him brought into the house, and then the excitement was so great that the people came near breaking into the house and hanging him."[22] After escaping the lynch mob, Leschi was secretly rushed to Steilacoom jail on November 16 for a quick trial the next day. Perhaps hoping that jail offered some measure of safety from the roving mob, Quiemuth turned himself over to Governor Stevens immediately after Leschi's trial (which had ended with a hung jury).[23] He too was sent to the governor's mansion in Olympia en route to Steilacoom to stand trial. This time, however, the governor was not able to protect the prisoner in his charge. On this November night, the fates of the brothers, as well as their places in historical memory, diverged.

On the night on November 18, 1856, three white male settlers and Betsy Edgar, Quiemuth's cousin, escorted Quiemuth to the governor's mansion as an overnight stopover.[24] Although the *Pioneer and Democrat* claimed that none of the escorts "dreamed for a moment of any danger to Quiemuth's life," the party's decision to travel under the cover of night suggests otherwise.[25] The group arrived safely and slept on the floor of Stevens's office, planning to undertake the next leg of their journey, to Steilacoom, in the morning. But sometime in the night, word got out about where Quiemuth could be found. Near five in the morning on November 19, a man burst into the governor's mansion, shot and fatally stabbed Quiemuth, and ran off into the night. His escorts later reported they were focused on Quiemuth's injuries or were impaired by the predawn darkness and did not get a look at the killer. "All was darkness," the escort H. E. Van Ogle later claimed. "We could not see who did this."[26] Another witness, James Longmire, remembered that as he awoke at the sound of the gunshot, "the lights were out," and only by the dim glow of the fire could he see Quiemuth crumpled on the floor.[27] Longmire claimed that he then ran to the door and saw "eighteen or twenty men outside the door."[28] Longmire's account suggests that the killer was only the boldest member of a posse. Van Ogle insisted that a mob of Indians had gathered outside the office to seek revenge for Quiemuth's death, but such a story is unlikely.[29] The fear Van Ogle expressed was an act of transference; the posse was not a group of vengeance-seeking Indians but most likely a mob of settlers intimidating the witnesses into silence.

Hazard Stevens later wrote of his father that "nothing that occurred during the whole war . . . caused him more regret and chagrin" than Quiemuth's murder in his office.[30] Governor Stevens immediately assumed the murder was a plot set by army general Wool to embarrass him for demanding the murder trials of Indian war leaders. Quiemuth's assassination threatened to show that Stevens had no control over the volunteers and territorial law, just as Wool charged.[31] Presumably to temper the criticism against him, Stevens demanded an investigation into the murder. The coroner's inquest found that Quiemuth had been killed by "parties unknown," but Stevens lodged a complaint against Joseph Bunting, the twenty-three-year-old son-in-law of James McAllister. Stevens and the *Pioneer and Democrat* suspected that Bunting was motivated by revenge and family honor to kill Quiemuth. After all, the McAllister family was linked to the rumor that Quiemuth had shot McAllister in the October 1855 ambush. Bunting was questioned but never charged with the murder.[32]

Joseph Bunting was freed due to lack of evidence and the investigation simply ended. A handful of later reminiscences implied that people feared social condemnation for naming the assassin. Some settlers refused to allow Quiemuth's murderer to face prosecution in a legal order they did not consider legitimate. The problem for some settlers was that the territorial courts could not be trusted to support the racial order that settlers believed ensured their safety as the minority population in the region. One witness to the murder later wrote, "We had a pretty clear idea of the murderer, but at that time suspicions were unsafe to mention, a white man's life being rarely lost in repaying the cruelty of a redskin."[33] This distrust of territorial courts persisted even though the court judgments often favored settlers over Indians. As one settler later reminisced: "It was much easier to convict and punish an Indian than it was a white man" in those days.[34]

Like so many other cases of murdered Indians, Quiemuth's death was officially considered the work of "parties unknown." His body was interred near Fort Nisqually. Leschi was buried nearby after his execution fifteen months later. Quiemuth's surviving sons, Moses and George, took the surname of Leschi in the 1890s to honor their uncle and remember his legal execution. The leaders' remains were moved together to a new cemetery on Nisqually Prairie in 1895, although the *Tacoma Ledger* reported some difficulties in locating Quiemuth's original gravesite. When the tribe lost access to the prairie cemetery in the 1918 Fort Lewis condemnation, Leschi was reinterred at a Puyallup cemetery, but the location of Quiemuth's final resting spot is unknown.[35] Quiemuth's story, name, and physical remains seemed to have vanished by the early twentieth century.

Quiemuth's life ended that November night in 1856, but he soon became a haunting presence in his brother's story. One settler vaguely recalled that Quiemuth's death "had the effect of keeping Leschi out longer than he would have remained unexecuted under other circumstances."[36] Although Quiemuth's name does not often emerge in documentary evidence from the period, his story is pivotal to understanding the focus on due process in the Historical Court and the development of the historical record more broadly. The space between Quiemuth's and Leschi's deaths—in their own time and in narratives constructed since—brings attention to historical contingency, to what *could have been* Leschi's fate, and what was forgotten because it was not. While Quiemuth's murder was an embarrassment for Stevens, Leschi's trials could prove that U.S. legal institutions dominated over legal pluralism and kept order in the territory. Leschi's legal drama stretched out for over a year and served as a battleground between Stevens's supporters and his critics. As one historian put it, "The longer [Leschi] managed to avoid the death penalty, the more significance his death seemed to acquire."[37] Leschi gained fame because settlers used his case to debate the norms of due process, but Quiemuth's assassination revealed what was at stake if due process—the bedrock of state law—failed and "frontier justice" or legal pluralism prevailed.[38] Death at the hands of the state, rather than of vigilantes, may have rescued Leschi from historical oblivion.

Contested Legal Practice

John Le Clair (Nisqually) told anthropologist Marian Smith in 1935 about the death of his grandfather, a trapper and doctor, a story that illustrates dominant South Puget Sound Native legal culture in the mid-nineteenth century. Le Clair's grandfather, a Native man from White River, married a Nisqually woman and treated his brother-in-law for an illness. When the sick man failed to improve, his brothers killed the doctor, believing him responsible for the man's condition. "His people at White River were going to fight about it," Le Clair recalled, "but the Nisqually paid them a lot of money and goods, and things were all right."[39] Le Clair's story exhibits important aspects of Native South Puget Sound legal culture. The killing was a matter between kinship groups, not a village-wide concern. The Nisqually family members killed the doctor because they believed he was using his power to harm the family.[40] That the doctor's people at White River sought payments for satisfaction in the matter showed that homicide was not necessarily considered a threat to public order—unless its effects went unanswered and a retaliatory cycle ensued.[41] Coast Salish villagers at the time, like other nineteenth-century Native societies, practiced retaliation in the form of blood revenge, although families generally frowned upon acts of retaliation.[42] This aversion to conflict explains why arbiters like Leschi enjoyed high esteem within their communities and across the region. Native people in the Puget Sound region often found ways to resolve conflicts to the satisfaction of all parties through common understandings of kinship responsibilities and gifting.[43]

From the 1830s through the 1850s, various newcomers to South Puget Sound accommodated these legal practices and thus acquiesced in legal pluralism. The traders at the HBC Puget's Sound Agricultural Company at Nisqually honored some established indigenous legal customs while maintaining some practices of their own. The British sometimes resorted to corporal punishment for infractions by Native employees, but, as Tolmie learned, punishment needed to be accompanied by payments to Native workers and gifts to village headmen to maintain good relations. Leschi and Quiemuth likewise acted as traditional arbiters while accommodating some British legal understandings of property rights. The brothers reportedly helped to capture an Indian who had injured a Hawaiian HBC employee in a dispute that began when the HBC shepherd shot the Indian man's hunting dog to protect the company's flock. This arrangement of legal plurality and accommodation worked because the British recognized their dependence upon Native labor and Nisquallies appreciated the benefits of HBC trade goods, wages, and protection from northern Indian raiders.[44]

When American settlement began in the area, the newcomers assumed their claims would be protected by U.S. law and rejected the established hybrid legal culture in theory but not necessarily in practice. American settlers in South Puget Sound were far outnumbered by HBC employees and Indians and did not challenge local practices until they had the military power to enforce their own notions of law. American officials found the first opportunity to establish a more visible military presence shortly after the United States claimed jurisdiction over the Puget Sound region in 1846. In accordance with Native legal practice ordered around kinship, a group of Snoqualmie men traveled to Fort Nisqually on May 1, 1849, to investigate a report that a Nisqually headman, Lahalet, had mistreated his Snoqualmie wife. Gunfire erupted between Nisqually and Snoqualmie family members at the fort, and one American bystander was inadvertently killed. While the fort traders knew of the history of tense relations between Snoqualmie and Nisqually families, American officials in Oregon, encouraged by panicked reports of the shooting from American settlers, interpreted this event as a concerted Indian attack on white presence.[45] Leschi and Quiemuth offered to arbitrate through a gift exchange and negotiations between high-status headmen.[46] But territorial authorities, and especially settlers, were not interested in this kind of solution. Settlers failed to understand an incident at Fort Nisqually within the plural legality of the fur trade and instead interpreted it as a threat to American security. What reportedly began as a family matter between Snoqualmies and Nisquallies turned into an opportunity for Americans to exercise public legal authority.[47]

Oregon territorial governor Joseph Lane threatened to send troops on an expedition against the shooters but in the end decided to build Fort Steilacoom to enhance the U.S. military presence in the area.[48] Initially, the American authorities offered a reward to the Snoqualmie headman if he agreed to deliver up the murderers; this policy quickly changed when officials realized that Snoqualmie slaves could be turned in as "murderers," according to Native legal practice.⁴⁹ At the new American post, territorial officials conducted their own investigation and placed six Snoqualmie Indians on trial for murdering the American man and found two guilty.⁵⁰ The first term of court held on Puget Sound, which was included within Oregon Territory's jurisdiction, convened specifically to put the Snoqualmie men on trial. Thus, from the beginning of the territorial court's operation in the region, the procedures of state-centered law were worked out through Indians. In an event unprecedented in the region, Indians watched as the territorial government publicly hanged the two Snoqualmie men.⁵¹ The American authorities thereby attempted to send a message to all Indians about the new order, but whether Native people of South Puget Sound received the intended message is doubtful.

American law operated on the principle that justice was impersonal and abstract and that the decision of the court was final, no matter whether all parties were satisfied. But two Snoqualmie men were killed for the death of one American, and the situation may have looked much like uneven retaliation to the families of the Snoqualmie men. The prompt hanging by state authority did not fit within established Native legal practice and would have been seen as an act of aggression that gave the families of the hanged men the responsibility of avenging their deaths or receiving compensation to their satisfaction.⁵² When the Nisqually headman Lahalet (who had been suspected of abusing his wife) died from an illness in the winter of 1849–50, Indians reportedly attributed his death to the vengeful power of a Snoqualmie medicine man angered by the executions of the previous fall.⁵³ U.S. authorities initially failed to understand, or chose not to see, that their actions fueled a response within local Native law rather than having the effect of cowing Indians to surrender to American will. At least in early public exercises of legal authority, U.S. officials tried to deny the existence of a Native legal order and the hybrid legal practices that had maintained peace.

After American officials became more familiar with local custom, however, they did sometimes make accommodations to Native law and recognize legal plurality. In the spring of 1856, a white settler who had lost property in the war shot and killed three Snoqualmie Indian men who had served as U.S. scouts. The government rectified the situation by paying out presents to Snoqualmie families and promising that the killer would be brought to justice.⁵⁴ Around the same time, a Steilacoom settler killed an old Indian man without cause, and the government again doled out gifts and made promises of punishment.⁵⁵ Two years later, in the summer of 1858, a lieutenant with the U.S. Army recorded the investigation of the murder of Goliah, an Indian man stabbed and robbed by a soldier. The soldier, John Crawley, was apprehended still wearing blood-stained clothes and in possession of Goliah's cash.[56] A few days into the investigation, the lieutenant reported: "The Indians are impatient about Goliah and want the matter settled. They want the Indian paid for or want the murderer hung." Crawley was questioned but soon released by the court, and Goliah's family was paid $100 for its loss.[57]

The territorial government was unwilling to punish white murderers but would respect Native legal conventions to maintain peace. This form of remediation reflected an understanding of violence as a wrong demanding compensation rather than a crime against the state. In places where state power was weak, government officials recognized that compensation helped them to maintain tenuous jurisdiction over settlers and Indians alike.[58] The fact that the killers were not punished indicated to Native people that gifting and exchange, rather than courts, was the most effective means of finding legal common ground with Americans. The legal order in the region in the 1840s and 1850s was created through dynamic negotiation; the United States did not always extend hegemonic legal authority the moment it claimed the right to do so.

Legal plurality was disconcerting to some local settlers of the region, who insisted that a legitimate government would not accommodate Indians' customs. They saw U.S. officials' compensation to victim's families as evidence of the ineffectual nature of federal authority and territorial courts. The story of Goliah and Crawley, for example, appeared in the local press under the headline "The Price of an Indian," which lampooned the principle of exchange for conflict resolution and criticized the officials' capitulation to Native law.[59] Later reminiscences ignored the clear avenues for conflict resolution at their disposal and characterized the 1850s as lawless and dangerous—a period when settlers courageously defended themselves from hostile Indians as they laid the foundations of American institutions. Ironically, many settlers sought to move their interactions with Indians outside of the jurisdiction of territorial courts because Anglophone legal culture, like that of the Coast Salish, was infused with norms of reciprocity. European natural law traditions held that retributive violence was a fundamental rule of human society. While indigenous people in territorial Washington initially appealed to the principle of reciprocity in this syncretic form, after the war and when military power shifted, settlers increasingly emphasized blood revenge to subvert federal jurisdiction.⁶⁰ While reporting Quiemuth's death and Bunting's release in November 1856, the *Pioneer and Democrat* declared it a "melancholy fact" that settlers who lost loved ones in the war would seek revenge on Indians to "enforce the old Levitical law wherever and whenever an opportunity presents itself."⁶¹ Especially after the 1855–56 war, settlers manipulated the federal government's tenuous hold on the territory by insisting upon federal support while simultaneously working against federal jurisdiction in South Puget Sound.

Some homesteaders excused violence against Indians in the same terms as vigilantism: settlers took action to maintain order in "new" American territories that lacked legitimate legal institutions.⁶² In 1892, James McAllister's daughter, Sarah Hartman, wrote an imaginative reminiscence of the circumstances surrounding Quiemuth's murder that illustrates this perspective.⁶³ She began her narrative by describing how her father was on a "peace mission" when he was ambushed and killed, effectively characterizing McAllister as innocent and Indians as treacherous. She offered gory details of where the bullets pierced her father's body and of how Connell was cut to pieces and his limbs scattered "in every direction."⁶⁴ Although her account appears to be largely fabricated, the way she imagined these events surely made for compelling reading for audiences expecting titillating tales of the "Wild West."⁶⁵

Curiously, Hartman recounted details of Quiemuth's murder in her essay although she was only four years old at the time. She claimed to remember lying in bed at the McAllister home when she heard a voice say: "I am going to kill the old dog." Another voice replied: "Kill the old dog but don't kill the young one," and a hand reached into the girl's room and removed a pistol from the nightstand. A few minutes later someone returned the pistol and whispered, "I shot the dog." The exchange suggests that certain settlers purposefully chose to kill Quiemuth and spare Leschi. While Hazard Stevens reported that his father intervened to save Leschi from the lynch mob, Hartman claimed that settlers alone determined who would live and die and thus characterized the era as one of familial governance. The story also placed the murder weapon in the McAllister home, which symbolically connected the act of vengeance to its justified location with this family. By starting her narrative with the hideous details of the rangers' deaths, Hartman excused settlers' extralegal brutality as an apt answer to unimaginably savage attacks.

Hartman's narrative celebrated pioneer conquest over both treacherous Indians and an ineffectual judiciary.⁶⁶ Hartman perceived territorial law as hostile to settlers' interests and well-being: "Those who had relatives who had been killed began to arrest the murderers, bringing them to trial. The law cleared every one but Leschi, whom they hung." Actually, settlers did not generally call for officials to arrest Indians whom they believed had killed their relatives and were more in the habit of killing first and asking questions later. "The Indians who killed father were cleared by law," Hartman hyperbolized, "but did not escape justice." To illustrate her point, Hartman claimed that Quiemuth had in fact stood trial and admitted to killing McAllister; the man's knife and gun were even produced as evidence. In her mind, the judge heard this confession but nevertheless acquitted Quiemuth. All of a sudden, Hartman claimed, "the lights were extinguished and a shot was heard. When they were relighted, Quilemuth [Quiemuth] was found shot and stabbed." At that point, legal authorities turned on the settlers: "They cleared those Indians who killed father, but they tried everyway to hang those that killed father's murderers." In her imagination, the friendly inquest into Joseph Bunting's involvement in Quiemuth's assassination took on the dimensions of a witch hunt. Although in the end only Indians died in this drama, "it was no fault of the law those Indians received their just dues."[67] The reality that settlers killed Indian men before they could stand trial was immaterial to Hartman's narrative; an Indian trial in territorial court was the same as none at all because the courts were unwilling to punish Indians.

Hartman referenced Quiemuth's death in order to demonstrate the injustice settler families suffered under the corrupt territorial courts. She used Quiemuth's imagined acquittal to argue that settlers' innate sense of fairness, rather than federal institutions, built "civilization" on the frontier. Even Ezra Meeker, the sympathetic juror in Leschi's first trial, later charged that honest settlers seemed to receive "no redress through our courts" because bribed jurymen protected the interests of the powerful.[68] Richard Slotkin describes the mythic representation of the "compleat American" as "one who defeated and freed himself from both the 'savage' of the western wilderness and the metropolitan regime of authoritarian politics and class privilege."[69]

Consequently, many settlers understood vengeance killings as "private" interactions between individuals and resisted formal legal structures that curtailed their ability to "discipline" Indians.[70] Some settlers' revenge killings enflamed rather than resolved conflicts by ignoring both Native laws that existed prior to American settlement and the syncretic legal forms that the British traders and U.S. officials had created with indigenous neighbors to ensure stability in the region.[71] There are several crucial differences between settler vigilantism and Puget Sound Native revenge killings, however. Native people recognized certain killings as justified for the protection of the family, such as killing a bad doctor or a raider in battle. Although American settlers shared the notion of justifiable homicide, not all chose to grant Native people the rights to engage in it. Non-Indians who pursued revenge killings after the war did not attempt to negotiate with the families of the Indians they identified as murderers because intimidation was part of the motivation for killings and resolving the matter to the satisfaction of all parties was not. After securing military power over Native people, some non-Indians pursued a legal double standard: Indian lawbreaking was a threat to an orderly society, while non-Indians' personal acts of vengeance were justified to defend family and white superiority.

Quiemuth's murder exemplified a campaign of terror against local Indians after the war, and although his was a high-profile assassination, it was not unique. Settlers who targeted Indians for violence excused the actions as retributive afterward. Joseph Brannon and James Lake, two militiamen whose family members were killed by Indians at the White River settlement, illustrate this point. During the war, Brannon and his company opened fire on an Indian camp and took three prisoners. Brannon claimed that the prisoners carried proof that they had been involved in the murder of settlers at White River, and they were promptly executed. Near the conclusion of the war, Brannon shot and severely wounded an Indian prisoner, Mowitch, on his way to stand trial. Lake succeeded in killing Mowitch soon afterward and claimed to know the Indian had been present at White River. Lake announced in his court defense that his actions were justified to "relieve this unhappy territory of those savages who are so engaged in the destruction of the lives and property of our citizens." Lake and Brannon intervened before Mowitch entered the territorial court system on the assumption that only settlers could be trusted to avenge the dead and secure authority over Indians. Territorial authorities did little to stop such behavior; Lake was convicted of murder but was released with a verbal reprimand, and Brannon went on to kill several more Indian men he claimed were responsible for his brother's death.[72] Settlers seemed to tolerate a few individuals' acts of terror directed toward Indians, even if the trade-off was living with paranoia and insecurity as a result. In an effort to maintain local control over Indians, some settlers entered into pacts of silence to shield white murderers from punishment while claiming to fear Indian reprisals. In 1858 the *Puget Sound Herald* cautioned settlers against the practice of loudly "boasting and threatening" to kill certain Indians because Native people notoriously spied on settlers and would spread "[unfriendly] feelings towards the whites."[73] H. E. Van Ogle, one of the witnesses to Quiemuth's assassination, insisted that the settlers did not divulge the killer's name for their own protection, since the Indians outnumbered them and would surely initiate a blood feud.[74] However, the pacts of silence were more likely instituted to keep federal authority at a distance. Authorities were in fact outnumbered by armed settlers and had to consider their own safety when they attempted to indict white men for crimes against Indians. In May 1856, Tolmie investigated the shooting death of an Indian HBC employee at Fort Nisqually known as "One-Armed John." Accompanied by female Indian witnesses and informed by the dying man's description, Tolmie went to Camp Montgomery to pick out the volunteer militiaman responsible for the deed. The witnesses pointed out the shooter, but, as the officers stood by, the soldiers leveled their guns at Tolmie and threatened to kill the witnesses. The group barely escaped with their lives, and the accused man never stood trial, thanks to the protection of his fellow militiamen.[75] Rather than serving as protection from Indian reprisals, vows of silence maintained a legal order controlled by local settlers.

Although settlers' vernacular culture may have invoked the "Levitical law" as a justification for killing, some settlers meted out revenge in a generalized rather than specific fashion. After a group of five settlers—which included both McAllister's eldest son George and his son-in-law Joseph Bunting—shot Too-a-pi-ti while serving a writ for his arrest for McAllister's death, the fact that numerous Indians had been killed in the name of a single white man did not escape notice.[76] The editor of the *Puget Sound Herald*, Charles Prosch, wrote sarcastically in 1859 about the nature of "law" in the region: "Quiemuth was killed in the Governor's office by relatives of McAllister . . . and the Indians say that George McAllister killed one-armed John on the reservation, and now the law comes in and claims Too-a-pi-ti, all for the same offence. We thus get three or four Indians for every white man." Furthermore, Prosch noted that some settlers gained power by refuting the legitimacy of due process and the decisions of the courts: "It is now pretty well established that we got the wrong Indian when we hung Leschi . . . and consequently we must eventually have the right offenders."[77] His tongue-in-cheek editorial pointed out that local authorities who prosecuted Indian warriors as criminals and revenge-seeking settlers who used the pretext of law to kill Indians colluded to create a legal farce that only prolonged the instability of the region.

Federal authorities also complained about settlers' unchecked violence against Indians because such actions limited their power in the territory. When Lieutenant August Kautz heard about Too-a-pi-ti's shooting, he declared himself "very much disgusted with these transactions" and determined to lodge complaints with the War Department in Washington, D.C.[78] Settlers' acts of violence no doubt made the army lieutenant's job of keeping the delicate peace more difficult.[79] Indian agent Wesley Gosnell, meanwhile, saw retributive killings as a serious threat to his ability to control Indians on the reservation. Gosnell noted in late 1857 that the Nisqually families on the reservation were uncooperative with his construction efforts "in consequence of ten Indians being killed, on the reservation 'by some white persons.'"[80] After the murder of One-Armed John, Gosnell requested troops to protect Nisquallies from "unprincipled white men."[81] There is no evidence that the governor sent troops or took steps to indict settlers for murdering Indians on or off the reservation at that time.

Governor Stevens was not particularly concerned with Indians' safety, but he was invested in the reputation of the territory and his own political career. He wanted Congress to pay veterans' benefits to volunteer soldiers and war debts to the territory, but this was unlikely as long as Washington settlers were reputed to be "Indian exterminators."[82] Indian agent Sidney Ford explained to Stevens that Quiemuth's killing "cast upon the people of the Territory an imputation of lawlessness," which the governor surely saw could reflect badly upon him when he sought higher political appointments.[83] Prosch, who believed pursuing the prosecution of Indian war veterans as criminals to be a senseless waste of territorial resources, charged that Stevens only turned to the courts to counteract the "charge so strongly used against us in Congress, of wantonly killing Indians."[84]

Given that Washington Territory had erupted into war during Stevens's treaty tour, it is not surprising that Stevens supported murder indictments against war leaders, in part to make a point about the authority of U.S. law and his own control over civil affairs in the territory.[85] Stevens hoped to make an example out of Indians who defied his treaty terms and local settlers who disapproved of his decisions. This would set a precedent that territorial civil law applied to Indians.[86] This message gained the full support of Indian agent Gosnell, who claimed that the government's unwillingness to indict Indian "murderers" created a disagreeable feeling among the "friendly Indians as well as the citizens." The agent was convinced that settlers would continue to take "illegal revenge" until they gained faith in the legal system.[87] Stevens claimed that punishing the Indian leaders would bring a conclusion to the war, but Nisquallies had already ceased fighting. Leschi's indictment was actually meant to send two messages: one to territorial settlers that the territorial courts would support their desire for revenge and legitimize their racialized social order, and one to Congress that the war had been fought responsibly and U.S. authority did extend over the territory. Leschi's indictment was thus an effort to redeem the reputations of the governor and the settlers alike, and it laid the groundwork for a historical narrative that celebrated the inherent morality and *legality* of early settlers. The territorial courts claimed to represent the justice-loving instincts of early American settlers even though the courts were forced to take action on Leschi's case to defuse settlers' extralegal actions. The celebratory narrative of settlers building legal institutions in the wilderness—a story so clearly at odds with the struggles over legal authority in the territorial period—helps to explain why Leschi's legal drama overshadowed Quiemuth's murder and many others like it in the 1850s.

The stakes were high in the trials of Leschi and the other war leaders. Indian agents saw the function of U.S. law as an important step in "civilizing" Indians and educating them on legal principles. But this was a precarious proposition, for if the court failed to uphold the principle of justice on which it was purportedly based, Indians would reject U.S. law and the officials who sought to extend legal authority over the region. In an appeal to Governor Fayette McMullin for a pardon for Leschi, Tolmie conjectured that if Leschi were executed for an offense of which Indians believed him innocent, the Indians' "notions of justice" would be "outraged" and they would lose all faith in the "white chiefs" to make decisions on future matters.[88]

During Leschi's trials, the territorial courts did offer Nisqually people opportunities otherwise closed to them while protecting them (albeit inconsistently) from settlers' retributive violence. While Nisquallies were powerless to bring about justice in the case of Quiemuth, they could exert some influence in Leschi's trial through legal counsel. Nisquallies hired a lawyer and raised a retaining fee of $300 with an agreement to pay another $500 when Leschi was acquitted.[89] After the Territorial Supreme Court denied Leschi's appeal, Nisquallies asked the governor for clemency in the case.[90] The judicial process moved slowly enough for Nisquallies to try to affect the outcome in various ways, but overall, Native people were disappointed with the legal order. Chief Seattle, Patkanim, and several other regional leaders were brought to Olympia to view the spectacle of Leschi's court trial. Rather than recognizing the superiority of territorial courts as Indian agents had hoped, Patkanim was so unimpressed with the weak evidence offered that he petitioned the territorial governor for his former enemy's release.[91]

Frustrated by the court, Nisqually people turned to federal authorities and appealed to the syncretic legal culture that had maintained peace before the war. Invoking the principles of retaliation and reciprocity and noting that the newspapers reported Quiemuth's death as an act of revenge by a murder victim's family member, Indians argued that the score was essentially settled.[92] "The general opinion of the Indians under my charge," wrote Indian agent Sidney Ford to Governor McMullin, "is that Quiemuth having been killed, it would be but fair and just that Leschi should go unpunished—that they will be satisfied to let the matter thus drop and consider it even—but if Leschi is executed they will not consider it right."[93] The Indian agent reported that "trouble will follow the execution of Leschi."[94] Despite these predictions, McMullin denied clemency for Leschi. He was apparently more moved by a petition signed by 700 settlers opposed to clemency, in addition to a handful of settlers' threats to burn the governor in effigy if he did not follow through with Leschi's hanging.[95] As evinced in both Quiemuth's and Leschi's deaths, the tail wagged the dog in Washington Territory.

Quiemuth's murder and Leschi's execution took place in a context in which emboldened settlers embarked upon a terror campaign to assassinate Native political leaders and federal officials struggled to assert at least the appearance of authority through due process. By examining the brothers' fates together, we can locate fissures in the progressive narrative of territorial settlement. Rather than a story of pioneers bringing order to the wilderness, we see one of some settlers ignoring the established legal order and working against the efforts of federal institutions. Leschi's case allowed later settlers to point to the existence of law-and-order in the territory and ignore settlers' roles in subverting it. The brothers' experiences became features of a dialectical story: Leschi's legal execution was needed to help forget Quiemuth's extralegal assassination.

Creating a Legal Past

The ways settlers later reminisced about the era of Quiemuth's murder in particular and retributive violence in general reveals how changing attitudes contributed to historical amnesia. Arthur Denny, a prominent Seattleite who penned his reminiscences in 1888, characterized American law as progressive and denounced the lynching of Indians as low-class and backward.[96] He began by listing instances in which Indians were hanged without trial for killing white settlers (therefore assuming the Indians' guilt), including a story of an Indian man who killed his wife and was lynched the same day. Three white men were arrested for the deed, but only one stood trial, and he was eventually acquitted.[97] Denny provided this example for his readers as a cautionary tale against lynching, based on the assumption that it would initiate Indian blood feuds: "[Lynching] is a most dangerous method of punishing crime and settling grievances amongst civilized men and where savages are involved it is no better. I have no doubt that two white men . . . were killed to compensate for the one Indian executed by the mob for killing his squaw."[98] Denny wished to commemorate his respectable Seattle family and their accomplishments by drawing a distinction between settlers of his class and those rough characters who bypassed law and order. Since revenge killing was evidence of savagery—no better than Indian ways—Denny condemned the actions of settlers who did not properly display the distinctions between the "civilized" and the "savage" races. Denny characterized settlers' vernacular legal culture as less civilized—less American—and wrote the competing syncretic system of justice out of existence.[99]

While Denny chose to see retributive justice as irrational, he also assumed that Indians could and would recognize the supremacy of the American legal system through firsthand experience: "If they commit crimes against whites and are dealt with and convicted under due process of law, I am very sure that the effect is much more likely to be salutary, and the penalty imposed accepted as a final settlement by the friends of the offenders."[100] Denny used Indians as the ventriloquist's dummy to argue for the universal appeal of due process in the U.S. legal system, despite the fact that Indians criticized the process that took Leschi's life. Thus, Denny's narrative crafted an argument for the logic, superiority, and inevitable growth of U.S. legal institutions. Denny used Indians as foils; Indians' law was absent or irrational, and settlers' superior "dispassionate" system of justice would be so irresistible that Indians would eventually welcome the order it brought to their lives. In Denny's historical revision, the state developed legal dominance in the region through enlightened persuasion rather than coercion.[101] Denny's narrative illustrates how Washingtonians at the turn of the twentieth century celebrated their predecessors as heroes by accentuating some narratives of violence and silencing others.

Other non-Indian writers at the turn of the twentieth century also contributed to changing understandings of settler violence against Indians while defending their ancestors' actions. Van Ogle, one of Quiemuth's escorts to the governor's mansion, penned an unpublished story that defies both chronology and belief.[102] Although Leschi's first trial ended in a hung jury, Van Ogle reordered the chronology of events and claimed that Quiemuth turned himself over to authorities immediately after the trial because he was depressed about his brother's conviction and execution. Van Ogle recalled that Quiemuth was not only upset by the way that Leschi was killed by hanging—a dishonorable death for a warrior—but was especially confused about the operations of a legal system that would intervene in a blood feud: "White man kill Injun. Injun kill him. They hang him like dog. No fair!" Van Ogle used Quiemuth as a ventriloquist's dummy to defend the rationality of the courts and lampoon Native principles of reciprocity and retaliation. Then, incredibly, Van Ogle claimed that Quiemuth literally begged to be shot: "Leschi—my brother, they hang him. You . . . not let em hang this Injun. Shoot him all same Boston soldier."[103] This account justified Quiemuth's murder as a killing that satisfied *Indians'* sense of justice. Yet Van Ogle's narrative contains an obvious contradiction: Why would Quiemuth turn himself over to the law only to ask to be killed outside of it? Van Ogle's account characterized Quiemuth as averse to due process in order to highlight Quiemuth's supposed resistance to a rational, "civilized," legal order.

The only other eyewitness known to have penned memories of Quiemuth's death was James Longmire, who submitted his reminiscences to the *Tacoma Ledger* for an essay competition.[104] Longmire was one of Quiemuth's trusted escorts to the governor's office on the night of his murder.[105] Longmire held solid pioneering credentials that added validity to his narrative. He was on the first wagon train to cross the Naches Pass in 1853, volunteered to fight in the war, climbed Mt. Rainier, and became a successful entrepreneur. He was remembered as "that splendid pioneer."[106] Longmire claimed that Quiemuth turned himself in because he believed the governor would clear him of all charges and that he even offered to lead Longmire to "lots of gold" if the governor did not kill him.[107] Perhaps there is some truth to this assertion. Quiemuth may have shrewdly assessed that the territorial government operated on personal favors and influence, or he may have acted as an arbiter and offered to compensate Longmire to settle the government's grievance. It is also possible that Longmire presented this anecdote to make Quiemuth into a foil for his own honorable intention to uphold due process and territorial law.

The settlers' written memories at the turn of the twentieth century were not consciously misleading productions, but they did follow the conventions of pioneer reminiscences and the rules of their contemporary moment, which often aimed to celebrate settlers' accomplishments.[108] The legal system, one of the bedrocks of American civilization, must appear simultaneously inevitable and hard-won through the work of pioneering individualists. These reminiscences eventually lost currency when professional historians adopted disciplinary standards that questioned the veracity of pioneer memories, and when popular representations of Indians shifted to sympathetic depictions that focused on their lamentable disappearance.[109] New narratives made settlers' stories of Quiemuth and the violence in the years surrounding his death into mere fantasies of an elderly cohort. However, a part of the purpose behind settler reminiscences survived in popular memory: the inevitable domination of state jurisdiction over Indians represented by Leschi's trial. The other part, of righteous pioneers battling dark forces that threatened to overtake them at any moment—represented in the vernacular legal culture surrounding Quiemuth's death—did not. Indeed, the survival of the first narrative required the suppression of the latter in the twentieth century as state power grew in the West. In addition, non-Indians increasingly decried Indians' unjust dispossession and the deceptive intent of treaties, and this sympathy focused solely on Leschi.

Haunting and Exoneration

Leschi's descendants found ample archival sources detailing Leschi's upstanding character, compassion in wartime, and unfair legal treatment for use in the 2004 Historical Court. Early and mid-twentieth-century historians followed the "paper trail" left from the 1850s and 1890s to write narratives that effectively re-inscribed Leschi's importance, dismissed Quiemuth's contributions, and weighed the significances of their deaths differently. The popular narrative convention of "great man" history meant that writers focused on singular actors who ostensibly embodied social ideals. Leschi and Stevens came to represent two opposing visions and ways of life, and Quiemuth was simply squeezed out.[110] In these historians' versions of the Medicine Creek Treaty, Leschi distinguished himself as the single true leader of the Nisqually Tribe. Meeker printed an account from an eyewitness, who claimed that Leschi had refused to sign the treaty but who was silent on Quiemuth's actions. Writing nearly fifty years after the fact, Meeker was singularly focused on foreshadowing the famous legal battle between Stevens and Leschi—a battle Quiemuth did not live long enough to play a clear role in. Later authors repeated the narrative of Leschi's prominence at the treaty, perhaps because it built dramatic tension and sympathy for a man whose death sentence was so well-documented.[111]

Writers in the first half of the twentieth century tended to characterize Leschi as a firebrand and dismiss his older brother as accommodating, naive, and even corrupt. Historian W. Bonney explained in 1932 that "poor, trusting Quiemuth" did not understand how the war could engender so much resentment and chose to surrender to authorities because he thought the governor was a good man.[112] In Archie Binns's 1940 historical novel, *Mighty Mountain,* set on the Nisqually Delta in 1854, a non-Indian boy asks an older relative whether the Indians will have to sign the coercive treaty. The relative explains that Quiemuth will certainly agree to it. When the boy counters that Quiemuth is "not important," the elder relative responds that it was Governor Stevens's sneaky tactic to appoint Quiemuth as chief because he would do anything to please the governor. When the boy conjectures that the Nisquallies would have selected Leschi as their leader if given the choice, the elder relative agrees, but reasons, "I'd say the Governor recognized that when he chose the lesser brother."[113] This fictional exchange characterizes Quiemuth as a pawn and Leschi as the principled and true chief. Stevens became the tyrannical straw man and therefore allowed territorial settlers to appear law-abiding *and* sympathetic to Indians, imbued with a sense of color-blind justice *and* paragons of American virtue. Quiemuth's actual life and death complicates this simple story by revealing the unsavory side of American culture, institutions, and territorial settlement.

By reading the evidence in the colonial archive against the grain and listening to the silences, another history of Washington emerges. The excited newspaper coverage of Leschi's legal fate details the many legal opportunities afforded him. Even in denying his appeal in 1857, the Territorial Supreme Court justice congratulated the legal system for offering Leschi "deliberate impartiality . . . at every stage of the proceedings," despite the "spirit of indignation and revenge" permeating the region.[114] At Leschi's resentencing in 1858, the judge reminded the prisoner that "the law is not vindictive."[115] Behind the declarations that "civilized" order had replaced a savage state of nature lies profound insecurity. That is, focusing on due process in Leschi's trials made a point that settlers and authorities were primarily concerned with the *appearance* of due process. If Washington should be civilized because it upholds the rule of law, non-Indians' historical narratives focus upon due process rather than extralegal violence. In this way, some narratives can overtake others by force.[116]

What did this history of settler violence and narrative production mean for the Historical Court? Leschi's descendants found ample archival sources detailing Leschi's legal treatment. The same archive that helped later authors build Leschi's reputation at Quiemuth's expense also informed a case for Leschi's exoneration. Leschi's conviction resulted in an official record, which gave his descendants something to argue against and correct.[117] Cynthia Iyall admitted that she felt that Quiemuth should have gotten more attention in the Historical Court, but there was not the same "paper trail" on which to base testimony and evidence of injustice against him.[118] The Committee to Exonerate Chief Leschi knew that it had to privilege archival documents in order to convince non-Indian allies of the truth in its claims. Quiemuth's story, placed beside his more famous brother's, allows for an assessment of the archives in such quasi-legal justice initiatives. Did the Historical Court and Leschi's exoneration set a precedent for historical justice that only judicial wrongs can be righted? Can Quiemuth's assassination ever receive public acknowledgment, since the perpetrators left little reliable documentary evidence of their deed?

Public memories of Quiemuth have faded since his death for a number of reasons. The public contest over Leschi's conviction and execution made Leschi a household name and simply overshadowed the fates of other war leaders. Leschi's hanging before a gathered crowd likely left a greater impression on public consciousness than Quiemuth's nighttime murder in the company of a few. Perhaps Quiemuth's sons' decision to adopt their uncle's name reinforced the perception that Leschi's legacy was more important. Or perhaps the reason that Quiemuth did not achieve the same public recognition as his brother is a combination of these factors. But no less real is the possibility that Leschi has been remembered because his case demonstrated due process and deviated from the general pattern of violence against Indians while Quiemuth's did not. Leschi's case was extraordinary while Quiemuth's was all too common.

Leschi's retrial in 2004 focused on due process, on laws of war, and on the ample reports of the legal drama in the territorial courts. But what was left out of the legal framing of Leschi's case? The climate of violence that terrorized indigenous people in South Puget Sound in the 1850s did not enter into Leschi's retrial. No one mentioned the compacts of silence that protected white settlers who killed Indians and no one mentioned how legal authorities offered tacit support to extralegal murders. To mention these truths would have rendered others untenable. How could law vindicate both Leschi and itself if Quiemuth's story revealed it as a tool of colonialism? The petitioners were able to convince politicians and judges to reevaluate Leschi's case, but Quiemuth's story could not be told because of the limits of even symbolic court rules that prompted expert witnesses to rely on written records and lawyers to create legal arguments based on established U.S. law. The short time available for the Historical Court also put pressure on the participants to focus on Leschi's case. Furthermore, the judges could make a decision on Leschi's case without indicting anyone in particular for wrongdoing—Leschi was simply exonerated because of jurisdictional error—but Quiemuth's assassination would involve probing into non-Indian settlers' actions and state responsibilities toward Indian murder victims.

After Quiemuth died unceremoniously, he entered a new existence as a ghost. Cecelia Carpenter explained that the spirit of a murdered person "would be condemned to roam aimlessly about until his death was avenged" or the account was squared.[119] The judges in the Historical Court admitted that Leschi should not have been convicted of murder, but Quiemuth's assassination remains unaddressed. Nisqually elders continue to consider how to bring peace to Quiemuth. A road on the reservation was named in his honor, and in 1993 the Thurston County Historic Commission voted to name the highest point in the county Quiemuth Peak.[120] When representatives from Fort Lewis asked the tribal chairwoman for permission to name a training facility after Leschi, she agreed but asked for at least a building to be named after Quiemuth.

Although elders have long told Quiemuth's story, the matter of justice has become more pressing since Leschi's exoneration. "We don't want to forget what [Quiemuth] went through," Iyall stated. Quiemuth, like Leschi, lives on as a symbol of tribal experiences. "My great uncles have reminded me that lots of Indian men went through the same thing [as Quiemuth]," Cynthia Iyall said. "We'd like to honor them in the future. Maybe one ceremonial act can ease the pain."[121] The tribe has sponsored a number of commemorative events and ceremonies in the years following the Historical Court that have pointedly included Quiemuth. In February 2008, the tribe hosted the "Honor and Celebration of Brothers," a daylong series of ceremonies and speeches. About 100 people participated in a run from the Lakewood memorial and Leschi's grave to Chief Leschi

School, where the audience listened to speeches and watched dance and drum performances. Swinomish linguist and historian Cecelia LaPointe-Gorman said of the event: "This is a healing process today."[122] And that process continued. A few months later, the Nisqually Tribe coordinated with officials at Joint Base Lewis-McChord to hold the first annual Leschi-Quiemuth Honor Walk on Range 91, the prairie that had belonged to the tribe before the 1917–18 condemnation. Elders riding in buses convened with walkers to visit significant sites on the prairie. Most of the tribal members saw family allotments and cemeteries for the first time.[123] Significantly, these annual events incorporate both the commemorative and the historical landscape of South Puget Sound, connecting Leschi's and Quiemuth's lives to elders' stories and tribal homelands.

The commemorative events and ceremonies are important to tribal members, but, unlike the Historical Court, they do not make demands on the state. As Peggy McCloud explained to me in 2007, part of the problem with the silence around Quiemuth was that his murder was known and felt but not acknowledged at the state level. A ceremony might ease the pain, but haunting will continue. As Avery Gordon notes, ghosts bring about change by showing the limits of the possible and the impossible. "The ghost is . . . pregnant with unfulfilled possibility, with the something to be done that the wavering present is demanding," Gordon writes. "This something to be done is not a return to the past but a reckoning with its repression in the present."[124] Leschi's exoneration brought Quiemuth's injustice into stark relief and makes his absence visible. "The Quiemuth story is just as interesting as Leschi's," Iyall said. "We'll work on that. Part two."[125]

Conclusion

Courts of law (even symbolic ones) offer participants the possibility of vindication: the sense that one's stories can be endorsed as truth, that one's conception of fairness can be affirmed as just. Courts draw upon principles and rules that reflect society's ideals and can therefore act as a means of reform or protection of tradition. Reformers and conservatives, descendants of colonizers and the colonized, and aggrieved and responsible parties alike are drawn to judicial remedies because they offer venues for telling stories about who we are as people and as a society. Given this context, the major question of this book is not whether Leschi's 1857 conviction conformed to legal standards, or even whether the court rendered a just decision. Rather, the more revealing question is why this society turns to courts at all.[1]

Leschi's 1857 trials accomplished something for territorial settlers and officials that a summary execution or amnesty could not. Leschi's trials were but one legal mechanism in a multipronged colonial strategy to dispossess Indians of land. Leschi's procession through the territorial court system provided non-Indian settlers with a way to construct Indians' dispossession as civilized and lawful. Whether defending Leschi or prosecuting him, some non-Indians turned to Leschi's case to demonstrate their commitment to fostering a community of laws. Leschi's lengthy legal case, unlike extralegal "revenge" killings of Indians, served as the basis for later claims about settlers' fidelity to tradition and respect for state-centered law. Leschi's judicial execution also served a purpose for indigenous communities. It became a focal point for outrage against the history of Puget Sound settlement, galvanizing their resistance and providing a starting place for historical counter narratives. And the courts, like other liberal institutions throughout the late nineteenth and early twentieth centuries, offered a means by which colonized people could resist the damaging effects of these technologies of rule.

The 2004 Historical Court likewise accomplished something for Leschi's descendants, public historians, state officials, and legal professionals that a ceremony, governor's apology, or legislative resolution could not. As a form of tribunal, the event enabled Nisqually and Puyallup leaders to achieve cultural goals of honoring elders and oral traditions. In the context of Nisqually political and social imperatives, the court reflected the leaders' claim to the tribe's national status (rather than a minority population) and illustrated indigenous survivance.[2] The Native representatives gave testimony within a Western legal format, but they also expanded the boundaries of legal performance to include Indians' perspectives and ways of knowing. Public historians used the court to educate and initiate public dialogue about state history and social responsibility in a multicultural society. The narrow focus on a single court case, meanwhile, allowed state officials to reflect on legal rules rather than passing judgment on settler ancestors and the larger processes that enabled colonial settlement.

Most important, the symbolic court offered each party a moral victory in an adversarial setting. Every participant, whether arguing for or against exoneration, whether descended from Leschi or from non-Indian immigrants, could be lauded for doing the right thing by insisting on the truth. This was both a meaningful and a painless solution, for it seemed to answer a demand for justice within established channels without compromising the authority of the state. As postcolonial scholars point out, settler colonial nations have devised strategies, derived from liberal theory, for resolving questions of moral legitimacy while enhancing their human rights reputations, particularly in relation to indigenous populations.[3] Although neither a state-sponsored event nor a "real" court, the Historical Court functioned to publicly legitimize a legal order drawn from colonial and liberal traditions—one Indians and non-Indians alike have come to rely upon to secure their interests and protect their rights. The 2004 event reaffirmed public perception of courts as inclusive spaces where truth is proclaimed and justice is achieved, even though Indians alone had to make compromises in order to access even a makeshift courtroom.

Because it is drawn from conservative and reformist currents, the Historical Court revealed a tension in the judicial approach to history. Does a court decision relieve the present of the burdens of the past, or does it reveal the ongoing operations of the past in the present? Carl Hultman opined that the Historical Court's legalistic format was ideal for historical inquiry: "We have a process that's . . . supposed to allow for the ending of conflicts, a finality. You don't just argue on forever about things."[4]

Chief Justice Gerry Alexander echoed this sentiment, claiming that an adversarial setting was best equipped to find truth and end debate, no matter how long ago the conflict began. Yet the Historical Court was not like other courts, because it navigated memories and historical narratives in addition to evidence and legal facts. "You are an historical court," John Ladenburg reminded the judges in his closing statement. "You have the right to examine all the history . . . all the things that have happened and transpired in our society since [the events of the 1850s]." The Historical Court engaged with a century of Nisqually and non-Indian social, political, and cultural interactions in South Puget Sound. Over time, storytellers deposited their own experiences, perspectives, and shifting concerns into Leschi's story. By 2004, stories about Leschi reflected generations of reciprocal influences, social interactions, and political negotiations. The public memorials, place-names, and texts dedicated to Leschi in the region illustrate how one man has come to signify a great deal more than a single legal decision. The testimony in the court made a case for the ongoing usefulness of the past; rather than being a roadblock to reconciliation, remembering and witnessing represented the pathway to progress.

The Native representatives who gave testimony and supported the exoneration interpreted the court's decision less as a destination and more as part of a journey. Along with a more general education program of language revitalization and traditional values, many Native leaders consider recognition of past wrongs and a heartfelt apology from the United States to be important steps in healing Native communities and peoples.[5] When the Washington legislature approved the apology resolution, Nisqually tribe member Tom Iyall declared: "It was a good step in starting the healing that needs to be done."[6] For Leschi's descendants, the Historical Court honored not only a relative but also ancestral wisdom and prophecy. These elements build Native identity and pride, qualities that Native leaders believe are necessary to empower their children. The judges' decision in the Historical Court was based on Western legal arguments but also contributed to Nisqually cultural survival.

Some Native leaders interpreted the Historical Court's public pronouncement of Leschi's exoneration as indicative of the state's willingness to reform. The exoneration could be a starting point from which Native people of South Puget Sound could press the state to address grievances with renewed vigor. Perhaps the exoneration signaled the beginning of an era in which Indians' righteous claims for fair treatment would find purchase. Puyallup tribal elder Ramona Bennett spoke at a Chief Leschi

School assembly shortly after the exoneration to educate the students about what the exoneration could mean for them. "It's an opportunity for the state to stop treating one Indian like a criminal," Bennett said. "It's just one Indian, but you know they've got to start some place."[7] Leschi's exoneration was symbolic, but elders argued that the effects need not be limited to the abstract and rhetorical. From Native perspectives, it was important that Leschi's wrongful conviction be corrected, but the judges' decision did not mark the end of the work of Leschi's story. Leschi's exoneration was part of a process of decolonization and healing, not its singular, finalizing event.

It was not only Native people who hoped that the Historical Court would become part of a longer process of reflection and social progress. Shortly before the Historical Court, Committee to Exonerate Chief Leschi member Melissa Parr explained in a radio interview that the court was a crucial educational opportunity for non-Indians. "It's [about] a sense of place," Parr insisted. "You live in Washington, you need to know the history of where you live. . . . You have [chosen] to be a part of the society so you need to look at what happened in this society and take responsibility."[8] Parr suggested that immigrants to Washington in particular had a social responsibility to listen and learn the truth; education has transformative potential that would compel people to moral action.

In accordance with this ideal, John Ladenburg concluded the petitioners' case by configuring Leschi's exoneration as a mode of communal cleansing, an act for social renewal. As a first step in this process, Ladenburg appealed to the judges to "do the simple justice of declaring the truth." The attorney argued that just such a collective self-improvement was possible by righting a wrong from so many years ago. "We do this not for Leschi alone," Ladenburg declared. "We do this not for Leschi's descendants alone, we do this not for the Nisqually tribe and the tribes of the Northwest alone. . . . [It is] for us, all of us." He then appealed to the panel of judges in the Historical Court to "let your verdict . . . sweep away the memory and pain and injustice inflicted upon Leschi, and let it leave the calm waters of reconciliation and brotherhood for all the people of Washington." The judges' decision could signal the conclusion of pain as well as freedom from guilt for having caused pain. The notion that the present must be liberated from the grip of the past is a Western goal and progressive concept.[9] Reflecting on the significance of the Historical Court afterward, Ladenburg claimed that the most important aspect of the court was that "tribal history" was vindicated over that of the "white man."[10] This

Pierce County executive, whose ancestors had immigrated to the region in the 1870s and had maintained relationships with Nisqually Indians since, found satisfaction in this outcome.[11]

But some Washingtonians felt threatened by what they perceived as the court's decision to endorse Nisqually histories and criticize territorial settlers. A handful of letters to the editor published in regional newspapers following the Historical Court offer a glimpse into the nature of this persistent controversy. The writers variously assessed the Historical Court to be a "kangaroo court," a "worthless exercise" that wasted taxpayer money, and a "travesty" in which judges, "who took oaths to uphold our laws and constitution," pursued a case without merit to "pander to the Nisqually Indians." One Puyallup resident charged that the Historical Court simply created a "false history" that served two functions: enhance Indians' sense of victimization and entitlement and allow liberals to feel cleansed by "practicing 'good' discrimination and indicting their racist ancestors."[12] "I hope they all feel better now," one man wrote to the *Tacoma News-Tribune*. "But as usual no one bothered to ask the victim's relatives if justice had been served. I wonder who isn't resting in peace now."[13] Rather than ending debate on the matter, the Historical Court decision seemed to reinvigorate it.

Many people hoped that Leschi's 2004 exoneration would initiate a new era for the tribe, but these letters to the editor show that at least some non-Indians in the region resisted historical revisions that validated Indian perspectives. These writers were not the first Tacomans to respond to a Nisqually court case with the charge that Indians deserve no "special rights" or to argue that standing up to Indians' demands would spare taxpayer trouble and expense. They were not the first Puget Sound residents to respond to Nisqually oral traditions by claiming such ways of transmitting knowledge endangered the integrity of "universal" rules, cherished principles, and the belief that history is composed of verifiable textual evidence. They were not the first to claim that Indian histories were politically motivated while settlers' narratives objectively reflected reality. A century before the Historical Court, Benjamin Shaw, the translator at the Medicine Creek Treaty, publicly reprimanded writers like Ezra Meeker for revising the history of the treaty and criticizing Governor Stevens. Shaw insisted that he needed to defend the celebratory narrative of the territorial period, lest the public grow so comfortable with the stories told by "Indiomaniacs" that "in time they might be considered as History."[14] The petitioners in the Historical Court pushed against a strong current when they endeavored to insert their perspectives into a long-standing historical narrative.

Whatever the narratives of progress, in 2004 the notion that "tribal history" could win endorsement over "white man's history" in a public forum remained alarming for some. The fear that Indians' perspectives might discredit inherited and long-cherished histories—despite the fact that non-Indian perspectives dominate the public realm—reveals a deep discomfort with the prospect of confronting the colonial past and its legacies. The arguments expressed in the letters to the editor showed that the Historical Court decision did not reflect and institute radical social change, but they also illustrate why the petitioners insisted on the court in the first place. Although the Historical Court was open to a public audience, the participants carefully selected the speakers to control the contours of debate. As the letters to the editor suggest, the petitioners had good reason not to give their testimony in an open forum and invite public opinion.

The letter writers' claims that the non-Indian participants were motivated by "white guilt" to create a court that only made Indians feel more entitled deserves further consideration. To what extent is the present generation responsible for the deeds of its predecessors? The writers denied that there was an error in need of correction, clearly in disagreement with Melissa Parr's assertion that Washingtonians needed to reexamine their history and take responsibility for it. Liberalism celebrates the sanctity of the individual subject; if a progressive government ensures equal opportunities and treatment under the law, one's achievements (or lack thereof) flow from individual merit. Inherited privileges and cross-generational grievances have no place in this formula. One can point to liberal ideology to argue that inheritance and cross-generational anger should neither confer benefits nor compel responsibilities in the present. Society is most fair if history stays safely in the past. However, as appealing as progress and clean slates may be to some, people live in a world formed by the past; we have all inherited history.

The format of the Historical Court in fact reinforced the perception that the impact of colonialism was (and is) only "real" in Indian history and experienced only in Indian psyches. The Native American representatives' testimony was personal and emotional in a way the expert testimony was not. One way to show that non-Indians' lives were also shaped by history would have been to allow personal and honest testimony from non-Indians. It would be an educational statement indeed if an Olympia farmer, Tacoma businessman, or Fort Lewis soldier took the stand to reflect on how his or her wealth, land, and privileges were made possible by U.S. colonialism. Perhaps time for the Historical Court was too limited for such a feature, or perhaps the narrow legal question of Leschi's 1857 conviction worked against a more holistic reckoning with the past that might engender a general sense of social responsibility in the present.

After the judges declared Leschi symbolically exonerated, one journalist wrote that the people of Chief Leschi "have a much better ending to their story, and we whites have a better one for ours, too."[15] Despite the judges' goal to put an end to the controversial legal question, the stories of Leschi and the legacies of colonialism did not end on December 10, 2004. The Historical Court must be located in its own political and cultural context, not seen as the apex of progressive history that moves ever closer to perfection. As John and Jean Comaroff have written, "Even contemporary celebrations of timeless truths may quickly become monuments to passing moments—and regimes."[16] The definitions of law, history, and even justice will continue to evolve just as certainly as they claim their bases in immutable truth.

The testimony presented in the Historical Court, as well as the organization of the event, revealed the tensions and unsettling contradictions of historical justice. The Historical Court represented a victory for Leschi's descendants, a call to action for Native elders, a boon to legal authority, and a confirmation of American settlers' just intentions and liberal achievements in the region. The court performances celebrated Western law even as the judges admitted that the law could be perverted to unjust ends. Leschi symbolized another set of contradictions. He was a model for resistance to U.S. domination and an example of a peaceful arbiter who valued cooperation and accommodation. Leschi signified the enduring active presence of the past as well as an attempt to seize control of it, a representative of a shared, multicultural collective memory and evidence of its impossibility in a settler state. His story was constructed from the same colonial archive it was meant to correct and gives notice of ghosts that it does not confront. These contradictions are not simple curiosities emerging from an obscure public history event; these contradictions illustrate the work of historical narratives in a liberal context.

Courts serve an important mediating and limiting function in a liberal settler state. They offer spaces of discursive exchange, and they maintain a balance between tradition and reform under the authority of the state. Stories, meanwhile, help us to construct (and deconstruct and reconstruct) the world and the relations that order it. The participants in the Historical

Court inherited a series of events that they did not choose and could not undo. And yet, remarkably, they agreed that rather than allow the past to make them, they would tell new stories and take action to make the world that they wanted.[17] "While some of us debate what history is or was," wrote Michel-Rolph Trouillot, "others take it into their own hands."[18] Engaging with the past and discussing the failures and silences of history is neither simple nor easy. But that engagement minimizes the distinction between words and deeds and makes the quest for justice perpetually important.

NOTES

ABBREVIATIONS USED IN NOTES

CSCPC Cecelia Svinth Carpenter Private Collection, Tacoma
HCIJ   DVD, Historical Court of Inquiry & Justice, TVW Television Network, Olympia, December 10, 2004
JWC   James Wickersham Collection, MSS TS-120, box 1, folder 3, Washington State Historical Society
NAA   National Anthropological Archives, Suitland, Md.
NARA   National Archives and Records Administration, Washington, D.C.
PNRO   National Archives, Pacific Northwest Regional Office, Seattle
UWSC   University of Washington Library and Special Collections, Seattle
WSHS   Washington State Historical Society Research Center, Tacoma

PREFACE

1. I honored a request from one non-Indian interviewee to remove material for fear of professional repercussions as well.

INTRODUCTION

1. Rob Carson, "Second Chance at Justice," *Tacoma News-Tribune*, December 9, 2004; Gregory Roberts, "Historical Court Clears Chief Leschi's Name," *Seattle Post-Intelligencer*, December 11, 2004, B1.

2. Sarah Kershaw, "Chief's Retrial, 146 Years in the Making," *New York Times*, December 5, 2004.

3. Interview with Cynthia Iyall.

4. Carpenter, "How It All Began," CSCPC; interview with Cynthia Iyall.

5. Interview with Melissa Parr; interview with Cynthia Iyall.

6. Early on, the group worked with the in-house tribal attorney, Bill Tobin, and legal advisers Tina Kuckkahn and Robert Anderson to consider the legal remedies available to them. Petitioners' Memorandum of Law, submitted by the Descendants of Chief Leschi and the Nisqually Indian Tribe on December 7, 2004, p. 2, courtesy of Cecelia Carpenter; Carpenter, "How It All Began," CSCPC; Kluger, *Bit-

ter *Waters of Medicine Creek*, 263; interview with Tina Kuckkahn; interview with Robert Anderson.

7. Now Joint Base Lewis-McChord.

8. The judges in the Historical Court were Gerry Alexander (Washington Supreme Court), Susan Owens (Washington Supreme Court), Ronald Cox (Division One Court of Appeals), Karen Seinfeld (retired, Division Two Court of Appeals), Daniel Berschauer (Thurston County Superior Court), Donald Thompson (retired, Pierce County Superior Court), and Theresa M. Pouley (Lummi Tribal Court).

9. Interview with Gerry Alexander; email correspondence with Gerry Alexander; email correspondence with Sharon Hultman; Interview with Carl Hultman; HCIJ.

10. Interview with Cynthia Iyall; interview with Tina Kuckkahn; Letter from Gerry Alexander to Cynthia Iyall, July 23, 2004, courtesy of Cecelia Carpenter; "Our Views: Chief Leschi Exonerated," *Olympian*, December 17, 2004, 9A.

11. Amin, *Event, Metaphor, Memory*, 3.

12. See Hess, *American Social and Political Thought*.

13. Goldberg, *Racist Culture*, 5.

14. Many foundational liberal thinkers were involved with colonial enterprises and developed their philosophies based on the relative status of European and non-European peoples at the height of European imperialism. Fitzmaurice, "Liberalism and Empire," 122; Armitage, "John Locke, Carolina, and the *Two Treatises of Government*," 602. See also Parekh, "Liberalism and Colonialism."

15. Wolfe, *Settler Colonialism and the Transformation of Anthropology*, 2–3.

16. Fitzmaurice, "Moral Uncertainty," 383–84.

17. In an effort to work through the contradictions between liberal ideals and colonial practice, seventeenth-century English philosophers developed the progressive theory of history, which held that the European state perched on the top position and non-Europeans were less advanced and inferior. Accordingly, English writers claimed that Native Americans were devoid of civil society and acted against natural laws of commerce when they refused to sell their land, and thus Indians held neither claim to universal forms of rationality nor possession of their land. Fitzmaurice, "Moral Uncertainty," 387, 399, 408; Ivison, *Postcolonial Liberalism*, 45; Young, "Reconsidering American Liberalism," 166; Grandin, "Liberal Tradition in the Americas," 77–78; MacMillan, *Sovereignty and Possession*, 9. For more on dispossession and natural law, see Arneil, *John Locke and America*; Pagden, *The Fall of Natural Man*; Williams, *The American Indian in Western Legal Thought*; and Tully, *An Approach to Political Philosophy*.

18. Fitzmaurice, "Liberalism and Empire," 122–23; Fitzmaurice, "Moral Uncertainty," 409. Liberal discourse informed early abolitionists and human rights advocates. Lauren, "A Human Rights Lens on U.S. History," 15–17, 20.

19. Indian nations' engagement with U.S. courts has resulted in a unique body of law. Harring, "Indian Law, Sovereignty, and State Law," 442, 444. For more on this body of law, see Felix Cohen, *Handbook of Federal Indian Law*. For a history

of indigenous and U.S. interpretations of sovereignty, see Deloria and Lytle, *The Nations Within*. For more on the European discourse of sovereignty as an assimilationist concept, see Williams, *The American Indian in Western Legal Thought*; David Wilkins, *American Indian Sovereignty and the U.S. Supreme Court*; and Alfred, "Sovereignty," 460–74.

20. Ivison, *Postcolonial Liberalism*, 45–46.

21. Morefield, *Covenants without Swords*, 25. Late nineteenth-century idealist liberal thinkers developed a theory of social responsibility to explain why rational, free individuals should care about others and about their communities. This reform impulse in the United States, known also as the Social Gospel, was coupled with emotional responses to images of poverty and suffering. Lauren, "A Human Rights Lens on U.S. History," 23–24.

22. The logic of progressive reform remained committed to liberal principles in that assimilation meant giving up those markers of difference that did not align with a dominant set of cultural and political values defined by Euro-Americans. Goldberg, *Multiculturalism*, 4–5.

23. During the World War II era, reformers seized on the liberal internationalist discourse of "human rights" to point out the discrepancy between U.S. liberal rhetoric projected in the international realm and the realities for indigenous peoples within the nation. However, U.S. reticence to participate in international accords or governing bodies in which the United States might be held to account limited American Indians' claims in the international realm. The 1960s signaled a shift in thinking from the assimilationist standard toward a new one of integration, but the impulse to protect a core American culture remained. Borgwardt, "FDR's Four Freedoms," 51–54. Liberal pluralism "allows" other voices to add themselves to the "mainstream." Political philosopher John Rawls posited that modern liberal pluralist states maintain egalitarianism by tolerating different social groups' beliefs and practices as long as they do not reject the essentials of democracy. However, "tolerance" suggests repugnance, and those in positions of authority have the greatest power to define the core values of democracy, thus maintaining exclusions while appearing to support egalitarianism. Liberal pluralism assumes that the state maintains neutrality in the face of individual and group differences. However, U.S. policies and legal decisions have failed to remain neutral when it comes to indigenous claims. Mendus, *Toleration and the Limits of Liberalism*, 149–50; Goldberg, *Multiculturalism*, 6; Stam and Shohat, "Contested Histories," 300; Rawls, "Political Liberalism," 171.

24. Henry Louis Gates Jr., "Good-Bye, Columbus," 205.

25. Goldberg, *Multiculturalism*, 7–8. See also Konkle, *Writing Indian Nations*; and Steinberg, *Diversity and Multiculturalism*, xi–xiii.

26. Wolfe, *Settler Colonialism and the Transformation of Anthropology*, 168.

27. Political theorist David Theo Goldberg characterizes the paradox of liberal pluralism: "The more ideologically hegemonic liberal values seem and the more

open to difference liberal modernity declares itself, the more dismissive of difference it becomes and the more closed it seeks to make the circle of acceptability." Goldberg, *Racist Culture*, 6–7.

28. I borrow the term "cultural logic" from Patrick Wolfe, who defines it as the persistent ideology in settler colonial contexts that leads to the creation and perpetuation of cultural, economic, and other structures of practical disenfranchisement for indigenous people. Wolfe, *Settler Colonialism and the Transformation of Anthropology*, 201–2.

29. The 1924 General Citizenship Act declared Native peoples to be American citizens while still allowing for tribal citizenship. Nobles, *The Politics of Official Apologies*, 16.

30. Duncan Ivison argues that it is possible to create a postcolonial liberal democracy that joins the twin indigenous political goals of minimizing forms of domination over indigenous people "whilst also promoting the capabilities of individuals and groups to modify and contest the norms and practices that govern them." Ivison, *Postcolonial Liberalism*, 11–12. Taiaiake Alfred argues that true decolonization will only be achieved by dismantling "white society's entrenched privileges and the unreformed structure of the colonial state"—not through indigenous leaders' submission and cooperation with liberal state-sponsored and government-regulated processes. Alfred insists that Native leaders participate in their own colonization when they accommodate Western cultural values and accept integration into their political and economic systems. He argues against accommodation because "indigenous governance systems embody distinctive political values, radically different from those of the mainstream." Alfred, "Native American Political Traditions," 18–19; *Wasáse*, 20–21. For more critiques of accommodation, see also Fanon, *Wretched of the Earth*; Alfred, *Peace, Power, Righteousness*; and Greymorning, *A Will to Survive*. For more on injecting indigenous traditions and perspectives into the liberal institution of the academy, see Mihesuah, *Natives and Academics*.

31. James, "Memory, Identity, and Diversity in BC," 53; Barkan, "Introduction: Historians and Historical Reconciliation"; Gibney et al., *Age of Apology*; Barkan and Karn, *Taking Wrongs Seriously*.

32. Between 1974 and 1994, at least fifteen truth and reconciliation commissions were established in nations around the world as part of a transition from dictatorial to democratic rule. These served as blueprints for the South African Truth and Reconciliation Commission (1996–98), which in turn inspired numerous others into the twenty-first century. This turn to commissions and tribunals can be traced to the Nuremburg Trials, which prompted international discussions of human and individual rights and possible recourses for citizens harmed by state action. Phelps, *Shattered Voices*, 77–78; Vora and Vora, "The Effectiveness of South Africa's Truth and Reconciliation Commission," 302–3; Rebecca Cook, "Leschi Trial Culminates Historical, Family Mission," *Olympian*, December 6, 2004.

33. Mooney, Knox, and Schacht, *Understanding Social Problems*, 351. The Florida state legislature in 1993 established a fund to compensate the survivors of the 1923 Rosewood Massacre. Nobles, *The Politics of Official Apologies*, 142. U.S. settlements to Native Americans have hinged on legal promises made in treaties to tribes as independent political entities. Congress and U.S. courts have investigated political and legal injustices against Native American tribes stemming from abrogated treaties and the misconduct of the Bureau of Indian Affairs, starting with the Indian Claims Commission in 1946. One of the most recent settlements came in December 2009 in *Cobell v. Salazar*, a class-action suit based on the Bureau of Indian Affairs' mismanagement of Individual Indian Money Accounts. For the settlement agreement text, see the Department of the Interior website: http://www.doi.gov/ost/cobell/index.html (April 2, 2011).

34. Bongani Finka, Foreword, in Magarrell and Wesley, *Learning from Greensboro*, viii.

35. For more on the Tulsa, Wilmington, and Greensboro cases, see Brophy, *Reconstructing the Dreamland*; Hirsch, *Riot and Remembrance*; Cecelski and Tyson, *Democracy Betrayed*; and Magarrell and Wesley, *Learning from Greensboro*. For a complete listing of truth and reconciliation commissions around the world from 1974 through 2011, see Hayner, *Unspeakable Truths*.

36. Nobles, *The Politics of Official Apologies*, 149–53.

37. Hunt, *Inventing Human Rights*, 204–5; Nobles, *The Politics of Official Apologies*, 3.

38. Lyle Marshall quoted in Nobles, *The Politics of Official Apologies*, 23–24. The implications of liberal historical philosophy can be seen in the Native American "apology" resolution signed by President Barack Obama in December 2009. The text of the resolution, appended to a defense spending bill and passed without much media attention, offered an apology "for the many instances of violence, maltreatment, and neglect inflicted on Native peoples by citizens of the United States" but also maintained that the resolution did not authorize or support any legal claims against the United States. The U.S. government would acknowledge its own role in the colonial violence inflicted upon Native Americans up to a point. That point was reached when the past threatened to invade the present, which could mean a change in legal or political power over contested resources. If past action could be connected to present claims, the U.S. government could lose authority over Native Americans and their lands. Rob Capriccioso, "A Sorry Saga: Obama Signs Native American Apology," *Indian Country Today*, January 20, 2010, http://indiancountrytodaymedianetwork.com/2010/01/a-sorry-saga-obama-signs-native-american-apology (April 3, 2011); Associated Press, "A Symbolic Apology to Indians," *New York Times*, October 7, 2009, http://www.nytimes.com/2009/10/08/us/politics/08brfs-ASYMBOLICAPO_BRF.html?_r=3&scp=2&sq=apology%20native%20americans&st=c&.(July 25, 2013).

39. For more on truth and reconciliation commissions and transitional democracies, see Minow, *Between Vengeance and Forgiveness*; and Wiebelhaus-Brahm, *Truth Commissions and Transitional Societies*.

40. Phelps argues that public acknowledgment of stories is an act of compassion and respect for humanity that the injustice and its ensuing silence had long denied. Phelps, *Shattered Voices*, 9. Notably, only Native "representatives" offered testimony of suffering in the Historical Court; they alone appeared to be impacted by the past and in need of reform.

41. Nobles argues that apologies (a similar symbolic act) open up a "new conversation" on historical matters, while reparations end the conversation. Reparations suggest the debt has been paid and the matter can be forgotten. Nobles, *The Politics of Official Apologies*, 141.

42. Alfred, "Restitution Is the Real Pathway." See also James, "Wrestling with the Past"; Daniels, "An Age of Apology"; and Cunningham, "Saying Sorry," 285–93.

43. Wolfe, *Settler Colonialism and the Transformation of Anthropology*, 201–2.

44. Bevernage, "Writing the Past Out of the Present," 115.

45. Cultural anthropologists and ethnohistorians note how non-Western societies recall history episodically and outside of linear chronology. Rappaport, *Politics of Memory*, 11–13.

46. Interview with John Ladenburg.

47. Trouillot, *Silencing the Past*, 26–27.

48. Campbell, "Settling Accounts," 971. In one sociological case study, researchers found that American university students ranked slavery as the nation's "primary sin." This is supported by many recent efforts to remember slavery without directly taking responsibility for it. Schwartz, Fukuoka, and Takita-Ishii, "Collective Memory," 266.

49. Lisa Ford describes "settler sovereignty" as a process in which settlers claimed legal jurisdiction over indigenous territory and peoples by denying the legitimacy of indigenous land claims and customary law in the peripheries of empire. Ford, *Settler Sovereignty*, 2, 9; Blackhawk, "Look How Far We've Come," 13–14.

50. Sturken, *Tangled Memories*, 1.

51. Calloway, *First Peoples*, 3; Amin, *Event, Metaphor, Memory*, 3–4.

52. Goldberg notes that modernity's "commitment to continuous progress" in terms of "material, moral, physical, and political improvement" is a standard the West took to be its own values universalized. Goldberg, *Racist Culture*, 4.

CHAPTER 1

1. Cole Harris, "How Did Colonialism Dispossess?," 177. See also Williams, *The American Indian in Western Legal Thought*; and Tomlins, "The Many Legalities of Colonization," 1–20.

2. Cole Harris, "How Did Colonialism Dispossess?," 167.

3. Benton, *Law and Colonial Cultures*, 260.

4. Cole Harris, *Making Native Space*, xvii.

5. Cheyfitz, "Savage Law," 109.

6. Cole Harris, *Making Native Space*, xvii.

7. As anthropologist Thomas Thornton points out, "Relationships with place are a matter of not just living and evolving in specific environments but also of imagining them." Thornton, *Being and Place among the Tlingit*, 7.

8. "Lushootseed" is a combination of two Puget Salish words meaning "salt water" and "language." Testimony of Connie McCloud, HCIJ; Thrush, "The Lushootseed Peoples of Puget Sound Country"; Thrush, *Native Seattle*, xvi; Carpenter, *The Nisqually, My People*, 17; Haeberlin and Gunther, "The Indians of Puget Sound," 7; Smith, *The Puyallup-Nisqually*. I use the terms "Southern Coast Salish," "Puget Salish," and "Lushootseed" somewhat interchangeably in this book, although I use the term "Lushootseed" to draw attention to language specifically. I use the term "Whulshootseed" to refer to the Nisqually and closely adjacent groups in the nineteenth century to allow for greater geographic specificity while also taking into consideration historically fluid tribal identities.

9. Carpenter relied heavily upon anthropologist's writings and served as the main liaison between the tribe and non-Indians interested in tribal history up to her death in 2010. Carpenter taught Indian history in her classroom using primary sources in Leschi's case. She was most interested in exonerating Leschi because of the effect it would have on the way state history would be taught. Interview with Cecelia Carpenter, February 21, 2007.

10. This story has been reprinted several times. The earliest recorded version of the flood epic was in an 1865 manuscript by George Gibbs (probably recorded in 1854), first published in Clark, "George Gibbs' Account," 322, 324. Beckham, "George Gibbs, 1815–1873," 148. Another account of the Nisqually origin story appeared in the *Tacoma Daily Ledger* in 1886. A. B. Rabbeson, "An Indian Legend: How the Nisqually Tribe Was Saved from Extinction," *Tacoma Daily Ledger*, July 7, 1886, p. 4. The same story, excluding some of Rabbeson's more offensive language, was published in 1890 by Myron Eells in "The Religion of the Indians of Puget Sound"; and reprinted in Carpenter, *The Nisqually, My People*, 148–49.

11. Carpenter, *The Nisqually, My People*, 123–24.

12. The origin story explains that the Changer also introduced the people to the spirit powers, who had their own independent will. Although out of human control, these figures were not beyond human influence. Individuals could enter into relationships with guardian spirits with the understanding that each party had obligations and responsibilities to the other. Carpenter, *The Nisqually, My People*, 124–25; Klingle, *Emerald City*, 19.

13. Carpenter, *The Nisqually, My People*, 51.

14. An important spring event across Coast Salish communities is the First Salmon Ceremony, conducted to announce the start of the annual King salmon run. King Salmon, the story goes, gave himself to the people so that they might

be fed. In return, the people honor King Salmon when he arrives each year with a community-wide ceremony in which he is cooked and eaten. The bones are respectfully returned to deep water in the hope that he will tell the other salmon to come to the people. Stories warned of the consequences for people who did not treat the salmon with respect or failed to conduct the ceremony. The ceremony maintains the relationship between salmon and the community; the act of returning the bones to the river is a gesture of respect that ensures the continuation of the people, the fish, and the river. Klingle, *Emerald City*, 22; Hilbert and Bierwert, *Ways of the Lushootseed People*, 14, 16; Carpenter, *The Nisqually, My People*, 160; Gunther, "An Analysis of the First Salmon Ceremony," 614–16.

15. I follow Peter Nabokov's definition of "myth" as a sacred story that involves nonhuman actors, is set in an earlier world, and is considered to communicate absolute truth. Nabokov defines a "legend" as a story of events featuring human actors, transpiring in today's world, and considered historical and factual. Nabokov, *Forest of Time*, 66.

16. Carpenter, *The Nisqually, My People*, 1–2.

17. The migration legend was also printed in *Messages from Frank's Landing*, a book that Carpenter contributed to and reviewed for accuracy. Wilkinson wrote that the legend comes from "tribal accounts." Wilkinson, *Messages from Frank's Landing*, 19. Anthropologists Teit and Boas noted stories of a relatively recent migration of "a considerable number" of interior Native people to the west side of the Cascades. Boas noticed linguistic similarities between the Upper Nisqually villagers and the ancestors of Sahaptin speakers on the Columbia Plateau and concluded that there was a recent wave of immigrants across the mountains who intermarried with Salish peoples. Teit, "The Middle Columbia Salish," 108.

18. The prefix Ni- may have been added by French traders. Native peoples most often named their communities after places rather than the other way around, as is common in Western culture. Thornton, *Being and Place among the Tlingit*, 103; Carpenter, *Where the Waters Begin*, 14.

19. Carpenter, Pascualy, and Hunter, *Nisqually Indian Tribe*, 14; Thornton, "Anthropological Studies," 214–15; Waterman, *Puget Sound Geography*, 264–328.

20. Basso, *Wisdom Sits in Places*, 34; Thornton, "Anthropological Studies," 211.

21. Vancouver's mission grew out of a sovereignty dispute with Spain after a Spanish commander seized a British ship in Nootka Sound. Vancouver was ostensibly on a scientific mission to survey the region, although he pointedly renamed some Spanish landmarks to support the British claim. Lewarne, "Snohomish County in the 'Second Great Age of Discovery,'" 36; Rochester, "George Vancouver."

22. Legal theorists of the Age of Discovery Franciscus de Victoria and Hugo Grotius combined natural law and religious justifications for Europeans' right to inhabited land. In the seventeenth century, English legal colonizing discourse shifted to focus on the commercial potential of the land. According to Robert Williams, English discourse characterized Indians as "the dehumanized entry barrier to the

lawfully mandated sovereignty over the underutilized, savage lands of the New World." Williams, *The American Indian in Western Legal Thought*, 13, 193–94, 199, 228; quote from p. 194.

23. Cole Harris, *Making Native Space*, 47–48, 52.

24. Carpenter, *Fort Nisqually*, 188; Harmon, *Indians in the Making*, 26; Galbraith, "Early History," 234. For more on Hawaiians in the Pacific Northwest, see Koppel, *Kanaka*; and Barman and Watson, *Leaving Paradise*.

25. White, *Land Use, Environment, and Social Change*, 15.

26. Harmon, *Indians in the Making*, 37.

27. Some European introductions to the region, especially pigs and sheep, caused environmental changes detrimental to Native livelihoods. Even so, Leschi and Quiemuth helped the Hudson's Bay Company shepherds and honored the British legal notion that domesticated animals were mobile private property. Meeker, *Reminiscences*, 210–11; Cary C. Collins, "In a Familiar yet Foreign Land"; White, *Land Use*, 22, 32–33; Cronon, *Changes in the Land*, 129–30.

28. Cole Harris, *Making Native Space*, xxiii.

29. Specifically, the Supreme Court ruling in *Johnson v. McIntosh* (1823) and the government's practice of selling parcels of land to settlers in the West before purchasing it first from Indians. Banner, *How the Indians Lost Their Land*, 150.

30. On the religious aspects of Manifest Destiny, see Stephanson, *Manifest Destiny*, 5–6. For more on the concept of progress and imperatives of capitalism as important factors in nineteenth-century North American colonialism, see Cole Harris, *Making Native Space*, 52.

31. Raibmon, "Unmaking Native Space," 58.

32. Wolfe, "Settler Colonialism and the Elimination of the Native," 388.

33. Raibmon, "Unmaking Native Space," 58.

34. In Frantz Fanon's words, colonial agents created a world "divided into compartments." Fanon quoted in Cole Harris, *Making Native Space*, xxiv. See also Scott, *Seeing Like a State*, 3–4.

35. "The geography of dispossession," Harris argues, "is explained more precisely when the powers that effected it are disaggregated." Cole Harris, "How Did Colonialism Dispossess?," 179.

36. J. B. Harley writes: "As much as guns and warships, maps have been the weapons of imperialism." Harley, "Maps, Knowledge, and Power," 282.

37. Quoted in ibid., 279.

38. Harmon, *Indians in the Making*, 43; Buerge, "Wilkes Expedition."

39. Brückner, *Geographic Revolution*, 237; Nisbet, *Mapmaker's Eye*, 76–77.

40. Buerge, "Wilkes Expedition."

41. Speech of Slugamus Koquilton of the Muckleshoot reservation, in Pierce County Pioneer Association, Program, "Commemorative Celebration," 11; Buerge, "Wilkes Expedition."

42. Thornton, *Being and Place among the Tlingit*, 128, 134.

43. Nineteenth-century geography texts purported to show the Enlightenment notion of universal categories and signs, which did not account for Native geography of kinship connections, spiritual realms, and family claims to specific sites. Harley, *New Nature of Maps*, 154.

44. Morrissey, *Mental Territories*, 29. Several geographers have taken Israel as an important case study, noting that the landscape has been renamed as part of a larger process of claiming Israeli historic attachment to land conquered since 1948 while simultaneously erasing Palestinian-Arab historical presence. Cohen and Kliot, "Place-Names in Israel's Ideological Struggle"; Falah, "The 1948 Israeli-Palestinian War."

45. Buerge, "Wilkes Expedition"; Meany, *Origins of Washington Geographic Names*, vii.

46. Thornton, "Anthropological Studies," 215; Waterman, *Puget Sound Geography*, 264–328.

47. Great Britain and the United States signed the Treaty with Great Britain, in Regards to Limits Westward of the Rocky Mountains, or the Oregon Treaty, in 1846. Douglas C. Harris, "The Boldt Decision in Canada," 148; Brückner, *Geographic Revolution*, 225; Nisbet, *Mapmaker's Eye*, 26.

48. Morrissey, *Mental Territories*, 29.

49. Nash, "The Changing Experience of Nature," 1602.

50. Morse, *North American Atlas* (New York: Harper and Brothers, 1842), in David Rumsey Historical Digital Map Collection (September 16, 2007).

51. Harley, "Maps, Knowledge and Power," 290–92.

52. Brückner, *Geographic Revolution*, 168.

53. August Mitchell, "New Map of Texas, Oregon, and California with the Regions Adjoining, Compiled from the More Recent Authorities" (Philadelphia: S. August Mitchell, 1846), in Washington State, Secretary of State, Historic Maps Digital Collection, www.secstate.wa.gov/history/maps_results.aspx (September 17, 2007).

54. Buchanan, "Dialectic Variants of the Nisqually Linguistic Root Stock of Puget Sound," 31; Wilkes, *Narrative of the United States Exploring Expedition*, vol. 5, 136; Meany, *Origins of Washington Geographic Names*, 189; Carpenter, *The Nisqually, My People*, 17.

55. See Cole Harris, *Making Native Space*, xvii.

56. Harley, *New Nature of Maps*, 188.

57. Schwantes, *Pacific Northwest*, 118–19, 121, 125; White, *Land Use*, 37–38.

58. Isaac Stevens led a team through Washington Territory as part of the 1853 Pacific Railroad Survey Act, a congressional program created to find the most economical and practical railroad routes to the Pacific Ocean. Boime, *Magisterial Gaze*, 129; J. W. Trutch, J. A. Preston, and G. W. Hyde, "Preston's Sectional and County Map of Oregon and Washington: West of the Cascade Mountains" (Chicago: A. H. Burley, Stationer, and New York: Ferd. Mayer & Co., Engraver, 1856), in Washing-

ton State University Libraries, Digital Map Collection; "Atlas of North America," by Henry Darwin Rogers of Boston and A. Keith Johnston, Geographer to the Queen (London, 1857), in David Rumsey Historical Digital Map Collection (September 15, 2007); J. H. Colton and Co., "Territories of Washington and Oregon" (New York, 1853), Washington State, Secretary of State, Web archive.

59. James Tilton, Surveyor General of Washington, "Washington Territory West of the Cascade Mountains" (Philadelphia: Wagner & McGuigan, 1857), Washington State, Secretary of State, Web archive. In 1855 the surveyor general of Washington Territory projected the mileage of surveyed land west of the Cascades would nearly double by the end of 1857. "Governor's Message," *Puget Sound Courier*, December 14, 1855.

60. Boime, *Magisterial Gaze*, 127–28.

61. On Preston's 1856 map, the area east of the Nisqually River is blank (the location of most Nisqually villages). A small star representing the location of a mill just east of Olympia gives the only indication of human land use. The mill suggested a specifically commercial kind of development that would entice potential emigrants and investors alike. Morrissey wrote that early maps of the Northwest "connected their users to national, economic, legal, and political systems" by representing land as "state-regulated property, accessible for private individual ownership, a commodity to be bought and sold on the market." Morrissey, *Mental Territories*, 29.

62. This shared notion led to an 1857 dispute between the Puget Sound Agricultural Company, which retained its pasturelands at Nisqually under the Oregon Treaty, and American settlers concerned about the effect of the international treaty on the status of their homestead claims. When the company sent out surveyors to establish the boundary line of its claim, an armed group of Americans "rebelled" and stopped the survey by a show of force. Meeker reported: "Many of the settlers looked upon the company as interlopers, pure and simple, without any rights they were bound to respect." Meeker, *Pioneer Reminiscences of Puget Sound and the Tragedy of Leschi*, 120–22; quote from p. 122. Cole Harris, *Making Native Space*, 49.

63. Wesley Gosnell to J. W. Nesmith, September 30, 1857, Bureau of Indian Affairs reports, PNRO.

64. Meeker, *Pioneer Reminiscences of Puget Sound and the Tragedy of Leschi*, 120–21. The origins of the Muckleshoot Tribe can be traced back to the establishment of the reservation between the White and Green Rivers following the 1855–1856 war. The name of the reservation was derived from the prairie on which it was established, and the people—all descended from Duwamish and Upper Puyallup ancestors—became known as Muckleshoot Indians over time. Muckleshoot Indian Tribe, "History of the Muckleshoot Indian Tribe and its Reservation."

65. Thrush, *Native Seattle*, 53.

66. Cole Harris, *Making Native Space*, 271.

67. Harmon, *Indians in the Making*, 113.

68. G. M. Wheeler, *Report upon the United States Geographic Surveys West of the One-Hundredth Meridian* (Washington, D.C.: Government Printing Office, 1889), 214; quoted in Boime, *Magisterial Gaze*, 140.

69. White, "Treaty of Medicine Creek," 173.

70. Wheeler quoted in Boime, *Magisterial Gaze*, 140. For more on the Wheeler Survey, see Short, *Representing the Republic*.

71. The commissioner of Indian Affairs suspected in 1869 that a portion of the Nisqually reservation was "incorrectly labeled" and ordered the survey to be done. The 1871 surveyor "corrected" the mistake by shaving off a half-mile strip, which included a cemetery. The Nisqually people moved their ancestors' remains and complained for years afterward that the land was unlawfully taken. Without access to geometric survey equipment of their own, they were powerless to argue their case in terms officials would respect. Records of the Washington Superintendency of Indian Affairs, 1853–74, Letters from the Commissioner 1861–74, M5, roll 8, PNRO; Carpenter, *The Nisqually, My People*, 189–91. The exact location of Leschi's first resting place, from 1858 to 1895, is not precisely known. The *Tacoma Daily News* for July 3, 1895, claimed that his remains were initially buried on the Huggins ranch (although this may have been Quiemuth's burial site), and a speech by H. F. Jones implied that his body was buried at Fort Nisqually. H. F. Jones Papers, TS-26, box 1/31, WSHS.

72. The railroad terminus would eventually go further north, to the Puyallup reservation and future site of Tacoma. Within two decades, the Puyallup lands were leased out and thrown open for sale. White, "Treaty of Medicine Creek," 178–79, 201–2.

73. Reddick and Collins, "Medicine Creek to Fox Island," 377–78; Harmon, *Indians in the Making*, 58. The law granted 320 acres to each male citizen over 18 who arrived in the territory before 1850, and if such a male citizen was married before 1851, his wife was also entitled to 320 acres. Male citizens who arrived after 1850 but before 1854 were entitled to 160 acres. In order to receive perfect title, the land had to be occupied for four years. Settlers who arrived after 1854 could acquire 160 acres of surveyed or unsurveyed land for $1.25 per acre. White, *Land Use*, 37–38.

74. Gibbs labeled the act "the great primary source of evil" in the territory because it prompted settlers to displace Native families with impunity. Gibbs, *Indian Tribes of Washington Territory*, 28.

75. U.S. Government, Northwest Ordinance, 1787, Section 14, Article 3, http://www.ourdocuments.gov/doc.php?flash=true&doc=8 (July 1, 2011).

76. Banner, *How the Indians Lost Their Land*, 190.

77. Reddick and Collins, "Medicine Creek to Fox Island," 377.

78. Schwantes, *Pacific Northwest*, 118–19, 125.

79. Beckham, "George Gibbs," 102–3.

80. Boxberger, "The Not So Common," 64.

81. Between 1854 and 1860, three survey commissioners used Gibbs's knowledge

of the region, attesting to his reputation as an authority. Hinsley, *Savages and Scientists*, 51–52; Miller, *Regaining Dr. Herman Haeberlin*, 83.

82. See introduction in Carstensen, "Pacific Northwest Letters of George Gibbs," 190–98.

83. Jackson, First Annual Message to Congress, Case for the Removal Act; Calloway, *First Peoples*, 230.

84. The treaty promised Indians monetary payments, hunting and fishing rights, agricultural and industrial schools, and a doctor to provide medical care. Reddick and Collins, "Medicine Creek to Fox Island," 36.

85. Beckham, "George Gibbs," 155.

86. Gibbs, *Indian Tribes of Washington Territory*, 30.

87. The right to fish in usual and accustomed places is known as the "reserved right" clause in the Stevens treaties. Beckham, "George Gibbs," 111–12.

88. Gibbs, *Tribes of Western Washington and Northwestern Oregon*, 183. Gibbs exchanged letters with Hudson's Bay Company employee Edward Huggins about Coast Salish vocabulary in 1869. Huggins informed him that "Nisquallies have no names for the moons, neither can [they] learn to count past fourth." Such perceptions among local European traders may have informed Gibbs's claim, fifteen years earlier, about Nisquallies' "vague" sense of numbers. This perception may have persisted until 1878, when Skokomish missionary Myron Eells indicated in his field notes that Huggins had misunderstood Lushootseed linguistic structure (prefixes) in relation to sequential numbers. Letter from Edward Huggins to George Gibbs, July 10, 1869, American Indian Northwest Coast manuscripts, MS 699, NAA; Myron Eells, Vocabulary 1878, MS 658, ibid.

89. Cole Harris calls demographic data and cartography "egregious simplifications and effective colonial tools." Cole Harris, "How Did Colonialism Dispossess?," 176.

90. Gibbs, *Indian Tribes of Washington Territory*, 36, 42.

91. Smallpox hit Puget Sound in 1782 or 1783 and may have cut the Native population of the region in half within 50 years. Wilkes noted the deep impacts of disease along the mouth of the Columbia River in the early 1840s. After European and American presence in the region increased, Native South Puget Sound villagers suffered a series of deadly epidemics: measles in 1847, smallpox again in 1853, and syphilis through the 1850s. Wilkes, *Narratives of the United States Exploring Expedition*, 5:149; White, *Land Use*, 27. See Robert Boyd, "Pacific Northwest Measles Epidemic of 1847–1848."

92. A few months before Gibbs presented his population figures, Edmond Starling estimated the Nisqually population at 80. Starling quoted in Reddick and Collins, "Medicine Creek to Fox Island," n6; Gibbs, *Indian Tribes of Washington Territory*, 40–42; Marian Smith, "The Puyallup of Washington," 11.

93. Reddick and Collins, "Medicine Creek to Fox Island," 18–22.

94. Trigger, "Past as Power," 12.

95. Jefferson, *Notes on the State of Virginia*, 163.

96. Nabokov, *Forest of Time*, 75; Calloway, *First Peoples*, 18. See Vine Deloria Jr., *Red Earth, White Lies*, chap. 4; and Fogelson, "A Final Look."

97. Beckham, "George Gibbs," 102–3.

98. Hinsley, *Savages and Scientists*, 52–53.

99. Nineteenth-century linguists referred to Whulshootseed as the Nisqually dialect and categorized it within the Nisqually language group (that is, Lushootseed) and Salish language family. Carpenter, *The Nisqually, My People*, 17; Hilbert and Bierwert, *Ways of the Lushootseed People*, 31; Miller, *Regaining Dr. Herman Haeberlin*, 83–84; Beckham, "George Gibbs, 1815–1873," 155, 193; Carpenter, "George Gibbs Remembered," 9.

100. Buchanan, "Dialectic Variants of the Nisqually Linguistic Root Stock of Puget Sound," 30; Carstensen, "Pacific Northwest Letters of George Gibbs," 197; Smithsonian Institution and Library of Congress "Ethnography" museum display, Library of Congress, Washington, D.C., 2007; Miller, *Regaining Dr. Herman Haeberlin*, 70.

101. Hinsley, *Savages and Scientists*, 52.

102. Bieder, *Science Encounters the Indian*, 9–13.

103. Trigger, "Past as Power," 17–19.

104. Gibbs exchanged letters with William Tolmie, Edward Huggins, Edwin Eells, and James G. Swan. Miller, *Regaining Dr. Herman Haeberlin*, 84.

105. Letter from James G. Swan to George Gibbs, July 20, 1855, American Indian Northwest Coast manuscripts, MS 970, NAA. Proto-anthropologists had reason to be suspicious. One Twana man recalled that the people disliked the missionary on the Klallam reservation, Myron Eells, and when he asked for vocabulary words "they would give him all sorts of dirty, nasty words" and laugh when he tried to use them. Elmendorf, *Twana Narratives*, 5.

106. Nabokov, *Forest of Time*, 35. Among Tlingits, for example, stories, placenames, and songs were the property of the individual storyteller, through inheritance, permission, the instruction of a spirit guardian, or personal innovation. Thornton, *Being and Place among the Tlingit*, 134–35.

107. Hilbert, *Haboo*, ix–xv.

108. Clark, "George Gibbs' Account," 322–23; Prosch, *Reminiscences of Washington Territory*, 44–45. Vi Hilbert and Jay Miller point out that the flood epic's hero figure is now called dəwiʔ (pronounced duh-wee-[glottal stop]), and because Lushootseed shifts the sound of N to D, the hero is likely named after the biblical figure Noah, although the story itself is much older. Peter, *Susie Sampson Peter*, 129.

109. One of Meany's undated (post-1912) speeches mentions one archaeologist's attempt to teach University of Washington students how to pronounce Salish words: "His study . . . gravitated to the minute consideration of the guttural phonetics. He illustrated the making of the sounds by displaying beef throats obtained at the slaughter house." Meany considered the models an "extreme [example] of

the effort to introduce the laboratory method into the study of Indian linguistics." Meany speech, "Opportunities for Linguistic Research among the Indians of the State of Washington," 6–7, Edmond Meany Papers, 84–15, UWSC; "Pronunciation of Indian Names," *Seattle Sunday Times*, October 7, 1906, p. 11; Waterman, *Puget Sound Geography*, vii. Elmendorf explained that one of his Skokomish informants, Frank Allen, warmed up to him when Elmendorf made an effort to pronounce Salish words correctly. "This struck him as quite different from what he had experienced with any other white person," Elmendorf wrote in 1940. Elmendorf, *Twana Narratives*, xxxiv.

110. As J. B. Harley has pointed out in other colonial contexts ranging from seventeenth-century Algonquin New England to nineteenth-century Gaelic Ireland, the cartographer's task was to Anglicize indigenous place names. The resulting maps "were a medium in a wider colonial discourse for redescribing topography in the language of the dominant society." Harley, *New Nature of Maps*, 179.

111. Meany appeared to operate under Daniel Webster's notion of correct pedagogical recitation: "The true pronunciation of the name of a place, is that which prevails in and near the place." Webster offered an early example of a linguistic practice that demonstrated how the agenda of Americanizing hinged on a territorializing ideology. That is, if American English speakers come to dominate a new territory, their pronunciation of the Native place-name will be the true one. Brückner, *Geographic Revolution*, 260–61.

112. Benton, *Law and Colonial Cultures*, 15.

113. For a case study of one Puyallup man's attempts to broker economic advantages by playing off tensions among federal paternalism, local land speculators, and railroad corporate greed, see Nathan E. Roberts, "The Death of Peter Stanup."

114. Quote from the Washington State Supreme Court decision in *State v. Towessnute* (1916). Wilkinson, *Messages from Frank's Landing*, 53.

115. As Harris notes of non-Native British Columbians, "a few found much to appreciate or pity in native lives" and some even supported Natives' calls for expanded reserve lands. "But even kindness," Harris explains, "was situated within the assumptions of the civilization/savage binary." Cole Harris, "How Did Colonialism Dispossess?," 170.

116. Here I draw on the concept of "imperialist nostalgia" from Rosaldo, "Imperialist Nostalgia."

117. Cary C. Collins, "Hard Lessons in America," 6–7; Cary C. Collins, "In a Familiar yet Foreign Land."

118. Waterman identified Sicade as a Muckleshoot man of Puyallup extraction. Sicade told anthropologist Hermann Haeberlin in the mid-1910s that his grandfather, Stann, was head shaman of the Nisqually who went to war in 1855–56. Haeberlin and Gunther, "Indians of Puget Sound," 76. Sicade's biographer, Oscar H. Jones, noted in 1936 that Sicade's maternal grandfather was chief of the Puyallup Indians and that his grandfather's brother was a revered arbiter who joined French

Jesuit missionaries in converting coastal peoples to Catholicism. Collins, "In a Familiar yet Foreign Land."

119. Konkle, *Writing Indian Nations*, 36.

120. The publishers of Sicade's speech pointed out to their readers that "some points in the tradition as it came to Mr. Sicade do not tally with contemporary records." Henry Sicade, "The Indians' Side of the Story," 490.

121. Ibid., 491–92.

122. Following one story of a Nisqually military engagement in the North Puget Sound, Sicade explained that the storyteller always concluded with instructions for the audience: "Some day, you may be called to defend our fair lands and waters. Remember your forbearers knew how to fight; we shall expect you to fight and die for our fair lands and waters if need be." Sicade, "The Indians' Side of the Story," 491–503; Sicade, "Henry Sicade," 2–12.

123. Sicade, "The Indians' Side of the Story"; Cary C. Collins, "In a Familiar yet Foreign Land."

124. Sicade, "The Indians' Side of the Story."

125. Collins, "In a Familiar yet Foreign Land."

126. Peter's parents were Mary Martin and John Kalama. Carpenter, Pascualy, and Hunter, *Nisqually Indian Tribe*, 97.

127. Carpenter, "George Gibbs Remembered," 9; Indian Claims Commission Docket 197 (*Nisqually et al. v. U.S.*), PNRO; Boxberger, "The Not So Common," 65.

128. Boxberger, "The Not So Common," 73–74; John Dodge, "Nisqually Tribe Has New Tool for Separating Wild, Raised Salmon," *Olympian*, September 22, 2012; Leslie Kaufman, "Seeing Trends, Coalition Works to Help a River Adapt," *New York Times*, July 20, 2011. In 2000, Washington tribes collectively employed more scientists in fisheries than did the State of Washington. Wilkinson, *Messages from Frank's Landing*, 94.

129. Lauren Benton argues that a colonized group's participation in an imposed order was not necessarily collaboration, just as any form of rejection was not necessarily resistance. Groups could simultaneously collaborate with an imposed order and resist its effects. Benton, *Law and Colonial Cultures*, 17.

CHAPTER 2

1. In situations in which Native peoples challenged or hindered colonials' self-interest, they could be excluded from the rights-bearing status of rational actors and subjected to a separate standard. This reflects political theorist Georgio Agamben's characterization of the "state of exception," in which governments suspend normal functions of law and ignore international convention while nevertheless claiming to apply the law. The result is that certain individuals can be categorized, at the government's discretion, into an extralegal status. Agamben, *State of Exception*, 24, 87.

2. Philip Deloria, *Indians in Unexpected Places*, 20. John Fabian Witt argues that

the peculiar legal status of Indians in the nineteenth century (at once independent nations and domestic dependencies) contributed to U.S. officials' confusion over how to apply the laws of war to western conflicts with Indians. Witt, *Lincoln's Code*, 336.

3. Interview with Robert Anderson.

4. Witt, *Lincoln's Code*, 81, 84–85, 128.

5. Military historians describe the "American way of war" as both legally justified and especially destructive. Witt provides a relevant example: "Enlightenment rules stand alongside wars of extermination on the Indian frontier." Witt, *Lincoln's Code*, 5–6.

6. Lepore, *Name of War*, x–xi.

7. Lee, "Mind and Matter," 1136.

8. Witt, *Lincoln's Code*, 4, 8–9.

9. Schwantes, *Pacific Northwest*, 120.

10. White, *It's Your Misfortune and None of My Own*, 155–56.

11. Olympia became the new capital of the territory and the Democratic stronghold of the region. The Republican legislature took office in 1861. Bancroft and Victor, *History of Washington, Idaho, and Montana*, 77; Oldham, "Governor Isaac Stevens Selects Olympia"; Dennis Weber, "The Creation of Washington Territory," 27–34. For more on how frontier newspaper editors influenced public opinion about the role of violence in their communities, see Hoffert, "Gender and Vigilantism on the Minnesota Frontier."

12. The *Pioneer and Democrat* first consolidated in January 1854, and Goudy was elected territorial printer on January 27, 1855, at the age of twenty-six. Goudy's connection with the paper ended in August 1856. Bancroft and Victor, *History of Washington, Idaho, and Montana*, 77. Goudy commanded Company C during the war. Himes, "History of the Press of Oregon," 354. Goudy was likely not the only newspaper employee who participated in the war. The *Pioneer and Democrat* skipped an issue near the start of the war, explaining on November 9, 1855, that "the hands in the office were either acting as volunteers or engaged in the work of fortifying Olympia." Meany, "Newspapers of Washington Territory," 265.

13. Kunsch, "Trials of Leschi," 71–72. One writer for the *Puget Sound Courier* argued against a new law voiding marriages between white men and women of half Native ancestry by noting that most of the territory's "founding fathers" had Indian wives. "Pocahontas at a Discount," *Puget Sound Courier*, May 31, 1855.

14. January 23, 1858, in Reese, *Nothing Worthy of Note Transpired Today*.

15. White, *Land Use, Environment, and Social Change*, 37.

16. Stevens, *Life*, 1:281.

17. Wesley Gosnell to Isaac Stevens, December 31, 1856, Bureau of Indian Affairs, Letters of the Superintendents of Indian Affairs for Washington Territory, 1856–74, NARA; Asher, *Beyond the Reservation*, 61–62.

18. Native people were only part of his concern. Stevens considered the close

relationships between Hudson's Bay Company employees and local Indians as a challenge to American sovereignty in the region. Kluger, *Bitter Waters of Medicine Creek*, 52.

19. "Indian Treaty," *Pioneer and Democrat*, December 30, 1854.

20. "Medicine Creek Treaty: Address by Colonel B. F. Shaw before the Annual Meeting of the Oregon Historical Society," *Portland Oregonian*, December 26, 1903, Clarence Bagley Scrapbook, vol. 2, p. 121, UWSC. Meeker dismissed Shaw's account as partisan favors to his benefactor, Governor Stevens, who provided Shaw with positions of prominence "only upon conditions that [Stevens] will be law." "Ezra Meeker's Interesting Address before State Historical Society," *Tacoma Daily Ledger*, January 24, 1904, Clarence Bagley Scrapbook, vol. 2, p. 112, UWSC.

21. Priscilla Wald argues that *Dred Scott* represented an attempt to legislate the disappearance of Indians by judging them to be neither citizens nor aliens, and thus not legally representable. Taney quoted in Wald, "Terms of Assimilation," 76.

22. Asher, *Beyond the Reservation*, 62.

23. For an example of how perceptions of the hegemony of U.S. law break down in frontiers, see Hoffert, "Gender and Vigilantism on the Minnesota Frontier," 358.

24. See William Tolmie letter, February 12, 1858, William Tolmie Papers, UWSC.

25. "Gov. Stevens' War," *Pioneer and Democrat*, October 26, 1855; "No Cause for Alarm," *Puget Sound Courier*, August 31, 1855; "To the People," *Puget Sound Courier*, August 24, 1855; "Governor Stevens' War," *Puget Sound Courier*, October 19, 1855. Quote from "To the People," *Puget Sound Courier*, August 31, 1855. The editor specifically criticized a group of government officials for bungling the U.S. government's plan to purchase Cuba from Spain by unilaterally threatening to break the neutrality agreement if Spain refused the sale. The Whig newspaper's concern for international diplomacy was an outgrowth of the larger sectional debate over the expansion of slavery into the Caribbean. See May, "Epilogue to the Missouri Compromise."

26. Meeker, *Pioneer Reminiscences of Puget Sound and the Tragedy of Leschi*, 226-27.

27. Meeker, *Seventy Years of Progress in Washington*, 345-46, 348.

28. Testimony of Shanna Stevenson, HCIJ.

29. Prosch, *Reminiscences of Washington Territory*, 46-49; "Trouble with the Indians," *Puget Sound Courier*, October 5, 1855.

30. Philip Deloria argues that in the "ambiguous period" immediately following treaties, Americans used representations of Indian violence to express anxiety over their limited power to control Native people. Deloria, *Indians in Unexpected Places*, 21.

31. Ostler, *Plains Sioux and U.S. Colonialism*, 350.

32. Tolmie later recalled a conversation with Leschi and Quiemuth as they considered their options: "Mason urged these Indians to go to Olympia, in part for their own safety, as some whites were threatening them, but that was to them the lion's den." William Tolmie to Fayette McMullin, January 12, 1858, Clarence Bagley

Papers, box 21, UWSC, printed in the *Truth Teller,* February 25, 1858; James McAllister to Washington Territorial Superintendent of Indian Affairs, October 16, 1855, reprinted in Reese, *Leschi, the Officers, and the Citizens,* 7.

33. Tolmie quoted in Meeker, *Pioneer Reminiscences of Puget Sound and the Tragedy of Leschi,* 211; "Wars and Rumors of Wars," *Puget Sound Courier,* September 28, 1855; "Fort at Seattle," *Puget Sound Courier,* October 5, 1855.

34. Meeker, *Pioneer Reminiscences of Puget Sound and the Tragedy of Leschi,* 283; Carpenter, *The Nisqually, My People,* 170; *Pioneer and Democrat,* October 26, 1855; *Pioneer and Democrat,* November 9, 1855; *Puget Sound Courier,* November 16, 1855; "Governor's Message," *Puget Sound Courier,* December 14, 1855; Olson, "Our Leschi: The Making of a Martyr," 22; Kluger, *Bitter Waters of Medicine Creek,* 133–36.

35. Philip Deloria, *Indians in Unexpected Places,* 20; "Governor Stevens' War," *Pioneer and Democrat,* October 26, 1855; "Governor Stevens' War," *Puget Sound Courier,* October 19, 1855; "A New Man at the Mill," *Puget Sound Courier,* November 16, 1855; "No Cause for Alarm," *Puget Sound Courier,* August 31, 1855.

36. *Pioneer and Democrat,* November 9, 1855, pp. 1–2. The *Courier* identified Quiemuth and "Klow-ow-it" as the leaders of the Nisqually warriors without mention of Leschi. "Latest from Our Troops," *Puget Sound Courier,* November 30, 1855.

37. In the same issue of the *Pioneer and Democrat,* Rabbeson wrote an eyewitness account of the death of Moses and named Leschi as present at the scene. *Pioneer and Democrat,* November 9, 1855, pp. 1–2. The *Puget Sound Courier* did not name Leschi specifically in their report of the ambush on Connell's Prairie. *Puget Sound Courier,* November 16, 1855. Several months earlier the *Courier* printed rumors of a Klickitat attack on Puget Sound, but dismissed such an attack as unlikely because most Indians were friendly. "Prospect of Indian Disturbances," *Puget Sound Courier,* August 24, 1855; "No Cause for Alarm," *Puget Sound Courier,* August 31, 1855. Those critical of Stevens insisted that Indians had legitimate complaints the governor had failed to address. Harmon, *Indians in the Making,* 88. Those friendly to Stevens claimed that Hudson's Bay Company employees "tampered with" their Native neighbors in a conspiracy to push Americans out of the region. Urban Hicks and W. W. Plumb, in Reese, *The Northwest Was Their Goal,* 2:111, 247; Mary Perry Frost, *Tacoma Sunday Ledger,* June 26, 1892, reprinted in Reese, *They Came to Puget Sound,* 83; *Pioneer and Democrat,* November 9, 1855, pp. 1–2.

38. Letter from Isaac Stevens to the Office of the Superintendent of Indian Affairs, May 31, 1856, WSHS, "Leschi" Web archive.

39. Eckrom, *Remembered Drums,* 74. Tolmie blamed himself for identifying Leschi as an important figure to American officials. Meeker, *Pioneer Reminiscences of Puget Sound and the Tragedy of Leschi,* 211.

40. *Pioneer and Democrat,* November 16, 1855, pp. 1–2.

41. Ibid., February 15, 1856, p. 1.

42. Shelton, *Wisdom of a Tulalip Elder,* 30.

43. *Pioneer and Democrat,* March 20, 1857.

44. In 1856, Governor Stevens described how "the Indians, believed to be the most reliable, in direct violation of their solemn word, commenced the war." Letter from Isaac I. Stevens to Superintendent of Indian Affairs, May 31, 1856, WSHS, "Leschi" Web archive.

45. Harmon, *Indians in the Making*, 87.

46. White, "Treaty at Medicine Creek," 120. The editor of the *Courier* suggested that the narrative of inevitable Indian war needlessly heightened anxieties and bolstered baseless rumors in the months before the start of the fighting in South Puget Sound: "'Wars and rumors of wars' with the Indians, are getting to be too old a story in this part of the world, for us to loose [sic] our senses before they actually happen." "No Cause for Alarm," *Puget Sound Courier*, August 31, 1855.

47. In a letter to Secretary of War Jefferson Davis several months later, Stevens claimed there were "many cases" in which Indians had killed their white friends. Isaac Stevens to Jefferson Davis, March 21, 1856, in Reese, *Leschi and the Indian War of 1855*, 21; Acting Governor Charles H. Mason to the Third Annual Session of the Legislative Assembly, December 7, 1855, in Charles M. Gates, *Messages of the Governors of the Territory of Washington*, 17. See also Olson, "Our Leschi: A Story of Puget Sound History," 47–48; and Olson, "Our Leschi: The Making of a Martyr," 34.

48. Rabbesson, "The Truth of History," 148.

49. Harmon, *Indians in the Making*, 88–89.

50. U.S. Supreme Court Chief Justice John Marshall wrote in *Johnson v. McIntosh* (1823) that under the "Doctrine of Discovery," the European nation had the legal and "exclusive right to extinguish the Indian title of occupancy, either by purchase or by conquest." Quoted in Williams, *The American Indian in Western Legal Thought*, 313. Banner argues that Marshall's reasoning did not reflect actual land acquisition practices, which were structured around a series of legal transactions. Conquest was not sufficient to secure title to land in legal terms, and a treaty with Indian consent was needed (no matter how coercive the circumstances). Banner, *How the Indians Lost Their Land*, 229.

51. Letter from Samuel James to William Tolmie, March 22, 1856, box 1, folder 4, William Tolmie Papers, UWSC; Testimony of John Swan in the second trial printed in the *Washington Republican*, April 10, 1857, courtesy of Cecelia Carpenter; *Puget Sound Courier*, February 4, 1856, reprinted in Vaughn, *Puget Sound Invasion*, 57; "Proclamation," *Puget Sound Courier*, January 25, 1856.

52. He reasoned that the fact that Indians had not attacked these settlers was proof that they were supplying the hostile forces with food and ammunition. Message of Governor Isaac Stevens to the Third Annual Session of the Legislative Assembly, January 21, 1856, in Charles M. Gates, *Messages of the Governors of the Territory of Washington*, 32. Captain Maxon wrote to the governor in March 1856 that he considered the "old-time employees of the Hudson's Bay Company . . . guilty of treason." Snowden, *Rise and Progress of an American State*, 484; "United States v.

Charles Wren, Lyon A. Smith, and John McLeod," 34th Congress, 3rd sess., 1857, S.E. Doc. 41, pp. 24–28 (Serial 881).

53. Olson, "Our Leschi: The Making of a Martyr," 29; Kunsch, "Trials of Leschi," 72; C.R.J., "Marshal Law—By a Citizen" and Isaac I. Stevens, "Proclamation," *Puget Sound Courier*, April 25, 1856.

54. President Pierce merely scolded Stevens for the unnecessary martial law declaration, and the situation deescalated by the summer. C.R.J., "Marshal Law—By a Citizen," *Puget Sound Courier*, April 25, 1856; Olson, "Our Leschi: The Making of a Martyr," 28; Judge Edward Lander to Secretary of State W. L. Marcy, May 22, 1856, in *Message of the President of the United States*, August 4, 1856, 26, Washington State, Secretary of State, Web archive, http://www.sos.wa.gov/history/publications_view _pdf.aspx?pub=68&p=28&i=SL_unitedmessage/SL_unitedmessage.pdf; Francis Chenoweth to Governor Fayette McMullan, March 6, 1858, http://www.sos.wa .gov/history/publications_view_pdf.aspx?pub=68&p=1&i=SL_unitedmessage/SL _unitedmessage.pdf; Kunsch, "Trials of Leschi," 72.

55. Originally published in the *San Francisco Evening News and Herald*, reprinted in the *Pioneer and Democrat*, February 15, 1856.

56. *Pioneer and Democrat*, February 15, 1856; Message of Governor Isaac Stevens to the Third Annual Session of the Legislative Assembly, January 21, 1856, in Charles M. Gates, *Messages of the Governors of the Territory of Washington*, 25–26; see legislative resolution introduced by Maxon in *Pioneer and Democrat*, January 22, 1858.

57. *Puget Sound Courier*, February 29, 1856; Isaac Stevens to Jefferson Davis, March 21, 1856, in Reese, *Leschi and the Indian War of 1855*, 20.

58. "Arrival of Governor Stevens," *Puget Sound Courier*, January 25, 1856; "Prospects of a Treaty," *Puget Sound Courier*, January 4, 1856; Faust, "Telling War Stories."

59. Message of Governor Isaac Stevens to the Third Annual Session of the Legislative Assembly, January 21, 1856, in Charles M. Gates, *Messages of the Governors of the Territory of Washington*, 40; "Letter from Gov. Stevens," *Pioneer and Democrat*, January 29, 1858.

60. Stevens asked Indian agents to set rewards for the other four war leaders as well. Stevens described the Indian war leaders as "notorious murderers" and opined that "men guilty of such acts should at least be tried, and if convicted, punished." Isaac Stevens to George Wright, October 4, 1856, in Field, *Washington Territorial Militia in the Indian Wars of 1855-56*, 45. Cited in Crooks, "Quiemuth, Part I," 6.

61. Wilma, "Isaac Ingalls Stevens."

62. William Morrow to Fayette McMullin, January 11, 1858, Washington State, Secretary of State, Web archive, http://www.sos.wa.gov/history/publications_view _pdf.aspx?pub=148&p=23&i=SL_mcmullincorrespondence/SL_mcmullincorre spondence.pdf.

63. Colonel Wright wrote to Leschi's lawyers before his second trial to inform them of his promise of protection to Leschi and expressed his hope that Leschi would not be hanged, even if convicted. *Pioneer and Democrat*, March 12, 1858.

64. "Isaac Stevens, Our First Territorial Governor, and the Trial of Leschi," *Tacoma News-Ledger*, October 22, 1916. This legal contradiction was clearly recognized in the 1850s. See "How to Serve a Writ," *Puget Sound Herald*, April 22, 1859.

65. Testimony of Alexandra Harmon, HCIJ.

66. Meeker, *Pioneer Reminiscences of Puget Sound and the Tragedy of Leschi*, 421–23.

67. Kunsch, "Trials of Leschi," 80; Meeker, *Pioneer Reminiscences of Puget Sound and the Tragedy of Leschi*, 423.

68. Evan, "The Trial of Leschi"; and court material reprinted in the *Washington Republican* and *Pioneer and Democrat*, 1857–58, all in CSCPC; Meeker, *Pioneer Reminiscences of Puget Sound and the Tragedy of Leschi*, 424–25.

69. Much of the court's opinion focused on the question of jurisdiction raised in the appeal. Although the indictment charged Leschi for a crime committed in the Third District in Pierce County and he was convicted in the Second District in Thurston County, the court declared that Leschi had not been denied the right to a fair trial. Testimony of Alexandra Harmon, HCIJ; Allen, *Reports of Cases Determined in the Supreme Court of the Territory of Washington*, 14–20; "Proceedings of the Supreme Court," *Pioneer and Democrat*, December 25, 1857; "Opinion of the Court," *Pioneer and Democrat*, January 8, 1858.

70. Kunsch, "Trials of Leschi," 26; Witt, *Lincoln's Code*, 4; McFadden's argument was echoed in "How to Serve a Writ," *Puget Sound Herald*, April 22, 1859.

71. Opinion of Justice McFadden in *Territory of Washington v. Leschi*, December term, 1857. Allen, *Reports of Cases Determined in the Supreme Court of the Territory of Washington*, 15.

72. Clark allegedly "procured an Indian to make an affidavit" that would lead to the sheriff's arrest. Meeker, *Pioneer Reminiscences of Puget Sound and the Tragedy of Leschi*, 442. Clark may have hatched the plan after reading section 20 (regarding the sale of liquor to Indians) and the new amendment to the laws regulating trade with Indians, which was published in the newspaper two weeks before Leschi's execution date. "Two Acts in Relation to Indian Affairs," *Pioneer and Democrat*, January 8, 1858; "Leschi," *Pioneer and Democrat*, January 22, 1858; "Mass Meetings of the Citizens of Washington Territory," *Pioneer and Democrat*, January 29, 1858.

73. Oliver Perry Meeker was two years older than his brother Ezra and was active in territorial affairs in the 1850s. *Pioneer and Democrat*, January 29, 1858; Olson, "Our Leschi: A Story of Puget Sound History," 57–58.

74. Meeker, *Pioneer Reminiscences of Puget Sound and the Tragedy of Leschi*, 437.

75. *Pioneer and Democrat*, February 5, 1858.

76. Schmitt, "Execution of Chief Leschi," 33–34.

77. George Williams, Pierce County Sheriff, and J. M. Bachelder, U.S. Commissioner of the Second Judicial District, "To the Citizens of Pierce County," *Truth*

Teller, February 3, 1858. Williams and Bachelder were denounced in Olympia's indignation meeting. Meeker, *Pioneer Reminiscences of Puget Sound and the Tragedy of Leschi*, 436.

78. Olson, "Our Leschi: A Story of Puget Sound History," 59.

79. George Williams to Governor McMullin, January 21, 1858, reprinted in Reese, *Leschi, the Officers, and the Citizens*, 88 and *Pioneer and Democrat*, January 29, 1858.

80. Reese, *Nothing Worthy of Note Transpired Today*, 153–54.

81. *Truth Teller*, February 25, 1858; quoted in Reese, *Leschi, the Officers, and the Citizens*, 117–21.

82. Schmitt, "Execution of Chief Leschi," 35.

83. Starting in 1893, Meeker compiled materials created during and immediately after Leschi's trials. Meeker excelled at personal promotion and entrepreneurship. Huggins to Fuller, October 20, 1901, Edward Huggins Papers, WSHS; Howard Clifford, "Ezra Meeker's Quest for Klondike Gold," 28.

84. Popular American sentiment in the late nineteenth century held that Indians were traditional, uncivilized, of the past, and rapidly vanishing. Raibmon, *Authentic Indians*, 7.

85. Meeker, *Pioneer Reminiscences of Puget Sound and the Tragedy of Leschi*, 205.

86. Meeker organized the Oregon Trail Monument Expedition to place historical markers along the route in an effort to advertise the Northwest and remind younger generations of previous heroics. Wrobel, *Promised Lands*, 109. Meeker's book revived public debate about the events of 1855 and 1856. See Edward Huggins to Ezra Meeker, September 28, 1903, for Huggins's response to Meeker's draft, including pointed criticism about a reference to Leschi. In a letter to a friend, Edward Huggins described the public interest around the 1855–56 war and commented: "I always avoided getting into a newspaper controversy about this 'Leschi' business, and the Indian war in general, although I was frequently very sorely tempted to reply to some of the extraordinarily exaggerated stories." Huggins to Fuller, April 9, 1899, and April 16, 1899, Edward Huggins Papers, UWSC.

87. See accounts by Urban Hicks, John McCarty, and Erastus A. Light, all first printed in the *Tacoma Sunday Ledger* in 1892 and 1893 and reprinted in two volumes of Reese, *The Northwest Was Their Goal*, 100 (Hicks, vol. 1), 439, 468 (McCarty and Light, vol. 2); Olson, "Our Leschi: A Story of Puget Sound History," 69.

88. Olson, "Our Leschi: A Story of Puget Sound History," 68.

89. Raibmon argues that scholars tend to focus on the actions of bureaucrats and officials because they are reluctant to confront the mundane practices of colonialism by regular people. Policy makers are easily othered—they are not us—and so the blame for colonialism can be heaped upon them. Settlers thus appear as "hapless bystanders rather than full participants in colonialism." Raibmon, "Unmaking Native Space," 76–77. Similarly, Andrew Bacevich argues that critics of the American war in Iraq and Afghanistan heap blame onto George W. Bush and a small handful of his closest advisers but fail to recognize the deep cultural roots

of American militarism that intertwine American interests with American values. Bacevich, *New American Militarism*, 4–5.

90. Meeker held a paternalistic view of Indians, which was typical for the period. See Meeker, *Pioneer Reminiscences of Puget Sound and the Tragedy of Leschi*, 222–25. Carpenter used quotes from Meeker's book for her testimony, especially pp. 206–11. Ironically, Meeker's legal and political perspectives could also undercut the petitioners' legal case in 2004. Meeker described Indian nationhood and land title as fictional, and, although he characterized Leschi as a principled combatant, he denied that Nisquallies had reason to resist land loss and that they had the right to commence war. Meeker, *Seventy Years of Progress in Washington*, 349. The writings produced at the turn of the twentieth century had various results. On the one hand, older non-Indians taught a younger generation of Washingtonians negative stereotypes about their indigenous neighbors and dismissed the legal force of Indian treaties. On the other hand, Meeker's sympathy for Leschi heavily influenced twentieth-century historians. In the second half of the century, writers used Meeker's work to create romantic depictions of prereservation Indian life and exalt Leschi as a tragic victim. By the close of the century, Leschi had been used to promote a variety of liberal critiques of American culture, from capitalism and environmental destruction to racism and militarism. See Binns, *Mighty Mountain*; Chaplin, "Only the Drums Remembered"; Emmon, *Leschi of the Nisquallies*; Vaughn, *Puget Sound Invasion*; and Eckrom, *Remembered Drums*.

91. Interview with Thor Hoyte.

92. Bacevich, *New American Militarism*, 4–5. Michael Moore's documentary *Fahrenheit 9/11* opened at number one in U.S. theaters in the summer of 2004. Dawson and Schueller, *Exceptional State*, 13.

93. Bacevich argues that Americans' tendency to conflate liberty with consumerism leads to imperialist wars justified as a defense of Americans' freedom. Bacevich, *Limits of Power*, 5–11.

94. Kluger, *Bitter Waters of Medicine Creek*, 282.

95. Wald, "Supreme Court Goes to War," 38–39; Dorf, *No Litmus Test*, 131, 133; Lepore, "Dark Ages," 28–29.

96. Sikkink, *Justice Cascade*, 190–91.

97. The "War on Terror" is a label applied to U.S. military operations fighting against networks identified by the United States as "terrorist organizations." The military operations in this "war" commenced in Afghanistan immediately following al-Qaeda's coordinated attacks on the United States on September 11, 2001. The "War on Terror" label later extended to encompass the U.S. war in Iraq, which began in March 2003. For more on the ambiguous meaning of the label, see Raz, "Defining the War on Terror."

98. Sikkink notes that since the story at Abu Ghraib broke, reports from the Red Cross and leaked official documents indicate that the practices of degrading and inhumane treatment were widespread and long-standing, occurring at black sites

around the world as well as at Guantánamo Bay. Sikkink, *Justice Cascade*, 197–98; Lepore, "Dark Ages," 32; Wald, "Supreme Court Goes to War," 39, 41; *New Yorker*, "The Abu Ghraib Pictures"; White House, Office of the Press Secretary, "George W. Bush Speech."

99. *Hamdi v. Rumsfeld*, 124 S. Ct. 2633 (2004); *Rasul v. Bush*, 124 S. Ct. 2686 (2004).

100. The petitioners also did not address Chief Justice John Marshall's characterization of Indian tribes in *Cherokee Nation v. Georgia* as "domestic dependent nations," which implied a lesser sovereign status. Military historian Harold Selesky observed colonists' ambivalence toward war with Indians as early as the seventeenth century. Frustrated that indigenous people did not fight in standard European fashion, colonists decided they could not engage in "civilized" warfare with Indians. Similarly, the *Pioneer and Democrat* denounced Indian attacks on settlers as murder but characterized rangers' ambush on unarmed Indians in a mountain camp as a successful military operation. Selesky, "Colonial America," 61–62; *Pioneer and Democrat*, April 25, 1856.

101. Asher, *Beyond the Reservation*, 134.

102. Acting Governor Mason expressed this view when he wrote in December 1855 that the "ink was scarcely dry" on the peace treaties before Indians "barbarously murdered our unoffending citizens." Testimony of Kent Richards, HCIJ.

103. Testimony of Eugene Ham, HCIJ.

104. Richards offered the examples of the imprisonment of Santa Anna in the Texas Revolt, the postwar imprisonment of Confederate president Jefferson Davis, and the trial and execution of Henry Wirz for atrocities committed at Anderson Prison. Testimony of Kent Richards, HCIJ. For more on shifts in U.S. laws of war in the period from the 1840s to the 1860s, see Witt, *Lincoln's Code*.

105. Evangelista, *Law, Ethics, and the War on Terror*, 73.

106. Ibid., 62, 75–76.

107. Wald, "Supreme Court Goes to War," 38–39; Katyal and Tribe, "Waging War, Deciding Guilt," 1286; Lepore, "Dark Ages," 28, 31–32. In fact, the military commission created in 2001 had antecedents, such as Winfield Scott's military commissions in 1847. See Witt, *Lincoln's Code*, 122–26.

108. In 2009, President Barack Obama announced that his administration would "abandon the Bush administration's term" because "it argues in court for the continued detention of prisoners at Guantánamo Bay, Cuba." Glaberson, "U.S. Won't Label Terror Suspects."

109. Fort Lewis Range Officer John Weller described Leschi Town as "a complex urban combat challenge with applicability world-wide. It's the army's first digital-data-capture combat town, with sophisticated systems that provide unit commanders real-time and post-exercise information on what the event looks like as it unfolds." Interview with John Weller, August 15, 2007; email correspondence with John Weller.

110. Leschi Town was conceived in 2000, was built and financed in a year, and was a regular part of training procedure in 2004. Sarah Wilkins, "Exercise Culminates 18 Months of Preparation for Iraq"; interview with John Weller, August 15, 2007.

111. Lepore, "Dark Ages," 31–32.

112. Interview with anonymous.

113. Blee, "Quest for the Legal Enemy," 55.

114. Bancroft quoted in Dippie, "The Moving Finger Writes," 90.

115. Bacevich, *New American Militarism*, 2.

116. Indians "reached to the ambivalence at the core of progress," Brian Dippie explains, because Americans "coveted what the Natives had and would not be denied, but [also] sought assurances that their actions were just and moral." Dippie, "The Moving Finger Writes," 90.

117. Wolfe, *Settler Colonialism and the Transformation of Anthropology*, 2.

CHAPTER 3

1. For more on the training of Coast Salish oral historians, see Hilbert, *Haboo*, ix. For more on the reliability of oral history for chronicling major historical events, see Nabokov, *Forest of Time*, 73–75; and Cruikshank, *Do Glaciers Listen*, 23. For a classic defense of the historical value of oral traditions and analytical methodologies for oral sources, see Vansina, *Oral Tradition as History*.

2. Niezen calls this "strategic essentialism." Niezen, *Public Justice*, 229.

3. Schwartz, Fukuoka, and Takita-Ishii, "Collective Memory," 255.

4. Sarah Kershaw, "Chief's Retrial, 146 Years in the Making," *New York Times*, December 5, 2004.

5. Critical legal theorists argue that "law is politics," and, just as we do not expect disagreement to cease in politics, in law we should not expect dissent to disappear. Tushnet, "Critical Legal Theory," 81.

6. James Clifford, *Predicament of Culture*, 329.

7. Walter Benjamin's "The Storyteller," quoted in Fields, "What One Cannot Remember Mistakenly," 155–56.

8. Floss Loutzenhiser, "Oldest Nisqually Recalls Tribe's Old Days," in *Tacoma News-Tribune and Sunday Ledger*, February 27, 1966, p. 26.

9. Stanley, "When Counter Narratives Meet Master Narratives," 14.

10. As the next chapter will show, Ezra Meeker used Indian stories in *Pioneer Reminiscences of Puget Sound and the Tragedy of Leschi*.

11. Floss Loutzenhiser, "Oldest Nisqually Recalls Tribe's Old Days," in *Tacoma News-Tribune and Sunday Ledger*, February 27, 1966, 26; Carpenter, Pascualy, and Hunter, *Nisqually Indian Tribe*, 62; Vaughn, *Puget Sound Invasion*, 47.

12. Eckrom, *Remembered Drums*, 20; Wilkinson, *Messages from Frank's Landing*, 16; Billy Frank Jr., "The Importance of Oral History," WSHS, "Leschi," Web archive.

13. Public perceptions of tribal divisions could harm the tribal council's efforts to negotiate with courts, regional businesses, and government agencies. Cornell, *Return of the Native*, 206.

14. Bierwert, *Brushed by Cedar, Living by the River*, 270.

15. Ibid., 267.

16. Angelbeck and McLay, "Battle at Maple Bay," 368.

17. Vi (Taqwseblu) Hilbert (1918–2008) coauthored Lushootseed grammars and dictionaries and published books on Lushootseed stories and traditions. Hilbert identified respect for the Creator, Earth and the Spirits, honesty, generosity, compassion, cleanliness, and industriousness as Lushootseed values imparted through stories. Hilbert, *Haboo*, x. All of the stories presented in this chapter come from previously recorded accounts or from a limited number of interviews I conducted from 2006 to 2010. I do not attempt or claim to present all previously unrecorded Native stories of Leschi here.

18. Cruikshank, *Social Life of Stories*, xii–xiii.

19. Because much of the content of Native stories of Leschi is not remarkably different from non-Indian sources, I make a point of highlighting moments of divergence from narratives published in non-Indian reminiscences and texts to explain their unique meaning in Coast Salish contexts. The point is not to determine a firm distinction between Western and Native history but to explore, through the multivocality of oral histories, the features and accomplishments of stories about Leschi.

20. Anna Lee Walters (Pawnee/Otoe) elaborates this concept in terms of two principal sequences of tribal history: "The first starts at the beginning and works its way toward the present. The second starts with the present and works its way back to the beginning." Nabokov, *Forest of Time*, 71.

21. Carpenter, *Leschi*, 7. Squally Prairie is also known as Nisqually Prairie and Muck Creek Prairie.

22. Legend of the Changer told by George Leschi. Wickersham, "Nusqually Mythology," 345–51. George Gibbs recorded two Nisqually versions of the "Star Child" epic in the 1850s about high-status girls who took stars—men of the upper world—as husbands. Clark, "George Gibbs' Account," 320; Peter, *Susie Sampson Peter*, 91.

23. Wilkinson, *Messages from Frank's Landing*, 101.

24. According to Bierwert, the fundamental distinction between the intellectual traditions of Native people and those of Western social scientists is that, for the former, "the chronicling and commentary of social life involves—wholly and unequivocally—relationship to other sacred beings that have agency in and of themselves." Gene Hunn writes that natural things share with people "intelligence and will, and thus have moral rights and obligations." Bierwert, *Brushed by Cedar, Living by the River*, 7, 42. Hunn quoted on p. 230.

25. Interview with Joseph Kalama, August 3, 2010.

26. Nabokov, *Forest of Time*, 147.

27. Carpenter, *Leschi*, 8, 11; Haeberlin and Gunther, "The Indians of Puget Sound," 56; Harmon, *Indians in the Making*, 37; Taylor, "Anthropological Investigation," 454; Testimony of Connie McCloud, HCIJ.

28. The Nisqually traded coastal shell money for Columbia dried salmon. The shells the Klickitat received were an important commodity further inland, among the Native people of the northern Rockies. Haeberlin and Gunther, "The Indians of Puget Sound," 11; Carpenter, *Leschi*, 11.

29. The Klickitat are closely associated with the Yakama people and speak Sahaptin, or Ichishkíin Sɨnwit, a variant of the Plateau Penutian language of south-central Washington and northern Oregon. See Beavert and Hargus, *Ichishkíin Sɨnwit*. Tolmie identified Leschi as a headman in 1858. Tolmie Papers, box 2/3, UWSC. Paul Leschi testified in 1952 that in the winter months Leschi had a home at Dominick's Prairie, or Dawes Place. Testimony of Paul Leschi, June 9, 1952, Indian Claims Commission Docket 197 (*Nisqually et al. v. U.S.*), PNRO, pp. 1, 5; interview with Bret Ruby, August 1, 2007; Department of Public Works, GIS map, "Native American Place Names."

30. Paul Leschi did not know the exact number, but claimed Leschi owned "plenty" of horses. Testimony of Paul Leschi, June 16, 1952, Indian Claims Commission Docket 197 (*Nisqually et al. v. U.S.*), PNRO, pp. 5–6; Carpenter, *Leschi*, 8, 11; Haeberlin and Gunther, "The Indians of Puget Sound," 56; Harmon, *Indians in the Making*, 37; Taylor, "Anthropological Investigation," 454. For more on siab status, see Suttles, *Coast Salish Essays*, 6.

31. Shelton, *Wisdom of a Tulalip Elder*, 29–30; interview with Mary Leschi by Ezra Meeker, n.d., Leschi Biography File, WSHS.

32. In a related note concerning the incest taboo, elder Willie Frank jokingly informed a newspaper journalist in 1966 that "Indians are taught not to marry too much in the tribe . . . that way get to be midgets." Loutzenhiser, "Oldest Nisqually Recalls Tribe's Old Days," 26–27; H. K. Haeberlin Ethnographic Notebooks, 30, NAA; Raibmon, *Authentic Indians*, 19, 26; Haeberlin and Gunther, "The Indians of Puget Sound," 52; Bierwert, *Lushootseed Texts*, 103; Curtis, *The North American Indian*, 74; Taylor, "Anthropological Investigation," 459–60.

33. Miller, *Problem of Justice*, 2; Harmon, *Indians in the Making*, 23, 27; Allen quoted in Elmendorf, *Twana Narratives*, 160.

34. KUOW, "In Person" radio program, interview, Cynthia Iyall with Megan Sukys.

35. Edward Huggins to Fuller, September 11, 1900, Edward Huggins Papers, WSHS; Harmon, *Indians in the Making*, 23; Miller, *Problem of Justice*, 2; Carpenter, Pascualy and Hunter, *Nisqually Indian Tribe*, 7.

36. Interview with Mary Leschi by Ezra Meeker, n.d., Leschi Biography File, WSHS.

37. Harmon, *Indians in the Making*, 27.

38. Angelbeck and McLay, "Battle at Maple Bay," 383–84.

39. Kalakala was also known as "Jenny." Charles Eaton would later lead the vol-

unteer militia against his father-in-law. Their marriage must have placed Kalakala in an awkward position during the war when Eaton's Rangers sought to arrest Leschi. Cynthia Iyall, "Families Rightfully Take Great Pride in Name, Lineage," *Olympian*, December 17, 2004, 9A; Letter from Edward Huggins to Frank Cole, December 8, 1901, Edward Huggins Papers, WSHS; interview with Cecelia Carpenter, February 21, 2007; Carpenter, Pascualy, and Hunter, *Nisqually Indian Tribe*, 31.

40. Carpenter, *The Nisqually, My People*, 168–69.

41. Wilkinson, *Messages from Frank's Landing*, 14; KUOW, "In Person" radio program, interview, Cynthia Iyall with Megan Sukys. For a recent example of the "race war" narrative, see Kluger, *Bitter Waters of Medicine Creek*.

42. Wilkinson, *Messages from Frank's Landing*, 9–10.

43. Testimony of Billy Frank Jr., HCIJ. See also James Wickersham, "The Indian Side of the Puget Sound Indian War," October 9, 1893, p. 5, JWC.

44. Waterman, *Puget Sound Geography*, 19.

45. Anthropologists Boas and Teit (1928) gave the Mashel (or "Mica'l") villagers autonomous band status, and Spier (1936) and Swanton (1952) followed suit. Billy Frank Jr. insisted in 1963 that the Mashel villagers were considered a part of the Nisqually Tribe. Smith, *Takhoma*, 68–69; Teit, "The Middle Columbia Salish," 108; Spier, *Tribal Distribution in Washington*, 26; Swanton, *The Indian Tribes of North America*, 428.

46. White, "Treaty of Medicine Creek," 32; Harmon, *Indians in the Making*, 34, 86; Crook, "Quiemuth, Part I," 4.

47. Harmon, *Indians in the Making*, 86; Miller and Boxberger, "Creating Chiefdoms," 272.

48. White, "Treaty at Medicine Creek," 36.

49. Wickersham, "The Indian Side of the Puget Sound Indian War," October 9, 1893, p. 2, JWC.

50. Interview with Mary Leschi by Ezra Meeker, n.d., Leschi Biography File, WSHS. Meeker wrote about Leschi's secret gold cache as a source of his wealth, which enabled him to give so much at the potlatch. Meeker, *Pioneer Reminiscences of Puget Sound and the Tragedy of Leschi*, 209.

51. Another, more literal, interpretation of Mary's story is that Leschi chose not to disclose the location because he did not want to initiate a gold rush. He may have heard from relations in Oregon that gold miners had a disastrous impact on Natives' ability to maintain access to their land. The first major gold rush in the Northwest was at Jacksonville, Oregon Territory, in 1852, and was followed by a number of smaller rushes in central Washington throughout the decade. Schwantes, *Pacific Northwest*, 128, 132. The local newspapers in the 1850s regularly reported on gold discoveries and routes to the nearest sites. See, for example, "Departures of More Gold Miners," *Puget Sound Courier*, July 27, 1855; "Best Route to the Mines" *Puget Sound Courier*, August 3, 1855; "Gold Mines," *Puget Sound Courier*, August 10, 1855.

52. Wickersham, "The Indian Side of the Puget Sound Indian War," October 9, 1893, pp. 2, 5, JWC. "Luke" is the phonetic approximation of the Whulshootseed name lu'kʷ. Nisquallies also knew him as "Buyachlt." Kluger, *Bitter Waters of Medicine Creek*, 96; Elmendorf, *Twana Narratives*, 34.

53. Wickersham, "The Indian Side of the Puget Sound Indian War," October 9, 1893, p. 5, JWC; Tyee Dick, a man of complicated loyalties, reported that Hiaton gave a speech encouraging other headmen to sign the treaty. Tyee Dick's name appears as E-la-kah-ha on the Medicine Creek Treaty, and he later reported that he signed because he thought it a mistake to fight the Americans. He was sometimes identified by this name as Sluggia's accomplice in turning Leschi over to territorial authorities, and was rumored to have been in possession of Leschi's pistol after the war. Meeker, *Pioneer Reminiscences of Puget Sound and the Tragedy of Leschi*, 244–45; Carpenter, Pascualy, and Hunter, *Nisqually Indian Tribe*, 25–27; Vaughn, *Puget Sound Invasion*, 61; Harmon, *Indians in the Making*, 84.

54. Frank quoted in Wilkinson, *Messages from Frank's Landing*, 14.

55. Ibid., 18.

56. Angelbeck and McLay, "Battle at Maple Bay," 359, 383.

57. Elmendorf, *Twana Narratives*, xxx–xxxi. The Skokomish are Twana speakers with communities on the south end of the Olympic Peninsula.

58. See Harmon, *Indians in the Making*, for more on Puget Sound Native identity formation.

59. Schwartz, Fukuoka, and Takita-Ishii, "Collective Memory," 267.

60. Frank Allen quoted in *Twana Narratives*, 153.

61. Raibmon notes that the practice of burning Indian villages can be traced back to Robert Gray's 1793 voyage in which he torched a village on Vancouver Island. Raibmon, "Unmaking Native Space," 70.

62. Barsh, "Ethnogenesis and Ethnonationalism," 155–58; Suttles, *Coast Salish Essays*, 15–25.

63. Interview with Peggy McCloud. It is not clear when the elder's relocation to Lummi occurred, although some forced relocations to reservations took place in the early 1870s. For example, in 1871, Indian agent Edwin Eells requested that Port Townsend officials demolish Indians' houses and escorted the displaced families to the Skokomish reservation. Eells also reportedly threatened to "burn out" Indian communities he encountered off the reservations. Harmon, *Indians in the Making*, 112–13. In any case, the important aspect of the elder's story is not chronicling a specific moment but rather making associations among her personal experience, Leschi's actions, and the shared Native experience of relocation in the region.

64. This order reportedly brought the resentment of the young warrior, Sluggia, who would later turn his uncle Leschi over to territorial authorities for trial. Meeker, *Pioneer Reminiscences of Puget Sound and the Tragedy of Leschi*, 210.

65. Interview with Cecelia Carpenter, February 21, 2007; Shelton, *Wisdom of a Tulalip Elder*, 29–30.

66. Allen quoted in Elmendorf, *Twana Narratives*, 154.

67. Olson, "Our Leschi: The Making of a Martyr," 34.

68. Allen quoted in Elmendorf, *Twana Narratives*, 156.

69. According to Meeker, Benjamin Shaw provided George Himes with the account in 1904. Meeker, *Pioneer Reminiscences of Puget Sound and the Tragedy of Leschi*, 427. Shaw was not a disinterested observer of territorial events in the 1850s; as an outspoken defender of Governor Stevens, Shaw charged that Native eyewitness accounts were unreliable and denounced the "Indiomaniacs" who gave credence to Native memories of the events leading up to the war. Speech, n.d., and letter to the editor of the *Portland Oregonian*, n.d. (probably January 1904), Benjamin Shaw Papers, MS 412, Oregon Historical Society, Portland; "Did Leschi Sign the Medicine Creek Treaty?" *Seattle Post-Intelligencer*, January 31, 1904, p. 25.

70. Speech, n.d., and letter to the *Portland Oregonian*, n.d., Benjamin Shaw Papers, Oregon Historical Society, Portland.

71. Cynthia Iyall said that Wa He Lut's warrior mentality was remembered in Nisqually oral traditions. "They say that while cleaning his gun, [Wa He Lut] was often heard to exclaim, 'Yep, we have one more good ride in us.'" Cynthia Iyall interview with Melissa Parr, September 20, 2004, "Leschi," WSHS, Web archive, http://stories.washingtonhistory.org/leschi/yelmjim.htm.

72. Cecelia Carpenter also highlights this crucial turn in the war and includes in her booklet a photograph of Hah-pa-ce-wud, who had to flee across the sandspit at Green River when Patkanim's scouts attacked Leschi's forces. The *Courier* noted that Patkanim's forces succeeded in killing a medicine man in a battle, but also killed women and children in an attack on a "house belonging to Leschi's band." Carpenter, "Leschi," 34; Allen quoted in Elmendorf, *Twana Narratives*, 156; "Patkanim," *Puget Sound Courier*, February 29, 1856.

73. At least as early as 1849, Hudson's Bay Company officials recognized this animosity; the Nisqually relied upon the HBC fort for arbitration in disputes with Snoqualmie men. See Harmon, *Indians in the Making*.

74. According to Allen and Carpenter, Sluggia, enticed by the reward of blankets, lured Leschi to territorial authorities. Sluggia convinced his uncle that he could safely come out of hiding in the mountains, but soldiers promptly arrested Leschi and put him in jail. Carpenter, "Leschi," 37–38; Eckron, *Remembered Drums*, 154.

75. Meeker, *Pioneer Reminiscences of Puget Sound and the Tragedy of Leschi*, 210; interview with Cynthia Iyall by Melissa Parr quoted in "Leschi," WSHS, Web archive, http://stories.washingtonhistory.org/leschi/leschitrial/betrayal.htm.

76. Sluggia's immoral behavior challenged Nisqually values and therefore called for an act of retributive justice. In 1857, Wa He Lut shot and killed Sluggia. Settlers interpreted Wa He Lut's action as an attempt to police tribal loyalty, but Wa He Lut and Leschi were related and the responsibility of restoring moral order went to Wa He Lut; he was the first cousin of Leschi's mother, a relationship synonymous with mother's brother. In a famous photograph taken in about 1880, Wa He Lut,

sitting upright with an air of defiance, poses with a shotgun beside a table displaying a human skull. A blanket hangs behind the scene as backdrop, all suggestive of the popular story of Sluggia's demise. Someone scrawled beneath the image: "A Nisqually Indian, He fought with Leschi in 1855–56, He killed Sluggia, Leschi's betrayer." Carpenter, "Leschi," 40; WSHS, "Leschi," Web archive; Marian Smith, *The Puyallup-Nisqually*, 162–63; Eckrom, *Remembered Drums*, 166–67; Reese, *Nothing Worthy of Note Transpired Today*, 124; *Seattle Post-Intelligencer*, August 7, 1896; cited in Schmitt, "Execution of Chief Leschi," n13. This story of betrayal and revenge reveals Nisqually values of family obligation, proper routes to status, and justice. As time went on, the story's lessons expanded to emphasize the threat Sluggia had posed to Nisqually nationhood as well. According to Billy Frank Jr., Wa He Lut killed Sluggia for "treason." Wilkinson, *Messages from Frank's Landing*, 17.

77. Alexandra Harmon reported that Sluggia received a reward for the service, testified in Leschi's defense in his first trial, and was murdered before he could offer the same testimony in Leschi's second trial. At the time of Sluggia's death it was still unclear whether Leschi would receive a fair trial from the Nisqually perspective. The Historical Court presented an occasion in which Carpenter's strategically framed story was, in a subtle way, undermined by previous Native accounts fixed in time when they became a part of the historical record. Testimony of Alexandra Harmon, HCIJ.

78. Redwing Cloud, "Chief Leschi's Name Restored," *Indian Country Today*, January 4, 2005. For more on Leschi's incarceration, see *Pioneer and Democrat*, February 5, 1858, and February 26, 1858.

79. Wilkinson, *Messages from Frank's Landing*, 18; Carpenter, "Leschi," 45. Lieutenant August Kautz wrote in his diary on February 19, 1858: "There was a large crowd to witness the execution, but few Indians." Reese, *Journals of August Kautz*, 154.

80. "Execution of Leschi," *Pioneer and Democrat*, February 26, 1858, p. 2. Father Louis Rossi claimed he was present at Leschi's final moments at the scaffold. Concerned for his immortal soul because he had never been baptized, Rossi encouraged Leschi to convert and renounce all but one of his wives just prior to his execution. Rossi's account was not translated into English until 1946, when it appeared in C. T. Conover, "Hanging of Leschi," *Seattle Star*, May 22, 1946. A full translation is now available: Rossi, *Six Years on the West Coast of America*, 141–42. See also Wortley, "Perceptions and Misperceptions," 157–61; and Reese, *A Documentary History of Fort Steilacoom*, 53. Shaw depicted a Catholic Leschi giving himself over to death: "[Leschi] made the sign of the cross, and said in his own Nisqually tongue . . . There is the Father, this is the Son, this is the Holy Ghost; these are all one and the same, Amen." The hangman, Charles Grainger, reported forty years later that Leschi calmly climbed the scaffold, told the official he was prepared, and then died without a struggle. Meeker, *Pioneer Reminiscences of Puget Sound and the Tragedy of Leschi*, 427. August Kautz wrote an account of Leschi's statement on February 6,

1858, similar to Rossi's, but he claimed that Leschi's comments took place during formal legal proceedings witnessed by several people in Leschi's cell, days before his execution. See Reese, *Leschi, the Officers, and the Citizens*, 57–58.

81. When Leschi spoke to James Swan about the war in January 1856, Leschi reportedly stated that he "entertain[ed] a most deadly hatred" toward Simmons, considered him the cause of the war, and suggested that if Simmons were removed Leschi would gladly stop fighting and "treat with some good man." "Leschi," *Puget Sound Courier*, January 25, 1856. When Simmons was confirmed as Indian agent for Washington Territory in the spring of 1856, a writer for the *Courier* expressed disappointment because "*all* the Indians loath" him. *Puget Sound Courier*, April 25, 1856.

82. "The Tragedy of Leschi" contribution by Laura B. Downey Barlett, *Puyallup Valley Tribune*, January 24, 1930. Copy available in Nisqually Vertical File, WSHS.

83. Cary C. Collins, "In a Familiar yet Foreign Land."

84. Ibid.

85. Allen quoted in Elmendorf, *Twana Narratives*, 159–60. Other sources agree that after his death Leschi's body was carried off in a wagon for private burial. Meeker reported that Dan Mounts, the agent at the Nisqually reservation, helped to retrieve Leschi's body, while Peggy McCloud said that she heard that John McCloud, a former HBC employee who had married a Puyallup woman, gathered Leschi's body. Meeker, *Pioneer Reminiscences of Puget Sound and the Tragedy of Leschi*, 454; interview with Peggy McCloud.

86. Carpenter writes about religion in the "simplest form possible" because anthropologists inappropriately "attempt to put Indian religious customs into scientific molds." Carpenter, *The Nisqually, My People*, 123.

87. "For [Wa He Lut] and many of his contemporaries, their abilities as Indians to match Americans' military and political strength was far less important than their ability as individuals to use their power effectively. . . . Neither the treaties nor the war had robbed all indigenous people of that ability." Harmon, *Indians in the Making*, 94.

88. Billy Frank Jr., "The Importance of Oral History," WSHS, "Leschi," Web archive.

89. James McCloud oral history, "Listening to Leschi," ibid.

90. De Laguna quoted in Nabokov, *Forest of Time*, 90.

91. Interview with Cynthia Iyall; Haeberlin and Gunther, "The Indians of Puget Sound," 60.

92. Leschi's half-sister Margaret married into the Iyall family, which made Cynthia Iyall an "indirect" descendant of Leschi. Carpenter, "How It All Began," CSCPC; Kluger, *Bitter Waters of Medicine Creek*, 261; interview with Cynthia Iyall.

93. Mitchell, "The Naming Ceremony," 18–19.

94. Interview with Cynthia Iyall.

95. Wa He Lut School is located on land belonging to Willie Frank on the Nisqually River and was initially supported on profits from Frank's Landing Smoke

Shop. In 1987 the school was deemed eligible for federal funding. Interview with Peggy McCloud; "Tribe Opens Its Own School," *Tacoma News-Tribune*, January 28, 1975; Heffernan, *Where the Salmon Run*, 179, 218–22.

96. Tomas Alex Tizon, "A Matter of Justice and Honor," *Los Angeles Times*, December 28, 2004.

97. Cynthia Iyall, "Why Is It So Important to Exonerate Chief Leschi?" *Olympian*, March 5, 2004.

98. KUOW, "In Person" radio program, interview, Cynthia Iyall with Megan Sukys; Redwing Cloud, "Chief Leschi's Name Restored," *Indian Country Today*, January 4, 2005.

99. Cynthia Iyall, "Why Is It So Important to Exonerate Chief Leschi?" *Olympian*, March 5, 2004.

100. MSNBC.com, "Court Acquits Chief Hanged in 1858."

101. Daes, "Protecting Knowledge," 233.

102. Interview with Peggy McCloud.

103. Carroll, "The Aesthetic and the Political," 44.

104. Interview with Cecelia Carpenter, February 21, 2007.

105. Emphasis mine. Kershaw, "Chief's Retrial, 146 Years in the Making."

CHAPTER 4

1. According to philosopher Henri Bergson, this dual function of memory explains how the past shapes perception of the present: "Memory does not consist in a regression from the present into the past, but, on the contrary, in a progress from the past into the present." Guerlac, *Thinking in Time*, 122; quote from p. 171.

2. In doing so, Frank framed Leschi within "tradition," which, as Paul Ricoeur explains, is "an ongoing dialectic between our being-effected by the past and our projection of a history yet-to-be-made." Kearney, "Between Tradition and Utopia," 24; quote from p. 36.

3. Connerton, *How Societies Remember*, 1.

4. Harmon, *Power of Promises*, 8.

5. Friday, "Performing Treaties," 159.

6. Harmon, "Indian Treaty History," 361, 365; Barsh, "Ethnogenesis and Ethnonationalism," 155–58; Suttles, *Coast Salish Essays*, 15–25. For a treatment of the formation of tribal identity and government in the nineteenth century more generally, see Cornell, *Return of the Native*, 79–84.

7. Konkle, *Writing Indian Nations*, 5.

8. Reddick and Collins, "Medicine Creek to Fox Island," 379–80; Carpenter, *Fort Nisqually*, 175; William Tolmie to Edward Huggins, August 20, 1853, Edmond Meany Papers, 93-31, UWSC; William Tolmie to Fayette McMullen, January 12, 1858, Clarence Bagley Papers, box 21, B146cp, vol. 1A, UWSC; Carpenter, *Leschi*, 8, 11; Taylor, "Anthropological Investigation," 454; Miller, *Problem of Justice*, 2; Harmon, *Indians in the Making*, 23, 27; Carpenter, *Leschi*, 15–16.

9. Billy Frank Jr., "The Importance of Oral History," WSHS, "Leschi," Web archive.

10. "To the People," *Puget Sound Courier*, August 24, 1855; Haeberlin and Gunther, "The Indians of Puget Sound," 9, 59; Gibbs, *Indian Tribes of Washington Territory*; Waterman, *Puget Sound Geography*, 16, 19; Curtis, *The North American Indian*, 67; Testimony of Herbert Taylor Jr., Indian Claims Commission Docket 197 (*Nisqually et al. v. U.S.*), PNRO, August 7, 1953, pp. 5, 7; Angelbeck and McLay, "Battle at Maple Bay," 361, 378.

11. KUOW, "In Person" radio program, interview, Cynthia Iyall with Megan Sukys. Miller and Boxberger argue that no convincing evidence exists that Coast Salish communities recognized village leaders as "chiefs" until American officials created the concept to expedite treaty negotiations in the Northwest. They contend that, by the 1920s, the concept of chief as a formal political leadership position became so deeply ingrained in the minds of Puget Sound Salish people that "many believed it had always been so." Miller and Boxberger, "Creating Chiefdoms," 278.

12. June McCormick Collins, "Influence of White Contact," 173; Angelbeck and McLay, "Battle at Maple Bay," 382; Miller, *Problem of Justice*, 62–64.

13. Traders and Indians used the jargon across the Northwest to communicate basic information. William Tolmie described Chinook jargon as "a vile compound of English, French, American & the Chenooke dialect"—a "miserable medium of communication" incapable of conveying complex concepts. Tolmie quoted in Harmon, *Indians in the Making*, 33; Meany, *Origins of Washington Geographic Names*, 46.

14. Friday, "Performing Treaties," 159–60; Harmon, *Indians in the Making*, 84.

15. Friday, "Performing Treaties," 165. The editor of the *Courier* criticized how the balance of appropriations from the Medicine Creek Treaty went to headmen rather than distributed equally among the Indian population. "To the People," *Puget Sound Courier*, August 24, 1855.

16. The handwritten text of the Medicine Creek Treaty is available at U.S. Office of Indian Affairs, Records of the Washington Superintendency, microfilm A12046, reel 63, UWSC.

17. Based on the 1838–39 census conducted by the Hudson's Bay Company, slaves composed 11 percent of the total Nisqually population. Taylor, "Anthropological Investigation," 424.

18. U.S. Office of Indian Affairs, Records of the Washington Superintendency, microfilm A12046, reel 63, UWSC.

19. Harmon, *Indians in the Making*, 88; Taylor, "Anthropological Investigation," 460; Raibmon, "Unmaking Native Space," 70.

20. Letter from Tolmie to McMullen, January 12, 1858, William Tolmie Papers, box 2/3, UWSC.

21. Leschi had good reason to be suspicious. Stevens entered the treaty negotiations with the expectation that all of the Indians on the east side of Puget Sound would eventually be removed and concentrated onto one reservation. He wrote

this uncertainty into the treaty by granting the president the power to relocate the tribes to new reservations at any time and to allot the reservation into family plots at the president's discretion. Records of the Proceedings of the Commission to Hold Treaties with the Indian Tribes in Washington Territory and the Blackfoot Country, U.S. Office of Indian Affairs, Records of the Washington Superintendency, microfilm A12046, reel 63, UWSC; Prucha, *American Indian Treaties*, 252–53; Wickersham, "The Indian Side of the Puget Sound Indian War," October 9, 1893, p. 5, JWC; Deposition of Jerry Meeker, Puyallup, March 25, 1927, p. 636, Duwamish et al., Court of Claims of the United States, no. F-275, 647, evidence for plaintiff and defendant, box 46, Northwest Ethnohistory Collection, Center for Pacific Northwest History, Western Washington University, Bellingham; Wilkinson, *Messages from Frank's Landing*, 14.

22. Quote from "Leschi," *Puget Sound Courier*, January 25, 1856; Scorpion, "Removing the Indians," and Iota, "The Indian Agency," *Puget Sound Courier*, November 30, 1855; "Reply to Scorpion," *Puget Sound Courier*, December 7, 1855; "McDonald's Island" and M. T. Simmons, "Notice," *Puget Sound Courier*, January 4, 1856.

23. Harring, *Crow Dog's Case*, 253.

24. Carpenter, *The Nisqually, My People*, 171; Wilkinson, *Messages from Frank's Landing*, 19.

25. Carpenter, Pascualy, and Hunter, *Nisqually Indian Tribe*, 8; interview with Cecelia Carpenter, February 21, 2007.

26. Connerton, *How Societies Remember*, 37.

27. Harmon, *Indians in the Making*, 104.

28. Collins, "Hard Lessons in America," 6–7; Caster, "Father Hylebos, St. George's Indian School and Cemetery, and St. Claire's Mission Church," 11–14; Miller, *Problem of Justice*, 83.

29. Oral history of James McCloud, WSHS Web archive. For Willie Frank's account of his experiences at St. George School and Cushman Indian School, see Heffernan, *Where the Salmon Run*, 23–25.

30. The allotment process began around Puget Sound a decade before the federal policy because of the unique conditions of the region, particularly the clauses in Washington Indian treaties that allowed for hunting and fishing off the reservations. Superintendent R. H. Milroy hoped that individual allotments would serve as an inducement to bring Indians to the reservations so they could be more closely managed by Indian agents. Harmon, *Indians in the Making*, 113–14; U.S. Senate, *Allotted Nisqually Indian Lands*, 21; Hoxie, *A Final Promise*, 76–77.

31. Hoxie, *A Final Promise*, 80, 148–49; Ashley and Hubbard, *Negotiating Sovereignty*, 69–70.

32. Gallacci, "Planning the City of Destiny," 293, 296; U.S. Senate, *Allotted Nisqually Indian Lands*, 16–17; Carpenter, *The Nisqually, My People*, 221; interview with Thor Hoyte.

33. By the time the Dawes Act had run its course as federal Indian policy in 1934,

Indian-owned land in the United States had fallen from 138 million to 52 million acres. McDonnell, *Dispossession of the American Indian*, vii. See also Hoxie, *A Final Promise*; and Carlson, *Indians, Bureaucrats, and Land*.

34. See "The Lummis Lose," *Seattle Post-Intelligencer*, March 31, 1897, p. 5; and "Indians and Game," *Seattle Post-Intelligencer*, March 3, 1904, p. 4.

35. *Goudy v. Meath*, 203 U.S. 146 (1906).

36. "Indians and Game," *Seattle Post-Intelligencer*, March 3, 1904, p. 4.

37. The General Allotment Act and other legislation in the 1880s resulted in a surge in federal Indian cases by the turn of the century. Harring, *Crow Dog's Case*, 5.

38. Carpenter, *The Nisqually, My People*, 220–21; Elmendorf, *Twana Narratives*, 22–23, 34. Billy Frank Jr. said in the Historical Court: "We don't want to go back to them days when . . . we could not exercise our ceremonies out in public. We had to go underground, out in the woods and hide. Slahal games—we had to hide when we played Slahal games. We had to hide when we talked our language."

39. Meany, "Ezra Meeker, the Pioneer," 124–25.

40. Carpenter, Pascualy, and Hunter, *Nisqually Indian Tribe*, 40; Meeker, *Pioneer Reminiscences of Puget Sound and the Tragedy of Leschi*, 255–56.

41. Meeker, *Pioneer Reminiscences of Puget Sound and the Tragedy of Leschi*, 242, 245, 250–51. I follow Cecelia Carpenter's spelling of "Hiaton," although Meeker published his name as "Hiton" and the *Puget Sound Courier* spelled his name "Hyton."

42. "Chief Leschi's Body," Tacoma (newspaper title unknown), July 2, 1895, Leschi Biography File, WSHS.

43. Songs and dances were deplored by white missionaries, who considered them "heathen" practices. Reservation agents around Puget Sound discouraged competitive games and contests on the assumption that such practices were immoral and wasteful, although competition likely helped to dissipate antagonism between families forced to live together on reservations. Miller, *Problem of Justice*, 83; June McCormick Collins, "Indian Shaker Church," 399–401, 409; Irwin, "Freedom, Law, and Prophecy," 35–36.

44. "Ceremonies [that] have as one of their defining features the explicit claim to be commemorating continuity . . . play a significant role in the shaping of communal memory." Connerton, *How Societies Remember*, 48.

45. "Leschi's Bones Reburied," *Tacoma Ledger*, July 4, 1895, Nisqually Biography File, WSHS; White, "The Great Race of 1941," 127, 134. The prominent non-Indians in attendance, as reported by the *Ledger*, included a city treasurer; attorney James Wickersham; a professor; Indian commissioner J. J. Anderson; and several former HBC employees and their families. Both the Nisquallies and their non-Indian neighbors celebrated the Fourth of July with gatherings and games. Even as the Indian agents cracked down on Indian social and spiritual practices, the Fourth of July celebration appeared as evidence of patriotic sentiments and the success of assimilation programs. See letter from Milroy to Q. Smith, Commissioner of Indian Af-

fairs, July 2, 1877, and Letter to Q. Smith, Commissioner of Indian Affairs, August 1, 1877, both Robert H. Milroy Letterpress Copybook, UWSC; and Bierwert, "Remembering Chief Seattle," 298. For more on how African Americans used Fourth of July celebrations for political purposes, see Fabre, "African American Commemorative Celebrations in the Nineteenth Century," 76. For more on tribal leadership goals and Coast Salish public relations strategies during the Depression, see White, "The Great Race of 1941."

46. A delegate of men from several tribes disinterred Leschi's and Quiemuth's remains and delivered them in coffins to the church. Haeberlin and Gunther, "The Indians of Puget Sound," 61; "Leschi's Bones Reburied," *Tacoma Ledger*, July 4, 1895.

47. "Leschi's Remains," *Tacoma Daily News*, July 3, 1895, p. 1; "Chief Leschi's Body," unnamed newspaper, July 2, 1895; "Leschi" biography file, UWSC; "Leschi's Bones Reburied," *Tacoma Ledger*, July 4, 1895.

48. One study of media content in the Skagit County (north of Seattle) from the 1910s to 1987 revealed that half of the reporting on Indians focused on contentious treaty rights issues, "which were represented as opposing white interests." White, "The Great Race of 1941," 132.

49. Interview with Cecelia Carpenter, February 21, 2007.

50. "Leschi's Bones Reburied," *Tacoma Ledger*, July 4, 1895; "Leschi's New Grave," *Seattle Post-Intelligencer*, July 4, 1895.

51. "Leschi's Bones Reburied," *Tacoma Ledger*, July 4, 1895.

52. Meeker, *Pioneer Reminiscences of Puget Sound and the Tragedy of Leschi*, 457.

53. "Payment to the Indians," *Pioneer and Democrat*, January 8, 1858; "Leschi's Bones Reburied," *Tacoma Ledger*, July 4, 1895.

54. Carpenter, Pascualy, and Hunter, *Nisqually Indian Tribe*, 37, 54–55; Oral history of James McCloud, WSHS Web archive.

55. Oral history of James McCloud, WSHS Web archive.

56. The Tacoma journalist claimed that several children were disinterred in the confused search for Quiemuth's remains. His body was then identified by a rusted knife lodged in the rib cage and a skull shattered from the murderer's bullet, which is not consistent with accounts of Quiemuth's death. "Leschi's Bones Reburied," *Tacoma Ledger*, July 4, 1895.

57. Ibid.

58. U.S. Senate, *Allotted Nisqually Indian Lands*, 21; Wilkinson, *Messages from Frank's Landing*, 23.

59. Interview with Bret Ruby, August 30, 2007.

60. Letter from Superintendent E. H. Hammond to the Commissioner of Indian Affairs, December 17, 1917, Letters from the Commissioner at Cushman Indian School, 1917–18, PNRO.

61. Archambault, *Fort Lewis*, 7.

62. Letter from Superintendent E. H. Hammond to the Commissioner of Indian

Affairs, February 25, 1918, Letters from the Commissioner at Cushman Indian School, 1917–18, PNRO; Wilkinson, *Messages from Frank's Landing*, 27; Kautz quoted in Heffernan, *Where the Salmon Run*, 28.

63. Hammond had an interest in relocating Nisqually families nearby since the Cushman School was in financial crisis for much of this period and he continuously sought much-needed funds through increased student attendance. Charles Roberts, "The Cushman Indian Trades School and World War I," 223; Letter from Superintendent E. H. Hammond to the Commissioner of Indian Affairs, February 25, 1918, Letters from the Commissioner at Cushman Indian School, 1917–18, PNRO.

64. It is unclear whether the sections of land Sicade assessed belonged to Indian allottees. Cary C. Collins, "In a Familiar yet Foreign Land." The Indian board appraised the land at $93,760, and the county assessed it at $70,662. The parties compromised on $75,840. On average, out-of-court settlements of non-Indian land suits netted 15 percent to 55 percent higher values over the county's offer, compared with the 7 percent increase the Nisqually allottees received. It was the opinion of an Interior Department investigator that the Nisqually lands were considerably more valuable than those owned by non-Indians at the time of the condemnation. The army and county did not offer a fair appraisal, and the assistant U.S. attorney did not diligently research the appraisals before making a compromise. U.S. Senate, *Allotted Nisqually Indian Lands*, 2–3, 22, 25–33; Carpenter, *The Nisqually, My People*, 227; Letter from the Acting Secretary of the Interior to the President of the United States Senate, "Indians of Nisqually Reservation, Wash.," *Senate Reports*, vol. 1.

65. Carpenter, Pascualy, and Hunter, *Nisqually Indian Tribe*, 17.

66. The Pierce County superior court decided individual allottee awards on May 6, 1918. The payments ranged from $100 to $8,000, depending on the claim and improvements, and most payments were distributed and spent under the Indian agent's supervision. Joseph Kalama recounted how armed soldiers forced allottees from their homes when the deadline arrived. Interview with Joseph Kalama; U.S. Senate, *Allotted Nisqually Indian Lands*, 1, 49–50.

67. Wilkinson, *Messages from Frank's Landing*, 27.

68. Carpenter, Pascualy, and Hunter, *Nisqually Indian Tribe*, 8; U.S. Senate, *Allotted Nisqually Indian Lands*, 11–14.

69. U.S. Senate, *Allotted Nisqually Indian Lands*, 2.

70. L. F. Michael's report to the Commissioner of Indian Affairs, August 24, 1918; quoted in Carpenter, *The Nisqually, My People*, 228.

71. Peter Kalama (1860–1947) graduated from Chemawa in 1885 and worked as a translator. His mother was Mary Martin, a Nisqually woman; his father was John Kalama, a Hawaiian Native employed by the Hudson's Bay Company. John Kalama died sometime before 1880, and Peter and his mother moved in with Henry Martin. As an adult, Peter worked in government service on the Warm Springs Reservation and was involved in the Indian Shaker Church. U.S. Census, Nisqually reservation, 1880, PNRO; interview with Cecelia Carpenter, February 21, 2007; "Indian Tribe

Leader Dies," *Tacoma News-Tribune*, May 8, 1947; U.S. Senate, *Allotted Nisqually Indian Lands*, 36–38; Teit, "The Middle Columbia Salish," 107.

72. Interview with Cecelia Carpenter, February 21, 2007; interview with Joseph Kalama.

73. Kalama quoted in Carpenter, *The Nisqually, My People*, 229–30.

74. U.S. Senate, *Allotted Nisqually Indian Lands*, 7.

75. George Walter quoted in Heffernan, *Where the Salmon Run*, 28. Congress approved a payment of $85,000 for the twenty five displaced Nisqually families with $6,000 earmarked for relocating cemeteries within seven months. Carpenter, *The Nisqually, My People*, 242–43; U.S. Senate, "Indians of Nisqually Reservation, Wash."

76. James Goudy, the same man who brought suit against Pierce County for imposing state tax on Indian allotments in 1906, worked as Ballard's informant, interpreter, and guide. Kluger, *Bitter Waters of Medicine Creek*, 96.

77. A 1919 report on Charlie's case suggests that he was waiting to inherit the Henry Martin allotment along with his half-sister, Sallie Jackson. The report indicated that Sallie's nephew Peter Kalama was prepared to care for his aging relatives. Charlie and Sallie likely found shelter on the Martin allotment after Charlie spoke with Ballard. Carpenter, *The Nisqually, My People*, 235; interview with Cecelia Carpenter, February 21, 2007; "'Nisqually Charlie' with His Wife after Eviction from Their Home, 18 May 1917," by Arthur C. Ballard, American Indian Northwest Coast manuscripts, MS 4527 (049), NAA.

78. See Photograph Collection, NAA.

79. Ballard later submitted the photograph as evidence for the Muckleshoots' Indian Claims Commission case.

80. U.S. Senate, *Allotted Nisqually Indian Lands*, 19.

81. Congress approved the money for grave relocation in 1924, but the tribe could not find a new cemetery plot in time and had to reapply for the appropriation. In 1929, the tribe received $6,000 for reburial costs. Carpenter, *The Nisqually, My People*, 242–43.

82. U.S. Senate, *Allotted Nisqually Indian Lands*, 19–20.

83. Gibbs, *Tribes of Western Washington and Northwestern Oregon*, 204; Aronsen and Urcid, "Inventory and Assessment of Human Remains and Funerary Objects," p. 31, NAA. Some of the Nisqually remains sent to the Smithsonian from this period were returned to the tribe in 2007. See Les Blumenthal, "Nisqually Tribe to Receive Remains of 6 Members," *Seattle Times*, June 3, 2007.

84. The speech is undated but refers to an introduction by William F. Bonney, secretary of the Washington State Historical Society and active local historian from the 1900s through the 1930s. H. F. Jones Papers, TS-26, box 1/31, WSHS.

85. Sally Sicade, "Henry C. Sicade: A Short Sketch by His Daughter," ca. 1928; interview with Cecelia Carpenter, February 21, 2007; Letter from Henry Sicade to Ezra Meeker, April 29, 1918, Ezra Meeker Collection, box 5/28, MS-2, WSHS.

86. According to the *Tacoma Daily News*, army trucks and personnel were loaned out to help move "two or three ancient Indian burial grounds" in April 1918. "Indians Last Resting Place Must Be Moved," *Tacoma Daily News*, April 19, 1918. In 1924 a monument was unveiled at the grave of Patkanim that only recounted his role in ceding land to the U.S. and fighting "for the white people." Meany, "Chief Patkanim," 187. Ezra Meeker attended the dedication ceremony for the memorial to Lieutenant William Slaughter. In his 1919 address at the dedication of the Slaughter memorial, the secretary of the Washington State Historical Society, W. P. Bonney, described 1855 and 1856 as a time when "the blood-curdling whoop of the savage vied in horror with the blood-dripping scalping knife." Bonney quoted in Meany, "Monument for Indian War Heroes," 178; Eckrom, *Remembered Drums*, 176. The Connell Prairie memorial is located near Buckley, Washington.

87. Meeker, *Pioneer Reminiscences of Puget Sound and the Tragedy of Leschi*, 212, 457.

88. Ibid., 453.

89. Bierwert, "Remembering Chief Seattle," 297.

90. Meeker, *Pioneer Reminiscences of Puget Sound and the Tragedy of Leschi*, 447.

91. "Leschi's Bones Reburied," *Tacoma Ledger*, July 4, 1895. St. George's Indian School opened on land deeded to the Bureau of Catholic Indian Missions between Pierce and King counties, in present-day Federal Way. Castor, "Father Hylebos," 15–16, http://www.federalwayhistory.org/powercms/files/FtHylebosJuly92009.pdf. For more on the Catholic Church's influence among Salish tribes, see Schoenberg, *A History of the Catholic Church in the Pacific Northwest*. Billy Frank Jr. later used this idea in 2004 when he said that Leschi sacrificed himself so that his people could maintain the rights secured by the Medicine Creek Treaty. Billy Frank Jr., "The Importance of Oral History," WSHS, "Leschi," Web archive.

92. The Indian Citizenship Act, which was controversial among Native people at the time and remains so, passed on June 2, 1924. Frank Iyall was among the delegates to Washington, D.C., who petitioned for the passage of the Act. Interview with Joseph Kalama; Carpenter, Pascualy, and Hunter, *Nisqually Indian Tribe*, 91.

93. Carpenter, *The Nisqually, My People*, 239.

94. Carpenter, Pascualy, and Hunter, *Nisqually Indian Tribe*, 9; U.S. Senate, *Allotted Nisqually Indian Lands*, 35–49. According to Carpenter, three main Nisqually families remained on the reservation after the condemnation to form the core of the tribe: the Kalama, the Wells, and the McCloud families. Interview with Cecelia Carpenter, February 21, 2007.

95. The Nisqually Tribe approved the 1946 constitution 17–0 out of a total of 37 eligible voters. U.S. Government, Department of the Interior, Bureau of Indian Affairs, "Constitution and Bylaws of the Nisqually Indian Community," 1, 7; Carpenter, *The Nisqually, My People*, 252–54. Carpenter's family lost two allotments in the condemnation. Carpenter's uncle, Walter Ross, was included in the tribal membership roll, but her mother was excluded. The 1946 Nisqually constitution created a

committee to review membership for the people displaced in the condemnation, but the prospect of per-capita payments following the Indian Claims Commission decision worked against expanding tribal membership. This trend changed in 1974, when the decision in *U.S. v. Washington* forced the tribe to open its rolls and include the 210 people on the list that was first drawn up by Peter Kalama following the condemnation. Interview with Cecelia Carpenter, February 21, 2007; Carpenter, Pascualy, and Hunter, *Nisqually Indian Tribe*, 9.

96. Carpenter, "Indian Memories of My Childhood," 282.

97. Indian Claims Commission Docket 197 (*Nisqually et al. v. U.S.*), PNRO. The Nisqually Tribe asked for about $12 million but accepted a settlement of $87,000 over thirty years after the claim was filed. Carpenter recalled that the Nisqually claim was one of the last filed under the Indian Claims Commission and that it was hurt by previous Squaxin and Steilacoom claims, which had included some Nisqually territory in their settlements. Interview with Cecelia Carpenter, February 21, 2007.

98. Congress established the Indian Claims Commission in 1946. Cornell argues that the lobbying efforts of the National Congress of American Indians was an early indication of the growing political power of supratribal politics, which paved the way for the 1960s and 1970s Indian political resurgence. Cornell, *Return of the Native*, 120. The Indian Claims Commission was beset with problems and delays. By the time it ended in 1978, 285 cases had been settled and $800 million had been paid out to tribes. Some scholars argue that the Indian Claims Commission was part of a larger trend in U.S. policy toward ending services to Indian tribes. The Indian Claims Commission took effect only a few years before the United States initiated tribal terminations. Calloway, *First Peoples*, 447–49; Harmon, *Indians in the Making*, 211.

99. Iyall paraphrased an interview with Ida and Paul in her possession. Interview with Cynthia Iyall; Carpenter, Pascualy, and Hunter, *Nisqually Indian Tribe*, 62.

100. Cornell, *Return of the Native*, 214–16.

101. The phrase "The people of Chief Leschi" was repeatedly used in the Historical Court.

102. U.S. Senate, *Allotted Nisqually Indian Lands*, 3.

103. State law allowed only hook-and-line fishing. U.S. Senate, *Allotted Nisqually Indian Lands*, 9; Carpenter, *The Nisqually, My People*, 247.

104. According to Charles Wilkinson, Willy Frank and "other Nisqually fishermen" obtained a federal court injunction in 1937. Wilkinson, *Messages from Frank's Landing*, 40; Paul Andrews, "Old Willie Frank Last Full Blood," reprinted in the *Bellingham Herald*, June 26, 1979, p. 4A; Carpenter, *The Nisqually, My People*, 248.

105. "Indian Tribe Leader Dies," *Tacoma News-Tribune*, May 8, 1947; Alex Tizon, "25 Years after the Boldt Decision: The Fish Tale That Changed History," *Seattle Times*, February 7, 1999.

106. *Tulee v. State of Washington*, 315 U.S. 681, 62 S.Ct. 862, 86 L.Ed. 1115 (1942).

107. A liberal construction of treaty language means judges read treaties on the assumption that Indians retained all rights not explicitly given up. A narrow construction assumes that treaties granted rights to Indians and therefore allowed no other rights than those explicitly stated. Hanson, "The Law of Indian Fishing Rights in Washington," 83–86.

108. U.S. Senate, *Allotted Nisqually Indian Lands*, 38; Wilkinson, *Messages from Frank's Landing*, 27–28.

109. American Friends Service Committee, *Uncommon Controversy*, 108. See, for example, Associated Press, "Shots fired, 60 arrested in Indian-fishing showdown," *Seattle Times*, September 9, 1970.

110. Harmon, *Indians in the Making*, 233; Chrisman, "The Fish-In Protests at Franks Landing."

111. Sturken, *Tangled Memories*, 48.

112. Ibid.

113. Quotes from Rod Cardwell, "Inscription on Monument Indicts Settlers Who Hanged Chief Leschi," *Tacoma News-Tribune*, April 12, 1964, p. 1; and Rod Cardwell, "9 Bitter Words, Etched in Granite, Recall Leschi's Death on Gallows," *Tacoma News-Tribune*, April 16, 1964, p. 1.

114. Haller quoted in Meeker, *Pioneer Reminiscences of Puget Sound and the Tragedy of Leschi*, 209. Meeker's characterization of Haller as a "defender" of Leschi is especially interesting given Haller's military past. In the 1850s Oregon Territory campaign, Haller hastily convened military commissions to justify the execution of Wenneste Indian warriors accused of killing non-Indian settlers. Haller may have been critical of the fact that Leschi was put on trial in a civilian court. Witt, *Lincoln's Code*, 332.

115. Olson, "Our Leschi: The Making of a Martyr," 35.

116. Sturkin, *Tangled Memories*, 63.

117. Savage, *Standing Soldiers, Kneeling Slaves*, 90.

118. Sturken, *Tangled Memories*, 17–18.

119. Savage, *Standing Soldiers, Kneeling Slaves*, 90.

120. Ibid., 106.

121. Interview with Cecelia Carpenter, June 10, 2006.

122. Cardwell, "Nine Bitter Words Recall Chief's Death."

123. Ibid.

124. *Tacoma News-Tribune*, April 16, 1964, p. 1.

125. Steilacoom mayor George Salazar argued that Indians had in fact been invited. One of those featured at the unveiling was Wilbur Lyle Rice, whose great-great-grandmother's aunt was the wife of Leschi, according to the newspaper reporter. *Tacoma News-Tribune*, April 16, 1964, p. 1.

126. "Indians Urging LBJ to Reorganize Bureau," *Tacoma News-Tribune*, April 17, 1964, p. 5.

127. Thrush, *Native Seattle*, 170.

128. Bruyneel, *Third Space of Sovereignty*, 123–24, 150–51.

129. *United States v. Washington*, 384 F. Supp. 312 W.D. Wash. (1974).

130. Zelma McCloud quoted in Heffernan, *Where the Salmon Run*, 8.

131. Harmon, *Indians in the Making*, 230–31; Heffernan, *Where the Salmon Run*, 172, 178–79. Other important effects of the Boldt decision include return-migration to the reservation, new economic opportunities for treaty tribes, and a continuing and sometimes contentious process of allocating fish among eligible tribes. Miller, "The Press, the Boldt Decision, and Indian-White Relations," 78.

132. Billy Frank Jr., "The Importance of Oral History," WSHS, "Leschi," Web archive.

133. Bruce Miller's study of local newspapers in the Skagit Valley in northwestern Washington concluded that the nature and volume of reporting about Indians and Indian issues changed during periods of intense competition over salmon resources. Negative reporting resulted in deteriorated public opinion of Indians and Indian issues in the rural Skagit Valley. See Miller, "The Press, the Boldt Decision, and Indian-White Relations." In the forty years since the Boldt decision, newspapers in urban western Washington seem to have trended toward more dynamic depictions of tribes although I could not locate a study of media depictions or public opinion polls focused on the recent past.

134. Interview with Cecelia Carpenter, February 21, 2007.

135. Carpenter, "How It All Began," CSCPC.

136. Redwing Cloud, "Chief Leschi's Name Restored," *Indian Country Today*, January 4, 2005.

137. Interview with Cynthia Iyall; interview with Cecelia Carpenter, February 21, 2007.

138. Interview with Cynthia Iyall; interview with Cecelia Carpenter, February 21, 2007.

139. Jennifer Lloyd, "Exonerate Chief Leschi of Murder, Say Tribe, Lawmakers," *Seattle Post-Intelligencer*, February 19, 2004.

140. Tomas Alex Tizon, "A Matter of Justice and Honor," *Los Angeles Times*, December 28, 2004.

141. Carpenter said; "I've always been very proud that [Leschi] was a Nisqually and not a Puyallup. Puyallup kept stealing him. . . . I wrapped my arms around him and held him as our chief." Interview with Cecelia Carpenter, February 21, 2007.

142. Tomas Alex Tizon, "A Matter of Justice and Honor," *Los Angeles Times*, December 28, 2004.

CHAPTER 5

1. Merry, "Courts as Performances," 37.

2. The participants in the court initiated what Lazarus-Black and Hirsch call "performances of hegemony and resistance that actively reshape legal conscious-

ness under conditions of postcolonial legal pluralism." Lazarus-Black and Hirsch, *Contested States*, 14.

3. Lazarus-Black and Hirsch write: "The decision to seek justice in court cannot be reduced to a simplistic calculation of whether or not one might 'win.' Rather, [legal] performance confronts the limits of hegemony." Ibid.

4. Interview with Cecelia Carpenter, February 21, 2007.

5. As Kent McNeil explains, although the U.S. and Canadian governments exercise sovereign authority over territory in the Pacific Northwest and *may* meet the requirements for prescriptive title in international law, "the legitimacy of that authority with respect to Indian nations . . . is questionable." McNeil, "Negotiated Sovereignty," 47.

6. Tomlins, "The Many Legalities of Colonization," 5, 19. See also Comaroff and Comaroff, *The Dialectics of Modernity on a South African Frontier.*

7. Tomlins, "The Many Legalities of Colonization," 5; Walters, "Histories of Colonialism, Legality, and Aboriginality," 819–24. See also McHugh, *Aboriginal Societies*; and Russell, *Recognizing Aboriginal Title.*

8. Carpenter, "How It All Began," CSCPC; interview with Cynthia Iyall.

9. Ibid.; Kluger, *Bitter Waters of Medicine Creek*, 265.

10. Petitioners' Memorandum of Law, submitted by the Descendants of Chief Leschi and the Nisqually Indian Tribe on December 7, 2004, p. 2, courtesy of Cecelia Carpenter; Carpenter, "How It All Began," CSCPC; Kluger, *Bitter Waters of Medicine Creek*, 263.

11. Common law systems, in this case the one operating in the United States, are informed by English legal traditions and practices. Cotterrell explains the unique character of common law: "The net of law does not break precisely because of its flexibility and resilience and because many links in it are continually being replaced or repaired." Cotterrell, "Common Law Approaches," 10–12.

12. Asher, *Beyond the Reservation*, 198.

13. Nobles, *The Politics of Official Apologies*, 23–24; Niezen, *Public Justice*, 222, 225. For criticism of this soft power, also known as the "politics of pity," see Boltanski, *Distant Suffering*; and Antze and Lambek, *Tense Past.*

14. Interview with Cynthia Iyall; Kluger, *Bitter Waters of Medicine Creek*, 265.

15. "Eijiro Kawada, "Chief Leschi 'Appeal' Gets Legislative Support," *Tacoma News-Tribune*, March 7, 2004, B2; interview with Tina Kuckkahn. Ezra Meeker confirmed that the records of Pierce County burned on April 5, 1859. Meeker, *Pioneer Reminiscences of Puget Sound and the Tragedy of Leschi*, 418.

16. Interview with Cynthia Iyall.

17. Kluger, *Bitter Waters of Medicine Creek*, 266.

18. Heath Foster, "Victim of Racism Will Gain Posthumous Bar Membership," *Seattle Post-Intelligencer*, February 5, 2001.

19. Interview with Robert Anderson.

20. Kluger, *Bitter Waters of Medicine Creek*, 268; Associated Press, "Execution

to Exoneration Is Quest for Chief Leschi," *Yakima Herald-Republic*, September 16, 2003, 5B; Lewis Kamb, "Leschi Wasn't a Murderer, Tribe Says," *Seattle Post-Intelligencer*, September 15, 2003.

21. Interview with Tina Kuckkahn.

22. Kluger, *Bitter Waters of Medicine Creek*, 270.

23. Jennifer Lloyd, "Exonerate Chief Leschi of Murder, Say Tribe, Lawmakers," *Seattle Post-Intelligencer*, February 19, 2004.

24. Tomlins, "The Many Legalities of Colonization," 2.

25. Kluger, *Bitter Waters of Medicine Creek*, 270–71.

26. Washington State history textbooks contained very little Indian history, so Indian communities organized in the years after this resolution to write sections for inclusion. The Nisqually group met through 2011 to complete its addition. Interview with Joseph Kalama.

27. Washington State Senate, Senate Joint Memorial 8054, www.leg.gov/pub/billinfo/2003-04/Senate/8050-8074/8054_02112004.txt. See "Called Session," *Pioneer and Democrat*, February 5, 1858.

28. Chaplin, "Only the Drums Remembered."

29. Thrush, *Native Seattle*, 189–92. See also American Friends Service Committee, *Uncommon Controversy*.

30. Harmon, "Indian Treaty History," 362; Cornell, *Return of the Native*, 199. For more on Initiative 456, see Cohen, *Treaties on Trial*, 185–86.

31. Billy Frank Jr. is the longtime chairman of the Northwest Indian Fisheries Commission, created after the 1974 Boldt decision, which coordinates the resource management efforts of Northwest treaty tribes. Frank is the winner of multiple awards, including the Washington State Environmental Excellence Award from the State Ecological Commission (received on behalf of participating tribes, 1987) and the Albert Schweitzer Prize for Humanitarianism (1992). http://nwifc.org/about-us/. August 31, 2012; http://www.sos.wa.gov/office/osos_news.aspx?i=torb6mXHLOi%2F%2FdeGTaVxdQ%3D%3D. August 31, 2012.

32. Non-Indians' attitudes toward Indians after the Boldt decision differed between rural and urban areas in the state. Seattleites' public attitudes toward Native Americans did not appear to deteriorate during the fishing rights controversy, although animosity increased in outlying areas where the battles over resources took place. Miller, "The Press, the Boldt Decision, and Indian-White Relations," 78–79, 91. Washington tribes also own several Class III gaming facilities, which bring jobs and revenue to the state. By 2003, several tribes were in the position to donate casino revenue to political parties and lobbying efforts. The tribes' economic stature may have convinced local legislators to give the Leschi case consideration. Kluger, *Bitter Waters of Medicine Creek*, 271.

33. Elisabeth Bumiller, "Bush Lays Out Goals for Iraq: Self-Rule and Stability," *New York Times*, May 25, 2004.

34. Brooks, "New Patriotism and Apology for Slavery," 214, 223. A forthcoming book (Harvard University Press, 2014) appears to offer the related argument that America's human rights advocacy served as a way to restore U.S. moral leadership following national trauma. See Keys, *Reclaiming American Virtue*.

35. Murphy, *Multiculturalism*, 3, 6, 7.

36. Ibid., 7–8.

37. Simpson, "On the Logic of Discernment," 483; Murphy, *Multiculturalism*, 16–17. See also Kymlicka, *Finding Our Way*; Tully, *Strange Multiplicity*; Ivison, *Postcolonial Liberalism*; and Turner, *This Is Not a Peace Pipe*.

38. Wolfe, "Settler Colonialism and the Elimination of the Native," 387–88.

39. Engle, "Self-Critique, (Anti) Politics and Criminalization." See also Wendy Brown, "The Most We Can Hope For."

40. Niezen, *Public Justice*, 22–23.

41. Kluger, *Bitter Waters of Medicine Creek*, 273.

42. State of Washington, House of Representatives Resolution 4708, adopted March 4, 2004; Senate Resolution 8727, adopted March 4, 2004; Senate Joint Resolution 8054.

43. Kluger, *Bitter Waters of Medicine Creek*, 274.

44. Eijiro Kawada, "Chief Leschi 'Appeal' Gets Legislative Support," *Tacoma News-Tribune*, March 7, 2004, 1B.

45. Ibid.

46. Nobles, *The Politics of Official Apologies*, 108–9.

47. Letter from Senator Bill Finkbeiner, Senator Lisa Brown, Representative Frank Chopp, and Representative Richard DeBolt to Chief Justice Gerry Alexander, March 9, 2004; courtesy of Gerry Alexander.

48. Tomlins, "The Many Legalities of Colonization," 4.

49. Letter from Senator Bill Finkbeiner, Senator Lisa Brown, Representative Frank Chopp, and Representative Richard DeBolt to Chief Justice Gerry Alexander, March 9, 2004; Kluger, *Bitter Waters of Medicine Creek*, 270; Thomas Shapley, "Some Wrongs Are beyond Righting," *Seattle Post-Intelligencer*, September 26, 2004.

50. Kluger, *Bitter Waters of Medicine Creek*, 268; Washington State Legislature, "A History of the Legislature—Enabling Act."

51. Interview with Gerry Alexander; Letter from Chief Justice Gerry Alexander to Senator Bill Finkbeiner, Senator Lisa Brown, Representative Frank Chopp, and Representative Richard DeBolt, March 15, 2004; courtesy of Gerry Alexander; Kluger, *Bitter Waters of Medicine Creek*, 274, 276; Thomas Shapley, "Some Wrongs Are beyond Righting," *Seattle Post-Intelligencer*, September 26, 2004.

52. Letter from Gerry Alexander to Cynthia Iyall, March 25, 2004; courtesy of Gerry Alexander.

53. Interview with Tina Kuckkahn; Kluger, *Bitter Waters of Medicine Creek*, 275–76.

54. The compromise that created the Historical Court exhibits what Samuel

Weber describes as the "certain tension between ethical ideals and political reality . . . at work wherever the notion of justice is concerned." Samuel Weber, "In the Name of the Law," 234.

55. Interview with Tina Kuckkahn.

56. Letter from Gerry Alexander to Cynthia Iyall, July 23, 2004; courtesy of Gerry Alexander.

57. Interview with Thor Hoyte.

58. Interview with Tina Kuckkahn.

59. Nobles, *The Politics of Official Apologies*, 19.

60. Audra Simpson explains how the practice of claiming is such that indigenous culture and identity are required to be "discerned," or fixed and adjudicated, in settler societies. Indigenous people who make legal claims subject themselves to a "logic of property" in which the existence of their identities and intrinsic value of their culture are determined by others. Simpson, "On the Logic of Discernment," 479.

61. Ivison, *Postcolonial Liberalism*, 40.

62. Tomlins, "The Many Legalities of Colonization," 5, 15, 18–19; Wolfe, *Settler Colonialism and the Transformation of Anthropology*, 2, 5.

63. A tribunal technically refers to a body convened in the name of the public to investigate an event that does not fit into regular state-run judicial systems. Tribunals do not entail universal rules of procedure, and evidence and testimony are defined according to the specifics of the case under examination. International bodies such as the United Nations or independent nation-states have sponsored tribunals to address crimes against the public. The tribunal following the Khmer Rouge Genocide, the International Criminal Tribunal for Rwanda, and the Tribunal for the Former Yugoslavia are a few recent examples. Some, like the Nuremberg Trials, were endowed with power to enforce their rulings, while others, like New Zealand's Waitangi Tribunal, may only make recommendations for action. Vora and Vora, "The Effectiveness of South Africa's Truth and Reconciliation Commission," 302–3.

64. See Belgrave, *Historical Frictions*; and Byrnes, *Waitangi Tribunal*, 3.

65. Truth and reconciliation commissions call on states as moral actors to take responsibility for collective wrongdoing, persuade public opinion to follow supposedly universal imperatives of human rights, and proclaim themselves as different or changed from the older regime that perpetrated injustice. Between 1974 and 2004, at least twenty truth and reconciliation commissions were established in nations such as Argentina, Chile, El Salvador, and the Philippines as part of a transition from dictatorial to democratic rule. Phelps, *Shattered Voices*, 78; Vora and Vora, "The Effectiveness of South Africa's Truth and Reconciliation Commission," 302–3; Niezen, *Public Justice*, 180.

66. As Ronald Niezen puts it, a truth and reconciliation commission "becomes a venue for the articulation of memories pulled past the obstacles of repression, in-

hibition and avoidance of . . . emotional pain." Niezen, *Public Justice*, 183; Peters, "Literature," 253–54, 272–75.

67. Peters, "Literature," 275.

68. Interview with Carl Hultman; Limerick, *Legacy of Conquest*.

69. Harmon, "Writing History by Litigation," 9.

70. As critics point out, testimony alone has limited power to compel change and expand political power or individual rights. Scholars decry the "politics of pity," defined as the dynamic between spectator and victim testimony of transgenerational suffering, as a strategy that sacrifices indigenous sovereignty to the will of the colonizer. Such an approach is ineffective for indigenous decolonization, Alfred contends, because guilt is a conditioned cultural response specific to monotheistic belief and not a recipe for lasting peace and justice between nations. Chouliaraki, "Watching 11 September," 185–98; Boltanski, *Distant Suffering*, 12; Alfred, "Restitution Is the Real Pathway," 182, 185; Simpson, "The 'Problem' of Mental Health in Native North America," 376–79.

71. Mejia, "Indians Put Christopher Columbus on Trial," One World Org, July 20, 1998, http://ishgooda.org/racial/holid4.htm.

72. The Tribunal was held August 12–23, 1993. Churchill and Venne, *Islands in Captivity*, 1.

73. Testimony by Francis Boyle; Molina, *USA on Trial*, 5, 11–23, 274.

74. The People's Tribunal was created, staffed, and funded by the people of the Kanaka Maoli Nation. The United States declined the invitation to attend, but a large empty chair labeled "U.S. Representative" was placed in the tribunal chamber. Churchill and Venne, *Islands in Captivity*, 677–79.

75. In a gesture that many accepted as meaningful (and some criticized as empty), Congress responded to the People's Tribunal by passing a resolution apologizing for the illegal overthrow of the Hawaiian government. Congress declined the Tribunal's recommendations and ordered the Interior and Justice Departments to conduct a report on more "feasible" solutions. One of the legal advisers to the Committee to Exonerate Chief Leschi, Robert Anderson, worked on the Department of Interior report and thought of the event as an encouraging model for Leschi's case. Robert Anderson worked for Interior Secretary Bruce Babbitt at the time. Interview with Robert Anderson; Weyeneth, "Power of Apology," 13; Lander and Lander, with Na Maka o ka 'Aina, "Proceedings of the People's International Tribunal, Hawai'i 1993."

76. A good example is the Civic Council of Popular and Indigenous Organizations of Honduras (COPINH), which convened a trial of Christopher Columbus in Honduras in 1998 on charges of genocide, ethnocide, rape, and plundering. The trial had the blessing of the Honduran government, and the public performance was meant to bring attention to indigenous peoples' struggles for rights throughout Latin America. Notably, COPINH decided to convene the trial a year after members

of the organization removed a statue of Columbus from Tegucigalpa's city center, an act that drew criticism and ultimately hurt support for indigenous rights activism. "America's Christopher Columbus—on Trial," October 14, 1998, http://news.bbc.co.uk/2/hi/americas/192240.stm.

77. In 2009, the U.S. Supreme Court upheld the Hawaiian state court's decision that the wording of the apology did not prohibit the state from selling land on Maui before Native claims had been settled. Justice Samuel Alito argued that waiting to settle the Native land claim infringed on Hawai'i's state sovereignty. Adam Liptak, "Justices Limit the Reach of Apology to Hawaiians," *New York Times*, April 1, 2009, A19.

78. Alexander adds that although not a "huge fan" of politicizing issues that are legal in nature, he respects the right of citizens to assemble and petition the government for a redress of grievances. Interview with Gerry Alexander; email correspondence with Gerry Alexander, March 25, 2013.

79. Cahn, "An Anthropologist Examines the Lawyer Tribe," 293.

80. Byrnes, *Waitangi Tribunal*, 18.

81. Email correspondence with John Ladenburg, October 13, 2008. Hultman described the other problem with the innocence defense: Leschi could also have been considered an accomplice to murder even if he did not fire the bullet that killed Moses. Hultman, who was involved in building the petitioners' argument even though he served as respondents' counsel in the Historical Court, recalled that the combatant defense strategically addressed legal issues the case presented. Interview with Carl Hultman.

82. Robert Anderson's opinion was that Wilkinson's argument for Nisqually sovereignty and the military historians' testimony about laws of war were the most convincing to the justices. Interview with Robert Anderson; interview with Cecelia Carpenter, June 10, 2006.

83. John Ladenburg appealed to the judges' task by "marrying facts with law" to present the most persuasive case. Interview with John Ladenburg.

84. Cotterrell, "Common Law Approaches," 11.

85. Ann Fienup-Riordan noted of Yupiit Nation elders that their "testimony was an ideal view of the past recalled in the present in an effort to influence the future. The value of the testimony is not its documentation of the past." Fienup-Riordan quoted in Miller, *Problem of Justice*, 55.

86. Interview with Tina Kuckkahn; interview with Cynthia Iyall. Cecelia Carpenter said she also had doubts that there would be an exoneration at the beginning of the process, but she was confident the judges would rule in favor of exoneration. Interview with Cecelia Carpenter, February 21, 2007.

87. Also unlike other judicial decisions, the Nisqually Tribe handed out commemorative medals, gifted the participants, and held a dance at the capitol—all suggesting that the participants had felt confident about the outcome. Interview with Peggy McCloud.

88. Tomas Alex Tizon, "A Matter of Justice and Honor," *Los Angeles Times*, December 28, 2004.

89. Barkan and Karn, *Taking Wrongs Seriously*, 14.

90. Peters, "Literature," 253–54, 281. Weyeneth argues that a public pronunciation of a past mistake by a figure of authority is a form of apology. Weyeneth, "The Power of Apology," 16. I contend here that an apology, as such, should be unambiguous and include acceptance of responsibility.

91. Jennifer Lloyd, "Exonerate Chief Leschi of Murder, Say Tribe, Lawmakers," *Seattle Post-Intelligencer*, February 19, 2004, B1.

92. Alfred, "Restitution Is the Real Pathway," 183–84.

93. Interview with Thor Hoyte.

94. Thor Hoyte noted that the press attention was pleasantly surprising: "It hit all seven continents," he recalled. Ibid.

95. Melissa Parr quoted in Kluger, *Bitter Waters of Medicine Creek*, 284.

96. Tomlins, "The Many Legalities of Colonization," 19.

CHAPTER 6

1. "Quiemuth" is the most common spelling of the name in recent sources, so I reproduce it here. There are several other versions that attempt to phonetically approximate the Whulshootseed name, such as Iui-ee-muth, Quiemulth, and Quaymuth.

2. Interview with Peggy McCloud.

3. Gordon, *Ghostly Matters*, 8, 194.

4. Interview with Peggy McCloud.

5. Benton, *Law and Colonial Cultures*, 209.

6. Asher, *Beyond the Reservation*, 133.

7. In addition to Leschi, war leaders Wa He Lut, Kitsap, and Winyea were tried in civil courts after the war. Quiemuth was indicted, but he was murdered before he could stand trial. Winyea and Kitsap were tried and acquitted in 1856, and Wa He Lut was convicted but released in 1859. "Puget Sound News — Capture of Leschi, the War Chief," *Weekly Oregonian*, November 22, 1856, p. 2; Asher, *Beyond the Reservation*, 133.

8. Due process, which territorial courts usually followed, is not the same as fairness. Indians were prosecuted under a legal regime imposed upon them by force. Asher, *Beyond the Reservation*, 198.

9. Benton, *Law and Colonial Cultures*, 13, 209.

10. Harring, *Crow Dog's Case*, 283–84.

11. Benton, *Law and Colonial Cultures*, 260.

12. Gordon, *Ghostly Matters*, 6.

13. Boyd and Thrush, *Phantom Past, Indigenous Presence*, xi–xii. See also the introduction in Buse and Stott, *Ghosts*, 1–20; and Nabokov, *Forest of Time*, 147–48.

14. Huyssen, *Present Pasts*, 3–4.

15. Quiemuth was about ten years older than Leschi. Leschi and Quiemuth had different mothers, but Nisqually society made little or no distinction between half brothers and full brothers. Meeker wrote that Quiemuth guided the party of wagon road builders across the Naches Pass in 1853, while Leschi likely supplied the horses. Meeker, *Pioneer Reminiscences of Puget Sound and the Tragedy of Leschi*, 139, 150; Crooks, "Quiemuth, Part I," 3–4.

16. One newspaper editor noted that, as a consequence of the Medicine Creek Treaty, "the chief . . . of the Nisquallys, has been furnished with farm implements, &c., to a large amount, which he receives for his own benefit." "To the People," *Puget Sound Courier*, August 24, 1855.

17. James Longmire claimed that Quiemuth visited with Governor Mason in Olympia on October 20, 1855. Works Progress Administration, *Told by the Pioneers*, 137; Carpenter, *The Nisqually, My People*, 170; Meeker, *Pioneer Reminiscences of Puget Sound and the Tragedy of Leschi*, 283.

18. William Tolmie to McMullin, January 12, 1858, Clarence Bagley Papers, box 21, UWSC.

19. James McAllister took a donation land claim on the Nisqually Delta near to the spot where the Medicine Creek Treaty council took place. McAllister's daughter claimed that Leschi suggested the family move to this location. McAllister wrote to Charles Mason requesting that Leschi "be attended to as soon as convenient for fear he might do something bad." James McAllister to Washington Territorial Superintendent of Indian Affairs, October 16, 1855, reprinted in Reese, *Leschi, the Officers, and the Citizens*, 7. Meeker, *Pioneer Reminiscences of Puget Sound and the Tragedy of Leschi*, 215, 278; Reese, *They Came to Puget Sound*, 2–3; *Pioneer and Democrat*, November 9, 1855.

20. Michael Connell was a recent immigrant from Ireland who took a homestead in the White River Valley, about twenty miles east of Steilacoom. Connell's Prairie, where the militiamen were killed in the October 27 and October 31 ambushes, took its name from its location on Connell's claim. Meeker's account states that McAllister and Connell were killed on October 27. The *Puget Sound Courier* reported that McAllister and Connell had been joined on their mission by two Indian guides, one of whom was killed in the ambush while the other escaped and reported the deaths to his family at Nisqually. Isaac Stevens reported seven months after the incident that McAllister had been shot by his Indian guide, specifically naming Stahi. According to a manuscript written by Charles Eaton in 1917, Leschi confessed that he "engaged in the murder of McAlester but Towapite [Too-a-pi-ti] shot McAlister with two balls." Meeker's account with unnamed killers seems to have dominated. In 1924 the Washington Historical Society erected a monument on Connell's Prairie with the inscription: "Near here Indians lay in ambush and killed Lieutenant McAllister and Michael Connell, October 27, 1855." Wiley, *Pioneer and Democrat*, November 9, 1855; "Outbreaks of the Indians West of the Cascades," *Puget Sound*

Courier, November 16, 1855; "Captain Charles E. Eaton: Confession of Lesh-hi," Indian War 1855 Papers, T-141/2, WSHS; Meeker, *Pioneers Reminiscences*, 283; Letter from Isaac I. Stevens to Commissioner of Indian Affairs, May 31, 1856, WSHS Web archive, "Leschi"; "How to Serve a Writ," *Puget Sound Herald*, April 22, 1859; Author unknown, "Unsettling Events—Bonney Lake Battle," Tacoma Public Library Northwest Reading Room & Special Collections database.

21. J. Ross Browne, *Indian War in Oregon and Washington* (Washington, D.C.: 35th Congress, 1st Sess., Ex. Doc. No. 40 [January 25, 1858]), 11–12, reprinted in Reese, *Leschi, the Officers, and the Citizens*, 103–4; "Leschi, Quiemuth, etc.," *Pioneer and Democrat*, November 28, 1856; Crooks, "Quiemuth, Part I," 6; "Latest from our Troops," *Puget Sound Courier*, November 30, 1855.

22. Letter from Hazard Stevens to his grandmother, November 15, 1856, quoted in Crooks, "Quiemuth, Part I," 6.

23. Carpenter records the date as November 17, but Drew Crooks points out that most newspaper sources agree that Quiemuth turned himself in on November 18. Carpenter, *The Nisqually, My People*, 171; Crooks, "Quiemuth, Part II," 5.

24. Betsy Edgar was a Nisqually woman married to John Edgar, a Scottish Hudson's Bay Company employee. Betsy Edgar has been identified as Quiemuth's cousin and Leschi's niece and of Nisqually and Klickitat heritage. Eckrom, *Remembered Drums*, 54; Vaughn, *Puget Sound Invasion*, 49; Van Ogle, "Van Ogle's Memory of Pioneer Days," 279; Letter from Isaac Stevens to the Superintendent of Indian Affairs, May 31, 1856, WSHS Web archive, "Leschi"; Bancroft and Victor, *History of Washington, Idaho, and Montana*, 386; Works Progress Administration, *Told by the Pioneers*, 142.

25. "Leschi, Quiemuth, etc.," *Pioneer and Democrat*, November 28, 1856. James Longmire later recalled that he asked Quiemuth to be delivered to him for the trip to Steilacoom "after dark, for if he was seen someone would surely kill him." Works Progress Administration, *Told by the Pioneers*, 142–43.

26. Van Ogle, "Van Ogle's Memory of Pioneer Days," 281.

27. Longmire's story is devoid of the self-conscious need to both explain what he witnessed and entertain his reading audience. Laura B. Downey Bartlett added drama to Longmire's account when she reprinted it in 1930. She wrote: "After darkness had settled in the room, with no sound from any corner, someone—no one knew who—with voice unknown, raised a corner of the blanket and asked, 'Is this you, Longmire?' When he answered, 'Yes,' the life of Quiemal was taken without delay." *Puyallup Valley Tribune*, January 24, 1930, Nisqually Vertical File, WSHS.

28. Narrative of James Longmire, in Works Progress Administration, *Told by the Pioneers*, 143.

29. Poem of Quiemuth, TS-30, folder 3, p. 4, H. E. Van Ogle File, WSHS.

30. Stevens, *Life*, 3:241.

31. Longmire recalled: "At the moment when Governor Stevens rushed in, saying,

as he saw the dying chief, 'Who in H— has done this?' I replied, 'I do not know.' 'In my office, too,' he added. 'This is a club for General Woo[l].'" "James Longmire, Pioneer," *Tacoma Daily Ledger*, August 21, 1892, p. 10.

32. Joseph Bunting was married to McAllister's sixteen-year-old daughter Martha Ann in 1855. Hazard Stevens later claimed to know that Quiemuth murdered McAllister, but he appears to base this charge upon nothing more than rumor. Van Ogle, one of Quiemuth's escorts, later wrote that McAllister's knife was found on Quiemuth's belt, and Bunting had been asking questions about how Quiemuth would receive justice, although I believe these to be plot inventions. Van Ogle, "Van Ogle's Memory of Pioneer Days," 281; marriage notice of Joseph Bunting and M[artha] A[nn] E. McAl[l]ister, *Pioneer and Democrat*, October 12, 1855 and *Puget Sound Courier*, October 19, 1855; "Leschi, Quiemuth, etc.," *Pioneer and Democrat*, November 28, 1856, p. 2; Letter from Isaac Stevens to the Office of the Superintendent of Indian Affairs, May 31, 1856, WSHS, "Leschi" Web archive; "Leschi's Bones Reburied," *Tacoma Ledger*, July 4, 1895.

33. Van Ogle, "Van Ogle's Memory of Pioneer Days," 281.

34. In the fifteen murder prosecutions brought against white men for killing Indians between 1853 and 1864 in Washington Territory, there was a 13 percent conviction rate. There were also an unrecorded number of cases in which settlers were questioned and released or there was no legal action taken whatsoever. Prosch, *Reminiscences of Washington Territory*, 69; Asher, *Beyond the Reservation*, 114.

35. Crooks, "Quiemuth, Part II," 6; Van Ogle, "Van Ogle's Memory of Pioneer Days," 281; Van Ogle accounts, n.d., in Robert Hitchman Manuscript, 229, T-48/6, WSHS; The newspaper claimed that the bodies of three children were unearthed in the search for Quiemuth's tomb and his remains were only positively identified by a rusty knife in the ribcage and a bullet hole in the skull. "Leschi's Bones Reburied," *Tacoma Ledger*, July 4, 1895.

36. Interview with August Kautz published in the *Weekly Ledger*, April 14, 1893. Reprinted in Reese, *Leschi, the Officers, and the Citizens*, 149.

37. Olson, "Our Leschi: The Making of a Martyr," 26; Reese, *Nothing Worthy of Note Transpired Today*, 145.

38. Olson, "Our Leschi: The Making of a Martyr," 31.

39. Informants told Marian Smith that in cases of shaman killing, "a close relative of the slain man might long for revenge." Smith, *The Puyallup-Nisqually*, 67, 161.

40. For more on how Northwest Coast indigenous people understood shaman power and customs that supported killing shamans for the protection of the community, see Fiddler and Stevens, *Killing the Shamen*.

41. Interpersonal family conflicts could spark larger wars, but kinship connections could also end wars. Harmon, *Indians in the Making*, 93.

42. Sometimes settlers characterized murders of Indians as part of a Native

"blood feud" that erupted if one family refused to compensate another for the murder of a family member, which they believed led into a spiral of endless killing. Marian Smith explains the Puyallup-Nisqually notions of blood feuds in more detail, in *The Puyallup-Nisqually*, 161–63. See also Denny, *Pioneer Days on Puget Sound*, 68–69. George Gibbs wrote of the Puyallup, that if a killer or his kin refused to pay atonement, the victim's family could kill the perpetrator without repercussions. It was more common among the Twana and Clallams that the perpetrator's family saw retaliatory killing as deserving of like compensation, which led to "a prolonged bout of retaliatory feuding." Asher, *Beyond the Reservation*, 25–26; Ford, *Settler Sovereignty*, 35–36.

43. Skagit informants described precontact life as peaceful; families generally frowned upon acts of retaliation because of the danger posed to the kin group, and adults were praised when they received insults without retaliating. Asher, *Beyond the Reservation*, 25.

44. Meeker, *Reminiscences*, 201–11; Harmon, *Indians in the Making*, 50–53.

45. The Oregon Treaty, signed in 1846, set South Puget Sound under the jurisdiction of the United States. Carpenter, Pascualy, and Hunter, *Nisqually Indian Tribe*, 7. Two other Americans suffered gunshot wounds in the Fort Nisqually shooting, and one unnamed Indian child was fatally wounded. The American killed, Leander Wallace, apparently did not seek cover when the gunfire broke out because he did not suppose he was a target. The Hudson's Bay Company's *Nisqually Journal* writer interpreted this event as a Snoqualmie raid on the "fort Indians." *Nisqually Journal*, May 1, 1849. However, an American settler, Michael Simmons, immediately sent a report to Governor Lane in the Oregon Territory, claiming that American settlers feared for their safety and "hourly expected to be attacked by the Indians." Joseph Lane's report to the War Department, May 17, 1849, and Report of William P. Bryant to Joseph Lane, October 10, 1849, printed in Reese, *A Documentary History of Fort Steilacoom*, 63–65, 67; Meeker, *Pioneer Reminiscences of Puget Sound and the Tragedy of Leschi*, 444; Farrar, "The Nisqually Journal," 215–18.

46. Letter from William Tolmie to Governor Fayette McMullin, January 12, 1858, Clarence Bagley Papers, box 21, UWSC.

47. One of the major differences between Native American and Euro-American legal traditions is the private/public dimension. Native groups placed much of the power of law enforcement upon kinship groups, while U.S. laws and courts represented the exercise of public authority. Asher, *Beyond the Reservation*, 32.

48. Joseph Lane to William Tolmie, May 17, 1849, ibid.; Reese, *A Documentary History of Fort Steilacoom*, 65; Harmon, *Indians in the Making*, 54–56.

49. Extracts of Report of J. Quinn Thornton to Governor Joseph Lane as reported to the Secretary of War and Governor Lane's comments, in Reese, *A Documentary History of Fort Steilacoom*, 66.

50. Three of the Snoqualmie defendants were found to be "less guilty" than the

two convicted, and the last was assumed to be a slave and found innocent. Report of William P. Bryant to Joseph Lane, October 10, 1849, in Reese, *A Documentary History of Fort Steilacoom*, 67.

51. Asher, *Beyond the Reservation*, 130; Harmon, *Indians in the Making*, 56; Bagley quoted in Meeker, *Pioneer Reminiscences of Puget Sound and the Tragedy of Leschi*, 546–47.

52. Harmon, *Indians in the Making*, 57.

53. White, "Treaty at Medicine Creek," 35.

54. David Edwards Blaine wrote in June 1856 that Seattle settler Luther Collins indiscriminately murdered three of Patkanim's men who had joined the U.S. military in the war. Blaine reasoned that because Collins had lost property in the war, he sought indiscriminate revenge. Blaine and Blaine, *Memoirs of Puget Sound*, 167. White, "Treaty of Medicine Creek," 106, 116.

55. Ibid, 106.

56. July 17 and 18, 1858, in Reese, *Journals of August Kautz*, 217–20.

57. Crawley escaped indictment because no white witnesses had seen Goliah and Crawley together. Although Indian witnesses had seen the pair together, Indian testimony against whites was not admissible in court. Asher, *Beyond the Reservation*, 62; July 20, 1858, and September 16, 1858, in Reese, *Journals of August Kautz*, 221, 243; "The Price of an Indian," *Puget Sound Herald*, September 24, 1858.

58. Ford, *Settler Sovereignty*, 33.

59. "The Price of an Indian," *Puget Sound Herald*, September 24, 1858.

60. Ford described this frontier legal culture as "syncretic normativity of reciprocity and retaliation." In Georgia, before 1820, Ford notes that indigenous people defended reciprocity, which was exchange among equals rather than blood revenge. Ford, *Settler Sovereignty*, 35–36, 38.

61. "Leschi, Quiemuth, etc.," *Pioneer and Democrat*, November 28, 1856.

62. Six organized vigilante movements have been identified in Washington's territorial period, although data is scarce. Of the two vigilante movements identified in Pierce County (1856) and Steilacoom (1860), both were small and Indians were not targeted. Wunder, "Law and Order on the Frontier," 332–35; Boessenecker, *Against the Vigilantes*, 32; Richard Maxwell Brown, *Strain of Violence*, 96–97.

63. In 1892, Clinton Snowden, historian and editor of the *Tacoma Ledger*, announced an essay contest to promote Washington history at the Western Washington Exhibition at the Chicago World's Fair. For her winning essay, Sarah Hartman received round-trip tickets to the Chicago Fair in 1893 to represent the Washington "pioneer" for a national audience and publication in the *Ledger*. It is possible that Snowden supported Hartman's essay because of her view on the naming of Mount Rainier, which aligned with his own on this contentious local issue. Richards, "In Search of Pacific Northwest," 422; Reese, *They Came to Puget Sound*, i, iv, 23. Edward Huggins expressed doubt about the veracity of Hartman's memories published in Ezra Meeker's book, and described her essay as "full of untruths and ex-

aggerations." Edward Huggins to Ezra Meeker, September 28, 1903, Edward Huggins Papers, WSHS; Edward Huggins to Eva Emory Dye, May 27, 1904, "Unsettling Events" database, Tacoma Public Library Northwest Room & Special Collections. Historian J. A. Eckrom also noted that her account was inaccurate. J. A. Eckrom, "Murder in Governor's Mansion," *Tacoma News-Tribune*, January 4, 1981, p. 10.

64. Other settlers wrote that McAllister's body was slashed on the arms and legs as though from a knife fight. Hartman embellished such information into "mutilation" for dramatic effect. Sarah Hartman, "Old Pioneer Stories," *Tacoma Ledger*, March 19, 1893, Pioneers Vertical File, p. 10, WSHS.

65. Philip Deloria, *Indians in Unexpected Places*, 62. Wild West shows were an especially popular feature at the Midway in the Chicago World's Fair. Frederick Jackson Turner also gave his famous paper about the significance of the frontier in American history at the Chicago World's Fair. For more on the historical narratives produced in "Buffalo Bill" Cody's show and Turner's essay, see White, "Frederick Jackson Turner and Buffalo Bill."

66. Furniss, *Burden of History*, 18, 69.

67. Hartman, "Old Pioneer Stories," 15–16.

68. Meeker claimed that bribed jurors refused to convict cattle wranglers. Meeker, *Pioneer Reminiscences of Puget Sound and the Tragedy of Leschi*, 153.

69. Slotkin, *Gunfighter Nation*, 11.

70. Asher, *Beyond the Reservation*, 15.

71. Allen argues that vigilantes in Montana continued to lynch men long after the establishment of formal courts of law. Allen, *A Decent, Orderly Lynching*, xvii.

72. Meeker described Mowitch as a friendly and able hunter who, in the years before the war, gifted settlers with venison. Meeker, *Pioneer Reminiscences of Puget Sound and the Tragedy of Leschi*, 129–30; Military Department Correspondence, 1855–56, box 12, Trial James Lake folder, Washington State Archives, Olympia; Eckrom, *Remembered Drums*, 141, 147; White, "Treaty at Medicine Creek," 106; Snowden, *Rise and Progress of an American State*, 503; "Indian Shot," *Puget Sound Courier*, April 25, 1856.

73. April 23, 1859, in Reese, *Journals of August Kautz*, 330; *Puget Sound Herald*, March 26, 1858.

74. Poem, TS-30, folder 3, p. 4, H. E. Van Ogle File, WSHS.

75. Snowden, *Rise and Progress of an American State*, 503; Eckrom, *Remembered Drums*, 148; Reminiscences of Edward Huggins, *Tacoma Ledger*, October 21, 1900, in Clarence Bagley Scrapbook, vol. 4, p. 143, UWSC.

76. The *Puget Sound Herald* reported that the posse killed Too-a-pi-ti when he tried to escape. Kautz wrote in his diary that the Indians told Dr. Tolmie that Too-a-pi-ti had been fired upon "without any attempt to arrest" him and that he was only injured. "How to Serve a Writ," *Puget Sound Herald*, April 22, 1859; April 18, 1859, in Reese, *Journals of August Kautz*, 329.

77. "How to Serve a Writ," *Puget Sound Herald*, April 22, 1859. Charles Prosch and

George Lee published the *Puget Sound Herald* on the same press as the *Puget Sound Courier*, although they declared the new paper to be politically independent. "Salutatory," *Puget Sound Herald*, March 12, 1858.

78. April 18, 1859, in Reese, *Journals of August Kautz*, 329.

79. Kautz's kinship ties to Nisqually Indians did not guarantee his allegiance one way or the other. Kautz left Kitty for several months as he fought against Indians in the Oregon Territory. Reese, *They Came to Puget Sound*; interview with Cecelia Carpenter, February 21, 2007.

80. Wesley Gosnell to the Superintendent of Indian Affairs for Washington Territory, December 31, 1857, Bureau of Indian Affairs, Letters of the Superintendents of Indian Affairs for Washington Territory, 1856–74, NARA.

81. Wesley Gosnell to Isaac Stevens, February 18, 1857, ibid.

82. *Olympia Pioneer and Democrat*, February 27, 1857. Charles Prosch recalled fifty years later that Pierce County "became somewhat noted in early days for affairs of this kind, they having occurred quite frequently there." Prosch, *Reminiscences of Washington Territory*, 69.

83. Ford quoted in Asher, *Beyond the Reservation*, 113.

84. "How to Serve a Writ," *Puget Sound Herald*, April 22, 1859.

85. Stevens called for trials for Kitsap, Nelson, Leschi, Quiemuth, and Stahi. "Arrest of Kitsap," *Puget Sound Herald*, January 14, 1859; Asher, *Beyond the Reservation*, 133.

86. Harring provides a detailed study of the process by which U.S. law was extended over Indian tribes following the important case of *Crow Dog* in 1883. Although Leschi's case occurred several decades before *Crow Dog*, it suggests how civil law was extended over Indians in a more localized manner. Harring, *Crow Dog's Case*, 23.

87. Gosnell refused to protect Indians on the reservation if they had not had not been tried and acquitted of wrong-doing. Wesley Gosnell to Isaac Stevens, December 31, 1856, Bureau of Indian Affairs, Letters of the Superintendents of Indian Affairs for Washington Territory, 1856–74, NARA.

88. William Tolmie to Fayette McMullin, January 12, 1858, Clarence Bagley Papers, box 21, UWSC.

89. August Kautz wrote in his diary on December 11, 1857, that "a great many Indians are here [at Steilacoom] pleading for Leschi." Reese, *Journals of August Kautz*, 151; Wesley Gosnell to Isaac Stevens, March 31, 1857, Bureau of Indian Affairs, Letters of the Superintendents of Indian Affairs for Washington Territory, 1856–74, NARA.

90. Meeker, *Pioneer Reminiscences of Puget Sound and the Tragedy of Leschi*, 451.

91. Letter from Agent Wesley Gosnell to Isaac Stevens, December 31, 1856, Bureau of Indian Affairs, Letters of the Superintendents of Indian Affairs for Washington Territory, 1856–74, NARA; White, "The Medicine Creek Treaty," 116. Twelve headmen of Puget Sound tribes (none of whom were party to the Medicine Creek

Treaty) asked Fayette McMullin for a pardon for Leschi. McMullin replied that he had not yet decided what to do about Leschi. "Payment to the Indians," *Pioneer and Democrat*, January 8, 1856.

92. Asher, *Beyond the Reservation*, 26.

93. Ibid., 137–38. Fayette McMullin became governor in September 1857, following Stevens and Acting Governor Charles Mason. Washington State, Secretary of State, web archive, www.secstate.wa.gov/library/governor/gov_table.htm.

94. February 11, 1858, in Reese, *Journals of August Kautz*, 151.

95. January 21, 1858, in ibid., 143.

96. By the 1880s, Washington Territory was decidedly Republican. Denny's word choice of "lynching" (as opposed to 1850s newspaper reports of "hanging") drew a conscious connection to post-Reconstruction southern culture and politics that evoked negative judgment from Republicans. Johannsen, "The Secession Crisis and the Frontier," 416.

97. Denny, *Pioneer Days on Puget Sound*, 56.

98. Ibid., 56–57, 67–68.

99. Brad Asher reports that among the Twana—who lived close to where Denny placed this event—the husband had the right to kill an adulterous wife without fear of retaliation. Village headmen arbitrated in such matters and decided how restitution should be paid after considering the wife's offense, if any. In fact, a Nisqually informant told an ethnographer that when Leschi found out that his eldest wife, Sarah, had had intercourse with an unmarried man, he became enraged, cut her hair, and threatened to kill her. Quiemuth sheltered the woman until the matter was settled; Leschi exchanged gifts with his father-in-law and the couple reconciled. The story may have illustrated Leschi's good character because he did not seek the revenge due to him for his wife's adultery with a man of lower status. The event of a husband killing his wife would have been a matter for village headmen and kin groups to settle after considering the specific case, hardly requiring the arbitration of a white lynch mob. If the arbiters believed the husband had just cause to kill his adulterous wife, the vigilantes' actions would have been interpreted as an aggressive (not retributive) act, stirring up trouble where things were otherwise settled. Asher, *Beyond the Reservation*, 28. The informant, Henry Martin, Leschi's cousin, was born around 1841 and likely heard the story of Leschi from older relatives. H. K. Haeberlin Ethnographic Notebooks, notebook 30, NAA.

100. Denny, *Pioneer Days on Puget Sound*, 56–57, 67–68.

101. Benton, *Law and Colonial Cultures*, 255.

102. A biography of H. E. Van Ogle may be found in "The History of the Town of Orting," by Alice Rushton (1981), p. 312, H. E. Van Ogle File, WSHS.

103. "The Tragedy of Quiemuth," Van Ogle accounts, p. 3, Robert Hitchman Manuscript, T-48/6, M-229, WSHS.

104. Although he was not chosen as a winner, his essay was later published at least four different times. Reese, *The Northwest Was Their Goal*, 1:i.

105. Narrative of James Longmire, in Works Progress Administration, *Told by the Pioneers*, 140.

106. Oldham, "First Emigrant Train." Laura B. Downey Bartlett referred to Longmire as "splendid" in 1930. *Puyallup Valley Tribune*, January 24, 1930, Nisqually Vertical File, WSHS; Meeker, *Pioneer Reminiscences of Puget Sound and the Tragedy of Leschi*, 138.

107. Narrative of James Longmire, in Works Progress Administration, *Told by the Pioneers*, 142.

108. Trouillot, *Silencing the Past*, 53, 132, 151.

109. Elderly settler Edward Huggins lamented in 1901 that local newspapers no longer published local history—that is, settlers' reminiscences. Edward Huggins to Frank Cole, October 30, 1901, Edward Huggins Papers, F-12B, WSHS.

110. For a recent example of this narrative framing, see Kluger, *Bitter Waters of Medicine Creek*.

111. Emmons wrote that Leschi refused to sign after Quiemuth had placed his thumbprint next to the X. Emmons, *Leschi of the Nisquallies*, 191. Kaylene suggests that Leschi, along with other Nisqually leaders, simply left the treaty grounds in frustration before signing. Kaylene, *Judicially Murdered*, 47–48; Binns, *Mighty Mountain*, 180; Carpenter, *The Nisqually, My People*, 169; Meeker, *Pioneer Reminiscences of Puget Sound and the Tragedy of Leschi*, 255–56; interview with Cecelia Carpenter, February 21, 2007.

112. W. P. Bonney, "Leschi's Brother Foully Murdered While Sleeping in Stevens' House," *Tacoma Times*, February 5, 1932.

113. Binns, *Mighty Mountain*, 180.

114. *Leschi v. Washington Territory*, 1. Wash. Terr. 13 (1857). Appellate transcript can be accessed in Allen, *Reports of Cases Determined in the Supreme Court of the Territory of Washington*, 13–29.

115. *Territory of Washington v. Leshi* [sic], 1 F. Cas. 113, 250–51 (2nd Jud. Dist., Terr. Wash.) (1857), handwritten Supreme Court Records and Briefs, AR3-A-67, Washington State Archives, Olympia; quoted in Kunsch, "Trials of Leschi," 92.

116. Cruikshank, *Social Life of Stories*, 97.

117. Melissa Parr thought Leschi was more famous than his brother because there was something on the books that needed to be changed but nothing to "reverse" when it came to Quiemuth. Statement at the Pacific Northwest Historians Guild, April 20, 2007.

118. Interview with Cynthia Iyall.

119. Carpenter, *The Nisqually, My People*, 116.

120. Crooks, "Quiemuth, Part II," 6 and n26.

121. Seth Truscott, "Historical Court Exonerates Leschi," *Nisqually Valley News*, December 31, 2004, A2.

122. Scott Fontaine, "Hundreds Celebrate Leschi," *Indian Country Today*, February 27, 2008, p. 1.

123. Melissa Petrich, "Nisqually Revisit Land Ancestors Once Walked," *Northwest Guardian*, May 6, 2012. See also *Squalli Absch News* (*Nisqually Tribal News*), April 2013; *Squalli Absch News*, February 2011; and film of the 2009 Leschi-Quiemuth Honor Walk posted by the Nisqually Indian Tribe, http://www.youtube.com/watch?v=fZENfjOsETE (May 6, 2013).

124. Gordon, *Ghostly Matters*, 6, 183.

125. KUOW, "In Person" radio program, interview, Cynthia Iyall with Megan Sukys.

CONCLUSION

1. John Fabian Witt first posed this question concerning the trials of Dakota men in 1862. Witt, *Lincoln's Code*, 331–32; see also Herbert, "Explaining the Sioux Military Commission of 1862," 743.

2. The concept of survivance—the dynamic sense of indigenous presence in active resistance to the notion of disappearance—comes from Anishinaabe writer Gerald Vizenor. For an example, see Vizenor, *Survivance*.

3. Regan, *Unsettling the Settler Within*, 57.

4. Sarah Kershaw, "Chief's Retrial, 146 Years in the Making," *New York Times*, December 5, 2004, p. 20.

5. Interview with Tina Kuckkahn.

6. Scott Gutierrez, "Legislators Right Historical Wrong," *Olympian*, March 5, 2004. Courtesy of Cecelia Carpenter.

7. Peggy Andersen, "Young Puyallups Savor Chief Leschi's Win," *Tacoma News-Tribune*, December 11, 2004, A10.

8. KUOW, "In Person" radio program, interview, Melissa Parr with Megan Sukys, ca. late 2003.

9. Schwartz, Fukuoka, and Takita-Ishii, "Collective Memory," 255–56.

10. Interview with John Ladenburg.

11. Ladenburg recalled that his father, an electrician foreman, had often hired Nisqually workers. Ibid.

12. Richard Somers, "Exoneration Was Merely a Feel-Good Exercise," Letters to the Editor, *Tacoma News-Tribune*, December 17, 2004, B9; Richard Bethard, "Why Was Taxpayer Money Spent on Worthless Exercise?" Letters to the Editor, *Tacoma News-Tribune*, December 14, 2004, B6. In response to this letter, Chief Justice Alexander said that no taxpayer money had been spent and that all of the time he put into the exoneration was voluntary. Interview with Gerry Alexander; Brad Slusher, "Public Paid for Travesty of Leschi's Mock Retrial," Letters to the Editor, *Tacoma News-Tribune*, December 15, 2004, B7; Brian Venable, "Where Was Justice in 'Kangaroo Court'?" Letters to the Editor, *Tacoma News-Tribune*, December 15, 2004, B7.

13. Brian Venable, "Where Was Justice in 'Kangaroo Court'?" Letters to the Editor, *Tacoma News-Tribune*, December 15, 2004, B7.

14. Letter to the editor, *Portland Oregonian*, n.d. (probably January 1904);

Benjamin Shaw speech, Benjamin Shaw Papers, MS 412, Oregon Historical Society, Portland.

15. Knute Berger, "Ending an Indian War," *Seattle Weekly*, December 15, 2004.
16. Comaroff and Comaroff, *Dialectics of Modernity*, 2.
17. Colwell-Chanthaphonh, *Massacre at Camp Grant*, 101.
18. Trouillot, *Silencing the Past*, 153.

BIBLIOGRAPHY

ARCHIVAL SOURCES
Bellingham, Washington
  Center for Pacific Northwest History, Western Washington University
    Northwest Ethnohistory Collection
Olympia, Washington
  Gerry Alexander Papers (access by request)
    Correspondence concerning the Leschi Senate Resolution and
      Historical Court
  Washington State Archives
    Military Department Correspondence, 1855–56
    Supreme Court Records and Briefs, 1857
Portland, Oregon
  Oregon Historical Society
    Benjamin Shaw Papers
Seattle, Washington
  National Archives, Pacific Northwest Regional Office
    Bureau of Indian Affairs reports
    Indian Claims Commission Docket 197 (*Nisqually et al. v. U.S.*)
    Letters from the Commissioner at Cushman Indian School, 1917–18
    Records of the Washington Superintendency of Indian Affairs, 1853–74
    U.S. Census, Nisqually reservation, 1880
  University of Washington Library and Special Collections
    Clarence Bagley Papers
    Clarence Bagley Scrapbook
    Edward Huggins Papers
    Edmond Meany Papers
    Robert H. Milroy Letterpress Copybook
    William Tolmie Papers
    U.S. Court of Claims, *Duwamish et al. v. United States*, Microfilm A-7374
    U.S. Office of Indian Affairs, Records of the Washington Superintendency,
      Microfilm A-12046

Steilacoom, Washington
   Steilacoom Historical Museum Library
      Journals of August V. Kautz [transcription]
Suitland, Maryland
   National Anthropological Archives
      American Indian Northwest Coast manuscripts (MSS 970, 699, 658, 4527 [049]).
      Aronsen, Gary, and Javier Urcid. "Inventory and Assessment of Human Remains and Funerary Objects from Puget Sound and Grays Harbor Regions of Washington State in the National Museum of Natural History." National Museum of Natural History Repatriation Office, Case Report No. 92-007 (May 7, 1996).
      H. K. Haeberlin Ethnographic Notebooks (MS 2965)
      Photograph Collection, OPPS NEG 80-16446
Tacoma, Washington
   Cecelia Svinth Carpenter Private Collection (access by request)
      Carpenter, Cecelia Svinth. "How It All Began." Essay, ca. 2005.
      Evans, Elwood. "The Trial of Leschi."
      Personal communication concerning the Committee to Exonerate Chief Leschi
   Washington State Historical Society Research Center
      Robert Hitchman Manuscript
      Edward Huggins Papers
      Indian War 1855 Papers
      H. F. Jones Papers
      Leschi Biography File
      Ezra Meeker Collection
      Nisqually Vertical File
      Pioneers Vertical File
      H. E. Van Ogle File
      James Wickersham Collection
Washington, D.C.
   National Archives and Records Administration
      Bureau of Indian Affairs, Letters of the Superintendents of Indian Affairs for Washington Territory, 1856–74

INTERVIEWS AND CORRESPONDENCE

Gerry Alexander, April 30, 2007, Olympia, Washington. Email correspondence, March 25, 2013.
Robert Anderson, February 28, 2007, Seattle, Washington
Anonymous, August 9, 2007, Fort Lewis, Washington
Cecelia Svinth Carpenter, June 10, 2006 and February 21, 2007, Tacoma, Washington. Email correspondence, October 12, 2008.

Alexandra Harmon, February 28, 2007, Seattle, Washington
Thor Hoyte, February 21, 2007, Nisqually, Washington
Carl Hultman, March 12, 2007, Tacoma, Washington
Sharon Hultman, email correspondence, February 21, 2007.
Cynthia Iyall, February 21, 2007, Nisqually, Washington
Joseph Kalama, August 3, 2010, Nisqually, Washington
Tina Kuckkahn, March 1, 2007, Olympia, Washington
John Ladenburg, April 5, 2007, Seattle, Washington. Email correspondence, October 13, 2008.
Peggy McCloud, March 15, 2007, Puyallup, Washington
Melissa Parr, June 8, 2006, Olympia, Washington. Statement at the Pacific Northwest Historians Guild, April 20, 2007, Tacoma, Washington.
Bret Ruby, August 1 and August 30, 2007, Fort Lewis, Washington
Bill Tobin, May 18, 2007, Vashon Island, Washington
John Weller, August 15, 2007, Seattle, Washington, and August 30, 2007, Fort Lewis, Washington. Email correspondence, October 14, 2008.

RADIO, TELEVISION, AND AUDIOVISUAL MATERIALS

BBC News Online. "America's Christopher Columbus—on Trial." October 14, 1998. http://news.bbc.co.uk/2/hi/americas/192240.stm. October 11, 2007.
David Rumsey Historical Digital Map Collection. http://www.davidrumsey.com/home. March 31, 2013.
Department of Public Works. GIS map, "Native American Place Names." Created for the Fort Lewis Cultural Resource Office, October 17, 2006. Courtesy of Bret Ruby.
KUOW. "In Person" radio program. Cynthia Iyall with Megan Sukys, ca. 2004. Courtesy of Cecelia Carpenter.
Lander, Puhipau, and Joan Lander, with Na Maka o ka 'Aina. "The Proceedings of the People's International Tribunal, Hawai'i 1993." VHS. Honolulu, Hawai'i, 1994. 84 minutes.
McIlveen, Rose. "Custer's Last Stand Takes Place in an IU Moot Courtroom." Indiana University website. http://www.iuinfo.indiana.edu/HomePages/100298/text/custer.htm. October 11, 2007.
Mejia, Thelma. "Indians Put Christopher Columbus on Trial." One World Org, July 20, 1998. http://ishgooda.org/racial/holid4.htm. October 11, 2007.
MSNBC.com. "Court Acquits Chief Hanged in 1858." December 11, 2004. http://www.msnbc.msn.com/id/6697065/ns/us_news/t/court-acquits-indian-chief-hanged/. March 19, 2012.
New Yorker. "The Abu Ghraib Pictures." www.newyorker.com/archive/2004/05/03/slideshow_040503. February 26, 2011.
Smithsonian Institution and Library of Congress. "Ethnography" museum display. June 2007, Washington, D.C.

Tacoma Public Library Northwest Room & Special Collections. Database. http://www.tpl.lib.wa.us/. Unsettling Events—Battles—Connell's Prairie Battle.

TVW and Washington State Supreme Court. *Historical Court of Inquiry & Justice.* Olympia, Wash.: TVW, 2004. DVD. 3 hrs., 26 min.

Washington State. Secretary of State. Web archive. http://www.sos.wa.gov/history. Classic Publications—Territorial and State Government; Classic Publications—Pioneer Life; Maps.

Washington State Historical Society. "Leschi: Justice in Our Time." Web archive. http://stories.washingtonhistory.org/leschi. March 19, 2012.

Washington State University Libraries. Digital map collection. http://www.westernwater.org/record/view/75240. October 9, 2012.

NEWSPAPERS AND NEWSLETTERS

Bellingham Herald (Bellingham, Wash.)
Bobcat Bulletin (Fort Lewis, Wash.)
Indian Country Today (New York, N.Y.)
Los Angeles Times
New York Times
Nisqually Valley News (Yelm, Wash.)
Northwest Guardian (Joint Base Lewis-McChord, Wash.)
Olympian (Olympia, Wash.)
Pioneer and Democrat (Olympia, Wash.)
Puget Sound Courier (Steilacoom, Wash.)
Puget Sound Herald (Steilacoom, Wash.)
Puyallup Tribal News (Puyallup, Wash.)
Puyallup Valley Tribune (Puyallup, Wash.)
Seattle Post-Intelligencer
Seattle Star
Seattle Times
Seattle Weekly
Squalli Absch News/Nisqually Tribal News (Olympia, Wash.)
Tacoma Daily Ledger
Tacoma Daily News
Tacoma News-Ledger
Tacoma News-Tribune and Sunday Ledger
Truth Teller (Steilacoom, Wash.)
Washington Republican (Steilacoom, Wash.)
Weekly Oregonian (Portland, Ore.)
Yakima Herald-Republic (Yakima, Wash.)

COURT RECORDS

Goudy v. Meath, 203 U.S. 146 (1906).
Hamdi v. Rumsfeld, 124 S. Ct. 2633 (2004).
Rasul v. Bush, 124 S. Ct. 2686 (2004).
Territory of Washington v. Leshi [sic], 1 F. Cas. 113 (2nd Jud. Dist., Terr., Wash.) (1857).
Tulee v. State of Washington, 315 U.S. 681 (1942).
United States v. Washington, 384 F. Supp. 312 (W.D. Wash. 1974).

OTHER SOURCES

Agamben, Giorgio. *State of Exception*. Translated by Kevin Attell. Chicago: University of Chicago Press, 2005.
Alfred, Gerald Taiaiake. "Native American Political Traditions." In *American Indians and U.S. Politics: A Companion Reader*, edited by John M. Meyer, 15–38. Westport, Conn.: Praeger, 2002.
———. *Peace, Power, Righteousness: An Indigenous Manifesto*. 2nd ed. Don Mills, Ont.: Oxford University Press, 2009.
———. "Restitution Is the Real Pathway to Justice for Indigenous Peoples." In *Response, Responsibility, and Renewal: Canada's Truth and Reconciliation Journey*, edited by Gregory Younging, Jonathan Dewar, and Mike DeGagné, 179–87. Ottawa, Ont.: Aboriginal Healing Foundation, 2009.
———. "Sovereignty." In *A Companion to American Indian History*, edited by Philip J. Deloria and Neal Salisbury, 460–74. Malden, Mass.: Blackwell, 2004.
———. *Wasáse: Indigenous Pathways of Action and Freedom*. Peterborough, Ont.: UTP/ Broadview Press, 2005.
Allen, Frederick. *A Decent, Orderly Lynching: The Montana Vigilantes*. Norman: University of Oklahoma Press, 2004.
Allen, John Beard, ed. *Reports of Cases Determined in the Supreme Court of the Territory of Washington from 1854 to 1879*. Vol. 1. San Francisco: Bancroft-Whitney Co., 1891.
American Friends Service Committee. *Uncommon Controversy: Fishing Rights of the Muckleshoot, Puyallup, and Nisqually Indians*. Seattle: University of Washington Press, 1970.
Amin, Shahid. *Event, Metaphor, Memory: Chauri Chaura, 1922–1992*. Berkeley: University of California Press, 1995.
Angelbeck, Bill, and Eric McLay. "The Battle at Maple Bay: The Dynamics of Coast Salish Political Organization through Oral Histories." *Ethnohistory* 58 (Summer 2011): 359–92.
Antze, Paul, and Michael Lambek, eds. *Tense Past: Cultural Essays in Trauma and Memory*. New York: Routledge, 1996.

Archambault, Alan H. *Fort Lewis.* Images of America Series. Charleston: Arcadia, 2002.

Armitage, David. "John Locke, Carolina, and the *Two Treatises of Government.*" *Political Theory* 32, no. 5 (October 2004): 602–27.

Arneil, Barbara. *John Locke and America: The Defence of English Colonialism.* New York: Oxford University Press, 1996.

Asher, Brad. *Beyond the Reservation: Indians, Settlers, and the Law in Washington Territory, 1853–1889.* Norman: University of Oklahoma Press, 1999.

Ashley, Jeffrey, and Secody Hubbard. *Negotiating Sovereignty: Working to Improve Tribal-State Relations.* Westport, Conn.: Praeger, 2004.

Bacevich, Andrew J. *The Limits of Power: The End of American Exceptionalism.* New York: Holt, 2009.

———. *The New American Militarism: How Americans Are Seduced by War.* New York: Oxford University Press, 2005.

Bancroft, Hubert Howe, and Francis Fuller Victor. *History of Washington, Idaho, and Montana, 1845–1889.* San Francisco: History Company, 1890.

Banner, Stuart. *How the Indians Lost Their Land: Law and Power on the Frontier.* Cambridge: Harvard University Press, 2007.

Barkan, Elazar. "Introduction: Historians and Historical Reconciliation." *AHR* Forum: Truth and Reconciliation in History. *American Historical Review* 114 (October 2009): 899–913.

Barkan, Elazar, and Alexander Karn, eds. *Taking Wrongs Seriously: Apologies and Reconciliation.* Stanford: Stanford University Press, 2006.

Barman, Jean, and Bruce McIntyre Watson. *Leaving Paradise: Indigenous Hawaiians in the Pacific Northwest, 1787–1898.* Honolulu: University of Hawai'i Press, 2006.

Barsh, Russel Lawrence. "Ethnogenesis and Ethnonationalism from Competing Treaty Claims." In *The Power of Promises: Rethinking Indian Treaties in the Pacific Northwest,* edited by Alexandra Harmon, 215–43. Seattle: University of Washington Press, 2008.

Basso, Keith. *Wisdom Sits in Places: Landscape and Language among the Western Apache.* Albuquerque: University of New Mexico Press, 1996.

Beavert, Virginia and Sharon Hargus. *Ichishkíin Sínwit: Yakama/Yakima Sahaptin Dictionary.* Seattle: University of Washington Press, 2009.

Beckham, Stephen Dow. "George Gibbs." In *Eminent Astorians: From John Jacob Astor to the Salmon Kings,* edited by Karen Kirtley, 91–114. Salem, Ore.: East Oregonian Publishing Company, 2010.

———. "George Gibbs, 1815–1873: Historian and Ethnologist." Ph.D. diss., University of California at Berkeley, 1969.

Benjamin, Walter. "The Storyteller: Reflections on the Works of Nikolai Leskov." http://slought.org/files/downloads/events/SF_1331-Benjamin.pdf. February 6, 2012.

Benton, Lauren. *Law and Colonial Cultures: Legal Regimes in World History, 1400–1900*. Cambridge: Cambridge University Press, 2001.

Bevernage, Berber. "Writing the Past Out of the Present: History and the Politics of Time in Transitional Justice." *History Workshop Journal* 69 (Spring 2010): 111–31.

Bieder, Robert E. *Science Encounters the Indian, 1820–1880: The Early Years of American Ethnology*. Norman: University of Oklahoma Press, 1986.

Bierwert, Crisca. *Brushed by Cedar, Living by the River: Coast Salish Figures of Power*. Tucson: University of Arizona Press, 1999.

———. "Remembering Chief Seattle: Reversing Cultural Studies of a Vanishing Native American." *American Indian Quarterly* 22 (Summer 1998): 280–304.

———, ed. *Lushootseed Texts: An Introduction to Puget Salish Narrative Aesthetics*. Lincoln: University of Nebraska Press, 1990.

Binns, Archie. *Mighty Mountain*. New York: Charles Scribner's Sons, 1940.

Blackhawk, Ned. "Look How Far We've Come: How American Indian History Changed the Study of American History in the 1990s." *Organization of American Historians Magazine: The American West* 16 (November 2005): 13–17.

Blaine, David Edwards, and Catherine Blaine. *Memoirs of Puget Sound: Early Seattle, 1853–1856*. Edited by Richard A. Seiber. Fairfield, Wash.: Ye Galleon Press, 1978.

Blee, Lisa. "The Quest for the Legal Enemy: Symbolic Justice during the War on Terror." *Radical History Review* 113 (Spring 2012): 55–65.

Boessenecker, John. *Against the Vigilantes: The Recollections of Dutch Charley Duane*. Norman: University of Oklahoma Press, 1999.

Boime, Albert. *The Magisterial Gaze: Manifest Destiny and American Landscape Painting, c. 1830–1865*. Washington D.C.: Smithsonian Institution Press, 1991.

Boltanski, L. *Distant Suffering: Morality, Media, and Politics*. Cambridge: Cambridge University Press, 1999.

Bonney, W. P. *History of Pierce County, Washington*. Vol. 1. Chicago: Pioneer Historical Publishing Company, 1927.

Borgwardt, Elizabeth. "FDR's Four Freedoms and Wartime Transformations in America's Discourse on Rights." In *Bringing Human Rights Home: A History of Human Rights in the United States*, abridged ed., edited by Cynthia Soohoo, Catherine Albisa, and Martha F. Davis, 40–67. Philadelphia: University of Pennsylvania Press, 2009.

Boxberger, Daniel L. "The Not So Common." In *Be of Good Mind: Essays on the Coast Salish*, edited by Bruce Granville Miller, 55–81. Vancouver: University of British Columbia Press, 2007.

Boyd, Colleen E., and Coll Thrush, eds. *Phantom Past, Indigenous Presence: Native Ghosts in North American Culture and History*. Lincoln: University of Nebraska Press, 2011.

Boyd, Robert. "The Pacific Northwest Measles Epidemic of 1847–1848." *Oregon Historical Quarterly* 95, no. 1 (Spring 1994): 6–47.

Brooks, Roy L. "The New Patriotism and Apology for Slavery." In *Taking Wrongs Seriously: Apologies and Reconciliation,* edited by Elazar Barkan and Alexander Karn, 213–33. Stanford: Stanford University Press, 2006.

Brophy, Alfred L. *Reconstructing the Dreamland: The Tulsa Race Riot of 1921, Race Reparations, and Reconciliation.* Oxford: Oxford University Press, 2002.

Brown, Richard Maxwell. *Strain of Violence: Historical Studies of American Violence and Vigilantism.* New York: Oxford University Press, 1975.

Brown, Wendy. "'The Most We Can Hope For': Human Rights and the Politics of Fatalism." *South Atlantic Quarterly* 103 (2004): 451–63.

Brückner, Martin. *The Geographic Revolution in Early America: Maps, Literacy, and National Identity.* Chapel Hill: University of North Carolina Press, 2006.

Bruyneel, Kevin. *The Third Space of Sovereignty: The Postcolonial Politics of U.S.-Indigenous Relations.* Minneapolis: University of Minnesota Press, 2007.

Buchanan, Charles M. "Dialectic Variants of the Nisqually Linguistic Root Stock of Puget Sound." *Washington Historical Quarterly* 1, no. 2 (1907): 30–35.

Buerge, David M. "The Wilkes Expedition in the Pacific Northwest." *Columbia* 1, no. 1 (Spring 1987): 17–32.

Buse, Peter, and Andrew Stott, eds. *Ghosts: Deconstruction, Psychoanalysis, History.* London: Macmillan, 1999.

Byrnes, Giselle. *The Waitangi Tribunal and New Zealand History.* Oxford: Oxford University Press, 2004.

Cahn, Edgar S. "An Anthropologist Examines the Lawyer Tribe." Book review. *Yale Journal of Law and the Humanities* 17 (Summer 2005): 293.

Calloway, Colin G. *First Peoples: A Documentary History of American Indian History.* 4th ed., Boston: Bedford/St. Martin's, 2012.

Campbell, James T. "Settling Accounts? An Americanist Perspective on Historical Reconciliation." *AHR* Forum: Truth and Reconciliation in History. *American Historical Review* 114 (October 2009): 963–77.

Carlson, Leonard A. *Indians, Bureaucrats, and Land: The Dawes Act and the Decline of Indian Farming.* Westport, Conn.: Greenwood, 1981.

Carpenter, Cecelia Svinth. *Fort Nisqually: A Documented History of Indian and British Interaction.* Tacoma: Tahoma Research, 1986.

———. "George Gibbs Remembered." *Nisqually Tribal News* 6 (September/October 1995): 9.

———. "Indian Memories of My Childhood." *Tacoma—Voices from the Past.* Tacoma: Pierce County Centennial Committee, 1988.

———. *Leschi: Last Chief of the Nisquallies.* 1986. Tacoma: Tahoma Research, 2004.

———. *The Nisqually, My People: The Traditional and Transitional History of the Nisqually Indian People.* Tacoma: Tahoma Research, 2002.

———. *Where the Waters Begin: The Traditional Nisqually Indian History of Mount Rainier.* Seattle: Northwest Interpretive Association, 1994.

Carpenter, Cecelia Svinth, Maria Pascualy, and Trisha Hunter. *Nisqually Indian Tribe*. Images of America Series. Charleston: Arcadia, 2008.

Carroll, David. "The Aesthetic and the Political: Lyotard." In *Jean Francois Lyotard: Critical Evaluations in Cultural Theory*, edited by Victor E. Taylor and Gregg Lamberts, 155–84. New York: Routledge, 2006.

Carstensen, Vernon. "Pacific Northwest Letters of George Gibbs." *Oregon Historical Quarterly* 54 (September 1953): 190–99.

Caster, Dick. "Father Hylebos, St. George's Indian School and Cemetery, and St. Claire's Mission Church." Document prepared for the Historical Society of Federal Way, 2004. http://www.federalwayhistory.org/powercms/files/FtHylebosJuly92009.pdf. November 10, 2012.

Cecelski, David S., and Timothy Tyson, eds. *Democracy Betrayed: The Wilmington Race Riot of 1898 and Its Legacy*. Chapel Hill: University of North Carolina Press, 1998.

Chaplin, Ralph. "Only the Drums Remembered: A Memento for Leschi." Tacoma: Dammeier Print, 1960.

Cheyfitz, Eric. "Savage Law: The Plot against American Indians in *Johnson and Graham's Lessee v. M'Intosh* and *The Pioneers*." In *Cultures of United States Imperialism*, edited by Amy Kaplan and Donald E. Pease, 109–28. Durham: Duke University Press, 1994.

Chouliaraki, Lilie. "Watching 11 September: The Politics of Pity." *Discourse and Society* 15 (May 2004): 185–98.

Chrisman, Gabriel. "The Fish-In Protests at Franks Landing." Seattle Civil Rights and Labor History Project. http://depts.washington.edu/civilr/fish-ins.htm. 25 July 2013.

Churchill, Ward, and Sharon H. Venne, comps. *Islands in Captivity: The Record of the International Tribunal on the Rights of Indigenous Hawaiians*. Cambridge: South End Press, 2004.

Clark, Ella. "George Gibbs' Account of Indian Mythology in Oregon and Washington Territories." *Oregon Historical Quarterly* 56 (December 1955): 293–325.

Clifford, Howard. "Ezra Meeker's Quest for Klondike Gold." *Columbia Magazine* 12 (Summer 1998): 24–29.

Clifford, James. *The Predicament of Culture: Twentieth-Century Ethnography, Literature, and Art*. Cambridge: Harvard University Press, 1988.

Cohen, Fay G. *Treaties on Trial: The Continuing Controversy over Northwest Indian Fishing Rights*. Seattle: University of Washington Press, 1986.

Cohen, Felix. *Handbook of Federal Indian Law*. Albuquerque: University of New Mexico Press, 1972.

Cohen, Saul B., and Nurit Kliot. "Place-Names in Israel's Ideological Struggle over the Administered Territories." *Annals of the Association of American Geographers* 82, no. 4 (December 1992): 653–80.

Collins, Cary C. "Hard Lessons in America: Henry Sicade's History of Puyallup Indian School, 1860 to 1920." *Columbia Magazine* 14 (Winter 2000/2001): 6–11.

———, ed. "In a Familiar yet Foreign Land: Reflections on the Life of Henry Sicade, Puyallup Tribal Elder and 'Cultural Broker.'" *Columbia Magazine* 19, no. 2 (Summer 2005): 9–17.

Collins, June McCormick. "The Indian Shaker Church: A Study of Continuity and Change in Religion." *Southwestern Journal of Anthropology* 6 (Winter 1950): 399–411.

———. "The Influence of White Contact on Class Distinctions and Political Authority among Indians of Northern Puget Sound." In *American Indian Ethnohistory: Coast Salish and Western Washington Indians*, vol. 2, edited by David Agee Horr, 89–204. New York: Garland, 1974.

Colwell-Chanthaphonh, Chip. *Massacre at Camp Grant: Forgetting and Remembering Apache History*. Tucson: University of Arizona Press, 2007.

Comaroff, John L., and Jean Comaroff. *The Dialectics of Modernity on a South African Frontier*. Vol. 2 of *Revelation and Revolution*. Chicago: University of Chicago Press, 1997.

Connerton, Paul. *How Societies Remember*. Cambridge: Cambridge University Press, 1989.

Cornell, Stephen. *The Return of the Native: American Indian Political Resurgence*. Oxford: Oxford University Press, 1988.

Cotterrell, Roger. "Common Law Approaches to the Relationship between Law and Morality." *Ethical Theory and Moral Practice* 3, no. 1 (March 2000): 9–26.

Crooks, Drew. "The Medicine Creek Treaty of 1854: A Turning Point in the History of Southern Puget Sound." *Occurrences* 24, no. 1 (Winter 2005–6): 6–11.

———. "Quiemuth: Remembering the Nisqually Indian Leader and His Tragic Murder in the Governor's Office, Part I." *Occurrences* 26, no. 1 (Winter 2008): 3–9.

———. "Quiemuth: Remembering the Nisqually Indian Leader and His Tragic Murder in the Governor's Office, Part II." *Occurrences* 26, no. 2 (Spring 2008): 3–7.

Cronon, William. *Changes in the Land: Indians, Colonists, and the Ecology of New England*. New York: Hill and Wang, 1983.

Cruikshank, Julie. *Do Glaciers Listen? Local Knowledge, Colonial Encounters, and Social Imagination*. Vancouver, B.C.: University of British Columbia Press, 2005.

———. *The Social Life of Stories: Narrative and Knowledge in the Yukon Territory*. Lincoln: University of Nebraska Press, 1998.

Cunningham, Michael. "Saying Sorry: The Politics of Apology." *Political Quarterly* 70, no. 3 (1999): 285–93.

Curtis, Edward S. *The North American Indian*. Vol. 9. Cambridge: Cambridge University Press, 1913.

Daes, Erica-Irene A. "Protecting Knowledge: Traditional Resource Rights in the New Millennium." In *Justice as Healing: Indigenous Ways*, edited by Wanda McCaslin, 231–39. St. Paul: Living Justice Press, 2005.

Daniels, Roger. "An Age of Apology?" *Distinguished Speakers Series in Political Geography* 7. Kingston, Ontario: Kashtan Press, 2003.

Dawson, Ashley, and Malini Johar Schueller, eds. *Exceptional State: Contemporary U.S. Culture and the New Imperialism*. Durham: Duke University Press, 2007.

Deloria, Philip. *Indians in Unexpected Places*. Lawrence: University Press of Kansas, 2006.

Deloria, Vine, Jr. *Red Earth, White Lies: Native Americans and the Myth of Scientific Fact*. New York: Scribner's, 1995.

Deloria, Vine, Jr., and C. Lytle. *The Nations Within: The Past and Future of American Indian Sovereignty*. Austin: University of Texas Press, 1984.

Denny, Arthur. *Pioneer Days on Puget Sound*. 1888. Fairfield, Wash.: Ye Galleon Press, 1965.

Dippie, Brian W. "The Moving Finger Writes: Western Art and the Dynamics of Change." In *Discovered Land, Invented Pasts: Transforming Visions of the American West*, edited by Jules David Prown et al., 89–115. New Haven: Yale University Press, 1992.

Dorf, Michael. *No Litmus Test: Law versus Politics in the Twenty-first Century*. Lanham, Md.: Rowman and Littlefield, 2006.

Eckrom, J. A. *Remembered Drums: A History of the Puget Sound Indian War*. Walla Walla, Wash.: Pioneer Press, 1989.

Eells, Myron. "The Religion of the Indians of Puget Sound." *American Antiquarian* 12 (March 1890): 69–84.

Elmendorf, William. *Twana Narratives: Native Historical Accounts of a Coast Salish Culture*. Seattle: University of Washington Press, 1993.

Emmons, Della Gould. *Leschi of the Nisquallies*. Minneapolis: T. S. Denison, 1965.

Engle, Karen. "Self-Critique, (Anti) Politics, and Criminalization: Reflections on the History and Trajectory of the Human Rights Movement." *New Approaches to International Law: The European and American Experiences*, edited by Jose Maria Beneyto and David Kennedy, 41–73. The Hague, The Netherlands: T.M.C. Asser Press, 2013.

Evangelista, Matthew. *Law, Ethics, and the War on Terror*. Boston: Polity, 2008.

Fabre, Genevieve. "African American Commemorative Celebrations in the Nineteenth Century." In *History and Memory in African American Culture*, edited by Genevieve Fabre and Robert O'Meally, 72–91. New York: Oxford University Press, 1994.

Falah, Ghazi. "The 1948 Israeli-Palestinian War and Its Aftermath: The Transformation and De-signification of Palestine's Cultural Landscape." *Annals of the Association of American Geographers* 86, no. 2 (June 1996): 256–85.

Fanon, Frantz. *The Wretched of the Earth*. New York: Grove Press, 1963.

Farrar, Victor. "The Nisqually Journal." *Washington Historical Quarterly* 10, no. 3 (July 1919): 205–30.

Faust, Drew Gilpin. "Telling War Stories: The Civil War and the Meaning of Life." *New Republic*, June 30, 2011. http://tnr.com/article/essay/magazine/89638/civil-war-remembrance. June 22, 2011.

Field, Virgil, ed. *Washington Territorial Militia in the Indian Wars of 1855–56*. Vol. 2 of *The Official History of the Washington National Guard*. Camp Murray, Wash.: Headquarters, Military Department, State of Washington, 1961.

Fields, Karen. "What One Cannot Remember Mistakenly." In *History and Memory in African American Culture*, edited by Genevieve Fabre and Robert O'Meally, 150–63. New York: Oxford University Press, 1994.

Fiddler, Thomas, and James Stevens. *Killing the Shamen*. Ottawa: Penumbra Press, 1985.

Fitzmaurice, Andrew. "Liberalism and Empire in Nineteenth-Century International Law." *American Historical Review* 117, no. 1 (February 2012): 122–40.

———. "Moral Uncertainty and the Dispossession of Native Americans." In *The Atlantic World and Virginia, 1550–1624*, edited by Peter C. Mancall, 383–409. Chapel Hill: University of North Carolina Press, 2007.

Fogelson, Raymond. "A Final Look and Glance at the Bearing of Bering Straits on Native American History." D'Arcy McNickle Center for the History of the American Indian. *Occasional Papers in Curriculum Series* 5 (1987).

Ford, Lisa. *Settler Sovereignty: Jurisdiction and Indigenous People in America and Australia, 1788–1836*. Cambridge: Harvard University Press, 2010.

Friday, Chris. "Performing Treaties: The Culture and Politics of Treaty Remembrance and Celebration." In *The Power of Promises: Rethinking Indian Treaties in the Pacific Northwest*, edited by Alexandra Harmon, 157–85. Seattle: University of Washington Press, 2008.

Furniss, Elizabeth. *The Burden of History: Colonialism and the Frontier Myth in a Rural Canadian Community*. Vancouver: University of British Columbia Press, 1999.

Galbraith, John S. "The Early History of the Puget's Sound Agricultural Company, 1838–1843." *Oregon Historical Quarterly* 55 (September 1954): 235–37.

Gallacci, Caroline. "Planning the City of Destiny: An Urban History of Tacoma to 1930." Ph.D. diss., University of Washington, 1999.

Gates, Charles M., ed. *Messages of the Governors of the Territory of Washington to the Legislative Assembly, 1854–1889*. Seattle: University of Washington Press, 1940.

Gates, Henry Louis, Jr. "Good-Bye, Columbus? Notes on the Culture of Criticism." In *Multiculturalism: A Critical Reader*, edited by David Theo Goldberg, 203–17. Cambridge: Blackwell, 1994.

Gibbs, George. *Indian Tribes of Washington Territory.* 1855. Fairfield, Wash.: Ye Galleon Press, 1978.

———. *Tribes of Western Washington and Northwestern Oregon.* Washington, D.C.: Government Printing Office, 1877.

Gibney, Mark, Rhoda E. Howard-Hassmann, Jean-Marc Coicaud, and Niklaus Steiner, eds. *The Age of Apology: Facing Up to the Past.* Philadelphia: University of Pennsylvania Press, 2007.

Glaberson, William. "U.S. Won't Label Terror Suspects as 'Combatants.'" *New York Times*, March 14, 2009, 1A.

Goldberg, David Theo. *Racist Culture: Philosophy and the Politics of Meaning.* Cambridge: Blackwell, 1993.

———, ed. *Multiculturalism: A Critical Reader.* Cambridge: Blackwell, 1994.

Gordon, Avery. *Ghostly Matters: Haunting and the Sociological Imagination.* Minneapolis: University of Minnesota Press, 1997.

Grandin, Greg. "The Liberal Tradition in the Americas: Rights, Sovereignty, and the Origins of Liberal Multilateralism." Forum: Liberal Empire and International Law. *American Historical Review* 117, no. 1 (February 2012): 68–91.

Greymorning, Stephen, ed. *A Will to Survive: Indigenous Essays on the Politics of Culture, Language, and Identity.* New York: McGraw Hill, 2004.

Guerlac, Suzanne. *Thinking in Time: An Introduction to Henri Bergson.* Ithaca: Cornell University Press, 2006.

Gunther, Erna. "An Analysis of the First Salmon Ceremony." *American Anthropologist* 28 (October–December 1926): 605–17.

Haeberlin, Hermann, and Erna Gunther. "The Indians of Puget Sound." *University of Washington Publications in Anthropology* 4 (September 1930).

Hanson, William L. "The Law of Indian Fishing Rights in Washington." In American Friends Service Committee, *Uncommon Controversy: Fishing Rights of the Muckleshoot, Puyallup, and Nisqually Indians*, 83–86. Seattle: University of Washington Press, 1970.

Harley, J. B. "Maps, Knowledge, and Power." In *The Iconography of Landscape: Essays on the Symbolic Representation, Design, and Use of Past Environments*, edited by Denis Cosgrove and Stephen Daniels, 277–312. Cambridge: Cambridge University Press, 1988.

———. *The New Nature of Maps: Essays in the History of Cartography.* Baltimore: Johns Hopkins University Press, 2002.

Harmon, Alexandra. *Indians in the Making: Ethnic Relations and Indian Identities around Puget Sound.* Berkeley: University of California Press, 2000.

———. "Indian Treaty History: A Subject for Agile Minds." *Oregon Historical Quarterly* 106, no. 3 (Fall 2005): 358–73.

———. "Writing History by Litigation." *Columbia* 4 (Winter 1990/91): 5–15.

———, ed. *The Power of Promises: Rethinking Indian Treaties in the Pacific Northwest.* Seattle: University of Washington Press, 2008.

Harring, Sidney L. *Crow Dog's Case: American Indian Sovereignty, Tribal Law, and United States Law in the Nineteenth Century.* Cambridge: Cambridge University Press, 1994.

———. "Indian Law, Sovereignty, and State Law: Native People and the Law." In *A Companion to American Indian History,* edited by Philip J. Deloria and Neal Salisbury, 441–59. Malden, Mass.: Blackwell, 2004.

Harris, Cole. "How Did Colonialism Dispossess? Comments from an Edge of Empire." *Annals of the Association of American Geographers* 94, no. 1 (March 2004): 165–82.

———. *Making Native Space: Colonialism, Resistance, and Reserves in British Columbia.* Vancouver: University of British Columbia Press, 2003.

Harris, Douglas C. "The Boldt Decision in Canada: Aboriginal Treaty Rights to Fish on the Pacific." In *The Power of Promises: Rethinking Indian Treaties in the Pacific Northwest,* edited by Alexandra Harmon, 128–54. Seattle: University of Washington Press, 2008.

Hayner, Priscilla B. *Unspeakable Truths: Transitional Justice and the Challenge of Truth Commissions.* 2nd ed. New York: Routledge, 2011.

Heffernan, Trova. *Where the Salmon Run: The Life and Legacy of Billy Frank Jr.* Seattle: University of Washington Press, 2012.

Herbert, Maeve. "Explaining the Sioux Military Commission of 1862." *Columbia Human Rights Law Review* 40 (2009): 743–98.

Hess, Andreas, ed. *American Social and Political Thought: A Reader.* New York: New York University Press, 2003.

Hilbert, Vi. *Haboo: Native American Stories from Puget Sound.* Seattle: University of Washington Press, 1985.

Hilbert, Vi, and Crisca Bierwert. *Ways of the Lushootseed People: Ceremonies and Traditions of Northern Puget Sound Indians.* Seattle: United Indians of All Tribes Foundation, 1980.

Himes, George H. "History of the Press of Oregon, 1839–1850." *Quarterly of the Oregon Historical Society* 3 (March–December 1902): 327–70.

Hinsley, Curtis M., Jr. *Savages and Scientists: The Smithsonian Institution and the Development of American Anthropology.* Washington, D.C.: Smithsonian Institution Press, 1981.

Hirsch, James S. *Riot and Remembrance: The Tulsa Race War and Its Legacy.* New York: Routledge, 2002.

Hoffert, Sylvia D. "Gender and Vigilantism on the Minnesota Frontier: Jane Grey Swisshelm and the U.S.-Dakota Conflict of 1862." *Western Historical Quarterly* 29 (Autumn 1998): 343–62.

Hoxie, Frederick. *A Final Promise: The Campaign to Assimilate the Indians, 1880–1920.* Lincoln: University of Nebraska Press, 1984.

Hunt, Lynn. *Inventing Human Rights: A History.* New York: W. W. Norton, 2007.

Huyssen, Andreas. *Present Pasts: Urban Palimpsests and the Politics of Memory*. Stanford: Stanford University Press, 2003.

Irwin, Lee. "Freedom, Law, and Prophecy: A Brief History of Native American Religious Resistance." *American Indian Quarterly* 21 (Winter 1997): 35–55.

Ivison, Duncan. *Postcolonial Liberalism*. Cambridge: Cambridge University Press, 2002.

Jackson, Andrew. First Annual Message to Congress, December 8, 1829. Our Documents. http://www.ourdocuments.gov/doc.php?flash=true&doc=25&page=transcript. November 9, 2012.

James, Matt. "Memory, Identity, and Diversity in BC." In *British Columbia Politics and Government*, edited by Michael Howlett, Dennis Pilon, and Tracy Summerville, 53–67. Toronto: Emond Montgomery, 2010.

——— . "Wrestling with the Past: Apologies, Quasi-Apologies, and Non-Apologies in Canada." In *The Age of Apology: Facing Up to the Past*, edited by Mark Gibney et al., 137–53. Philadelphia: University of Pennsylvania Press, 2008.

Jefferson, Thomas. *Notes on the State of Virginia*. 1787. Chapel Hill: University of North Carolina Press, 1995.

Johannsen, Robert W. "The Secession Crisis and the Frontier: Washington Territory, 1860–1861." *Mississippi Valley Historical Review* 39 (December, 1952): 415–40.

Katyal, Neal K., and Laurance H. Tribe. "Waging War, Deciding Guilt: Trying the Military Tribunals." *Yale Law Journal* 111, no. 6 (April 2002): 1259–310.

Kaylene, Anne. *Judicially Murdered*. Scappoose, Ore.: Melton, 1999.

Kearney, Richard. "Between Tradition and Utopia: The Hermeneutical Problem of Myth." In *On Paul Ricoeur*, edited by David Wood, 55–73. New York: Routledge, 1991.

Keys, Barbara. *Reclaiming American Virtue: The Human Rights Revolution of the 1970s*. Cambridge: Harvard University Press, 2014 (forthcoming).

Klingle, Matthew. *Emerald City: An Environmental History of Seattle*. New Haven: Yale University Press, 2007.

Kluger, Richard. *The Bitter Waters of Medicine Creek: The Tragic Clash between White and Native America*. New York: Knopf, 2011.

Konkle, Maureen. *Writing Indian Nations: Native Intellectuals and the Politics of Historiography*. Chapel Hill: University of North Carolina Press, 2004.

Koppel, Tom. *Kanaka: The Untold Story of Hawaiian Pioneers in British Columbia and the Pacific Northwest*. Vancouver, B.C.: Whitecap Books, 1995.

Kunsch, Kelly. "The Trials of Leschi, Nisqually Chief." *Seattle Journal for Social Justice* 5 (Fall/Winter 2006): 67–119.

Kymlicka, W. *Finding Our Way: Rethinking Ethnocultural Relations in Canada*. New York: Oxford University Press, 1989.

Lauren, Paul Gordon. "A Human Rights Lens on U.S. History: Human Rights at

Home and Human Rights Abroad." In *Bringing Human Rights Home: A History of Human Rights in the United States*, abridged ed., edited by Cynthia Soohoo, Catherine Albisa, and Martha F. Davis, 7–39. Philadelphia: University of Pennsylvania Press, 2009.

Lazarus-Black, Mindie, and Susan F. Hirsch, eds. *Contested States: Law, Hegemony, and Resistance*. New York: Routledge, 1994.

Lee, Wayne E. "Mind and Matter—Cultural Analysis in American Military History: A Look at the State of the Field." *Journal of American History* 93, no. 4 (March 2007): 1116–42.

Lepore, Jill. "The Dark Ages: Terrorism, Counterterrorism, and the Law of Torment." *New Yorker*. March 18, 2013, 28–32.

———. *The Name of War: King Philip's War and the Origins of American Identity*. New York: Knopf, 1998.

Lewarne, Charles P. "Snohomish County in the 'Second Great Age of Discovery.'" *Columbia* 22, no. 3 (Fall 2008): 36–41.

Limerick, Patricia Nelson. *The Legacy of Conquest: The Unbroken Past of the American West*. New York: W. W. Norton, 1988.

MacMillan, Ken. *Sovereignty and Possession in the English New World: The Legal Foundations of Empire, 1576–1640*. Cambridge: Cambridge University Press, 2006.

Magarrell, Lisa, and Joya Wesley. *Learning from Greensboro: Truth and Reconciliation in the United States*. Philadelphia: University of Pennsylvania Press, 2008.

May, Robert E. "Epilogue to the Missouri Compromise: The South, the Balance of Power, and the Tropics in the 1850s." *Plantation Society* 1, no. 2 (June 1979): 201–25.

McBryde, Isabel, ed. *Who Owns the Past?* Melbourne: Oxford University Press, 1985.

McDonnell, Janet. *The Dispossession of the American Indian, 1887–1934*. Bloomington: Indiana University Press, 1991.

McHugh, Paul. *Aboriginal Societies and the Common Law: A History of Sovereignty, Status, and Self-Determination*. Oxford: Oxford University Press, 2004.

McNeil, Kent. "Negotiated Sovereignty: Indian Treaties and the Acquisition of American and Canadian Territorial Rights in the Pacific Northwest." In *The Power of Promises: Rethinking Indian Treaties in the Pacific Northwest*, edited by Alexandra Harmon, 35–55. Seattle: University of Washington Press, 2008.

Meany, Edmond S. "Chief Patkanim." *Washington Historical Quarterly* 15, no. 3 (July 1924): 187–98.

———. "Ezra Meeker, the Pioneer." *Washington Historical Quarterly* 20, no. 2 (April 1929): 124–28.

———. "Newspapers of Washington Territory." *Washington Historical Quarterly* 13, no. 4 (October 1922): 251–70.

———. *Origins of Washington Geographic Names.* Seattle: University of Washington Press, 1923.

———. "Washington Geographic Names." *Washington Historical Quarterly* 8, no. 4 (October 1917): 265–90.

———, ed. "Monument for Indian War Heroes." *Washington Historical Quarterly* 10, no. 3 (July 1919): 177–81.

Meeker, Ezra. *Pioneer Reminiscences of Puget Sound and the Tragedy of Leschi.* Seattle: Lowman and Hanford, 1905.

———. *Seventy Years of Progress in Washington.* Seattle: Allstrum Printing, 1921.

Mendus, Susan. *Toleration and the Limits of Liberalism.* London: Macmillan, 1989.

Merry, Sally Engle. "Courts as Performances: Domestic Violence Hearings in a Hawai'i Family Court." In *Contested States: Law, Hegemony, and Resistance,* edited by Mindie Lazarus-Black and Susan F. Hirsch, 35–59. New York: Routledge, 1994.

Mihesuah, D., ed. *Natives and Academics: Researching and Writing about Native Americans.* Lincoln: University of Nebraska Press, 1998.

Miller, Bruce G. "The Great Race of 1941: A Coast Salish Public Relations Coup." *Pacific Northwest Quarterly* 89, no. 3 (Summer 1998): 127–35.

———. "The Press, the Boldt Decision, and Indian-White Relations." *American Indian Culture and Research Journal* 17, no. 2 (1993): 75–97.

Miller, Bruce G., and Daniel L. Boxberger. "Creating Chiefdoms: The Puget Sound Case." *Ethnohistory* 41, no. 2 (Spring 1994): 267–93.

Miller, Jay. *The Problem of Justice: Tradition and Law in the Coast Salish World.* Lincoln: University of Nebraska Press, 2001.

———. *Regaining Dr. Herman Haeberlin: Early Anthropology and Museology in Puget Sound, 1916–17.* Seattle: Lushootseed Press, 2007.

Minow, Martha. *Between Vengeance and Forgiveness: Facing History after Genocide and Mass Violence.* Boston: Beacon, 1999.

Mitchell, Dewey. "The Naming Ceremony." In *Ways of the Lushootseed People: Ceremonies and Traditions of Northern Puget Sound Indians,* edited by Vi Hilbert, 18–19. Seattle: United Indians of All Tribes Foundation, 1980.

Molina, Alejandro Luis, ed. *USA on Trial: The International Tribunal on Indigenous Peoples and Oppressed Nations in the United States, Mission High School, October 2–4, 1992.* Chicago: C & D Print Shop, 1996.

Mooney, Linda, David Knox, and Caroline Schacht. *Understanding Social Problems.* 7th ed. Wadsworth: Cengage Learning, 2011.

Morefield, Jeanne. *Covenants without Swords: Idealist Liberalism and the Spirit of Empire.* Princeton: Princeton University Press, 2004.

Morgan, Murray. *Puget's Sound: A Narrative of Early Tacoma and the Southern Sound.* Seattle: University of Washington Press, 1981.

Morrissey, Katherine G. *Mental Territories: Mapping the Inland Empire.* Ithaca: Cornell University Press, 1997.

Muckleshoot Indian Tribe, "The History of the Muckleshoot Indian Tribe and its Reservation." http://www.muckleshoot.nsn.us/about-us/overview.aspx. July 19, 2013.

Murphy, Michael. *Multiculturalism: A Critical Introduction*. New York: Routledge, 2012.

Nabokov, Peter. *A Forest of Time: American Indian Ways of History*. Cambridge: Cambridge University Press, 2002.

Nash, Linda. "The Changing Experience of Nature: Historical Encounters with a Northwest River." *Journal of American History* 86 (March 2004): 1600–1629.

Niezen, Ronald. *Public Justice and the Anthropology of Law*. Cambridge: Cambridge University Press, 2010.

Nisbet, Jack. *The Mapmaker's Eye: David Thompson on the Columbia Plateau*. Pullman: Washington State University Press, 2005.

Nobles, Melissa. *The Politics of Official Apologies*. Cambridge: Cambridge University Press, 2008.

Oldham, Kit. "First Emigrant Wagon Train across Naches Pass through the Cascade Mountains in the Fall of 1853." Washington Historical Society. HistoryLink.org. Essay #5053. http://www.historylink.org/essays/output.cfm?file_id=5053. November 19, 2007.

———. "Governor Isaac Stevens Selects Olympia as Capital of Washington Territory on November 28, 1853." Washington Historical Society. HistoryLink.org. Essay #5054. http://www.historylink.org/essays/output.cfm?file_id=5054. February 26, 2008.

Olson, Alexander. "Our Leschi: The Making of a Martyr." *Pacific Northwest Quarterly* 95 (Winter 2003/4): 26–36.

———. "Our Leschi: A Story of Puget Sound History." B.A. thesis, Stanford University, 2002.

Ostler, Jeffrey. *The Plains Sioux and U.S. Colonialism from Lewis and Clark to Wounded Knee*. Cambridge: Cambridge University Press, 2004.

Pagden, Anthony. *The Fall of Natural Man: The American Indian and the Origins of Comparative Ethnology*. Cambridge: Cambridge University Press, 1982.

Parekh, Bhiku. "Liberalism and Colonialism: A Critique of Locke and Mill." In *The Decolonization of the Imagination: Culture, Knowledge, and Power*, edited by J. N. Pieterse and B. Parekh, 81–98. London: Zed Books, 1995.

Perry, Adele. "The Colonial Archive on Trial: Possession, Dispossession, and History in *Delgamuukw v. British Columbia*." In *Archive Stories: Facts, Fictions, and the Writing of History*, edited by Antoinette Burton, 325–50. Durham: Duke University Press, 2005.

Peter, Susie Sampson. *Susie Sampson Peter: The Wisdom of a Skagit Elder*. Translated by Vi Hilbert and Jay Miller. Seattle: Lushootseed Press, 2005.

Peters, Julie Stone. "'Literature,' the 'Rights of Man,' and Narratives of Atrocity:

Historical Backgrounds to the Culture of Testimony." *Yale Journal of Law and the Humanities* 17 (Summer 2005): 253–83.

Phelps, Teresa Godwin. *Shattered Voices: Language, Violence, and the Work of Truth Commissions.* Philadelphia: University of Pennsylvania Press, 2004.

Pierce County Pioneer Association. Program. "Commemorative Celebration at Sequalitchew Lake, July 5, 1906." Tacoma: Washington State Historical Society, 1906.

Prosch, Charles. *Reminiscences of Washington Territory: Scenes, Incidents, and Reflections of the Pioneer Period on Puget Sound.* Seattle, 1904.

Prucha, Francis Paul. *American Indian Treaties: The History of a Political Anomaly.* Berkeley: University of California Press, 1994.

Rabbesson, Antonio B. "The Truth of History." *Oregon Native Son* (July 1899): 148–51.

Raibmon, Paige. *Authentic Indians: Episodes of Encounter from the Late Nineteenth Century Northwest Coast.* Durham: Duke University Press, 2005.

———. "Unmaking Native Space: A Genealogy of Indian Policy, Settler Practice, and the Microtechniques of Dispossession." In *The Power of Promises: Rethinking Indian Treaties in the Pacific Northwest,* edited by Alexandra Harmon, 56–86. Seattle: University of Washington Press, 2008.

Rappaport, Joanne. *The Politics of Memory: Native Historical Interpretation in the Andes.* Durham: Duke University Press, 1998.

Rawls, John. "Political Liberalism." In *American Social and Political Thought: A Reader,* edited by Andreas Hess, 171–78. New York: New York University Press, 2003.

Raz, Guy. "Defining the War on Terror." National Public Radio. http://www.npr.org/templates/story/story.php?storyId=6416780. September 5, 2012.

Reddick, SuAnn M., and Cary C. Collins. "Medicine Creek to Fox Island: Cadastral Scams and Contested Domains." *Oregon Historical Quarterly* 106 (Fall 2005): 374–97.

Reese, Gary Fuller, ed. *A Documentary History of Fort Steilacoom.* Tacoma: Tacoma Public Library, 1978.

———. *Leschi and the Indian War of 1855.* Tacoma: Tacoma Public Library, 1967.

———. *Leschi, the Officers, and the Citizens: Documents about the Role of Leschi of the Nisqually Indians in the Opening of the Indian War of 1855 and His Execution after the Close of the War.* Tacoma: Tacoma Public Library, 1986.

———. *The Northwest Was Their Goal: A Collection of Pioneer Reminiscences Published in Clinton Snowden's Tacoma Daily and Weekly Ledger, 1892–1893.* Vols. 1–2. Tacoma: Tacoma Public Library, 1984.

———. *"Nothing Worthy of Note Transpired Today": The Northwest Journals of August V. Kautz.* Tacoma: Tacoma Public Library, 1978.

———. *They Came to Puget Sound: Reminiscences of Pioneer Women as Published* in the *Tacoma Daily and Weekly Ledger, 1892–1893*. Tacoma: Tacoma Public Library, 1984.

Regan, Paulette. *Unsettling the Settler Within: Indian Residential Schools, Truth Telling, and Reconciliation in Canada*. Vancouver: University of British Columbia Press, 2010.

Richards, Kent. "In Search of Pacific Northwest: The Historiography of Oregon and Washington." *Pacific Historical Review* 50 (November 1981): 415–43.

——. *Isaac I. Stevens: Young Man in a Hurry*. Provo: Brigham Young University Press, 1979.Roberts, Charles. "The Cushman Indian Trades School and World War I." *American Indian Quarterly* 11 (Summer 1987): 221–39.

Roberts, Nathan E. "The Death of Peter Stanup: A Modern Indian Leader Whose Life Was Forfeited in the Puyallup Land Fight." *Columbia* 22, no. 3 (Fall 2008): 24–31.

Rochester, Junius. "George Vancouver." Washington Historical Society. HistoryLink.org. Essay #5359. http://www.historylink.org/index.cfm?DisplayPage=output.cfm&File_Id=5359. July 11, 2010.

Rosaldo, Renato. "Imperialist Nostalgia." *Representations* 26, Special Issue: Memory and Counter-Memory (Spring 1989): 107–22.

Rossi, Louis. *Six Years on the West Coast of America, 1856–1862*. Fairfield, Wash.: Ye Galleon Press, 1983.

Russell, Peter. *Recognizing Aboriginal Title: The Mabo Case and Indigenous Resistance to English-Settler Colonialism*. Toronto: University of Toronto Press, 2005.

Savage, Kirk. *Standing Soldiers, Kneeling Slaves: Race, War, and Monument in Nineteenth-Century America*. Princeton: Princeton University Press, 1997.

Schmitt, Martin. "Execution of Chief Leschi and the 'Truth Teller.'" *Oregon Historical Quarterly* 50 (March 1949): 30–39.

Schoenberg, Wilfred P. *A History of the Catholic Church in the Pacific Northwest*. Washington, D.C.: Pastoral Press, 1987.

Schwantes, Carlos A. *The Pacific Northwest: An Interpretive History*. Lincoln: University of Nebraska Press, 2000.

Schwartz, Barry, Kazuya Fukuoka, and Sachiko Takita-Ishii. "Collective Memory: Why Culture Matters." In *The Blackwell Companion to the Sociology of Culture*, edited by Mark D. Jacobs and Nancy Weiss Hanrahan, 253–71. Malden, Mass.: Blackwell, 2005.

Scott, James C. *Seeing Like a State: How Certain Schemes to Improve the Human Condition Have Failed*. New Haven: Yale University Press, 1998.

Selesky, Harold. "Colonial America." In *The Laws of War: Constraints on Warfare in the Western World*, edited by Michael Howard, George Andreopoulos, and Mark Shulman, 59–85. New Haven: Yale University Press, 1994.

Shelton, Ruth Sehome. *The Wisdom of a Tulalip Elder*. Transcribed by Vi Hilbert and translated by Vi Hilbert and Jay Miller. Seattle: Lushootseed Press, 1995.

Short, John. *Representing the Republic: Mapping the United States, 1600–1900*. London: Reaktion Books, 2001.

Sicade, Henry. "Aboriginal Nomenclature." *Mazama: Record of Mountaineering in the Pacific Northwest* 5 (December 1916): 251–52.

———. "Henry Sicade." In *History of Pierce County, Washington*, edited by William P. Bonney. Chicago: Pioneer Historical Publishing Company, 1927.

———. "The Indians' Side of the Story." In *Building a State: Washington, 1889–1939*, vol. 3, edited by Charles Miles and O. B. Sperlin, 490–503. Tacoma: Washington State Historical Society Publications, 1940.

Sicade, Sally. "Henry C. Sicade: A Short Sketch by His Daughter." *Puyallup Tribal News*, May 14, 2008. www.puyalluptribalnews.net/news/view/henry_sicade_revered_leader_of_puyallups/. May 1, 2013.

Sikkink, Kathryn. *The Justice Cascade: How Human Rights Prosecutions Are Changing World Politics*. New York: W. W. Norton, 2011.

Simpson, Audra. "On the Logic of Discernment." *American Quarterly* 59, no. 2 (June 2007): 479–91.

———. "The 'Problem' of Mental Health in Native North America: Liberalism, Multiculturalism, and the (Non)Efficacy of Tears." *ETHOS* 36, no. 3 (2008): 376–79.

Slotkin, Richard. *Gunfighter Nation: The Myth of the Frontier in Twentieth Century America*. New York: HarperCollins, 1992.

Smith, Allen. *Takhoma: Ethnography of Mount Rainier National Park*. Pullman: Washington State University Press, 2006.

Smith, Marian. *The Puyallup-Nisqually*. New York: Columbia University Press, 1940.

———. "The Puyallup of Washington." In *Acculturation in Seven American Indian Tribes*, edited by Ralph Linton, 3–36. New York: D. Appleton-Century, 1940.

Snowden, Clinton. *The Rise and Progress of an American State*. Vol. 3 of *History of Washington*. New York: Century History Company, 1909.

Spier, Leslie. *Tribal Distribution in Washington*. Menasha, Wis.: George Banta, 1936.

Stam, Robert, and Ella Shohat. "Contested Histories: Eurocentrism, Multiculturalism, and the Media." In *Multiculturalism: A Critical Reader*, edited by David Theo Goldberg, 296–324. Cambridge: Blackwell, 1994.

Stanley, Christine A. "When Counter Narratives Meet Master Narratives in the Journal Editorial-Review Process." *Educational Researcher* 36 (January/February 2007): 14–24.

Steinberg, Shirley R., ed. *Diversity and Multiculturalism: A Reader*. New York: Peter Lang, 2009.

Stephanson, Anders. *Manifest Destiny: American Expansion and the Empire of Right*. New York: Hill and Wang, 1996.

Stevens, Hazard. *The Life of Isaac Ingalls Stevens*. Vols. 1 and 3. Boston: Houghton Mifflin, 1900.

———. "The Pioneers and Patriotism." *Washington Historical Quarterly* 8 (July 1917): 172–79.

Sturken, Marita. *Tangled Memories: The Vietnam War, the AIDS Epidemic, and the Politics of Remembering*. Berkeley: University of California Press, 1997.

Suttles, Wayne. *Coast Salish Essays*. Seattle: University of Washington Press, 1987.

Swanton, John Reed. *The Indian Tribes of North America*. Washington, D.C.: U.S. Government Printing Office, 1953.

Taylor, Herbert C., Jr. "Anthropological Investigation of the Medicine Creek Treaty Tribes Relative to Tribal Identity and Aboriginal Possession of Lands." In *American Indian Ethnohistory: Indians of the Northwest*, edited by David Agee Horr, 401–73. New York: Garland, 1974.

Teit, James Alexander. "The Middle Columbia Salish." Edited by Franz Boas. *University of Washington Publications in Anthropology* 2, no. 4 (June 1928): 83–128. Thornton, Thomas. "Anthropological Studies of Native American Place Naming." *American Indian Quarterly* 21 (Spring 1997): 209–28.

Thornton, Thomas. "Anthropological Studies of Native American Place Naming." *American Indian Quarterly* 21 (Spring 1997): 209–28.

———. *Being and Place among the Tlingit*. Seattle: University of Washington Press, 2008.

Thrush, Coll. "The Lushootseed Peoples of Puget Sound Country." University of Washington Libraries. http://nooksack.lib.washington.edu/aipnw/thrush.html. July 18, 2013.

———. *Native Seattle: Histories from the Crossing-Over Place*. Seattle: University of Washington Press, 2007.

Tomlins, Christopher. *Law, Labor, and Ideology in the Early American Republic*. Chicago: American Bar Foundation, 1993.

———. "The Many Legalities of Colonization: A Manifesto of Destiny for Early American Legal History." In *The Many Legalities of Early America*, edited by Christopher Tomlins and Bruce H. Mann, 1–20. Chapel Hill: University of North Carolina Press, 2001.

Trigger, Bruce. "The Past as Power: Anthropology and the North American Indian." In *Who Owns the Past?* edited by Isabel McBryde, 11–35. Papers from the annual symposium of the Australian Academy of the Humanities. Melbourne: Oxford University Press, 1985.

Trouillot, Michele-Rolph. *Silencing the Past: Power and the Production of History*. Boston: Beacon, 1995.

Tully, James. *An Approach to Political Philosophy: Locke in Contexts*. Cambridge: Cambridge University Press, 1993.

———. *Strange Multiplicity: Constitutionalism in the Age of Diversity*. Cambridge: Cambridge University Press, 1995.

Turner, Dale. *This Is Not a Peace Pipe: Towards a Critical Indigenous Philosophy*. Toronto: University of Toronto Press, 2006.

Tushnet, Mark V. "Critical Legal Theory." In *The Blackwell Guide to the Philosophy of Law and Legal Theory,* edited by Martin P. Golding and William A. Edmundson, 80–89. Malden, Mass.: Blackwell, 2005.

U.S. Government. Northwest Ordinance. 1787. http://www.ourdocuments.gov/doc.php?flash=true&doc=8. July 1, 2011.

———. Department of the Interior, Bureau of Indian Affairs. "Constitution and Bylaws of the Nisqually Indian Community of the Nisqually Reservation, Washington." Washington, D.C.: Government Printing Office, 1951.

U.S. Senate, Committee on Indian Affairs. *Allotted Nisqually Indian Lands.* Washington, D.C.: Government Printing Office, 1920.

U.S. Senate. "Relief of Indians of Nisqually Reservation, Wash." *Senate Reports.* Vol. 1. 66th Cong., 3rd Sess., December 6, 1920–March 4, 1921. Washington, D.C.: Government Printing Office, 1921.

Van Ogle, H. E. "Van Ogle's Memory of Pioneer Days." *Washington Historical Quarterly* 13 (October 1922): 269–81.

Vansina, Jan. *Oral Tradition as History.* Madison: University of Wisconsin Press, 1985.

Vaughn, Wade. *Puget Sound Invasion.* Seattle: [Vaughn?], 1976.

Vizenor, Gerald, ed. *Survivance: Narratives of Native Presence.* Lincoln: University of Nebraska Press, 2008.

Vora, Jay A., and Erika Vora. "The Effectiveness of South Africa's Truth and Reconciliation Commission: Perceptions of Xhosa, Afrikaner, and English South Africans." *Journal of Black Studies* 34 (January 2004): 310–22.

Wald, Patricia. "The Supreme Court Goes to War." In *Terrorism, the Laws of War, and the Constitution,* edited by Peter Berkowitz, 37–68. Stanford: Hoover Institutional Press, 2005.

———. "Terms of Assimilation: Legislating Subjectivity in the Emerging Nation." In *Cultures of United States Imperialism,* edited by Amy Kaplan and Donald Pease, 59–84. Durham: Duke University Press, 1993.

Walters, Mark. "Histories of Colonialism, Legality, and Aboriginality." *University of Toronto Law Journal* 57, no. 4 (Fall 2007): 819–32.

Washington State Legislature. "A History of the Legislature—Enabling Act." Approved February 22, 1889. [25 U.S. Statutes at Large, c 180, p. 676.] http://www.leg.wa.gov/History/State/Pages/enabling.aspx. September 17, 2011.

———. House. Chief Leschi Apology Bill. HR 4708. Passed March 9, 2004.

———. Senate. Chief Leschi Apology Bill. SR 8727. 58th Leg. Passed March 9, 2004.

———. Senate. Chief Leschi Apology Bill. Senate Joint Memorial 8054. 58th Leg., 2004 sess. S-4704.1. http://apps.leg.wa.gov/documents/WSLdocs/2003-04/Pdf/Bills/Senate%20Joint%20Memorials/8054-Chief%20Leschi.pdf. March 19, 2012.

Waterman, Thomas Talbot. *Puget Sound Geography*. Edited by Vi Hilbert, Jay Miller, and Zalmai Zahir. Seattle: Lushootseed Press, 2001.

Weber, Dennis. "The Creation of Washington Territory: Securing Democracy North of the Columbia." *Columbia Magazine* 17 (Fall 2003): 27–34.

Weber, Samuel. "In the Name of the Law." In *Deconstruction and the Possibility of Justice*, edited by Drucilla Cornell, Michael Rosenfeld, and David Gray Carlson, 232–57. New York: Routledge, 1992.

Weyeneth, Robert. "The Power of Apology and the Process of Historical Reconciliation." *Public Historian* 23 (Summer 2001): 9–38.

Whaley, Gray H. *Oregon and the Collapse of Illahee: U.S. Empire and the Transformation of an Indigenous World*. Chapel Hill: University of North Carolina Press, 2010.

White, Richard. "Frederick Jackson Turner and Buffalo Bill." In *Frontiers in American Culture*, edited by James Grossman, 7–66. Berkeley: University of California Press, 1994.

———. *"It's Your Misfortune and None of My Own": A New History of the American West*. Norman: University of Oklahoma Press, 1991.

———. *Land Use, Environment, and Social Change: The Shaping of Island County, Washington*. Seattle: University of Washington Press, 1979.

———. "The Treaty of Medicine Creek: Indian-White Relations on Upper Puget Sound, 1830–1880." M.A. thesis, University of Washington, 1972.

White House. Office of the Press Secretary. "George W. Bush Speech at the United States Army War College, Carlisle, Pennsylvania, May 24, 2004." http://www.whitehouse.gov/news/releases/2004/05/20040524-10.html. October 11, 2007.

Wickersham, James. "Nusqually Mythology, Studies of the Washington Indians." *Overland Monthly* 32 (July–December 1898): 345–51.

Wiebelhaus-Brahm, Eric. *Truth Commissions and Transitional Societies: The Impact on Human Rights and Democracy*. London: Routledge, 2010.

Wilkes, Charles. *Narrative of the United States Exploring Expedition, 1838–1842*. Vol. 5. Philadelphia: Lea and Blanchard, 1845.

Wilkins, David E. *American Indian Sovereignty and the U.S. Supreme Court: The Masking of Justice*. Austin: University of Texas Press, 1997.

Wilkins, Sarah. "Exercise Culminates 18 Months of Preparation for Iraq." *Bobcat Bulletin* 3 (Fall 2004): 10.

Wilkinson, Charles. *Messages from Frank's Landing: A Story of Salmon, Treaties, and the Indian Way*. Seattle: University of Washington Press, 2000.

Williams, Robert, Jr. *The American Indian in Western Legal Thought: The Discourses of Conquest*. New York: Oxford, 1990.

Wilma, David. "Isaac Ingalls Stevens." Washington Historical Society. HistoryLink.org Essay #5314. http://www.historylink.org/index.cfm?DisplayPage=output.cfm&file_id=5314. March 12, 2013.

Witt, John Fabian. *Lincoln's Code: The Laws of War in American History.* New York: Free Press, 2012.

Wolfe, Patrick. "Settler Colonialism and the Elimination of the Native." *Journal of Genocide Research* 8, no. 4 (December 2006): 387–409.

———. *Settler Colonialism and the Transformation of Anthropology: The Politics and Poetics of an Ethnographic Event.* New York: Cassell, 1999.

Works Progress Administration. *Told by the Pioneers: Tales of Frontier Life as Told by Those Who Remember the Days of the Territory and Early Statehood.* Vols. 1–3. Olympia, Wash.: Works Progress Administration, 1937–38.

Wortley, W. Victor. "Perceptions and Misperceptions: A European Cleric's View of the American Indian." *Pacific Northwest Quarterly* 72 (October 1981): 157–61.

Wrobel, David M. *Promised Lands: Promotion, Memory, and the Creation of the American West.* Lawrence: University Press of Kansas, 2002.

Wunder, John Remley. "Law and Order on the Frontier: Justices of the Peace in Washington Territory." Ph.D. diss., University of Washington, 1974.

Young, James P. "Reconsidering American Liberalism." In *American Social and Political Thought: A Reader,* edited by Andreas Hess, 162–70. New York: New York University Press, 2003.

INDEX

Abu Ghraib prison, 72, 216–17 (n. 98)
Afghanistan War, 71, 215–16 (n. 89), 216 (n. 97)
"Age of apology," 14–15, 196 (n. 32), 197 (nn. 33, 38), 198 (n. 41)
Alexander, Gerry, 75, 78, 141, 253 (n. 12); Historical Court and, 5–6, 8, 53, 137; Historical Court format and, 6–7, 187; Historical Court idea and, 147, 148; Historical Court seeking truth and, 11, 81, 155, 187; Indian law and, 152, 242 (n. 78); Leschi exoneration announcement and, 9–10, 155, 157; Native American testimony and, 155–56; oral history and, 81, 82; Washington Supreme Court Leschi case possibility and, 145, 146–47, 149
Alfred, Gerald Taiaiake, 12, 158
Allen, Frank, 91–94, 95, 97–98
Al-Qaeda, 71, 216 (n. 97)
American Boundary Commission, 38–39
American exceptionalism, 77–79
American Indian Movement, 152
American values: colonialism and, 23–24, 77–78; Native American dispossession of land and, 78, 218 (n. 116); rule of law and, 23–24, 136–37; War on Terror and, 72, 216–17 (n. 98)
Ancestors, 21, 23, 26, 27, 47, 48, 49, 80, 98, 99, 100, 121, 122, 150, 200 (n. 17), 204 (n. 71); settlers and, 178, 186, 189
Anderson, Robert, 8, 141, 156, 241 (n. 75), 242 (n. 82)
Anglicizing language, 44, 207 (n. 110)
Anthropologists, 25, 91–92, 99, 120, 121, 166, 198 (n. 45); Nisqually Indians and, 89, 221 (n. 45), 225 (n. 86); proto-anthropologists, 41, 42, 43, 44
Apology, 141, 143, 187, 197 (n. 38), 198 (n. 41), 242 (n. 77), 243 (n. 90); to Leschi's descendants, 138, 139, 141, 145, 157, 186. *See also* Washington State legislature; "Age of apology"
Asher, Brad, 160
Assimilation, 13, 195 (n. 22); pain and suffering representing, 151; participation in symbolic gestures and, 158; selling land and, 111, 112; U.S. Indian policy and, 110, 111

Bacalabc, 87
Bacevich, Andrew, 71, 215–16 (n. 89)
Ballard, Arthur, 120–21, 232 (nn. 77, 79)
Bancroft, Hubert H., 77
Banner, Stuart, 30
Benjamin, Walter, 81
Bennett, Ramona, 187–88
Bering Strait migration theory, 41, 42

Berschauer, Daniel, 137
Bin Laden, Osama, 77
Binns, Archie, 180
Blockhouses, 59, 62–63
Boldt, George, 131, 132, 236 (nn. 131, 133), 238 (nn. 31–32)
Bonney, William P., 180
Brannon, Joseph, 172
Brooks, Roy, 143
Bunting, Joseph, 164, 170, 171, 173, 246 (n. 32)
Bureau of Indian Affairs, 45, 118, 127. *See also* U.S. Department of the Interior
Bush, George W.: Iraq War and, 72, 143, 215–16 (n. 89); War on Terror and, 70, 71, 74, 217 (n. 108)

Carpenter, Cecelia Svinth, 7, 25–26, 234 (n. 97); Committee to Exonerate Chief Leschi and, 139, 140; Historical Court of Inquiry and Justice idea and, 133, 147–48; Historical Court of Inquiry and Justice testimony and, 95–96, 216 (n. 90); innocence of Leschi and, 6, 93, 140, 154; land condemnation and, 118, 124–25, 233–34 (n. 95); Leschi exoneration and, 102, 133, 138, 139, 140, 152, 157, 199 (n. 9); Leschi stories and, 84, 86, 88, 92, 95–96, 142, 223 (n. 72); Nisqually migration legend and, 27, 41–42, 200 (n. 17); Nisqually reservation and, 109–10; Quiemuth and, 182; stone memorial to Leschi and, 129. *See also* Committee to Exonerate Chief Leschi
Cartography. *See* Mapping
Cascade Range, 27, 31, 87
Casey, Silas, 68
Catholic Church, 97, 124, 207–8 (n. 118)

Celebration of Brothers. *See* Leschi-Quiemuth Honor Walk
Central Intelligence Agency (CIA), 71
Central Washington University, 7
Changer, The, 26, 86, 199 (n. 12)
Chemawa Indian School. *See* Indian Industrial Training School
Chenoweth, Francis, 65, 66
Chief Leschi Elementary School, 159, 183, 187–88
Chief Leschi Schools, 99
Chinook jargon, 96, 107, 227 (n. 13)
Civil Practice Act of 1854 (Washington Territory), 55
Civil War, 74
Clark, Frank, 67, 68, 214 (n. 72)
Clifford, James, 81
Coast Salish Indians: chief role and, 39, 106, 227 (n. 11); disputing surveying teams, 45; fishing and, importance and significance of, 39, 127, 199–200 (n. 14); groups and geography of, 25, 199 (n. 8); Historical Court of Inquiry and Justice and, 5, 25, 49, 82, 91; Hudson's Bay Company (HBC) and, 29; Indian legal customs and, 166, 169; kinship expectations and, 87; legends and, 42–43, 199–200 (n. 14), 206 (n. 108); Lekwiltok raids and, 91; Leschi stories and, 25, 82, 84–86, 91, 95–96, 134; migration theories and, 41–42; oral history multiplicity of stories and, 84–86, 219 (nn. 17, 19); Puget Sound Indian War and, 109; relationship to land and, 29; settler memoirs and, 112; stone memorial to Leschi and, 128; treaties and, 105; tribal events and outsiders and, 113–14, 229–30 (n. 45); values expressed through stories, 85, 219 (n. 17); villages of, 92, 93. *See also* Nisqually Indians;

Puyallup Indians; Snoqualmie Indians; Squaxin Island Indians
Colonialism: American exceptionalism and, 78–79; American values and, 23–24, 77–78; children and, 101, 107; dispossession of Indian land and, 30, 49, 69–70, 185, 198 (n. 49); European right to uninhabited land and, 28–30, 200–201 (n. 22); Historical Court of Inquiry and Justice and, 15–16, 17, 22, 78–79, 152–53, 158, 190–91; Leschi exoneration and, 149, 152–53; liberalism and, 12, 14, 21, 24, 194 (nn. 14, 17), 196 (nn. 28, 30); mapping and demarcation and, 30–37, 201 (nn. 35–36), 202 (n. 43); misunderstanding Native needs and, 39, 40, 41, 205 (nn. 88–89); Native American resistance to, 24, 49, 208 (n. 129); pain and suffering and, 151, 241 (n. 70); place-names and, 32, 44, 207 (n. 110); postcolonial condition of Native Americans and, 149, 196 (n. 30); racism and, 30, 144; rule of law and, 13, 23–24, 138, 148; scientific method and, 37–38, 40, 49, 205 (n. 89); treaty negotiations and, 39; white settlers and, 16–18, 20–21, 49, 69–70, 182, 198 (n. 49), 215–16 (n. 89)
Columbia River, 32
Comaroff, Jean, 191
Comaroff, John, 191
Committee to Exonerate Chief Leschi: archival evidence supporting Leschi's exoneration and, 9, 181; building political will and, 141, 143, 152; choice of approximate justice and, 137–38, 158; considering Washington Supreme Court and, 141, 146, 147; enemy combatant argument and, 70–71, 154; establishment of, 6, 139; Historical Court of Inquiry and Justice as education and, 188; Historical Court of Inquiry and Justice design and, 6–7, 150–51, 152–53; Historical Court of Inquiry and Justice idea and, 147, 148, 149; legal remedies available and, 8, 140–41, 193–94 (n. 6); rule of law and, 140, 146. *See also* Carpenter, Cecelia Svinth; Iyall, Cynthia; Parr, Melissa
Common law, 23, 139, 140, 148, 155, 237 (n. 11)
Condemnation of land in Pierce County, 1917–18, 105, 117–22, 124, 126, 134, 165, 183, 231 (n. 64), 234 (n. 95). *See also* Pierce County Condemnation Board
Connell, Michael, 162, 170, 244–45 (n. 20)
Connell's Prairie, 2; memorial to white men killed and, 122, 233 (n. 86), 244–45 (n. 20); death of rangers and, 59, 60, 65, 67, 72, 122, 154, 211 (n. 37)
Cornezita, 87
Corporal punishment, 166
Cotterrell, Roger, 155
Cox, Ronald, 75, 137
Crawley, John, 169, 248 (n. 57)
Cushman Indian School, 48, 118, 121, 231 (n. 63)

Daes, Erica-Irene, 101
Dawes Act. *See* General Allotment Act of 1887
De Laguna, Frederica, 99
Deloria, Vine, Jr., 41
Democratic Party, 55, 60, 209 (n. 11)
Denny, Arthur, 176–77
Disease, 40, 205 (n. 91)
Dred Scott decision, 56, 210 (n. 21)
Duwamish Indians, 25

INDEX 283

Eaton, Charles, 88, 220–21 (n. 39), 244–45 (n. 20)
Eatonville, 87, 141
Edgar, Betsy, 163, 245 (n. 24)
Elmendorf, William, 91–92
Emmons, Della Gould, 129, 130, 252 (n. 111)
Enabling Act of 1889, 146
Enemy combatants: Historical Court of Inquiry and Justice and, 9, 21, 51–52, 53, 62, 71, 72, 73–75, 78, 154, 242 (nn. 81–82); legality of, 21, 51–52, 53, 70–71, 74, 75, 77, 154, 217 (nn. 102, 104, 107–8); Leschi's trials and, 8–9, 51, 65, 73
Environmentalism, 132, 142, 143, 236 (n. 131), 238 (n. 31)
Ethnography, 37, 38–39, 41–44, 46, 90
Ethnohistorical approach, 18–19, 198 (n. 45)
European contact: British crops and animals and, 29, 47–48, 162, 201 (n. 27), 244 (n. 16); European right to uninhabited land and, 28–30, 200–201 (n. 22); place-names and, 28–29, 32, 200 (n. 21)
Evergreen State College, The, 8

Filibusters, 57, 210 (n. 25)
Fishing rights, 106, 236 (n. 131), 238 (n. 32); Medicine Creek Treaty of 1854 and, 1, 39, 48, 107, 129–30, 131–32, 205 (nn. 84, 87); Nisqually Indian activism and, 127, 130, 131, 134, 142–43, 152, 234 (n. 104), 235 (n. 107); Nisqually Indian arrests and, 126–27, 130. *See also* Salmon
"Fish-ins," 127, 130, 131, 142
Ford, Sidney, 174, 176
Fort Lewis Army Base, 7, 120, 124, 132, 143; honoring Leschi and Quiemuth and, 182, 183; Leschi Town and, 75–76, 77
Fort Nisqually, 31, 41; Hudson's Bay Company (HBC) and, 29, 88, 166, 173; inadvertent shooting of American and, 167, 247 (n. 45), 247–48 (n. 50); Quiemuth burial and, 165, 204 (n. 71)
Fort Steilacoom, 55, 57, 63; establishment of, 88, 167; Puget Sound Indian War and, 94; Puget Sound Indian War beginnings and, 3, 58, 59. *See also* Steilacoom (town)
Foucault, Michel, 31
Fourth of July events, 113–14, 229–30 (n. 45)
Fox Island, 109
"Frame narrative," 19
Frank, Billy, Jr., 7, 86, 100; fishing rights and, 126–27, 132; Leschi message and, 91, 103–4, 106, 134, 226 (n. 2); Leschi stories and, 83–84, 89, 135; Leschi's vision of the future and, 96–97, 98; salmon and, 26–27, 143, 238 (n. 31)
Frank, Willy, 82–83, 89, 127, 225–26 (n. 95)
Frank's Landing, 99, 127
"Frontier justice," 160, 166, 169–70, 248 (n. 60)
Fur trade, 29, 44, 167

General Allotment Act of 1887, 111, 228–29 (n. 33), 229 (n. 37)
Geneva Convention, 74, 75
Genocide, 143, 151, 240 (n. 63), 241–42 (n. 76)
Gibbs, George, 38–40, 41–42, 43, 48, 204–5 (n. 81), 205 (nn. 88, 92)
Giveaways. *See* Potlatches
Gold, 90, 221 (nn. 50–51)
Goliah, 169

Gordon, Avery, 183
Gosnell, Wesley, 35, 174, 250 (n. 87)
Goudy, George, 55, 209 (n. 12)
Goudy, James, 111–12, 120, 232 (n. 76)
Great Britain: Indian trade and, 31; introducing crops and animals to Indians, 29, 47–48, 162, 201 (n. 27), 244 (n. 16); Oregon Treaty of 1846 and, 29, 202 (n. 47). *See also* Hudson's Bay Company
Greensboro Truth and Reconciliation Commission, 14
Guantánamo Bay prison, 71, 74, 76

Habeas corpus, 63, 71
Haller, Granville O., 128–29, 235 (n. 114)
Ham, Eugene, 7, 73, 75, 76, 154
Harmon, Alexandra, 7, 74–75, 156, 224 (n. 77)
Harring, Sidney, 161
Hartman, Sarah, 170–71, 248–49 (n. 63), 249 (n. 64)
Hawai'i, 151, 152, 241 (nn. 74–75), 242 (n. 77)
Hawaiians, 29, 48, 167, 231–32 (n. 71)
Hiaton, John, 90–91, 112, 115, 222 (n. 53), 229 (n. 41)
Hilbert, Vi, 85, 219 (n. 17)
Historical Court of Inquiry and Justice: antecedents and models for, 149–53; archival documentary evidence and, 8–9, 16, 70, 179; author's research approach to, x–xii, xiii, 10–11, 19–20; creation of, 100, 133, 139, 147–49, 239–40 (n. 54); criticism of, 189, 190, 253 (n. 12); enemy combatant argument and, 9, 21, 51–52, 53, 62, 71, 72, 73–75, 78, 154, 242 (nn. 81–82); exoneration announcement, 9–10, 187; exoneration of Leschi and, xi, 11, 16, 21, 70, 80, 91, 101, 102, 182, 188; expert witnesses and, 6–7, 8–9, 70, 73, 155, 156; "fact" and "law" and, 154–55, 242 (n. 83); failure to address larger issues of colonialism, 15–16, 17, 22, 78–79, 152–53, 158, 190–91; as form of apology and, 157, 243 (n. 90); human rights discourse and, 150, 151; judges of, 7–8, 137, 194 (n. 8); legalistic format and, 6–7, 8, 13, 186–87; Leschi as Nisqually leader and, 25, 103–4, 179, 234 (n. 101); Leschi message and, 103–4, 132, 133–35; Leschi stories and, 16, 81–82, 87–88, 89, 92–93, 95–96, 191–92, 224 (n. 77); Leschi's trials and, 5–6, 8–9, 24, 49, 51, 69, 138; liberalism and, 12, 13, 14, 48–49, 138; military base and training context and, 75–76, 77, 218 (n. 110); multiculturalism and, 13, 81; Native American testimony and, 7, 9, 13, 16, 17, 21–22, 25, 27, 80–81, 84, 89, 91, 100–102, 103–4, 136–39, 150, 154, 155–56, 186, 187, 190, 242 (nn. 85–86); Nisqually Indian involvement and, ix, xi, 7, 8, 22, 81, 186; Nisqually Indian sovereignty and, xii, 62, 72, 73, 104, 139, 242 (n. 82); oral history and, 16, 80–82, 100, 151, 186; performance of legality and, 8, 22, 136–39, 148–49, 156–58, 191, 236–37 (n. 2), 237 (n. 3); Quiemuth, absence of in, 22, 159, 162, 181, 182; Quiemuth as haunting of, 161, 165, 182; rule of law and, 23, 24, 50–51, 63, 153, 160; tribal history vs. "white man" history and, 16, 188–90; tribunal comparison, 150, 240 (n. 63); truth and reconciliation commissions model and, 14, 15, 16, 150, 240 (n. 65); truth seeking and, ix, 6, 11, 81, 82, 155, 187; truth telling

INDEX   285

and, 151, 241 (n. 70); U.S. Army testimony and, 7, 71, 73–74, 75, 76–77, 154; victim testimony and, 15, 198 (n. 40); war and legality and, 51–53, 74, 138, 242 (n. 82); War on Terror context of deliberations, 70, 71, 74–75

History textbooks, 101, 141, 142, 144, 145, 238 (n. 26)

Hohamish Indians, 35

Hoopa Indians, 15

Horne, Gerald, 8

Horses, 39, 59, 87, 90, 108, 220 (n. 30)

Hoyte, Thor, 8, 148, 156, 158

Hudson's Bay Company (HBC): employee marriages with Indians and, 29, 48, 62–63, 88, 231–32 (n. 71), 245 (n. 24); Fort Nisqually shooting incident and, 167, 247 (n. 45); fur trade and, 29; Indian legal customs and, 166–67, 223 (n. 73); Leschi and, 61, 67, 83; Leschi and Quiemuth and, 88, 162, 201 (n. 27); Puget Sound Indian War and, 62–63, 212–13 (n. 52); relations with Indians and, 31, 33, 57, 167, 173, 209–10 (n. 18), 211 (n. 37), 227 (n. 17); territorial government and, 55, 57, 63, 67, 212–13 (n. 52); U.S. citizenship and, 55, 62

Hultman, Carl, 8, 9, 72, 150, 156, 186, 242 (n. 81)

Hultman, Sharon, 8

Human rights, 13, 72, 74, 76, 139, 142, 143, 144–45, 150, 151, 152, 158, 186, 195 (n. 23)

Huyssen, Andreas, 162

Indian boarding schools, 28, 45, 46, 114, 118, 119; punishment and shame about Indian ways and, 110–11, 115

Indian casinos, x, 238 (n. 32)

Indian Claims Commission (ICC), 125–26, 234 (nn. 97–98)

Indian Industrial Training School, 46

Indian War Veterans Association, 69

International law: human rights discourse and, 144–45; war and legality and, 51–53, 71, 72, 73–74, 75, 138

International Tribunal on Indigenous Peoples and Oppressed Nations in the United States, 151

Iraq War, 70, 72, 215–16 (n. 89), 216 (n. 97); training for, 75–76, 143

Ivison, Duncan, 149

Iyall, Cynthia, 106, 223 (n. 71); Historical Court of Inquiry and Justice idea and, 100, 147, 148; Historical Court of Inquiry and Justice testimony and, 7, 80, 156, 242 (n. 86); Indian Claims Commission (ICC) claim filed by Nisqually Indians and, 125, 126; Sherman Leschi and, 6, 99–100, 135; as Leschi descendant, 6, 225 (n. 92); Leschi exoneration and, 6, 102, 133, 139, 141, 152; Leschi stories and, 95, 101; Quiemuth and, 181, 182, 183; Washington state legislature and, 141, 142, 145. *See also* Committee to Exonerate Chief Leschi

Iyall, Ida, 125

Iyall, Tom, 187

Japanese-American internment, 14

Jefferson, Thomas, 41

Johnson, Robert, 31

Joint Base Lewis-McChord military base. *See* Fort Lewis Army Base

Kalakala (daughter of Leschi), 88, 220–21 (n. 39)

Kalama, Peter, 48, 119–20, 126, 208 (n. 126), 231–32 (n. 71), 233–34 (n. 95)

Kanaka Maoli, 151, 241 (n. 74)
Kansas, 54
Kautz, August, 67, 68, 88, 153, 174, 249 (n. 76), 250 (nn. 79, 89)
Kautz, Georgiana, 118
King County, 2, 59
Kitsap, 243 (n. 7), 250 (n. 85)
"Kitty" (daughter of Quiemuth), 88, 250 (n. 79)
Klickitat Indians, 3, 27, 60, 87, 90, 211 (n. 37), 220 (nn. 28–29)
Koquilton, Chief, 31
Kuckkahn, Tina, 8, 147, 148, 156
Kwakwak'waka Lekwiltok Indians, 91

Ladenburg, John, 156, 157, 187, 242 (n. 83); enemy combatant argument and, 153–54; Pierce County and, 8, 140, 188–89, 253 (n. 11); war and legality and, 52, 72
Lahalet, 167, 168
Lake, James, 172
Lakewood, 46, 127–28, 135, 182
Lakota Indians, 41
Lander, Edward, 63, 66
Lane, Joseph, 167
LaPointe-Gorman, Cecelia, 183
Law, rule of: American values and, 23–24, 136–37; changing history and, 141–42; colonialism and, 13, 23–24, 138, 148; common law and, 23, 139, 140, 148, 155, 237 (n. 11); court system and, 144, 185; due process and, 50, 159, 161, 177, 180–81, 243 (n. 8); Historical Court of Inquiry and Justice and, 23, 24, 50–51, 63, 153, 160; Historical Court of Inquiry and Justice as symbolic of, 136–39, 148–49, 158, 236–37 (n. 2), 237 (n. 3); vs. Indian legal customs, 161, 167–69, 177, 247 (n. 47), 248 (n. 54); Indians defying treaty terms and, 174, 250 (n. 86); Native Americans and, 50, 148–49, 177, 208 (n. 1), 240 (n. 60); positive law and, 139–40; truth and, 81, 218 (n. 5); Washington Territory and, 50, 51, 63, 146, 160, 174–75, 250 (n. 85), 251 (n. 96). *See also* White settlers
Law of Nations, 28, 200–201 (n. 22)
Laws of war, 51–53, 58, 65, 72–75, 76, 77, 138, 181, 208–9 (n. 2), 217 (n. 104), 242 (n. 82)
Le Clair, John, 166
Le Roy, Bruce, 130
Leschi, Chief: appeals after trials and, 66, 67, 175–76, 180, 214 (n. 69); appointed sub-chief for treaty council and, 1, 39, 106, 107, 162, 180; as arbitrator, 123, 124; attempts to kill, before trial, 163; author's research approach to, 18–19; burial ground of, 37, 165, 204 (n. 71); charges and, 3, 50, 51, 163; death, as sacrifice and, 124, 233 (n. 91); descendants of, 6, 84, 99, 114, 115, 116, 133, 186, 225 (n. 92); due process for trials and, 50, 51, 66–67, 159, 160, 165, 176, 177, 180–81; as enemy combatant, 8–9, 21, 51, 52, 53, 65, 71, 72, 73, 75, 78, 216 (n. 90); fame of, x, 61, 165, 252 (n. 117); Fort Nisqually shooting incident and, 167; Governor Stevens and, 64, 170, 179, 180, 250 (n. 85); headstone of, 84, 122–24; as hero, 76, 77, 94; Hudson's Bay Company (HBC) and, 61, 67, 83, 88, 162, 201 (n. 27); indictment of, 3, 4, 8, 65, 66, 175; legal status and, 50, 51; length of time under trials and appeals and, 165, 185; death of McAllister and Connell and, 162, 163; death of rangers and, 3, 6, 9–10, 73, 211 (n. 37), 244–45 (n. 20); as Nisqually

leader, 25, 103–4, 144, 179, 234 (n. 101); Olympia, called to, 59, 72, 162, 210–11 (n. 32); Olympia, trial at, 66, 175–76; pronunciation of name and, x, 43; Puget Sound Indian War and, 58, 60–61, 62, 64–65, 91–95, 109, 244 (n. 19); Quiemuth and, 162, 179, 244 (n. 15); Quiemuth's death and, 165, 176; reburial, 1895, 113–16, 124, 165, 230 (n. 46); reburial, 1918, 116–17, 119, 121–22, 165, 232 (n. 81); relationship to land and, 27; seeking pardon for, 67–68, 175, 176, 214–15 (n. 77), 250–51 (n. 91); stone memorial to, 127–31; sympathy for, 1960s onward, 142–44; as traditional arbiter in Indian legal customs, 107, 166–67; on trial for murder, 54, 165, 175, 179, 185, 214 (n. 63), 250 (n. 89); on trial for murder, first time, 4, 8, 65, 163, 171, 178, 224 (n. 77); on trial for murder, second time, 4–5, 8, 51, 66, 67, 224 (n. 77); white settlers and, 24, 61, 92, 106, 165, 211 (n. 39). *See also* Leschi conviction; Leschi execution; Leschi exoneration; Leschi message; Leschi stories; Medicine Creek Treaty of 1854; Newspapers

Leschi, George, 99, 114, 115, 116, 124, 165

Leschi, Mary, 87, 88, 90, 95

Leschi, Moses, 165

Leschi, Paul, 125–26

Leschi, Sherman, 6, 99–100, 133, 135

Leschi conviction, 66, 67, 69, 77, 101, 157; court system and, 185; destruction of old records and, 65, 140; failure to address larger issues of, 97, 138; Historical Court of Inquiry and Justice and, 8, 9, 11, 15, 21, 49, 50, 152–53; Nisqually Indians and Historical Court and, 148–49, 150–51; sentencing and, 5; territorial government and, 65, 67, 160–61; Washington Supreme Court and, 146–47. *See also* Leschi exoneration

Leschi execution, 5, 6, 49, 68–69, 224 (n. 79); burial ground and, 165; court system and, 185; final words before death and, 96, 97, 123, 224–25 (n. 80); racism and, 142; rule of law and, 69; settlers trying to stop, 67–68, 214 (n. 72); stone memorial and, 127–28, 135; territorial government and, 142; white settlers and, 176

Leschi exoneration: American values and, 78; announcement of, 9–10, 155, 157, 187, 191; apology from Washington State and, 139, 141, 145; archival evidence supporting, 6, 16, 153–54, 181, 199 (n. 9), 252 (n. 117); colonialism and, 12, 148, 149, 152–53; court system and, 142, 144; coverage of, 10, 158, 243 (n. 94); criticism of, 189, 190; destruction of old records and, 140, 237 (n. 15); due process and, 159, 160; enemy combatant argument and, 8–9, 21, 53, 62, 71, 72; history textbooks and, 101, 141, 142, 144, 145, 238 (n. 26); human rights discourse and, 144–45; murder conviction as focus for, 152–53; Nisqually Indian claim to Indian Claims Commission (ICC) and, 125–26; Nisqually Indian exoneration action and, 11, 133, 139; Nisqually Indians, significance to of, 6, 9, 49, 80, 91, 100, 101, 102, 189; Nisqually Indians and announcement of, 10, 157, 242 (n. 87); Nisqually Indians and Historical Court and, 15–16, 21, 137–38; Nisqually Indian sovereignty and, 15–16, 140, 154, 242 (n. 82); pardon vs., 133; patriotism, 2000s and, 143–44; Quiemuth and, 183; proof of innocence not sought as basis for, 153–54, 182, 242 (n. 81); respondents needed for, 146–47; rule of law and, 11, 50–51, 140, 153–58, 161; as starting point for healing and, 187–88; symbolic rather than administrative, 147–48; U.S. Army objections to trials and, 76–77; Washington state legislature and, 141–42, 143, 144–45, 146–47, 150, 157, 158, 187; Washington Supreme Court involvement in, 22, 141, 142, 145, 146–47, 157, 158. *See also* Committee to Exonerate Chief Leschi; Historical Court of Inquiry and Justice

Leschi message: cooperation and goodwill and, 104, 106, 115, 132, 135; fighting for prairie reservation lands and, 110, 114, 120, 121, 125, 134; fighting for rights if necessary and, 22, 103–4, 114–15, 132, 191; fishing rights, 1960s and, 131, 134; Medicine Creek Treaty of 1854, non-signing by Leschi and, 106, 109, 114, 121, 134; Nisqually Indian claim to Indian Claims Commission (ICC) and, 126; Nisqually self-determination and, 134–35; as testimony in Historical Court, 103–4

Leschi place-names, x, xi

Leschi-Quiemuth Honor Walk, 183

Leschi stories, x, 81–102, 187, 191–92, 219 (n. 19), 251 (n. 99); betrayal by Sluggia and, 95–96, 222 (nn. 53, 64), 223 (n. 74), 223–24 (n. 76), 224 (n. 77); birth of Leschi, 86–87; cause of war and, 92–93, 96, 224–25 (n. 80), 225 (n. 81); childhood, 87; Coast Salish Indians and, 25, 82, 84–86, 91, 95–96, 134; denying U.S. power over Leschi in death, 97–98, 225 (n. 87); failures in war and, 94–95, 223 (n. 69); as fierce warrior, 93–94; final words before death and, 96, 97, 123, 224–25 (n. 80); innocence of Leschi and, 6, 80, 93, 140; Leschi as arbiter and, 88–89, 93; Leschi as compassionate in warfare and, 93, 95, 222 (n. 64); Leschi as headman and, 87, 220 (n. 29); Leschi execution and, 96–97, 224 (n. 79), 224–25 (n. 80); Leschi finding gold and, 90, 221 (nn. 50–51); after Leschi's hanging, 97–98, 225 (n. 85); Leschi promised a fair hearing and, 96; Leschi taking care of kin and, 87–88, 90; Medicine Creek Treaty of 1854 and, 88, 89–91, 108–9, 112, 124, 126; military training for men and, 83–84; Nisqually elders' pain and, 133–34; oral history vs. modern historical discourse and, 21–22, 82–83; published accounts of, 84; Puget Sound Indian War and, 91–95; reputed wealth of Leschi, 87–88; Snoqualmie Indians against Nisqually Indians and, 95, 223 (nn. 72–73); spirit helpers and, 87, 88, 90, 94, 97–98; successes in war and, 94, 95; told as ritual, 101; vision of future and, 85, 96–97, 98–100. *See also* Nisqually Indians; Oral history

Leschi Town, x, 75–76, 77, 217 (n. 109), 218 (n. 110)

Leschi War, 91, 109. *See also* Puget Sound Indian War

Liberalism, 16, 48–49, 152, 190, 195–96 (n. 27); American exceptionalism and, 77–78; American faith in, 139; assimilation and, 13, 195 (n. 22); colonialism and, 12, 14, 21, 24, 194 (nn. 14, 17), 196 (n. 30); dispossession of land from Native Americans and, 138; equality and, 138, 144, 149; Historical Court of Inquiry and Justice and, 12, 13, 14, 48–49, 138; indigenous people's rights and, 12–13, 194–95 (n. 19), 195 (n. 23); Leschi trials and, 66–67; progress and, 20, 198 (n. 52); social reform and, 13, 194 (n. 18), 195 (nn. 21–22)

Lincoln, Abraham, 74

Locke, John, 28, 29–30

Longhouse Education and Cultural Center (The Evergreen State College), 8

Longmire, James, 164, 178, 244 (n. 17), 245 (nn. 25, 27), 245–46 (n. 31), 251 (n. 104)

Luke, 90, 92, 94, 98, 112, 115, 116, 222 (n. 52)

Lummi reservation, 93, 222 (n. 63)

Lummi Tribal Court, 7

Lushootseed Indians. *See* Coast Salish Indians

Lushootseed language, 25, 87, 114, 199 (n. 8), 205 (n. 88); anglicizing and, 44; banning of, in schools, 28, 110; naming ceremonies and, 99; place-names and, 27–28

Maoris, 150, 153

Maple Bay, battle of, 91

Mapping, 30–37; anglicizing/removing indigenous place-names and, 28–29, 32, 44, 207 (n. 110); for immigrants and investors, 34–35; Indian groups named on, 33, 34; map-publishing and, 32–33, 34, 35; Native American dispossession of land and, 31, 32–33, 201 (n. 36), 202 (n. 43); Native American use of, 48; surveying and, 35–36

Marcy, William, 63

Marshall, John, 72, 212 (n. 50), 217 (n. 100)

Marshall, Lyle, 15

Martin, Charlie, 120, 232 (n. 77)

Martin, Henry, 114, 119, 251 (n. 99)

Mashel River, 87

Mason, Charles: as acting governor for Stevens and, 58, 59, 251 (n. 93); Puget Sound Indian War and, 62; Puget Sound Indian War beginnings and, 58, 59, 72, 162, 210–11 (n. 32), 217 (n. 102), 244 (nn. 17, 19)

Master narratives, 83, 84, 101, 102

McAllister, George, 173

McAllister, James, 162, 164, 170, 173, 244 (n. 19), 244–45 (n. 20), 246 (n. 32), 249 (n. 64)

McAllister, James (son), 163

McCloud, Connie, 7, 25, 27, 49, 87–88, 134, 151, 156

McCloud, James, 98, 110, 115

McCloud, Janet, 130, 131

McCloud, Peggy, 159, 183

McFadden, Obadiah, 66, 67

McMullin, Fayette, 65, 68, 175, 176, 250–51 (n. 91), 251 (n. 93)

Meany, Edmond, 43–44, 206–7 (n. 109), 207 (n. 111)

Medicine Creek Treaty of 1854: creating agricultural plots and, 111; farm implements and, 162, 244 (n. 16); fishing rights and, 1, 39, 48, 107, 129–30, 131–32, 205 (nn. 84, 87); forged Indian signatures and, 91, 115; headmen and, 107, 227 (n. 15); land for settlement from, 1–2, 34, 35–36, 56; Leschi and, 73, 107, 132, 144, 179, 180; Leschi grievances with, 1, 57, 89–91, 108–9, 130, 134, 227–28 (n. 21); Leschi headstone and, 124; Leschi refusing to sign and, 90–91, 106, 108, 112, 113, 121, 132,

179, 180, 252 (n. 111); Meeker interviewing Natives from, 112, 113; Native Americans ceding land for annuity payments and services, 35–36, 39, 107, 205 (n. 84); Nisqually Indian claim to Indian Claims Commission (ICC) and, 126; Nisqually Indian interpretation of Leschi and, 88, 91, 104–5, 106; Nisqually prairie land and, 1, 89–90, 108, 110; Nisqually Indian sovereignty and, 154; population based on, 40–41; Puget Sound Indian War and, 92; Quiemuth and, 1, 90, 106, 108, 121, 162, 180, 252 (n. 111); reservations and, 1, 39, 56, 57, 89–90, 108, 129, 227–28 (n. 21); saltwater vs. prairie peoples and, 39, 89–91, 222 (n. 53); sesquicentennial exhibition and, 6, 133; Isaac I. Stevens and, 1–2, 56, 73, 106, 189, 210 (n. 20), 227–28 (n. 21); treaty terms and, 1–2, 47, 107–8

Meeker, Ezra, 73, 122, 216 (n. 90), 244 (n. 15); autobiography of, 69, 70, 112–13, 115, 215 (nn. 83, 86), 218 (n. 10), 235 (n. 114), 248–49 (n. 63); Leschi headstone and, 84, 123–24; as Leschi trial juror, 65, 67, 171; Leschi trials and, 179–80; Medicine Creek Treaty of 1854 and, 112, 113, 115, 179; territorial government criticism and, 57, 189, 210 (n. 20), 249 (n. 68)

Meeker, Oliver Perry, 67, 214 (n. 73)

Memory, ix, x, xii, xiii, 10, 18, 22; American culture and, 17, 18, 122, 179, 191; forgetting and absence and, 159, 162, 163; as group process, 92, 110; oral tradition and, 84–85, 94, 125, 135; shaping present and, 19, 103–4, 120, 126, 146, 226 (n. 1); truth and, 10, 11, 16, 81

Messages from Frank's Landing (Wilkinson), 83–84

Mighty Mountain (Binns), 180

Miles, Joseph, 3, 6

Militias, territorial, 3, 55, 58, 60, 62, 63. *See also* Puget Sound Indian War

Mitchell, Dewey, 99

Mitchell, Samuel Augustus, 33, 34

Moses, Abram Benton, 3, 6, 72, 154, 211 (n. 37)

Mt. Rainier, 26, 178, 248–49 (n. 63). *See also* Ta-Co-Bet

Mowitch, 172, 249 (n. 72)

Muck Creek, 87, 109, 115

Muckleshoot Indians, 31, 36, 203 (n. 64)

Multiculturalism, 13, 144, 145, 152, 155, 186

Nabokov, Peter, 86

Naches Pass, 31, 34, 87, 178

Native American dispossession of land, 17–18, 37–39, 201 (n. 29), 202 (n. 44), 212 (n. 50); allotment sales and, 111, 228–29 (n. 33); American values and, 78; colonialism and, 30, 49, 69–70, 138, 185, 198 (n. 49); without "fair dealings," 38; mapping and demarcation and, 31, 32–33, 201 (n. 36), 202 (n. 43); Oregon Donation Land Act of 1850 and, 38, 55, 204 (n. 74); railroads and, 37, 204 (n. 72); scientific method and data and, 30, 37–38; South Puget Sound and, 30, 32–33, 37–39, 44

Native Americans: "age of apology" and, 14–15, 197 (nn. 33, 38), 198 (n. 41); assimilation and, 13, 110, 111, 195 (n. 22); Bering Strait migration theory and, 41, 42; burning villages and, 92, 93, 222 (nn. 61, 63); colonialism and, 14, 21, 24, 30,

39, 40, 41, 49, 205 (nn. 88–89), 208 (n. 129); court system and, 138–39; government boarding schools and, 28, 45, 46; historical justice and, 14–15, 18; Indian traditional histories and, 86, 219 (n. 24); language and, 41–42, 206 (n. 105); legal status and, 13–14, 50, 196 (n. 29), 208 (n. 1), 208–9 (n. 2); liberalism and adoption of sovereignty and, 12, 13; as "noble and dying breed," 69, 215 (n. 84); oral history vs. modern historical discourse and, 16, 17, 81; oral traditions as history and, 86, 219 (n. 20); Oregon Treaty of 1846 and, 29; postcolonial condition and, 149, 196 (n. 30); relationship to land and, 24–25, 30, 31–32, 39, 199 (n. 7), 201 (n. 29), 202 (n. 43); self-determination, 1960s and, 131; social progress theories and, 42; sympathy for, 1960s on, 143, 238 (n. 32); used as guides in new territory, 31, 33; viewed as criminal for resisting U.S. authority and, 60, 73

New Mexico, 54

Newspapers: Historical Court of Inquiry and Justice and, ix, 8; Historical Court of Inquiry and Justice criticism and, 189, 190; Indian fishing rights and, 127; Indian legal customs and, 169; Indian treaty rights and, 2, 114, 236 (n. 133); killing of Indians and, 172–73, 249 (n. 76); Leschi and Quiemuth reburials and, 113, 114, 115–16, 122, 165, 230 (n. 56), 246 (n. 35); Leschi execution and, 96; Leschi exoneration and, ix, 10, 158, 191, 243 (n. 94); Leschi stories and, 82–83; Leschi trials and, 65, 66, 180; Medicine Creek Treaty of 1854 and, 2; deaths of rangers and militiamen and, 65, 163; Puget Sound Indian War and, 60, 63, 64, 211 (nn. 36–37), 212 (n. 46); Puget Sound Indian War and Leschi and, 55, 61; Quiemuth's death and, 170, 173, 176, 178, 251 (n. 104); stone memorial to Leschi and, 127–28, 129

New York Times, ix, 6, 102

New Zealand, 150, 153, 240 (n. 63)

Nisqually Indians: activism over fishing rights and, 127, 130, 131, 134, 142–43, 152; allotments and, 48, 111, 117–18, 126, 183, 228 (n. 30), 231 (nn. 64, 66); ancestor signs and, 100; anthropologists analyzing and, 89, 221 (n. 45), 225 (n. 86); appeals relative to condemned land, 119–20; arrests from fishing and, 126–27, 130; author's research approach to, xii, 193 (n. 1); British crops and animals and, 29, 47–48, 162, 201 (n. 27), 244 (n. 16); civilizing era, 1870–1920s, 105–6; criminals vs. enemy combatants and, 73, 217 (n. 102); displacement of, 1918, 118–19, 124–25, 232 (n. 75), 233 (n. 94), 233–34 (n. 95); dispossession of land and, 37, 47, 48, 204 (n. 71); dispossession of land due to U.S. Army, World War I and, 116–24; eras of tribal crisis and, 104, 105–6; fishing rights and, 106, 126–27, 130, 131–32, 234 (n. 104), 235 (n. 107); geography of, 24, 25, 26, 27, 28, 44, 47; headman role and, 106–7, 227 (n. 11); Historical Court of Inquiry and Justice and, ix, xi, 7, 8, 22, 81, 186; Historical Court of Inquiry and Justice, and proving harm from Leschi's conviction and, 148–49, 150–51; Historical Court of Inquiry and Justice idea and, 148–49; Historical Court of

Inquiry and Justice testimony and, 13, 27, 80–81, 84, 89, 91, 100–102, 103–4, 136–39, 150; histories of, 25–27, 46–47, 92, 199 (n. 9); Indian boarding schools and, 28, 110–11, 114, 115, 118, 119; Indian Claims Commission (ICC) claim, 1950s, 125–26, 234 (n. 97); Indian guides and, 46, 207–8 (n. 118); Indian legal customs and, 166, 167, 172, 251 (n. 99); Indian ways kept, during "civilizing" period, 112, 113, 229 (nn. 38, 43–44); intertribal trade and, 87, 220 (n. 28); intra-Indian disputes and, 166, 167; language and, 28, 41–42, 47, 48, 99, 134, 199 (n. 8), 205 (n. 88), 206 (n. 99); Leschi as leader and, 25, 103–4, 144, 179, 234 (n. 101); Leschi message informing actions of, 103–4; Leschi stories and, x, 80, 82–83, 84, 85–91, 133–34; Leschi stories for future of tribe, 98–100, 101–2; Leschi's trial and, 175–76, 250 (n. 89); Leschi's vision of the future and, 99–100; marriages and, 87, 88, 220 (n. 32), 250 (n. 79); memorial practices, 124; migration legend, 27, 41–42, 200 (n. 17); named on maps and, 33, 34; naming ceremonies, 99; naming of, 27, 200 (n. 18); narrative discipline to present tribal goals and, 84, 219 (n. 13); oral history vs. modern historical discourse and, 47, 82–83, 208 (n. 122); origin story and, 26, 199 (nn. 10, 12); place-names and, 27–28, 32, 44, 200 (n. 18); population, 1840s and 1850s, 40, 205 (n. 92); prairie land and, 1, 39, 86–87, 89–90, 108, 110, 113, 114, 117, 120, 121, 134, 183; public relations, 1890s and, 114, 115; Puget Sound Indian War and, 3, 59–60, 62, 72, 211 (n. 36); Quiemuth, honoring of and, 159, 182–83; Quiemuth's death and, 176; reburial ceremony for Leschi and Quiemuth and, 113–16, 229–30 (n. 45), 230 (nn. 46, 56); relationship to land and, 26, 27, 28, 39, 47–48, 49; religion and, 98, 225 (n. 86); salmon and, 26–27, 48, 143, 199–200 (n. 14), 208 (n. 128); saltwater vs. prairie peoples and, 89–90; self-determination and, 106, 134–35, 158; shamans and, 98, 166, 207–8 (n. 118), 246 (nn. 39–40); slaves and, 108, 227 (n. 17); Snoqualmie Indians against, in war, 95, 223 (nn. 72–73); spirits and, 26, 87, 88, 89, 90, 91, 94, 97–98, 114, 199 (n. 12); stars and, 86, 219 (n. 22); stone memorial to Leschi and, 129, 130, 135, 235 (n. 125); transferring remains of people to new cemetery and, 121–22, 232 (n. 81), 233 (n. 86); U.S. citizenship and, 111; values expressed through stories, 88; voting membership, 1940s, 125, 233–34 (n. 95); Wa He Lut and, 72–73, 95, 223 (n. 71); warfare and, 3, 166, 246 (n. 41), 246–47 (n. 42), 247 (n. 43); white settlement resistance and, 17, 45–49; white settler interest in, 1890s and, 112–13; white settlers encroaching on land and, 88, 89, 110; white settler violence and, 47, 174, 250 (n. 87). *See also* Leschi exoneration; Leschi message; Medicine Creek Treaty of 1854; Nisqually reservation

Nisqually, My People, The (Carpenter), 92

Nisqually Prairie, 113, 165, 183, 219 (n. 21)

Nisqually reservation, x, 25; campaign of terror by settlers and, 174, 250

(n. 87); condemnation of land and, 117–18, 126, 127, 134, 165, 183, 231 (nn. 64, 66); forced relocation to, of Nisqually Indians, 93, 222 (n. 63); forced vacating of homes from, 118–19, 120–21, 232 (n. 77); increased land after war and, 3, 109–10; land loss, 1917–18, 116–24; land sales and, 111; land taken from, 37, 204 (n. 71); Leschi message and, 110, 134; Medicine Creek Treaty of 1854 and, 1, 108; Quiemuth and, 182; U.S. Army, World War I and, 117, 183. *See also* Nisqually Indians

Nisqually River, 3, 87, 126, 132, 203 (n. 61), 225–26 (n. 95)

Noncombatants, 73

North American Atlas (Morse), 32

Northern Pacific Railway, 37, 114, 204 (n. 72)

Northwest Indian Fisheries Commission, 7, 132, 238 (n. 31)

Northwest Ordinance of 1787, 38

Oklahoma Commission to Study the Tulsa Riots of 1921, 14

Olson, Alexander, 94

Olympia, 5; as capital of territory, 54, 55, 58, 63, 209 (n. 11); Leschi called to, 59, 72, 210–11 (n. 32); Leschi's travel to, to ensure peace, 59; Leschi trial and, 66, 175–76; Quiemuth called to, 59, 210–11 (n. 32); Quiemuth's travel to, to ensure peace, 59, 162, 244 (n. 17)

Olympian, 8

"One-Armed John," 173, 174

Oral history: Historical Court of Inquiry and Justice and, 16, 80–82, 100, 151, 186; Leschi stories and, 21, 80, 81, 82–83, 84–86, 219 (n. 19);

Nisqually migration legend as, 27, 200 (nn. 15, 17); Nisqually origin story and, 26, 199 (nn. 10, 12); prejudices against, 41, 43, 47, 189, 218 (n. 1); Wa He Lut and, 95, 223 (n. 71)

Oregon Donation Land Act of 1850, 33–34, 38, 55, 204 (nn. 73–74)

Oregon Territory, 32, 34, 35, 167–68

Oregon Treaty of 1846, 29, 33, 202 (n. 47), 203 (n. 62), 247 (n. 45)

Owens, Susan, 137, 147

Parr, Melissa, 6, 139, 158, 188, 190, 252 (n. 117). *See also* Committee to Exonerate Chief Leschi

Patkanim, 95, 175, 176, 223 (n. 72), 233 (n. 86)

Patriotism, 143–44

People's International Tribunal, 151, 241 (nn. 74–75)

People's Republic of Leschi, 131

Pierce County, 2, 59, 189, 250 (n. 82); condemnation of Nisqually reservation land and, 105, 117–18, 126, 231 (nn. 64, 66); Historical Court of Inquiry and Justice and, 7, 8, 140, 157; Leschi execution and, 67; Leschi trials and, 65, 237 (n. 15); opposition to Stevens and, 55, 57, 63; Puget Sound Indian War and, 62–63, 64; Puyallup allotment land loss and, 111–12

Pierce County Condemnation Board, 117

Pierce County Historical Society, 83

Pierce County Pioneer and Historical Association, 127–29

Pioneer and Democrat: Leschi execution and, 67, 96; Leschi trials and, 65, 66, 211 (n. 37); Medicine Creek Treaty of 1854 and, 56; Puget Sound Indian

War and, 55, 60, 61, 62, 63, 64, 209 (n. 12), 217 (n. 100); Quiemuth's death and, 163–64; white settler violence against Indians and, 170

Pioneer Reminiscences of Puget Sound and the Tragedy of Leschi (Meeker), 69, 70, 112–13, 123, 218 (n. 10), 235 (n. 114)

Positive law, 139–40

Postcolonial condition, 149, 196 (n. 30)

Potlatches, 87, 114, 221 (n. 50)

Pouley, Theresa, 137

Preston's Sectional and County Map of Oregon and Washington (1856), 34, 35, 203 (n. 61)

Prisoners of war, 52, 74

Progress and liberalism, 20, 198 (n. 52)

Prosch, Charles, 173, 174, 249–50 (n. 77), 250 (n. 82)

Proto-anthropologists, 41, 42, 43, 44. *See also* Anthropologists

Public Historians, 6, 11, 18, 133, 186

Puget Salish Indians. *See* Coast Salish Indians

Puget Sound, 2; mapping and demarcation and, 31, 32; naming of, 28. *See also* South Puget Sound

Puget Sound Agricultural Company, 29, 55, 166, 203 (n. 62)

Puget Sound Courier, 57, 58, 60, 63, 211 (n. 37), 212 (n. 46), 249–50 (n. 77)

Puget Sound Geography (Waterman), 28

Puget Sound Herald, 172–73, 249–50 (n. 77)

Puget Sound Indian War, 91–95, 109; beginnings of, 3, 57–60, 65, 72; Hudson's Bay Company (HBC) and, 62–63, 212–13 (n. 52); Indians blamed for starting, 60, 72; legality and, 77, 79; killing as legitimate action in war and, 72, 154, 217 (n. 100); deaths of McAllister and Connell and, 162–63; newspapers and, 55, 60, 61, 62, 63, 64, 209 (n. 12), 211 (nn. 36–37), 212 (n. 46), 217 (n. 100); Nisqually Indians and, 3, 59–60, 62, 72, 211 (n. 36); righteousness of, 70, 71; Snoqualmie Indians and, 95, 223 (nn. 72–73); trials of Indians after and, 97, 160–61, 243 (n. 7); twentieth century research on, 83, 120–21; U.S. Army and, 3, 57–58, 59, 60, 63–64, 94, 95; as violation of treaty, 73, 217 (n. 102); volunteer troops and, 58, 60, 62, 63–64, 69, 209 (n. 12), 220–21 (n. 39); white justification for, 61–62, 64, 212 (n. 47); White River Massacre and, 60, 61, 73. *See also* Leschi, Chief; Stevens, Isaac I.; War and legality; White settlers

Puyallup Indians, 46, 97, 114, 120, 207–8 (n. 118); cemetery of, 121, 122; Historical Court of Inquiry and Justice and, 7, 25, 49, 81, 133–34, 186, 189; land losses and, 111–12, 204 (n. 72); Leschi and, 134, 187–88, 236 (n. 141); Medicine Creek Treaty of 1854 and, 1; population count for treaty and, 40; Quiemuth and, 159; reservation and, 109, 110, 204 (n. 72)

Puyallup Indian School, 46, 48, 118, 122, 231 (n. 63). *See also* Cushman Indian School

Quiemuth, 87, 243 (n. 1); appointed chief for treaty council and, 1, 106, 162, 180; descendants of, 99, 114, 115, 116, 165, 181; due process failure and, 165–66; forgotten over time, 179, 181, 252 (n. 117); Fort Nisqually shooting incident and, 167; going into hiding, 162, 163; as guide for homesteaders, 162, 244 (n. 15); as haunting, 159, 161–62, 183; Hudson's Bay Company (HBC) and, 88, 162, 167, 201 (n. 27); internment, 165, 204 (n. 71); Medicine Creek Treaty of 1854 and, 1, 90, 106, 108, 121, 162, 180, 252 (n. 111); deaths of McAllister and Connell and, 163; Olympia, travel to, to ensure peace, 59, 210–11 (n. 32), 162, 244 (n. 17); reburial ceremony for, 113–16, 165, 230 (nn. 46, 56), 246 (n. 35); Isaac I. Stevens and, 162, 163–65, 180, 245–46 (n. 31), 250 (n. 85); story of, 162–66, 244 (n. 15); as traditional arbiter in Indian legal customs, 166–67, 251 (n. 99); turning himself in, 163, 178, 245 (n. 23)

Quiemuth, Bill, 115, 116

Quiemuth death, 183, 243 (n. 7), 245 (nn. 25, 27), 245–46 (n. 31); violence against Indians after war and, 172, 173, 174, 176; compared to Leschi execution, 22, 159–60, 165–66, 175, 176, 182; nature of killing of, 163–64, 246 (n. 32); settler stories about, 170–71, 176, 178, 179, 251 (n. 104)

Quiemuth Peak, 182

Rabbeson, Antonio, 3–5, 6, 65, 66, 67, 211 (n. 37)

Racial superiority, 42, 207 (n. 115), 210 (n. 21); land claims over Indians and, 30, 43, 56, 144; Puget Sound Indian War and, 58, 60, 61–62, 64; vengeance killings of Indians and, 172

Racism, 30, 129, 142, 144

Railroads, 34, 202–3 (n. 58); Native American dispossession of land and, 37, 204 (n. 72)

Rasmussen, Marilyn, 141–42

Reconciliation, 14, 17, 18, 187, 188. *See also* Truth and reconciliation commissions (TRCs)

Reparations, 14, 15, 150, 198 (n. 41)

Reservations, 39, 203 (n. 64), 204 (n. 72); counting Native people in treaty area for, 40; Fox Island council and, 109; U.S. Indian policies and, 56, 92, 93, 110, 222 (n. 63); white settlers and, 36, 37, 204 (n. 71). *See also* Medicine Creek Treaty of 1854; Nisqually reservation

Richards, Kent, 7, 9, 73

Roads, 34

Robnett, Mary, 8, 9, 23, 44, 49

Robson, Paul, 7, 51–52, 74, 75

Rumsfeld, Donald, 74

Sahaptin language, 87, 220 (n. 29)

Salmon, 36; environmental concerns and, 132, 143, 236 (n. 131); fishing rights and, 131, 132, 236 (n. 131); Nisqually Indians and, 26–27, 48, 143, 199–200 (n. 14), 208 (n. 128); scientific method and, 48, 208 (n. 128)

Sanchez, Dorian, 7, 80, 101, 138

Scientific data: counting Native people in treaty area, 39–40, 41, 205 (n. 89); Native American dispossession of land and, 30, 37–38

Scientific method: map-making and, 32; Native American dispossession of land and, 37; Native American languages and migrations and, 41–42; Native American languages and pronunciations and, 43–44; Native American legends and, 42–43, 206 (n. 106); salmon and, 48, 208 (n. 128)

Seattle, 5; Puget Sound Indian War and, 3, 61, 93; sympathy for Native

Americans and, 142–43, 176–77, 238 (n. 32)
Seattle, Chief, 175
Seattle Post-Intelligencer, 94, 112, 141
Second District Court, 65–66, 214 (n. 69)
Seinfeld, Karen, 137
September 11, 2001 terrorist attacks, 77, 216 (n. 97)
S'Gukugwas, 87
Shaw, Benjamin, 94, 189, 210 (n. 20), 223 (n. 69)
Shelton, Ruth, 93
Siab, 87, 88, 90, 93, 105, 107–8
Sicade, Henry, 97, 110, 122, 207–8 (n. 118); appraising Indian allotments and, 118, 231 (n. 64); South Puget Sound history and, 46–48, 208 (nn. 120, 122)
Simmons, Michael T., 40, 96, 106, 225 (n. 81), 247 (n. 45)
Skokomish Indians, 91–92, 222 (n. 57)
Slavery, 17, 54, 198 (n. 48)
Slotkin, Richard, 171
Sluggia, 95–96, 222 (nn. 53, 64), 223 (n. 74), 223–24 (n. 76), 224 (n. 77)
Smith, Marian, 166
Smithsonian Institution, 120, 121
Snoqualmie Indians, 25, 95, 167–68, 247–48 (n. 50). *See also* Patkanim
Social progress, 42
Southern Coast Salish Indians. *See* Coast Salish Indians
South Puget Sound, ix, x, xiii, 11; area of, 2, 5; disease and, 40, 205 (n. 91); histories of, 46–47, 208 (nn. 120, 122); Indian groups of, 25, 92; Indian land cessions and, 1–2, 17–18; Indian legal customs and, 166, 167–68, 246–47 (n. 42), 247 (n. 43), 247–48 (n. 50); mapping and demarcation and, 31, 32; Medicine Creek Treaty of 1854 and, 1–2, 39, 205 (n. 84); military population and, 143, 144; Native American dispossession of land and, 30, 32–33, 37–39, 44; Native American land ownership and, 36–37, 45; Native American population numbers and, 40; Native American relationship to land and, 24–25; Native Americans and court system and, 45, 185; Native Americans disputing surveying teams, 35–36; Native American suffering and, 36, 151; Nisqually legends and, 26, 27, 41–42, 200 (n. 17); Nisqually place-names and, 28, 32; place-names and, 39, 44, 46; territorial government and, 55; treaty negotiations and, 38, 39; warfare with Native Americans and, 53, 58; white migration routes to, 31, 34. *See also* Hudson's Bay Company; Puget Sound Indian War; White settlers
Sovereignty: Nisqually Indian Tribe, xii, 73, 124, 139, 152–54; U.S. law and policies regarding Indian tribes and, 12, 13, 28, 56, 194–95 (n. 19), 241 (n. 70); U.S settlers and, 49, 54, 55, 62, 64, 67, 198 (n. 49)
Spirits: The Changer, 26, 86, 199 (n. 12); Leschi and, 87, 88, 90, 94, 97–98; Leschi reburial and, 114; prairie land and, 89; warfare and, 91, 94
Squally, Andreya, 101
Squally Prairie, 86, 219 (n. 21). *See also* Nisqually Prairie
Squaxin Island Indians, 1, 25, 40, 234 (n. 97)
Stahi, 163, 244–45 (n. 20), 250 (n. 85)
Stars, 86, 219 (nn. 22, 24)
Steilacoom (town), xv, 5, 58, 67, 68, 135, 164, 168, 235 (n. 125), 248

(n. 62); Leschi's trial and, 65, 66, 163, 250 (n. 89); martial law and, 63; newspapers and, 57, 67; Quiemuth and, 163, 164
Steilacoom, John, 112, 115, 116
Stevens, Hazard, 163, 164, 170, 246 (n. 32)
Stevens, Isaac I., 9, 202–3 (n. 58), 244–45 (n. 20); appointing chiefs for treaty council, 1, 39, 106–7, 162, 180; arresting Indian leaders from war and, 3, 64, 174–75, 213 (n. 60), 250 (n. 85); declaring martial law and, 63, 213 (n. 54); establishing U.S. sovereignty and, 56, 209–10 (n. 18); Fox Island council and, 109–10; Indian grievances with treaty and, 47, 130, 211 (n. 37); Leschi and, 61, 64, 73, 170, 179, 180, 250 (n. 85); Medicine Creek Treaty of 1854 and, 1–2, 56, 73, 106, 189, 210 (n. 20), 227–28 (n. 21); Puget Sound Indian War and, 3, 61, 62–63, 64–65, 75, 212 (n. 47), 212–13 (n. 52); Quiemuth and, 162, 180; Quiemuth detention and, 163–64, 250 (n. 85); Quiemuth murder and, 164–65, 245–46 (n. 31); rule of law after war and, 174–75, 250 (n. 85); settlers' attitudes toward, 55, 57, 63, 64, 65, 66, 67, 165, 211 (n. 37); treaties with Indians and, 33, 104–5; treaty tour and, 1, 2, 39, 58, 62; volunteer troops and, 62, 63, 64; as Washington Territory governor, 54–55, 56, 57, 210 (n. 20), 251 (n. 93)
Stevenson, Shanna, 7
Strait of Juan de Fuca, 28
Stryker Brigades, 75
Surveying, 35–36, 45, 203 (nn. 59, 62)
Survival of the American Indian Association, 130
Survivance, 186, 253 (n. 2)

Swan, John, 109, 225 (n. 81)
Symbolic courts, for indigenous hearings, 151, 152, 241 (nn. 74–75), 241–42 (nn. 74, 76)

Ta-Co-Bet, 26, 27. *See also* Mt. Rainier
Tacoma, 5, 111, 114, 117, 131, 133, 142, 204 (n. 72)
Tacoma Academy of Sciences, 46
Tacoma Ledger, 114, 165, 178
Tacoma News-Tribune, 82, 83, 128, 129, 145, 189
Taney, Roger B., 56
Third District Court, 65, 214 (n. 69)
Thompson, Donald, 137
Thunderbird Plaza, 127–28
Thurston County, 2, 7, 55, 65, 68, 157
Thurston County Historic Commission, 182
Tobin, Bill, 8, 156
Tolmie, William Fraser, 40, 211 (n. 39), 227 (n. 13), 249 (n. 76); Hudson's Bay Company (HBC) and, 29, 166, 173; Leschi seeking advice from, 57, 58, 210–11 (n. 32); Leschi stories and, 84, 124, 220 (n. 29); Medicine Creek Treaty of 1854 and, 90, 106, 108; Puget Sound Indian War and, 162; trying to save Leschi, 67, 68, 175
Tomlins, Christopher, 142
Too-a-pi-ti, 163, 173, 174, 244–45 (n. 20), 249 (n. 76)
Torture, 76
Treaties, xi, 107, 210 (n. 30); arresting Indians defying terms of, 58, 73, 174; condemnation of land in violation of, 118; courts used by Native Americans for, 1890s, 113; fishing rights and, 126–27, 129, 234 (n. 104), 235 (n. 107); legalizing land for settlers and, 1–2, 38, 212 (n. 50); as living documents for Indians, 104–5, 132,

134; Native challenges and, 1960s, 131; public opinion toward, 132–33, 236 (n. 133); white backlash toward, 1960s on, 143
Treaty Trail (exhibition), 6
Tribunals, 150, 152, 240 (n. 63)
Trouillot, Michel-Rolph, 192
Truth and reconciliation commissions (TRCs), 151, 196 (n. 32), 240–41 (n. 66); Historical Court of Inquiry and Justice modeled on, 14, 15, 16, 150, 240 (n. 65)
Truth Teller, 67–69
Tualatin Academy, 46, 47
Tulalip Indians, 61, 93
Tulee v. Washington, 127
Tuskegee syphilis study, 14

United Nations, 101, 240 (n. 63)
U.S. Army: Historical Court of Inquiry and Justice and, 7, 71, 73–74, 75, 76–77, 154; Indian legal customs and, 169, 248 (n. 57); Leschi execution and, 68; Leschi trials and, 3, 65, 66, 73, 75, 76, 214 (n. 63); military trials and, 65; vs. militias, 63–64, 69; Nisqually reservation land condemnation and, World War I, 117–18, 183; Puget Sound Indian War and, 63–64, 94, 95; Puget Sound Indian War beginnings and, 3, 57–58, 59, 60; territorial government criticism and, 3, 63–64, 65, 76; vigilante killings and, 174; war and legality and, 58, 76, 154
U.S. citizenship for Indians, 110, 111, 112, 124, 131, 196 (n. 29), 233 (n. 92)
U.S. Congress, 241 (n. 75); backlash to sympathy for Indian treaty rights and, 143; General Allotment Act of 1887 and, 111; Indian Claims Commission (ICC) and, 125, 234 (n. 97); Nisqually condemned reservation land and, 119, 120, 232 (n. 75); territorial governments and, 54; veterans' benefits to volunteer soldiers and, 174, 175; Washington State creation and, 146
U.S. Constitution, 54
U.S. Department of Justice, 131, 241 (n. 75)
U.S. Department of the Interior, 117, 118, 119, 231 (n. 64), 241 (n. 75). *See also* Bureau of Indian Affairs
United States Exploring Expedition, 31, 32. *See also* Wilkes Expedition
U.S. Geographic Surveys, 37
U.S. Indian policies, xii; allotments and, 48, 92, 111, 228 (n. 30), 228–29 (n. 33), 229 (n. 37); assimilation and, 110, 111; forced relocation to reservations and, 56, 92, 93, 110, 222 (n. 63); Indian Claims Commission (ICC) and, 125–26, 234 (nn. 97–98); Nisqually condemned reservation land and, 119–20; treaties securing land for homesteaders and, 1–2
U.S. moral leadership, 144, 239 (n. 34)
U.S. Supreme Court, 201 (n. 29); *Dred Scott* decision, 56, 210 (n. 21); Hawaiian state sovereignty and, 152, 242 (n. 77); Indian legal status and, 56, 210 (n. 21); Native Americans and sovereignty and, 72, 217 (n. 100); *United States v. Washington*, 131, 132, 143; War on Terror enemy combatants and, 71, 72; *Worcester v. Georgia*, 72
United States v. Washington, 131, 132, 143
University of Colorado, 7
University of Washington, 7, 8, 141; Native American activism and, 131; Whulshootseed language and, 43–44, 206–7 (n. 109)

Upper Skagit Indians, 25, 85, 99
Utah, 54

Values: American, 23–24, 72, 77–78, 216–17 (n. 98); Coast Salish Indians and, 85, 219 (n. 17); Nisqually Indians and, 88, 223–24 (n. 76)
Vancouver, George, 28–29, 200 (n. 21)
Vancouver Island, 91
Van Ogle, H. E., 164, 173, 178, 246 (n. 32)
Vigilantes, 170, 172, 248 (n. 62), 249 (n. 71)

Wa He Lut, 72–73, 92, 93, 98, 115, 116, 223 (n. 71), 243 (n. 7); killing of Sluggia and, 95, 223–24 (n. 76)
Wa He Lut School, 99, 225–26 (n. 95)
Waitangi Tribunal, New Zealand, 150, 153, 240 (n. 63)
Wanatco, 87
War and legality, 209 (n. 5); enemy combatants and, 21, 51–52, 53, 70–71, 74, 75, 77, 154, 217 (nn. 102, 104, 107–8); Historical Court of Inquiry and Justice and, 51–53, 74, 138, 242 (n. 82); historical development of, 74; Indians without legal right to declare war and, 58, 60, 72–73; "Indian war" and, white justification for, 61–62, 212 (n. 50); international law and, 51–53, 71, 72, 73–74, 75, 138; Leschi execution and, 69; Leschi trials and, 65, 66–67, 77; noncombatants and, 73; Puget Sound Indian War and, 58, 62, 63, 73–74, 75, 79; War on Terror and, 21, 51, 70–71, 72, 74, 217 (nn. 107–108); Washington Territory and, 65, 214 (n. 64)
War on Terror, 216 (n. 97); American values and, 72, 216–17 (n. 98); cultural crisis and, 70–71, 216 (n. 93); enemy combatants and, 21, 51, 70–71, 72, 74, 217 (nn. 107–8); legality of, 53; questioning of, 70, 216 (n. 92)
Washington: congressional members from, 111, 143; courts used by Native Americans for fishing rights under treaties and, 126–27, 234 (n. 104), 235 (n. 107); courts used by Native Americans for treaty rights and, 111–12, 113, 115, 229 (n. 37); fish and game policies and, 126, 234 (n. 103), 235 (n. 107); Leschi apology and, 145; Leschi exoneration and, 139, 157; statehood and, 140, 146
Washington governors, 157, 251 (n. 93). *See also* Mason, Charles; McMullin, Fayette; Stevens, Isaac I.
Washington Senate Joint Memorial, 142, 143, 144–45
Washington State Capitol Museum, 10
Washington State Historical Court of Inquiry and Justice. *See* Historical Court of Inquiry and Justice
Washington State Historical Society, 6, 8, 84, 122, 130, 136, 244–45 (n. 20)
Washington State History Museum, 5, 75
Washington state legislature: asking Washington Supreme Court to review Leschi case, 145, 146; final resolutions on Leschi exoneration and apology, 145, 146, 187; Leschi exoneration and, 141–42, 143, 144–45, 157, 158, 187; Senate Joint Memorial and, 144–45
Washington Supreme Court, xi, 11; admitting Yamashita posthumously to bar and, 141; justices from on Historical Court and, 7–8, 137, 138; Leschi exoneration and, 22, 142, 157;

Leschi exoneration possibility and, 141, 145, 146–47, 158; Native Americans vs. settlers and, 45; Puyallup allotment land loss and, 111–12; *Tulee v. Washington*, 127

Washington Territorial Supreme Court: Leschi appeals and, 5, 66, 175, 180, 214 (n. 69); Leschi execution and, 142

Washington Territory, 209 (n. 13); court record decisions untouchable with statehood and, 146, 158; courts prejudiced against Indians and, 97, 165, 171, 246 (n. 34); court system and, 140–41, 165, 169–70, 172, 175, 185; Democratic Party and, 55, 209 (n. 11); denying Indians testimony in court and, 55–56, 248 (n. 57); due process and, 161, 180–81, 243 (n. 8); execution of Leschi and, 5, 67, 68, 70, 142; government corruption and, 54, 57, 63–64, 69, 160; government structure and, 54–55; "Indian experts" and, 38–40, 204–5 (n. 81); Indian legal status and, 56–57; legal plurality and, 161, 165, 166–67, 169; Leschi conviction and, 140–41; mapping and demarcation and, 34–35, 203 (n. 59); newspapers and, 54–55; Puget Sound Indian War and, 2–3, 54–70, 209 (n. 12); Quiemuth and law of, 161–62; rule of law and, 50, 51, 63, 146, 160, 174–75, 250 (n. 85), 251 (n. 96); Isaac I. Stevens as governor of, 54–55, 56, 57, 210 (n. 20), 251 (n. 93); war and legality and, 65, 214 (n. 64)

Washington Treaty Commission, 38

Waterman, T. T., 28, 32, 46, 89, 207–8 (n. 118)

Wheeler, George, 36–37

Whigs, 57, 210 (n. 25)

White River Massacre, 60, 61, 73, 172

White settlers: abuse of Indians and, 56; attitudes toward Stevens, 55, 57, 63, 64, 65, 66, 67, 165, 211 (n. 37); blockhouses for protection and, 59, 62–63; burning Native villages and, 92, 93, 222 (nn. 61, 63); violence against Indians after war and, 163, 172–74, 176, 179, 181–82, 250 (n. 82); colonialism and, 16–18, 20–21, 49, 69–70, 182, 198 (n. 49), 215–16 (n. 89); distrust of territorial courts, 165, 170–71, 172, 175, 249 (n. 68); expectations that Native Americans would disappear, 36, 40–41; expectations that Native Americans would surrender land, 12, 24, 36–37, 69–70, 203 (n. 61), 216 (n. 90); interest in Leschi, 1890s and, 112–13; land claims and, 33–36, 55, 56, 201 (n. 29), 203 (n. 62), 212 (n. 50); Leschi and, 24, 61, 92, 106, 165, 211 (n. 39); Leschi execution and, 67–68, 70, 97, 176, 214 (n. 72); Leschi's trial and, 185; deaths of McAllister and Connell and, 170, 249 (n. 64); Native American sovereignty, refusal of, 72, 73, 217 (n. 100); Nisqually Indian resistance to, 17, 45–49; Nisqually land, encroachment on and, 88, 89, 110; Oregon Donation Land Act of 1850 and, 33–34, 38, 55, 204 (nn. 73–74); perceiving Indians as contentious over treaty rights, 1890s, 114, 230 (n. 48); population increase, after 1870, 110; Puget Sound Indian War and, 58–60, 212–13 (n. 52); Quiemuth murder and, 159–60, 163, 164–65; Quiemuth murder stories and, 170–71, 176, 178, 179, 251 (n. 104); racial superiority to Natives and, 30, 144; relationship to land and, 25,

28, 29–30, 39, 47–48; reminiscences and, 177–79, 248–49 (n. 62), 252 (n. 109); reservations and, 36, 37, 204 (n. 71); rule of law and, 23, 50, 167, 179, 185; rule of law vs. blood revenge and, 169–70, 171–74, 176–77, 248 (n. 60), 249 (nn. 71, 76), 251 (n. 96); rule of law vs. Indian legal customs and, 168–69, 248 (n. 57); sale of liquor to Indians and, 67, 214 (n. 72); squatters, 37; sympathy for, 1910s, 122, 233 (n. 86); sympathy with Native Americans and, 45–46, 207 (n. 115); territorial government and, 54, 55, 57, 69, 160–61; U.S. Indian policies and, 56–57; vigilantes and, 170, 248 (n. 62); violent attacks on Indians and, 47, 92, 93, 170, 174, 177–79

Whulge. *See* South Puget Sound

Whulshootseed language, 25, 28, 206 (n. 99); pronunciations and, 43–44, 206–7 (n. 109), 207 (n. 111)

Wickersham, James, 90

Wild West, 170, 249 (n. 65)

Wilkes, Charles, 31, 32, 40

Wilkes Expedition, 31, 32. *See also* United States Exploring Expedition

Wilkinson, Charles, 7, 72, 83–84, 91, 154, 242 (n. 82)

Wilmington Race Riot Commission, 14

Witt, John Fabian, 53

Wolfe, Patrick, 15, 30

Wool, John E., 63–64, 65, 164, 245–46 (n. 31)

Worcester v. Georgia, 72

World War I, 117, 119, 120

World War II, 74, 128, 195 (n. 23)

Wright, George, 65, 214 (n. 63)

Yakama Indians, 2, 92, 220 (n. 29)

Yakima, 3

Yamashita, Takuji, 141, 144, 145, 146

Yll-whaltz, 87

www.ingramcontent.com/pod-product-compliance
Lightning Source LLC
Chambersburg PA
CBHW020753020526
44116CB00028B/127